The East in the West

Much European history and social theory has viewed the East as 'static' or 'backward', seeing in its institutions characteristics that have prevented modernisation. Such were the assumptions of Marx and Weber in the heyday of capitalism, and have also been held by many of those concerned with the 'European miracle' or 'the Uniqueness of the West'.

Jack Goody challenges these assumptions, beginning with the notion of a special Western rationality which enabled 'us' not 'them' to modernise. He then turns to 'rational' bookkeeping, which several social and economic historians have seen as intrinsic to capitalism, arguing that there was in fact little difference between East and West in terms of mercantile activity. Other factors said to inhibit the East's development, such as the role of the family and forms of labour, have also been greatly exaggerated. This Eurocentrism both fails to explain the current achievements of the East and misunderstands Western history. *The East in the West* starts to redress the balance and so marks a fundamental shift in our view of Western and Eastern history and society.

The East in the West

Jack Goody

St John's College, Cambridge

CAMBRIDGE
UNIVERSITY PRESS

Published by the Press Syndicate of the University of Cambridge
The Pitt Building, Trumpington Street, Cambridge CB2 1RP
30 West 20th Street, New York, NY 10011–4211, USA
10 Stamford Road, Oakleigh, Melbourne 3166, Australia

First published 1996

Printed in Great Britain at the University Press, Cambridge

A catalogue record for this book is available from the British Library

Library of Congress cataloguing in publication data applied for

ISBN 0 521 55360 1 hardback
ISBN 0 521 55637 2 paperback

WD

Contents

Figures

Tables

Acknowledgements

The material for this essay has been gathered over a number of years at the Indian Institute of Management, Ahmadabad, the Museum of Ethnology, Osaka, the Ecole des Hautes Etudes en Science Sociale, Paris, and in Cambridge, England. Most of the writing was done at the National Humanities Center, North Carolina, at the Wissenschaftskolleg in Berlin and at St John's College, Cambridge. I am grateful to all these institutions for their support.

I gave chapter one as a lecture on receipt of the Rezius Medal in Stockholm, Sweden; a preliminary version of chapter five was offered as the St John's College lecture at the University of East Anglia, and I have discussed other aspects of the thesis in many places, at the Chinese University of Hong Kong, the National University of Singapore, the Academia Sinica in Taiwan, the Wissenschaftskolleg zu Berlin, the National Humanities Center, North Carolina and especially at the University of Illinois, Urbana. I thank my hosts and audiences collectively for sitting through the presentation of earlier versions of these ideas.

Chapters of the book have been read by Malcolm Schofield and Geoffrey Lloyd (one), by Asha Sarabhai (four), by Shahid Amin (three and four) and all by Keith Hart. In addition I have been helped by Victor Mair, Joe McDermott, Juliet Mitchell, Norman Stockman and many others. The references to the trade in cloth owe much to Esther Goody's interest. My thanks are also due to the criticisms of anonymous readers, and I would like to thank Ruth Daniel for reading the proofs.

St John's College, Cambridge   JACK GOODY
March 1995

Introduction
The West's problem with the East

In Samuel Johnson's *Rasselas* (1759) the poet Imlac tries to explain to Rasselas the state of the world outside the Happy Valley.

In the Near East 'I conversed with great numbers of the northern and western nations of Europe; the nations which are now in possession of all power and all knowledge, whose armies are irresistible, and whose fleets command the remotest parts of the globe. When I compared these men with natives of our own kingdom and those that surround us, they appeared almost another order of beings. In their countries it is difficult to wish for anything that may not be obtained: a thousand arts, of which we never heard, are continually labouring for their convenience and pleasure; and whatever their own climate had denied them is supplied by their commerce.'

'By what means', said the Prince, 'are the Europeans thus powerful?; or why, since they can so easily visit Asia and Africa for trade or conquest, cannot the Asiatics and Africans invade their coast, plant colonies in their ports, and give laws to their natural princes? The same wind that carries them back would bring us thither.'

'They are more powerful, sir, than we', answered Imlac, 'because they are wiser; knowledge will always predominate over ignorance, as man governs the other animals. By why their knowledge is more than ours, I know not what reason can be given but the unsearchable will of the Supreme Being.'[1]

When did Europeans become conscious of their superiority over other nations?[2] Ethnic superiority is a universal feature of the human condition, the ethnocentric counterpart on the level of the group of the egocentricism that maintains the individual spirit. Such generalised superiority is not inconsistent with the presence of pockets of inferiority, with the recognition of inadequacies, with self doubts and self criticism. But at another level it emerges with especial clarity in group situations, as expressed by John of Gaunt's deathbed speech.

---

[1] *Rasselas*, p. 47.
[2] On the 'rediscovery' of the East in the later part of the eighteenth century, see Mannsåker 1990; Said 1978; and Schwab [1950] 1984.

> This royal throne of kings, this scepter'd isle,
> This earth of majesty, this seat of Mars,
> This other Eden, demi-paradise . . .   (*Richard II*, Act II, Scene i, 40–3)

What we do not find in Shakespeare is the expression of a generalised superiority of West over East that comes out so clearly in Johnson's statement in *Rasselas* in 1759, before the advent of the real Industrial Revolution (and of capitalism in that sense). There he correctly sees power and knowledge as being the attributes of the Europeans, especially military power and firepower, which recalls the theme of C. M. Cipolla's book, *Guns and Sails in the Early Phase of European Expansion 1400–1700* (1965). That power provides abundant trade goods and rests upon superior knowledge. So far so good. But such superiority is then given a permanent guise, being compared to the governance of man over the other animals, and that in turn is attributed to 'the unsearchable will of the Supreme Being'. However, the present superiority has not always existed, for it results from 'the progress of the human mind, the gradual improvement of reason, the successive advances of science'.[3] Meanwhile the application of reason is associated with the coming of Christianity, with the disappearance of 'the darkness of heathenism and the first dawn of philosophy'.[4]

This notion that Europeans were 'almost another order of beings' was not simple ethnocentricism, the result of defensive narcissism, but was based upon the achievements of the Renaissance, the Scientific Revolution and the Enlightenment. Hence the stress on knowledge, on reason (a concept which had come into fashion), on power and on trade. Yet while these achievements were recent, their roots were often seen to lie further back, in the deep structure of culture, in the heritage from the Greeks (or Germans) and in the favours of the Almighty (to a chosen people and to the coming of Christianity). In other words a historically specific advantage was generalised into a long-standing, indeed permanent, almost a biological superiority. Moreover the specific grounds for the superiority were not always well conceived, as a result of which Western historians, humanists and social scientists have often misunderstood the relationship between the East and the West. So too have some Eastern ones, blinded by the shattering effects of overseas expansion, of the advance of science, technology and knowledge more generally and finally of the coming of industry to Europe.

At the most general level, the contrast between Europe and Asia, with the consequent devaluation of the East, took root early in the history of

---

[3] Johnson 1759: 116.   [4] Johnson 1759: 186.

the West. The struggle between Greeks and Persians led to Asiatics being referred to as marked by despotic authority and barbaric splendour; in the *Politics* Aristotle saw them as more servile.[5] The medieval identification of Christianity and Europe reinforced these sentiments and following Aristotle, Montesquieu (1689–1755) again contrasted Europe's 'genius for liberty' with Asia's 'spirit of servitude': 'we shall never see there anything but the heroism of servitude, which held the despotic empire together because political relations are modelled on the filial piety.'[6] That contrast was challenged by the greater knowledge of the East resulting from the expansion of European trade in the seventeenth and eighteenth centuries: for China it was the Jesuits who insisted on a different perspective; for India it was the more perceptive merchants, travellers and administrators.[7] But the challenge rarely affected the general assessment of difference, as we see from Johnson's fantasy.

With the coming of the Industrial Revolution, the political contrast took a more specifically economic turn at the hands of the classical economists in England. Their views went back to Adam Smith's *The Wealth of Nations* in which he saw the poverty of the masses arising from the fact that the economy could not keep pace with the growth of the population. That feature had already concerned Montesquieu who ascribed excessive increase to hot climates; China was a stationary regime, neglecting natural liberty in favour of artificial regulations that checked commerce.

Among those influenced by the classical economists was Karl Marx, who lived in England between 1850 and 1883. Marx followed these earlier writers and more popular attitudes in seeing the static Asiatic state, based on irrigation, as ruling despotically over a servile peasantry. This was the Asiatic way of life. For profound reasons they were unable to follow the sequence of development that led from ancient society to feudalism and eventually to capitalism and then socialism. Marx's scheme of developmental stages were formalisations of widespread assumptions based upon European experience; they excluded Asia which took the road to a stagnant 'oriental' form of society, the road of 'Asiatic exceptionalism'.

By the time these economists were writing a considerable gap had opened up in the standard of living, in the accumulation of knowledge,

---

[5] 'Uncivilized peoples', including Asiatics, are more servile than Greeks or Europeans (*Politics* III, xiv, p. 6).
[6] Montesquieu [1989]: 280, 284.
[7] On the Jesuits and China, see Dawson 1967 and Mungello 1989.

as well as in the political systems between the East and the West. In the latter part of the eighteenth century western Europe had entered a period of self-sustaining growth so that Asia appeared static in comparison. The gap looked as though it was there to stay.[8] Again this advantage tended to be seen as reflecting a permanent state of affairs based upon long-standing social differences as the result of which the East had not experienced the growth of feudalism and its commercial centres, the communes that spread from northern Italy and heralded a civil society. Those actual and speculative advantages formed the background to the brilliant work of Max Weber. Weber produced a sounder basis for discussion than earlier writers like Hegel and more especially Herder who saw the difference with the Far East as due to 'the peculiar nature of the Chinese', by which he meant nature rather than culture since it arose from innate peculiarities.[9] That particular line of thinking can be dismissed; it is interesting only because it illustrates the extremes to which ethnocentricism can go – to racism in the literal sense. Weber's views require more serious consideration, especially as very similar ones still dominate much thinking in the social, political and historical fields. It is to those views, and the views of many others like him, that this book is addressed. Many Western specialists on Asia are well aware of their deficiencies, though others are mesmerized by the undoubted accomplishments of the West into giving them a global character (for example, rationality) when more specific factors would be appropriate, or into seeing the advantage in more long-standing terms than the evidence seems to warrant. If those failings are found among some specialists, including Eastern ones, they are yet more prevalent among historians, humanists and social scientists in the West, whose 'miraculous' Uniqueness constitutes a basic assumption of their work. What is at issue is the nature of the Uniqueness (which all societies obviously possess) in relation to the gap that grew up in this period.

In the nineteenth century there arose the specific question of the Uniqueness of the West in relation to the 'miracle' of self-sustaining growth, or in the eyes of others to the 'curse' of capitalism. The 'static' nature of the economics of Eastern society was seen to follow from the fact it did not possess adequate forms of rationality, of kinship, or of entrepreneurial skills, which were considered to be features of the West alone, as well as being critical to the major developments that had taken

---

[8] From the analytic standpoint, the term 'rapid growth' would be preferable since we do not know how 'self-sustaining' the growth will be, either for specific units or for the world as a whole.

[9] See the general account in Dawson 1967.

place there. Weber sees Europe as characterised by special forms of authority, rationality and economic ethic that allowed for the development of capitalism, whereas in Asia this outcome was inhibited by caste and kinship, as well as by the religious ethic. Both theories continue the humanist tradition that singled out the inheritance from Greece and Rome as conveying special virtues upon Europe. That ancient inheritance combined with the post-Renaissance search for rationality in knowledge and the economy enabled it to make the great leap forward, phrased in various ways as the Scientific Revolution, the Age of Reason and the Enlightenment, leading to 'modernisation', industrialisation and capitalism, the 'economic miracle' itself. Countless Western historians make similar assumptions in slightly different forms. Reduced to its ethnocentric bones, the question they pose to themselves is: 'What made us more fitted to be the torchbearers of modern society?'

I spoke of two classical theories. In addition we have various versions of 'world-systems theory'. Its advantage lies in its emphasis on the impact of recent changes on societies throughout the world. Its disadvantages are twofold. Firstly all other 'systems' or 'subsystems' are classified in relation to the West, i.e. as periphery or semi-periphery. While this division may represent an advance on a unitary concept of the Third World, it looks at the situation in terms of recent progress towards industrialisation; for example, Taiwan raised itself from periphery to semi-periphery since the post-war land reform.

The framework of such ideas has been the bread and butter of sociologists, historians, demographers, economists and, from a somewhat different angle, anthropologists. They have attempted to draw lines that not only overemphasised and deepened historically the differences (especially the critically relevant differences of which we have spoken) between the two parts of the Eurasian landmass, but also in my view those lines often overlooked the common heritage of the major societies of that region in the great Near Eastern civilisations, tending to 'primitivise' Eastern institutions, domestic, economic, religious and political, in unacceptable ways, at least in comparison with those of early modern Europe. From a broad, long-term standpoint we have to account for the subsequent divergence rather than the initial differences.

The facts have become increasingly apparent through major publications such as Needham's *Science and Civilisation of China*. The arguments relying on a long-standing advantage failed to take into account the fact that during the Middle Ages the East was pre-eminent in many fields. Moreover the discussion has become outdated by recent events in Asia, with the rapid growth of the economy, the technology and systems of knowledge, first in Japan and now in many other nations in the region.

Some decades ago it was clear, even to social scientists (historians did not yet have to face up to the problem: only practical men did), that Japan was worthy to be ranked among the industrial nations (the G7). How did this upgrading fit with current theories and popular prejudice? It was first assumed to be a case of Japanese exceptionalism. At the end of the 1950s, a scholar could put the question: 'Why did modern industrial capitalism arise in one East Asian society (Japan) and not in another (China)?'[10] Twenty years later another sociologist following this classic approach asked again, why Japan was 'the only non-Western country to have become a major industrial nation'.[11] The question behind this study remained that behind much of the work of Weber and Marx. In Parson's words, why did the Oriental civilisations never develop capitalism? The new gloss was that, largely since their days, Japan had become a world power. How was this to be explained? As 'the exception that proves the rule'?

For many in the West, scholars as well as the general public, the answer to the general question lay in the socio-cultural differences in the nature of their traditional societies, whether in the 'value system', the structure of the family, or another factor or combination of factors, that is to say, to internal differences. When Japan was brought into the analysis, a search was made for the similarities between Japan and western Europe, and hence for the differences of the former from China, which at that time had clearly not developed in the same way. Moulder argues that the differences between China and Japan were not all that great. What created the differences was the relative positions of Japan and China in the political economy of the world. While Japan was relatively autonomous and could adapt to the new situation, China (like most of the rest of the world) was said to be dominated by foreign capitalism, locked into 'a world system that disproportionately benefits others'.

The problem for this argument is that, while it recognises the internal similarities, it overstresses the external ones. For the same problem dogs the 'external' explanations of world-systems theory (developed by Wallerstein) that hampers the internal ones of Weberian theory. Both attempts have now suffered not only at the hands of Japan but since then from the development of the overseas Chinese communities of Hong Kong, Taiwan, Singapore and (though not Chinese in the same sense) Korea. All have undergone 'imperialist domination'; all have a similar

[10] Jacobs 1958: ix.   [11] Moulder 1977: vii.

culture to mainland China, which according to Moulder could only industrialise by undergoing a revolutionary Communist movement to loosen external ties. Events have amply demonstrated what is wrong with this analysis.

Others have provided more 'cultural' reasons. Some time ago the sociologist Bellah, following in the tradition of Parsons and Weber, argued that the religio-ethical tendencies in Japan prior to the Meiji Restoration provided a similar stimulus to economic and social development as Protestantism had played in the West.[12] That thesis has been taken up by Japanese writers like Morishima who argues that Japanese culture, especially its religion, explains these remarkable economic achievements. Now the goal posts have again been moved. Ten years later, and from a very different political position, Berger includes all east Asia as a second case which has generated 'a new type, or model, of industrial capitalism'. That type operates under 'non-democratic regimes and in non-"individualistic" cultures'.[13] It is akin to the notion of the alternative, collectivist form of capitalism put forward by a number of writers such as Redding, Rudner and Gellner. In other words this theory of the two capitalisms, one Western, one Eastern, meant that while they were unable to make it 'our way', they produced their own. The implication remains that they could not have modernised because of deep-structural features, a notion that needs to be challenged.

What is clear is that the superior achievements of the West can no longer be seen as permanent or even long-standing features of those cultures but as the result of one of the swings of the pendulum that has affected these societies over the millennia. The merest outline of a theory must begin by accepting the alternation. There remains of course a problem in explaining the pre-eminence of the West during the period between the Renaissance and the present day. Spectacular advances were made that ushered in the modern period. The result has been that European systems of industrial production, of intellectual activity (schools and universities), of health care, of bureaucratic government and to a significant extent of 'cultural' achievement, have established themselves, not without modification, throughout the world.

I am obviously not denying the importance for world history of these events and achievements associated with the Renaissance nor later with the Industrial Revolution and its aftermath, though comparisons with the East and the earlier West as well as some doubts about the way these claims are phrased lead me to entertain some queries. My main reservations have to do with the nature of the explanations for those

[12] Bellah 1957.   [13] Berger 1987: 141, 170.

changes, and their implications not simply for social science but for our perception of ourselves and of others. These reservations bear upon the way the changes have been characterised and upon the subsequent processes of 'development' in other parts of the world. It is often difficult to reconcile the developer's belief (a natural result of his calling) in the malleability of other social systems with the historical sociologist's belief in deep-structural differences. Indeed the latter appear to be belied by the fact that, while economic 'development' has had its setbacks in parts of the world (Africa, for example), in east Asia there have been major changes in the commercial and industrial spheres, as well as in many other areas of endeavour.

One tendency has been to ascribe to Europe the ability to modernise, whereas others could but copy. That argument can as well be applied to the West. It has been said of medieval economic life in Europe that 'What made it extraordinary was less the capacity to invent than the readiness to learn from others, the willingness to imitate, the ability to take over tools or techniques discovered in other parts of the world, to raise them to a higher level of efficiency, to exploit them for different ends and with a far greater degree of intensity'.[14] That widespread view assumes the occurrence of a radical break which only the West could make. But 'modernisation' is a continuous process and one in which regions have taken part in leap-frogging fashion. No one is endowed with unique features of a permanent kind that enable them alone to invent or adopt significant changes such as the Agricultural Revolution. What is critical is that the same kind of explanation has to be offered for the earlier superiority of the East as for the later achievements of the West. That is not what has happened. Academia is still stuck with its earlier theories which it is reluctant to abandon. I do not attempt to offer an account of the Rise of the West nor yet of the East, for I do not have the competence to do so. My intention is to revaluate the approaches we should be taking to such questions by querying the adequacy of our account of Western rationality, of Western commerce and of the Western family, in the way they relate to the process we loosely speak of as 'modernisation', 'industrialisation' or 'capitalism'.

In view of earlier achievements and later advances, what I regard as inadequate is any theory that claims to find something profoundly 'structural' in Asia that prevented these developments from taking place, or in Europe that advanced them. In looking at Europe, and specifically England, our natural egocentricity has often led us to assume a priority at deep, socio-cultural levels whereas the evidence for this is either thin

---

[14] Oakley 1979: 100.

or non-existent. The reasons for achievements in both West and East are more contingent. That leaves many questions to be asked and answered in a more particular, less ethnocentric way than has often been the case.

One resolution to the problem lies in looking at a wider span of world history than that from 1600 to the present day, and in modifying the emphasis so many of these theories give to events in western Europe.[15] To carry out such a wide-ranging re-examination of the specific reasons for Western pre-eminence lies well beyond the scope of the present essay. What I hope to do is to question many current assumptions about the Uniqueness of the West and so to lay the groundwork for better explanatory theories as well as for an improved understanding. As Berger remarks, what was earlier seen as an obstacle to development, namely Confucianism, came to be regarded as a facilitator. Now Mahayana Buddhism joins the queue, for 'the genius of the Chinese mind . . . succeeded in changing a radically world-denying religion into an essentially world-affirming one'. Certain components of the Western tradition, 'notably activism, rational innovativeness, and self-discipline' are now seen as elements of east Asian civilisation, whether in the great traditions or in folk culture. Individualism on the Western model, a theme much beloved by sociologists and historians, is not included and Berger does not think this element intrinsic, though it may appear as a consequence. In any case the net is already large enough to take in a multitude of fish. With parts of south-east Asia following the pattern of east Asia, similar questions have to be raised about Islamic values in Malaysia. When south Asia follows, as it shortly will, then Hinduism, Jainism and Sikhism will enter the picture so that little or nothing is excluded among the 'world religions'.

That seems to me correct. 'Culturalist' explanations for the rise of the West are problematic. So too are many 'institutionalist' ones.[16] In both cases the nature of the 'comparative advantage' allocated to these sets of factors needs to be re-examined with care. Some of these factors I look at in this book, beginning with rationality, going on to bookkeeping (*ragioneria*), then to levels of commerce at the time of European expansion, and the nature of the family and other groupings that were involved in trade and then in industry.

My conclusion is that we need to reconsider the East in the West. Let me give one example. Following the humanist tradition rather too closely, I earlier argued the West had a 'comparative advantage' due to the development of alphabetic literacy in Greece. That argument I now

[15] From a Near Eastern perspective, see Abu-Lughod 1989 and Adas 1993.
[16] See Vogel 1979.

regard as not entirely invalid but as exaggerated. Many of the achievements that are associated with the alphabet were also available to those
making use of logographic or other systems of writing. In pre-industrial
times, widespread literacy was not important for most purposes. In any
case the levels of reading and writing in societies with non-alphabetic
scripts were underestimated. That does not affect the socio-cultural
significance of writing in any way. But it does affect the way lines are
drawn between the East and the West in the context of scripts.

One problem constantly facing the enquirer is the kind of binarism that
looks at the world and in one of many possible ways says, or implies,
that there are two kinds of society, modern and traditional, advanced
and primitive, hot and cold, capitalist–industrialist as against pre-
capitalist–pre-industrialist, Worlds One and formerly Two as against the
Third World. That is the case even with many anthropologists. Those
concerned with their own intensive fieldwork inevitably set up a series of
binary comparisons, at least implicitly, between what they know about,
say the Asante of Ghana, and the European society from which they
come; or *vice versa*. On a general level the result tends to get phrased in
terms of binary categories (as between simple and complex and so on).
There seems to me a few, but very few, contexts in which this division is
useful, especially when one is experiencing a situation where individuals,
groups and even societies are shifting from one category to another. Even
if such a division were acceptable (and we are obviously forced to make
some broad categorisations), it is manifestly wrong to include the major
societies of Asia and of Africa in the same category, wrong from
the standpoint of 'contemporary development' and wrong from the
standpoint of the history of cultures.

Intellectually, we know that such a categorisation is all too crude and
useful for very few purposes. In practice it is part of our repertoire of folk
concepts. But the major problem we face in the present discussion has to
do not so much with binary divisions but with more sophisticated but
nevertheless insufficiently sophisticated ways of dividing the great
Oriental civilisations from our own. I have been deeply dissatisfied with
these types of vision, arising either from the binary or from the stage
approach, not only in a general, intellectual sense but because of my own
experience in and with Asia and Africa. In a short essay I can only point
to how another perspective can suggest some ways in which earlier
discussions have gone awry. For the wrong evaluation of the comparative
situation as between East and West also affects the West's understanding
of itself.

1   Rationality in review

The rise of the West has often been associated, by Westerners, with the possession of a rationality not available to others. That notion has taken two main forms. The classical humanist tradition regards itself as heir to Greek rationality, especially its invention of 'logic'. Another line of enquiry concentrates on a later period, the Renaissance, the Reformation or more usually the Enlightenment, and looks to special forms of rationality as enabling the West to take the lead in the economic and intellectual developments seen as associated with the modern world. Weber writes of this as the rationality of world-mastery and commentators have called it a specifically 'western rationality'.[1] His aim was to 'comprehend the distinctiveness of the West and especially modern Western rationalism and to explain it genetically'.[2] He posed the question why 'did not . . . the economic development there [in China and India] enter upon that path of rationalization which is peculiar to the Occident'.[3] Others have seen it as embedded in the growth of secularism, the end of magic, the beginning of experimental science and the Age of Reason. Either way the change emerges in the sixteenth, seventeenth or eighteenth centuries CE rather than two millennia previously.

I want to challenge both these scenarios from several angles. Firstly, I discuss briefly the evidence that rationality in a wide sense, as well as in its specialist form, logic, are attributes of all cultures, taking some general as well as some culturally specific forms. Secondly, this informal logic differs from the formal 'logic' of the Greeks whose typical instrument, the syllogism, is present only in the much more general form of sequential reasoning in oral cultures. The same is true of other forms of proof but I shall concentrate on syllogistic reasoning since Aristotle did. Thirdly, this specialised form has not been confined to the Greeks but is

[1] Schluchter 1981.
[2] Author's introduction, *Collected Essays in the Sociology of Religion*, quoted Schluchter 1981: 133.
[3] Weber 1958: 25.

11

found in other literate societies of the Near East and Asia, so that Europe cannot see itself as the sole beneficiary, or even perhaps the only victim, of these ways of reasoning. Finally, I discuss claims about the distribution of rationality in the wider sense, especially in relation to economic development.

Let me first clarify the definitional problem. Etymologically the word 'reason' comes from the Latin *ratio*, computation, hence ratio and rations. The meanings in the Oxford English Dictionary are given as:

1. a statement in explanation (that is, cause);
2. the power of comprehending, inferring or thinking, especially in orderly, rational ways (that is, intelligence).

Rationality is the capacity to reason, to apply logic, the latter being doubly defined as:

1. a science that deals with the canons and validity of inference and demonstration (that is, deductive, formal, philosophical 'logic' in a specialised sense);
2. the interrelation or sequence of facts or events when seen as inevitable or predictable (that is, logic in a more general sense). More directly, it is 'a generic truth-securing faculty'.[4]

The humanist argument holds that rationality or logic began with the Greeks. That is essentially the problem raised for Evans-Pritchard in his work on *Witchcraft, Oracles and Magic among the Azande* (1937) by Lévy Bruhl's contention that the 'primitive mind' was characterised by the absence of logic (and was therefore pre-logical) and by the failure to recognise contradiction. Evans-Pritchard on the other hand pointed to the logic behind Azande thought when, for example, they posed the question of why the granary wall collapsed just when certain people were sitting underneath. It was not enough to say it just happened, or did so by chance; some agency must have been at work.[5] He remarks of the Azande, 'they reason excellently in the idiom of their beliefs'.[6] Wrong outcomes of divinations, for example, were explained by assuming that witchcraft or some other force had distorted the workings of the poison oracle by which they tried to discover the truth. In general they did not ask questions that were not 'easily tested by experience'; rather they searched for 'the mystical forces which hang over a man and doom him in advance'. While they did not distinguish between what the anthropologist called natural and mystical causes, nevertheless their belief in witchcraft 'in no way contradicts empirical knowledge of cause and effect'.[7] In other words there exists a kind of logic, as well as some

---

[4] Gellner 1992: 26.   [5] Evans-Pritchard 1937: 69.
[6] Evans-Pritchard 1937: 338, 340, 341.   [7] Evans-Pritchard 1937: 73.

recognition of contradiction. Nevertheless purely oral cultures may inhibit the perception of how the oracle has failed in ways that are central to my general argument: 'the contradiction between his beliefs and his observations only becomes a generalised and glaring contradiction when they are recorded side by side in the pages of an ethnographic treatise, as a result of collecting "jottings" over many months of observation and enquiry. The contradictions in Zande thought are then readily seen . . . If he is conscious of a contradiction it is a particular one which he can easily explain in terms of his own beliefs.'[8] That is to say, literacy is critical in promoting scepticism and 'truth-securing' procedures. Scepticism about the oracle's verdicts existed, but was swallowed up by the more general faith in the system and by the difficulties of perceiving contradiction in oral discourse.

That discussion has to do with the question of societies and rationality. But there is another external, rather than actor-oriented, approach to the beliefs and practices of witchcraft and divination that pertains to individual acts in any society. We can consider these acts as irrational (or non-rational) in themselves in that as observers we do not see the effects as following from the putative causes. In talking of rationality and logic among the Azande, Evans-Pritchard was referring to procedures, to the entailment of argument and to inference. The alternative sees witchcraft and divination as irrational because of the nature of their basic premisses; in other words it applies largely external criteria to the entailment of the means–end relationships from a 'scientific' point of view rather than in terms of logical consistency. From this angle, the question of what is rational always presents a moving target, since science is necessarily changing its mind about cause and effect. This is a question to which I will return in considering contemporary Chinese divination.

These two approaches relate to the distinction between the universalist and the relativist positions. The first affirms the existence of global standards that can be used as a measure. The second assumes that every culture has a coherent system of beliefs which cannot be judged by external categories. Evans-Pritchard seemed to employ both and to argue not only that the Azande had their own logic but that actions of theirs could, in Parsons' terms, be considered as rational, non-rational or a-rational, depending upon whether or not the means–end relationship was 'intrinsic' by 'objective' standards (that is, by the Western academic observer). Once again there are two interrelated questions: whether societies are characterised by rationality or by a special type of rationality; and whether a particular action can be described as 'rational'

[8] Evans-Pritchard 1937: 319.

or 'logical'. In analysing Trobriand fishing using external criteria Malinowski pointed out that the islanders adopted 'rational' techniques in lagoon fishing but applied magical ones in the deep sea when there was greater uncertainty. Rationality and irrationality existed side by side. That theme has been followed up in studies of Western societies.[9] The opposition between 'utilitarian' and 'ritual', between rational and non-rational or even symbolic means, involves the application, at least implicitly, of specific external criteria regarding the relationship between types of 'cause' and 'effect' in different contexts in the same society. It does not directly address the more inclusive problem of different 'modes of thought', of different cultural forms of rationality or logic. Indeed the segmental approach runs somewhat counter to the holistic one. If we see rationality and logic as features of all societies, the problem remains of how extensive the application of rationality is in a particular society in terms of activities and individuals and of whether there is some analytic threshold we can usefully suggest to distinguish, for example, 'modern' from 'traditional'.

Much of the philosophical and anthropological debate on rationality has taken place in just such a dichotomised context, the modern West versus 'primitive' societies.[10] It takes a 'we' versus 'they' format, rationality against ritual. In the latter case action is to be interpreted as expressive or symbolic rather than as means–ends related. However the difference between Greek 'logic' and Azande logic cannot simply be dichotomised in this particular way nor just designated cultural and subjected to no further examination.

There are two other main ways of looking at the problem of rationality. The first is one taken by many anthropologists and psychologists, having to do with the presence and use of logic and logical procedures. That discussion goes back in particular to Lévy Bruhl's treatment of logical and pre-logical mentalities which following Aristotle has frequently turned on the use of syllogistic reasoning as the major difference, although others have referred to procedures of argument and proof in a broader sense. The second approach turns its attention to modernisation and to the emergence not of Greek thought but of Western science, the advent of which is seen as linked to the coming of capitalism. Like the first, this line of thinking has its roots in popular beliefs of a widely held kind, but its scholarly expression is associated with Max Weber and

[9] Malinowski 1948.
[10] That is the tenor of the work edited by Bryan Wilson entitled *Rationality* (1977) with papers by philosophers such as Winch, Gellner, Jarvie, MacIntyre, Agassi, Lukes and Hollis, and philosophically minded anthropologists such as Horton and Beattie.

the sociological tradition.[11] His 'central theoretical question' was 'how Occidental rationalism can be explained'.[12]

Lévy Bruhl had raised this problem of logic when comparing advanced (Greek and post-Greek) thinking with the operation of what he called the 'primitive mind'. Evans-Pritchard's reply was to demonstrate the logic, the interrelatedness, of Azande beliefs. His answer could be interpreted in a culturally specific sense, that each society had its own distinct logic. I do not think that is only how he meant it and certainly that was not how it was interpreted by those who followed his discussion – by Fortes in a lecture on the 'Mind' (in *Primitive Society*), by Gluckman in a thoughtful article on 'logic', by Horton and Finnegan in their subsequent work on 'modes of thought' and by Tambiah in his Morgan lectures on magic.[13] That all cultures have their own logic is in a sense a truism, or would be if it were possible to establish adequate boundaries; indeed individuals and groups have their own variants. But such a contention is clearly inadequate at any significant level of abstraction since many cultures display important similarities in their thinking, in their cognitive procedures, especially in respect of the search for an active cause behind the falling granary. If this were not so, if extreme cultural particularism held true, then it is difficult to see how there could be the considerable degree of communication that undoubtedly exists between neighbouring human groups. On the other hand neither Evans-Pritchard nor these subsequent writers were simply saying that all these logics, Greek and Azande, were the same; that is, they did not take an unrestricted, universalistic position. The Azande did have notions of contradiction, in dispute cases for example, just as they could argue logically, but they did not have the formal laws of contradiction nor yet the formal logical procedures that marked the Greeks of Aristotle's day. Let us look at that contrast in greater detail.

Syllogistic reasoning in Greece

For Aristotle, knowledge was built on previous knowledge. The *Posterior Analytics* begins 'All teaching and learning that involves the use of reason proceeds from pre-existent knowledge'.[14] The subject of this work is proof or demonstration (*apodeixis*), that is, argument producing scientific understanding (*epistēmē*). Aristotle conceives of a demonstrative science

---

11 'Among the social sciences sociology is most likely to link its basic concepts to the rationality problematic' (Habermas 1984: 3).
12 Habermas 1984: 6.
13 Gluckman 1949–50; Fortes 1954; Horton and Finnegan 1973; Tambiah 1990.
14 Aristotle (ed. and trans. Tredennick) 1960: 25.

as a system of demonstrations which are in turn a type of deduction (*sullogismos*). So while the *Prior Analytics* gives an account of deductions in general, the *Posterior* discusses the specific character of those deductions which are demonstrations.[15] The syllogism is described as a logos in which if something is posited, something else reasonably follows; in other words, as a form of sequential reasoning. This procedure was linked to the development of 'a demonstrative science' and to the enunciation of laws of syllogistic reasoning, described by Tredennick as perhaps Aristotle's 'greatest and most original achievement'.[16] Like forms of contradiction, it was connected with types of inference and proof, and characterised reasoning in formal 'logic' up to the development of modern procedures. The general format is well known:

> Every animal that breathes possesses lungs.
> Every viviparous (birth-giving) animal breathes.
> Therefore every viviparous animal possesses lungs.[17]

Or, perhaps more simply:

> All virtue is praiseworthy.
> Kindness is a virtue.
> Therefore kindness is praiseworthy.

I want to draw attention to three aspects of the Greek development of these highly decontextualised and universalistic statements. Firstly, it involved the establishment of the syllogism as a formal operation.

[15] R. Smith 1989: xiii.

[16] Aristotle (ed. and trans. Tredennick) 1938: 182.

[17] Barnes 1982: 30. Aristotelian logic is a logic of *terms* – elements (usually nouns and adjectives) which can figure in the subject or predicate position of a simple subject–predicate proposition. The schematic letters A, B, C stand as dummies for these elements. The syllogism is then constructed from two such propositions which share one of their terms and a conclusion deduced from them, for example

> If C is predicated of every B
> and B of some A
> then C is predicated of some A

The later Stoic school developed a logic of *propositions* which is now recognised as a system of greater scope and power than Aristotelian syllogistic. The Stoics too used dummy expressions, although typically not letters but ordinals – 'the first', 'the second' etc. Thus their first 'indemonstrable argument' (known since the Middle Ages as *modus ponens*) has the form:

> If the first, then the second.
> The first.
> Therefore the second.

A particular standard example:

> If it is day, then it is light.
> It is day.
> Therefore it is light.

I am most grateful to Dr M. Schofield for his extensive comments.

Secondly, there was the emergence of metatheory, that is, of commentaries and theories about those procedures. Thirdly, there was training in their use as part of the educational process, feeding back to at least a segment of the population. The syllogism itself required writing as a prerequisite, especially in the abstract Aristotelian form. The metatheory too required writing. Of course members of oral cultures are capable of adapting and commenting on procedures of computation or thought, though such comments would undoubtedly be more concrete and more restricted than if they were made in writing. But these comments tend either to get incorporated in a standardised utterance or to be tied to the passing moment since they remain unrecorded and hence not available for further scanning; either way the likelihood of incremental commentary is drastically reduced. Finally the teaching or use of the syllogism itself involves script in the general sense that writing dominates education in literate cultures. There is no reason why some cognitive tool that required writing to invent (such as the mathematical tables) cannot become part of oral transmission within a literate culture. Obviously the products of writing can influence not only oral traditions in literate societies but neighbouring oral cultures themselves. Nevertheless, writing is engaged at all three levels in these particular logical procedures.

There are two views about the nature of the syllogism. The humanist tradition sees the form of logic it embodies as deriving from the Greeks and as a fundamental contribution to the superior performance of the West. Others see it as universal, part of the built-in abilities of the human mind, like Chomsky's contention about syntax. This I take to be the position of Johnson-Laird in his book on *Mental Models* where he writes: 'How does a system of logic arise in the mind? Neither the principles of learning theory nor the assumptions of Piagetian lore appear to provide an adequate answer. By default, it seems that our logical apparatus must be inborn, though there is no account of how it could have become innately determined.'[18] Everything turns on whether the first sentence refers to logic in general or to 'logic' in the shape of the formal syllogism. The rest of the account suggests the latter. Yet in the work of the Russian psychologist, A. R. Luria, we find non-schooled peasants rejected the format, seeing the epitome of Aristotelian logic as irrational. Indeed I would suggest that not only is it a tool unknown (in that form) in oral cultures, but in literate ones it is typically seen as an instrument of the educated, often of the overeducated, the pedant, the logician.

Both theses, the humanist and the universalist (or 'rationalist'), have

[18] Johnson-Laird 1983: 39–40.

something to be said for them, but each is inadequate on its own. Forms of inferential reasoning, logic in the general sense we encountered among the Azande, are certainly found in all human societies (though not of course always used). But 'logic' in the shape of the syllogism is a formalised development of such reasoning, which is certainly *not* universal. Indeed in its most abstract form it clearly depends upon the use of an alphabet. As a result of the Greek adaptation of a Semitic script, Aristotle was able to produce a generalised version of the syllogism by substituting meaningless letters for the meaningful terms such as 'animal' giving a formula such as:

All $A = B$
All $C = B$
Therefore all $A = C$

No longer were the elements specific words or concepts: the grammar of 'logic' could now be universalised, globalised, by substituting phonetic symbols (letters) for words (semantic symbols), that is, by abandoning the lexicon. It is more difficult to take this step with logographic writing like Chinese because of the concrete references of the signs employed. However even the less abstract type of syllogism constitutes a formalisation of reasoning, of the largely implicit logical procedures of the Azande type, which results from putting them down in a visual format and so permits and encourages the reorganisation of both the information and the syntax. In the same way writing encouraged the development and formalisation of the notion of categories by placing them in lists, so that the constituent items became partly decontextualised, were provided with a beginning and an end (involving an additional kind of exclusion and inclusion) and given a definite hierarchical form, all characteristics of the written procedure.[19] The syllogism of the Aristotelian kind may well sound like nonsense to members of the Azande used to inferential reasoning of a more general type. That is even true for those members of societies with writing who have not been to school, as was vividly brought out in the study of the responses to verbal syllogisms carried out by Luria.

Working in Central Asia with peasants who had not been incorporated into the large collective farms then being organized in the Soviet Union, as well as 'progressive' peasants who had been collectivized, Luria found striking differences in the way these two populations responded to simple verbal syllogisms. For example, one noncollectivized (and presumably more traditional) peasant was posed the following problem: 'In a certain town in Siberia all bears are white. Your neighbor went to that town and he saw a bear. What color was that bear?' The peasant responded that there was no way for him to know what

19 See Goody 1977.

color that bear was, since he had not been to the town. Why didn't Professor Luria go to his neighbor and ask him what color the bear was? Such responses were typical and seemed to be more or less independent of the particular content of the problem. More sophisticated subjects (those who had been living on a collective farm for some time and had been exposed to new farm practices and new cultural traditions) responded very much as we might respond. That is, they simply said something like, 'Of course the bear must be white since you said only white bears live in that town.'[20]

The rejection of syllogistic reasoning is not confined to the uneducated. The limits of formal logic have been apparent to many. Francis Bacon accused Aristotle of rendering natural philosophy 'useless and disputatious' by making it subservient to logic.[21] That objection is related to an earlier remark that the first distemper of learning is 'when men study words and not matter', that is, when they neglect the truly scientific method.[22] These same procedures were also the subject of more satirical comment. Quine sees inductive logic as covering the main stem of philosophy, the theory of knowledge itself, whereas deductive logic is 'the systematic study of the logical truths'. The latter has been more colloquially defined by Lewis Carroll: '"Contrariwise", continued Tweedledee, "if it was so, it might be; and if it were so, it would be; but as it isn't, it ain't. That's logic."' The greater formalisation of such procedures was intrinsic to certain developments of knowledge in the classical world as we can see from the theorems of Euclid ending with the phrase, translated into Latin as QED, *Quod Erat Demonstrandum*. However, that any particular procedure, such as the syllogism, was intrinsic to later developments in European knowledge is less evident. Indeed to many the syllogism appears as a highly artificial form of proof largely reserved for logicians. In any case its use is contextual, for solving a particular kind of puzzle; it does not take over all our cognitive operations.

The varied responses remind us that these 'language games' (to use a phrase of Wittgenstein's) are precisely that. They face two ways. At one level they are seen by Aristotle (and by philosophers for the following 2,000 years) as intrinsic to rational knowledge. They were cognitive tools which indeed enabled the Greeks to formalise geometry and other sciences. On the other hand, they were formalisations of the obvious, fit for pedants (as the Russian peasant suggests), appropriate for children's games (as Carroll implies), and at times positively misleading for the accumulation of knowledge (as Bacon insists).

---

[20] Cole *et al.* 1971: 185.   [21] *Novum Organum*, First Book, 63, 54.
[22] *Advancement of Learning*, First Book, IV, 3.

Their formality derives from writing in a very direct way, for as we have seen the elements of the syllogism need not even be verbal. Aristotle substituted the abstract letters of the alphabet for linguistic units. It has been argued that without the use of (alphabetic) letters 'logic cannot become a general science of argument'.[23] But writing in the form of graphic representation was significant in other ways. It has even been suggested that the syllogistic procedure emerged from a graphic form. 'A premiss was probably represented by a line joining the letters chosen to stand for the terms.' That is speculation, but Aristotle may well have used a blackboard like modern logicians or mathematicians. He certainly appears to have owed something to mathematicians and, in a more abstract sense, the drawing of lines was critical, as in Plato's practice of definition by dichotomy (in a characteristically literate way).[24] That particular practice is criticised by Aristotle as 'a kind of weak syllogism' while others have described it as 'trivial and question-begging' for modern readers.[25] But what some see as the splitting of hairs and the drawing of lines is an essential element of such procedures.

Aristotle claimed his syllogistic (*sullogismos*) was a universal statement of logic. Later thinkers were so impressed by its elegance that for two millennia 'the Analytics were taught as though they constituted the sum of logical truth'.[26] Clearly that was not the case. Even his own scientific works do not follow these procedures, whose very written formality poses dangers not only for the spoken word but for logic itself. For example, the practitioner may be led into filling empty boxes that were possibly better left unfilled. Tredennick calls attention to Aristotle's desire for symmetrical tripartition, a procedure as capable of leading the enquirer astray as Plato's binary categories or the fourfold tables of later formalists.[27] Acknowledging that a purely formal logic detached from reality is a worthless instrument, he criticises Aristotle for expecting 'more correspondence between the conclusion of a syllogism and objective reality than is compatible with the conception of the syllogism as a process of thought'.

Later psychologists such as Vygotsky and more recently Johnson-Laird have seen the syllogism as just such 'a process of thought'. Other philosophers such as Barnes have viewed it not as an activity to be followed by the scientific researcher but as a way in which the results of an enquiry 'are to be systematically organised and displayed'.[28] In either

---

[23] Barnes 1982: 30.   [24] See Jackson 1920 and Einarson 1938.
[25] On Plato's 'dialectic' by dichotomous division, see W. and M. Kneale 1962: 9ff.
[26] Barnes 1982: 31.
[27] Aristotle (ed. Tredennick) 1938: 192.   [28] Barnes 1982: 38.

case the formal syllogism is clearly a cognitive tool constructed in and through the medium of the written word, that is, it is found only in a particular range of human society. This and similar tools are seen by humanists as being a specifically Greek creation that enabled Europe to develop rational and logical procedures as well as forms of knowledge not available to others, all of which contributed to the later pre-eminence of that continent. And the reason they arose in ancient Greece is customarily attributed to its love of argument and desire for forms of proof. Such an argument could not apply to logic and reason in the broad sense since these were certainly not absent from oral cultures. But if our argument about the literate nature of the formal syllogism is correct, we should expect to find it, at least in a non-alphabetic form, in other written civilisations. Not inevitably, for these are the results of specific historic developments, based on writing, and possibly achieved by adaptation rather than invention. But a process of adaptation nonetheless indicates that the situation was ripe for such a written development, of making implicit procedures explicit and changing their character in so doing.

What was the importance of these logical rules? They played some part in axiomatising knowledge in the Euclidian manner but they also served to rigidify it. In later periods in the West, as in the East, they appeared more frequently in religious (scholastic) debates than they did in scientific ones. However, the presence of 'logic' has sometimes been seen by historians of ideas as being a necessary tool, like mathematics in the developments of science. For science, as for logic and mathematics, we find wider and narrower definitions of the field. Some have seen science as 'the system of behaviour by which man acquires mastery of the environment', while others define it as an active process of knowledge-making.[29] The first of these definitions finds science everywhere; the second tends to see it in the Western tradition alone. However, even by the restricted criteria, we find science in the East, as Joseph Needham has amply demonstrated for China. Anthropologists usually opt for the wider definition and many observers have discerned rational, logical and technological action in the simplest societies. At the same time, formalised procedures, leading to the adoption of the experimental method, are clearly absent in oral cultures, though they begin to make their appearance in literate societies before the Greeks. G. E. R. Lloyd suggests that the Greek text *On the Sacred Disease* was the first explicitly to declare a body of beliefs to be magical and substitute a naturalistic explanation, thus separating the two spheres. But the simultaneous

[29] See Tambiah 1990: 8–9.

rejection of one explanation and the acceptance of a causal pluralism that embraced what we see as 'naturalistic' and 'magical' factors was present among the Greeks as it was among other peoples. Evans-Pritchard sees an implicit distinction being made by the Azande. That is what Malinowski demonstrated for the Trobriands. If we regard explicit recognition as essential, then when we look at earlier activity in the Near East, it is not clear that we find among the Greeks the actual emergence of a radical paradigmatic shift, although there were important changes of emphasis.

Returning to the syllogism, we find the humanist contention flawed, partly because the procedure itself was perhaps less important for seeking truth than they thought. But the notion that it formed part of a special form of rationality confined to the West lacks conviction when we look back and more widely at other cultures with writing.

Mesopotamia

The more specialist procedures found in ancient Greece seem to have specific prototypes in earlier written cultures. The French Assyriologist, Bottéro, has described embryonic syllogistic forms in ancient Mesopotamia which have to do with equivalences and empty boxes arising out of the creation of tables. The first takes the form of:

> if term 1 = term 2
> and term 2 = term 3
> then term 1 = term 3

Other procedures invite us to fill an empty box on the principle of analogy:

term 1	term 2
term 3	

term 1 is to term 2

as term 3 is to ?

At a less formal level, procedures of this general kind appear in all or most societies, since they relate to ways that cases are argued not only in court, and in less formal moots, but in discussions between individuals trying to establish that things are like this rather than like that.

It is sometimes suggested that the development of logic enabled the Greeks to move from divination and magic to science, with Greek astronomy originating in Mesopotamian astrology and divination. Bottéro argues that this typically European line of thinking is quite wrong. As in many other ways he sees the Greeks as 'tributaires des vieux Mésopotamiens'. In the first place, there were many Mesopotamian contributions to astronomy proper. Secondly, early divination itself became 'une connaissance de type scientifique' and already, in essence, a science;[30] with the accumulation of written records, it became deductive, taking into account not only actual outcomes (that is, the double gall-bladder in a sacrificial sheep) but all theoretically possible ones, with three and even seven deformations. In this evolution of divination Bottéro sees the development of a scientific method: 'this encyclopaedic curiosity; this way of approaching universal reality by way of knowledge that is analytic, indispensable, deductive, *a priori*; this "abstract" and scientific attitude to things was a definite acquisition by the human spirit.'[31] As I have argued with lists, this inquisitive spirit may well have been already in place, at least potentially; however it was writing that enabled it to develop in the manner described.[32] In this way there emerged a 'dialectique graphique' some fifteen centuries before the Greeks. That dialectic he illustrates by examining the use of the name of the god Marduk. Learned men elucidated or built up the meanings of a name by analysing the syllables, finding the equivalent in Sumerian words (for example, 'a' stands for 'water'), looking at the Akkadian equivalent (since writing was bilingual, like Latin in the European Middle Ages), and playing with the visual graphemes and the phonetic homophones. For example, the word A-sa-ri implied that Marduk was:

> The giver of agriculture;
> The founder of the partitioning of fields;
> The creator of cereals and hemp;
> The producer of all greenery.[33]

Some of these forms of discourse developed in Mesopotamia paved the way for increasingly precise scientific methods; others were precursors of syllogistic procedures; yet others involved language games that appeared to lead nowhere. All were encouraged by the use and development of the written word, or at least of graphic techniques.

In looking at Eastern societies I have excluded the Arab world of the Near East for a specific reason. It took over much of Greek learning and later introduced Aristotle to Europe after Islam began to penetrate the south of that continent. Not only did Islam fail to meet the criteria for an independent case but Greek methods of formal reasoning were known in some circles before they were in the West. In the early ninth century the seventh 'Abbāsid caliph, al-Ma'mūn, founded, or at least developed, the House of Wisdom in Baghdad where Greek philosophical and scientific works were translated into Arabic. The House had a

---

[30] Bottéro 1987: 157.   [31] Bottéro 1987: 168.   [32] Goody 1977.
[33] I have not done justice to Bottéro's careful explanation, but see 1987: 113ff., and preferably his 'Les noms de Marduk, l'écriture et la "logique" en Mésopotamie ancienne', in *Essays on the Ancient Near East: in memory of J. J. Finkelstein.*

magnificent library, with several astronomical observatories, and drew on the learned culture not only of Greece but of Persia and India in such fields as medicine, mathematics, philosophy, theology, literature and poetry. Iraq regarded itself as heir to all former civilisations but especially to the Greek. The works of Aristotle fascinated the élite because of his method of intellectual reasoning, and his influence was very prominent in the school of thought known as Mu'tazilism, which aimed at harmonising reason and faith. At this time Baghdad was the hub of Near Eastern trade, with its merchants sailing to Ceylon and as far as China.

Trade and conquest also took Islam to the Mediterranean. Already in the seventh century it had reached the Maghreb and soon made its mark on Sicily and Spain. While it did not introduce Greek reasoning to the West, it played an important part in its development. Syllogistic reasoning was already known in the scholastic philosophy of western Europe through the translations from Greek into Latin, and through the commentaries made by the sixth-century Roman scholar, Boethius. He translated Aristotle's *Organon* (six treatises on logic), wrote two short works on the syllogism and possibly a commentary on the *Prior Analytics*. But the other major works of Aristotle were not known in the West until they were translated largely from the Arabic, together with the commentaries of Avicenna, Averroës and Maimonides in the thirteenth century when they influenced the Dominican scholar, Albertus Magnus, to study nature. While the concept of reason did not dominate Arabic thought in the way it did the post-Enlightenment West, that thought was as well grounded in Aristotelian logic.[34] But let us turn from the West and the Near East to south and east Asia.

India, China and Japan

The fact that we find proto-syllogisms in Mesopotamia detaches that notion from the West, since the East too derived a great deal from that first Bronze Age society which formed one of the major contributors to the great Oriental civilisations. In what other of these societies do we see forms of syllogism? The data I want to discuss here are well known to specialists in the field. Nevertheless many of them, dazzled by the spectacular advances made in Europe in industrial capitalism (since 1780) and in knowledge systems (since the Renaissance), tend to search for the causes in differences in systems of rationality and 'logic'. What is clear is that types of syllogism existed throughout the East over a

---

[34] See Aziz Al-Azmeh 1986.

long span of time. A well-known Indian scholar divided that country's philosophy into three periods: the pre-logical (before the Common Era), the logical (to the eleventh century) and the ultralogical (to the eighteenth century).[35] We can dismiss the pre-logical phase, unless the reference is taken to be to the absence of formal 'logic' in the Greek sense. A more usual approach is to divide Indian logic itself into three periods: Old Nyāya (c. 250 BCE), Buddhist logic (sixth century CE) and New Nyāya. The Nyāya-sūtra belongs to the earlier period; the Nyāyapravesśa (the Buddhist introduction to logical methods, which had so great an influence in China as well as in India among Buddhists and Jains) belongs to the second period.[36] Even the early period already saw the appearance of a string of texts, of sūtras and commentaries that arose in the context of controversies among Buddhists, Brahmans and Jains. The early Nyāya-sūtra already elaborated a methodology of discussion and presented a so-called five-member syllogism:

> Proposition (pratijñā): there is fire on the mountain.
> Reason (hetu): because there is smoke on the mountain.
> Example (dṛṣṭānta): as in a kitchen – not as in a lake.
> Application (upanaya): it is so (i.e. it is so in the present case).
> Conclusion (nigamana): there is fire on the mountain.[37]

In later forms of Buddhist logic the five-membered syllogism was reduced and consisted either of the first three or last three parts. Guénon has pointed out that the last three resembled the Aristotelian deductive syllogism (modus ponens) while the first three represented an inversion, what Pierce and later Hanson have called 'retroduction'. The background of such formalisation is well brought out in an account of a treaty concluded in about 150 BCE between Menander, the Greek King of the Punjab, and the sage Nāgasena, which provides an early example of the formalisation of argument by scholars.

> The king said: 'Excellent Nāgasena, would you like to hold further discussion with me?'
> 'If you are willing to discuss like a wise man, O king, yes, indeed; but if you want to discuss like a king, then no.'
> 'How do the wise discuss, excellent Nāgasena?'
> 'In the discussions of the wise, O king, there is found unrolling and rolling up, convincing and conceding; agreements and disagreements are reached. And in all that, the wise suffer no disturbance. Thus it is, O king, that the wise discuss.'[38]

---

[35] Dasgupta 1922–55.   [36] Factor 1983: 183.
[37] For another translation, see Factor 1983: 187.   [38] Bocheński 1961: 421.

Out of such a context, discourse developed with strictly defined rules. There are some queries among those philosophers like Daye who claims that the *Nyāya* models are not inferences but 'formalistic explanations'; in other words that it is not deductive. But most scholars accept that there is no radical incompatibility between Nyāya methods and those of the *Analytics* or of *Principia Mathematica*. There are differences in any tradition but not such as to exclude inference as some have argued (for example, Hansen for China). After the emergence of a concept of universal law, concludes Bocheński, Indian logic developed uninfluenced by the West. While some important problems were unknown, it elaborated other theorems in the domain of relational logic that did not appear in the West until Frege and Russell. However in many respects it developed 'the *same problems* and reached the same solutions', providing 'an original and interesting variety of genuine formal logic'.[39]

A similar kind of analysis to that Bocheński applied to ancient Western and Indian logic has been extended to China. Two views emerge about Chinese logic. On the one hand there are statements by Munro, Graham, Hall and Ames that deny logic to Chinese thinking; Hansen claims that Later Mohist texts do not imply truth-claims. On the other hand Paul maintains that the syllogism does not necessarily have as its object the discovery of truth (as in the case of modern logic); it may be seen as 'a way of establishing identity and diversity-relations of/between concepts'.[40] In opposition to Hansen, he sees Neo-Mohist philosophers as developing a system of logic 'basically identical to what was generally considered logic in the West from Aristotle to Frege'.[41] Arguing against the view of those scholars that see only difference (and especially the thesis of Hansen who stresses what he considers to be the particular features of logic in China), Paul maintains that the Later Mohists expressly formulated the 'law of non-contradiction', the 'law of the excluded middle', and the 'Dictum de omni et nullo'. Moreover they conceived of these laws as laws, that is to say, they employed them as criteria of accepted language use and argument, and tried to abide by them (as well as by the 'law of identity'). Since it is precisely these principles that figure most prominently in the Aristotelian tradition, he concludes that the basic logical laws do not depend on particular presuppositions such as culture, language, ontology or truth concepts. There exists a universal logic.

While general parameters of language use undoubtedly exist, it is significant that the actual formulation of these rules of discourse occurs

---

[39] Bocheński 1961: 447.
[40] Paul 1993: 122.   [41] Paul 1993: 123.

only at a certain point in the development of human society, with the advent of writing. As with grammar, implicit rules existed before but their explicit formulation creates a different situation, mainly but not only for the literati. We have to take into account these cultural factors as well as more randomly distributed ones such as the specific features of the Aristotelian or Mohist tradition that interested Hansen or of other Eastern traditions such as the Buddhist. Indeed Paul takes a universalist position that overlooks some useful distinctions since he strongly supports the notion that there is a kind of 'universal rationality' and argues that there can be 'no illogical cultures', which leads him in turn to see Aristotelian syllogistic and 'Chinese' logic as 'basically the same'.[42] I would myself present the case on more specific grounds that link the formal syllogism to literate procedures, confining 'logic' in that limited sense to written cultures.

The problem was raised not only by Western scholars but by the Chinese themselves. Following the 1911 Revolution, some Chinese writers had attempted to look for forms of syllogistic reasoning in early Mohist texts such as *Kung-sun Lung Tzu* and the *Mo-King*.[43] One of these later efforts to re-establish a logical tradition in China was the work of Hu Shih, *The Development of the Logical Method in Ancient China*, presented as a thesis to Columbia University and published in Shanghai in 1922. Like other adherents to New China, the author believed that the development of science and philosophy (which he sees as bound up with one another) in modern China 'has greatly suffered for lack of an adequate logical method'.[44] The country needed to import new methods but these are only going to work if grafted on to local roots. He sees the Neo-Confucians of the Song (thirteenth to fourteenth centuries) as having led the tradition astray, mainly by neglecting the non-Confucian writers of earlier times. So his task was to revive an interest in the logic of ancient China.

The study of the *Kung-sun Lung Tzu* was taken up by Kou Pao-koh and his lead was followed by Joseph Needham who declared that 'Syllogistic reasoning is of course not infrequently implicit in ancient Chinese texts; the form is complete, for instance, in *Kung-sun Lung Tzu*'.[45] While much of this text was forged between 300 and 600 CE (and there is a substantial proportion of nonsense), it contains a pre-Han essay called 'The White Horse' which presents the following syllogism.

---

[42] Paul 1993: 120.   [43] Cheng 1965: 195.
[44] Hu Shih 1922: 6.   [45] Kou Pao-koh 1953: 200.

Is it admissible that a white horse is not a horse?
It is admissible.
Why?
'Horse' is that by which we name the shape, 'white' is that by which we name the
    colour. To name the colour is not to name the shape. Therefore I say, 'A
    white horse is not a horse'.

This obscure argument is explicated by the Sinologist, A. C. Graham,
who nevertheless points out that the author 'is playing a trick on us', but
it is also 'a relentlessly logical working out of the implications of its
suspect premises . . . it is a potentially instructive game'.[46] Once again
we find ambivalence. Chmielewski, who offers a more complicated translation, rejects the notion that this represents a form of the Aristotelian (or
the 'traditional') syllogism but sees it as 'an early Chinese anticipation of
the theory of classes', concerned with the relation of non-identity and the
disallowing of class inclusion.[47] It does however relate to such procedures
in a general way and it suffered from the same kind of sceptical
comments and jokes that we find in the West, especially from members
of other philosophical schools, coming from a counter-culture that
parodies formal logical procedures. For instance, a sophist was said to
have employed this argument in getting his horse across the frontier
when there was a ban on their export: a white horse is not a horse.[48]

Setting aside this particular form of quasi-syllogistic reasoning and the
later and more Aristotelian type of Buddhist 'logic' that I will return to in
talking of Japan, other schools developed forms of discourse that come
within the more general rubric of rationalising procedures. The early
rhetoricians dwelt upon the difference, a grammatical difference,
between objects and attributes, which was felt to be important in
grasping a better knowledge of the world, that is, in making statements
about it. That development was accompanied by the discovery (or
elaboration) of astral correspondences, another kind of step in the
formalising of knowledge. But thesis produced antithesis, and in the early

---

[46] Graham 1989: 85–90. For references to the celebrated thesis of Kung-sun Lung
    concerning the 'White horse is not horse', see Chi-yun Chen, 'Kung-sun Lung, white
    horse and other issues', *Philosophy East and West* 33 (1983) 341–54, which is part of a
    rebuttal of Hansen's linguistic determinism. That criticism is more explicit in his 1990
    article.
[47] Chmielewski 1962.
    1. Horse has not [the property of] rejecting–selecting colour.
    2. White horse had [the property of] rejecting–selecting colour.
    3. What has not [the property of] rejecting–selecting colour is not what has [the
       property of] rejecting–selecting colour.
    4. . . . White horse is not horse.
[48] Graham 1978: 19.

third century a measure of disillusion set in with such knowledge in general and with rhetorical knowledge in particular. The reaction among some philosophers took the form of rejecting logical distinctions or denying opposites, and of adopting a relativistic position that properties are impermanent. This position in turn was challenged by ethical philosophers.[49]

I have argued that scepticism of this kind is more evident in written cultures where it becomes cumulative in the sense that one writer comments upon a previous one, giving rise to a scholastic tradition of comment and criticism. In China Wang Ch'ing criticised both Confucians and Mohists for their attitude to spirits of the dead. Attention was continually drawn by him to fallacies in the writings of the literati on a variety of topics. He was engaged in a continual search for the truth, which led him to reject exaggerations, falsehood, fictitious influences and lies as well as imposters, all those who pretend to be something other than what they are. While the results of his enquiries differed from our own, he proceeded by looking at internal contradictions and external evidence in deciding upon auguries, omens and the like, subjecting the writings of his predecessors to a similar scrutiny. In this way a rationalising process was applied to divination, as Bottéro argues was the case in Mesopotamia.

The Mohists adopted arguments that were both utilitarian and individualist. They pursued logical problems such as the nature of identity and of argument as well as certain forms of quasi-syllogistic reasoning. Confucians like Mencius countered their general thesis, maintaining that morality could not be reduced to utility, even at the level of benefit to the community.[50] Later Confucians developed a different kind of formality in expanding the theory of the five elements while others elaborated the notion of the Yin and the Yang. Thinking in such symmetrical patterns is often held to characterise China, in opposition to the abstract and analytic thinking of the West; indeed Durkheim's analysis of 'primitive classification' included China for just such reasons, while others have also looked there for 'la pensée sauvage'. On this point Graham makes the important observation that while these schemes may be important in astronomy, alchemy and medicine, they are rare in classical philosophy and quite secondary in Neo-Confucian writings. In other words they were used in ways that were contextually specific to the domain and that changed over time. And, as he points out,

---

[49] I am indebted to E. B. Brooks, who is engaged in an account of the chronology of the Confucian *Analects* and to V. H. Mair for his interest and help.

[50] See Graham 1978.

'such "artificial" constraints have been common in the proto-science of Europe and elsewhere', despite the efforts of Aristotle.[51] So we cannot contrast a single 'mentality' in one region with that of another; the so-called rational or logical procedures were specific to certain contexts and certain times.

Writing of words like logic and logical (and the same would apply to rational), Paul queries their appropriateness for describing cultural differences. 'However carefully they may be defined and employed, usually they will be understood as also referring to fundamental logical laws, thus giving the impression that the differences are *much deeper* and more serious than it is actually possible for them to be.'[52] That is an important general point in our argument. Significantly the attempt of Hansen to understand Chinese thought through the uniqueness of language (a linguistic–pragmatic view) is linked to the idea that Chinese ethics are 'holistic and heteronomous and lacking the ideas of freedom, individualism, and personal dignity'.[53] However Graham maintains that most Chinese philosophy was directed to human needs where their thinking 'is of the same sort as our own moral and practical thinking'.[54] In the early period, he argues, the Chinese threw open their fundamental beliefs to 'the test of reason', qualifying this statement with the claim that they did not initiate 'a lasting tradition of rationalism' since the Confucian and Daoist classics assumed 'a scriptural authority'. Similar sequences involving hiatus and canonisation took place in the West where 'a lasting tradition' is presumed.[55] Neoplatonists treated Plato and Aristotle virtually as sacred books, an attitude that was accompanied by extreme scholastic ingenuity, a kind of overrationalisation which was also to be found in much medieval theology. But it was not at all the same critical thought that characterised the age of Socrates. In neither China nor the West, of course, did rational analysis (and activity) vanish but continued outside formal philosophy, although that is not clear from the works of many commentators.

To shift precociously to the question of economics, the notion that 'rationality' was not merely abandoned but altogether absent in China is a commonplace among writers on change and development.[56] In contrast to the situation in the West, they see dependence on

---

[51] Graham 1964: 50.   [52] Paul 1993: 121.
[53] Roetz 1993: 70; Hansen 1983.   [54] Graham 1964: 54.
[55] In a parallel process the Confucian classics, revived by the Song Neo-Confucians, were canonised by the fifteenth century. Rationalism and the investigation of things were set aside in favour of memorisation, recollection, textual studies and flowery comparisons. Creativity is said to have disappeared in favour of pure scholasticism.
[56] For example, Redding 1990: 136.

'paternalism' and 'personalism' as associated with conditions of insecurity and as opposed to the 'rationality' of an economic kind. That kind was linked by Max Weber with bureaucracy, with the depersonalised, non-patriarchal authority which he termed rational–legal, as distinct from traditional, which characterised the rest of the world. For him the magical garden of heterodox doctrine, as typified by Daoism, meant that neither a rational economy nor natural science could develop there. For Western scholars the position regarding science has now become untenable, largely through the work of Joseph Needham. Even if China did not develop the same experimental procedures and information systems as modern science, its contributions to the field were enormous. However, it is also plainly inadequate to view modern capitalism of the Western kind as the only type of 'rational' economy. China's earlier success in this field is clear from the volume of its exports, the complexity of its manufactures as well as the density and achievements of its population.[57] It reached high levels of profitable production (that is, mass production of a 'rationalised' kind) in response to both internal markets and to external demands from the West as well as from the Near East and south-east Asia.[58]

These external contacts brought with them influences from abroad. Since Indian logic was so caught up in religious discussion, it inevitably made its mark on China, Korea, Japan and those other areas of south-east Asia to which Buddhist writings spread, and which developed their own variants. Chinese monks travelled extensively in India during the early years of the Common Era seeking original texts. The north of the sub-continent had been influenced by the Greeks long before western Europe had experienced their achievements. As a result of Alexander's conquests in Asia, Greek cities were established, and with Greek cities there existed Greek theatres and Greek philosophers. There was also Greek art which, together with local forms, had such a profound influence on Ghandara and on Buddhist art more generally. With Buddhist art and Buddhist flowers, Buddhist logic (*inmyō*) reached Japan by way of China at an early date. In 653 CE, during the reign of Emperor Kōtoku, Dōshō left to study in China, and, together with the monk Jion (Tz'u-ên), worked under Hsüan-Tsang on the latest philosophy of the time, the doctrine of idealism (*wei-shih, vij-ñaptimātratā*), and schooled himself in logic (*inmyō*). In 661, during the reign of Saimei, he returned and introduced these procedures to Japan. Hsüan-Tsang himself had

---

[57] This suggestion is to measure success partly in sociobiological terms. However China's population was not only numerically large, it was well fed and highly 'cultured'.
[58] See Ledderose 1992.

made the round trip to India (629–45) and he later translated seventy-four Buddhist works in 1,338 volumes, while his *Record of the Western Regions (Hsi-yü chi)* is the most important work of its kind.[59] Again, the 'logic' we are dealing with is not confined to a single 'culture', though it may have local variants.

The Japanese themselves wrote many books on Buddhist logic: Hōtan's bibliography from the middle of the Tokugawa period lists eighty-four. Included in these volumes was *A Treatise on Thirty-three Fallacies*, while another offered a commentary on the doctrine of Four Types of Contradiction. These developments were not confined to Japan, since Genshin sent his work, 'Short Commentaries on the Four Types of Contradiction', to a Chinese master through the intermediary of Song merchants. It was a subject that had to be mastered by every monk. However Buddhist logic was generally regarded as an esoteric field to be transmitted secretly; many new works consisted of exegetical commentaries and in this contrasted with India and Tibet.

So Japan shared in a wider tradition of analysis that was not confined to its political boundaries, much as western Europe shared in the classical heritage. For that country adopted and modified the formula of reasoning, or syllogism, of Indian logic. One original Indian formula that was used as a model runs:

1. The conclusion: words are impermanent.
2. The reason: because they have been made.
3. The explanatory example: it is a fact of experience that whatever has been made is impermanent, as are jars, etc. It is a fact of experience that whatever is permanent has not been made, as with space.[60]

There were Japanese expressions of sequences or inferences made up of successively related judgements. The following is one of the well-known examples of such a loosely linked chain syllogism:

When the wind blows, it becomes dusty. If it becomes dusty, it becomes injurious to the eyes. If it becomes injurious to eyes, many people become blind, and then there appear many *samisen* (string-instrument) players. If there appear many *samisen* players, *samisens* are in great demand. If *samisens* are in great demand, cats are killed (to make the strings for this musical instrument). If cats are killed, rats increase in number. If rats increase in number, boxes are chewed, and become articles in great demand. Therefore, boxmakers become prosperous.[61]

These procedures are not identical to European formal logic, which remained much the same until the Renaissance and then became more

[59] Nakamura 1964: 543.
[60] Nakamura 1964: 545.   [61] Nakamura 1964: 534–5.

elaborate until it led up to the new logic of the latter part of the nine-teenth century. They seem rather to resemble children's games such as the 'Kid for Two Farthings', the riddle that ends the *Hagadah*, which is the Ashkenazi text read out at the Passover meal. As we have seen, for many people formal syllogisms partake of this very quality of an almost childish playing with words. They certainly belong to the same genre of 'language games', of the riddles of many cultures. The relationship between the loose forms of sequential reasoning, such as the Japanese syllogism, and popular forms of language game such as the riddle is obvious. While these popular forms are of course found in oral cultures, in my experience they are more frequent in societies with writing, especially among children whose use of them often seems to mimic the questioning procedures of their teachers at school.

Like classical Indian logic, forms of argument in China consisted of a logic of written dialogue, argument and commentary; while they often present themselves as oral, they had in fact been transformed by writing into a formal procedure. Coming from China the same kind of formalised argument appeared in Japan. In the Tendai sect the periodic examinations of state-supported student priests involved similar procedures. The official gazette of the Enryaku period (782–806) reports that five questions and ten problems were put and all of them had to be answered aloud. This was a step towards the ritualisation of logical discussion that some see as the origin of the argument in the Noh-drama. In this instruction the forms of *inmyō* as well as the discussion style (*rongi*) were both employed. Questions and answers were recited, accompanied by a gracious rhythm which assisted the exact memorisation of the written word (and hence its canonisation). Outside the Buddhist sphere, the practice of holding public discussions of lyric verse and of *The Tale of Genji* developed in various places; in the *utaawase* poems were discussed, again with questions and answers. Today the ritualised debate continues to be held at Mt Kōya. The answerers (*Rissha*), the questioners (*Monja*), the judge (*Tandai*), the stenographer (*Chūki*), and the manager (*Gyōji*) sit in pious attitude around the statue of the Buddha, while hymns are sung and the *sūtras* are read.[62] As in medieval Europe, this form of discussion was closely linked to religion. It was the absence of this religious component that made Greece so different; there learning was distinctly secular. Whereas in Japan, logical debate tended to become associated with Buddhist meetings and with the most pious kind of decorum.

[62] Nakamura 1964: 544–5.

Just as we have found disagreement about the presence of logic and rationality in India and China, so too a similar argument has occurred about Japan. According to the contemporary Japanese philosopher, Nakamura, India differed from China and Japan where he finds little by way of logical thinking.[63] His account, started in 1945–6, is an attempt to show the differences among Eastern societies (though it also points to many similarities, for example, in the spread of Indian logic) but in particular with Western systems. It is remarkable for its self-criticism (as Arthur Wright points out in the introduction) by a scholar trained in British and American philosophy and faced with the collapse of Japan in 1945. One of three chapters is entitled, 'The tendency to emphasize a limited social nexus' and another 'Non-rationalistic tendencies' that begins with a section on 'The tendency to neglect logical rules', which he links to the nature of the Japanese language. For instance, the frequent omission of subject is seen as possibly having 'something to do with the inexact character of the Japanese mode of thought in general', though he adds that in fact the subject is usually suggested by or can be inferred from the context.[64] Other section titles include the 'lack of logical coherence', and 'the slow development of logic in Japan'. It is an approach that is complicated by the fact that it merges the levels of popular usage (for example, language) with that of specialist knowledge.

Such self-criticism is not surprising, given the author's background in time and place. But despite this self-deprecating attitude, he also sees Japanese philosophy as grappling with 'the same kinds of problems as did philosophers in the West, in India, and in China', following much the same course of development as that found elsewhere.[65] In a later book he pursues the notion of parallel development in the history of ideas. Especially for the earlier periods, he points to the general similarities in levels of development in East and West. Even 'modern thought' he sees as appearing in Eastern countries, but only sporadically; it 'did not develop fully, and vanished in incipient stages'.[66] No one doubts that following the Renaissance Europe made significant advances. But Nakamura is here suggesting that there was the potentiality for 'modern thought' to have developed in the East.

I am not claiming that all types of formal logic, of the syllogism, are the same. But, as with lists and tables, the written forms of oral procedures of inference do have a strong element of similarity in both the East and West. It is possible that all derived in a shadowy way from Mesopotamian

---

[63] 'We need not despair completely, however, of the capacity of the Japanese people for logical thinking' since this is just a 'customary tendency' (p. 550).

[64] Nakamura 1964: 535.

[65] Nakamura 1967: i, v–vi.   [66] Nakamura 1975: 561.

forms which spread in both directions. Or that all were influenced by the eastward spread of Greek philosophy. My own preference would be to link the development more clearly with the adoption of writing but, even if we accept the diffusionist argument, India would have acquired formal syllogistic reasoning before *western* Europe. For that form of logic only arrived there at a much later date by way of Rome, which effectively prolonged the boundaries of the classical empires to the West. In other words, the East had as much claim to these Greek achievements as the West that was later to become the home for the development of industrial capitalism and of 'modern' knowledge systems.

Forms of argument exist in all societies, but these procedures we have discussed are not simply implicit in language or in oral culture, waiting to be written down. Oral man has rationality and logic, but he does not have these special forms of 'logic' and 'rationality' which are under discussion. Sequential reasoning, informal syllogistic reasoning, is not limited to the formal syllogism. The latter is a product of human creativity (and sometimes of dubious value) emerging in literate societies at specific places and particular times, not as an instant product of systems of writing. It is a consequence of, in the sense of following from, writing. But it was developed from embryonic forms such as we find in Mesopotamia and it has to be learned. It is a product of discovery and education, not something that is part of the 'unlearned' equipment of the child, part of an inbuilt language of thought which may well include sequential reasoning itself. On the other hand it belongs to the sphere of culture, not in that emergent sense that anthropologists often use the concept but in a concrete historical way which is in some, but not in all, respects incremental. 'Logic' in the limited meaning is developed in writing; logic in the broader sense is a pan-human phenomenon, a function perhaps of the very use of language in the process that Esther Goody calls 'anticipatory interactive planning'.[67]

Why should these developments in 'logic' have taken such homologous forms, despite the very different cultural backgrounds? Is it because of some ultimate truth about 'formal logic'? As we have seen, in the course of refuting the arguments of Hansen and others about the non-equivalence of axioms in Aristotelian and Mohist logic, Paul argues for the universality of logic and rationality. But the formal syllogism is not universal, even though parallel devices may be found in Europe and the East. How then did this parallelism arise? Diffusion was certainly a possibility. But for Greece and India we would stress the ferment of activity that followed the adoption of simplified writing systems at

[67] E. Goody 1995.

roughly the same period. Both regions had experienced earlier, more cumbrous systems of writing, in which some embryonic 'logical' procedures based upon the kind of reasoning found in oral societies were certainly developed. But in both these cases a relatively simple form of writing, probably originating in the same or parallel Semitic form, encouraged an outburst of literate activity which shifted attention from the dominant lists of the early logographic scripts to the more discursive 'argument' of alphabetic ones (until canonisation occurred). That activity included further attempts to formalise enquiry in writing, for the sage Nāgasena's approach, like that of Aristotle, was essentially the approach of a master of the written word. It also led to the more abstract syllogism where letters stood for concrete terms.

The argument I offer admits both of the psychic unity of mankind and of developmental or evolutionary sequences. Many anthropologists see these as opposed;[68] that was not the case with E. B. Tylor nor yet with Lewis Morgan and in work on the implications of literacy I too have insisted on the distinction between common abilities and differential capacities at the cognitive level. It is the latter that are influenced by changes in the mode of communication such as the introduction of writing. While I do not argue that what occurred was a total, revolutionary, paradigm shift in the manner of Kuhn, I do point to the advent of factors that help to change problem-formulation and problem-solving, to alter cognitive operations over the longer term and to add new capacities to many existing abilities.

There is no reason why all societies with writing should engage in similar activities. But the very operation of putting words in writing turns cognitive activity in the direction of such formalism. Different groups will produce variant procedures, but there are some family resemblances. Like many other innovations they may have come from elsewhere and been incorporated in the traditions of the host society, with some modifications but in substantially the same form. That seems to me the history of the formal syllogism.

Rationality and capitalism

Up to this point I have been speaking of the distribution of rationality in the sense of logical procedures, formal and informal, in the major societies of the Eurasian continent. But, as I mentioned in the opening discussion, there is another wider sense in which rationality of a looser

[68] Tambiah 1990: 1.

kind is considered to be characteristic of the West and which I have touched upon in discussing China. From one standpoint, this represents a *post hoc* argument having to do with modernisation and the adoption of rational procedures in religion, economics, administration and in knowledge systems: since it was the West that 'modernised' first, it must have been the more 'rational', at least in terms of 'formal rationality' as distinct from 'substantive rationality'. Formal rationality Weber sees as linked to the process of institutional differentiation with the associated separation of value spheres, creating tensions between them and giving rise to substantive irrationality. There is an obvious but limited level at which this claim has to be true, since those developments involved the application of rational thought. But is there any other, more meaningful sense in which different types of rationality were involved? Or do such statements represent purely retrospective accounts of what is assumed to have happened, that generalise contemporary (that is, modern) advantage into a deep-structural feature of a psychological or social kind?[69] Many folk beliefs insist that 'they' (the others) do not think like 'us', which is why they did not 'modernise'. On a more academic level I have considered the way that attachment to the humanistic tradition running from the Greeks has tended to lead scholars to neglect, even to primitivise, other parallel forms of discourse in the East. The same seems to be true when the discussion turns to rationality in the context of modern economic activity, where the focus of attention usually shifts to modern Europe. Such attitudes have been given an academic garb in the works of many writers in history, philosophy and the social sciences, but as we have seen the best known, the best argued, and most influential case was put forward by the German comparative historian and sociologist, Max Weber.[70] In his comments on Weber's achievements, Bendix observes that the Greeks were the first to develop a 'rational proof in geometry', which Indian geometry lacked. The West also took the lead in the formulation and use of 'rational concepts in historical scholarship and jurisprudence'. But he also suggests that government administration and economic enterprise came to be characterised 'by a rational systematisation for which there was no analogue in the Orient'. The Protestant

---

[69] In Habermas' comment on Weber's notion of rationality, the rationalisation of world view involves 'not merely a generalization of the domain of application of formal operations of thought [formal rationality], but a decentration of world-perspectives that is impossible without *a simultaneous change in deep-seated, moral–practical structures of consciousness*' (Habermas 1984: 176, my italics). That seems to me to go to the heart of the problem.

[70] See for example Gellner 1992, and the general trend of Habermas' discussion about rationality.

ethic merely explored one phase of that 'emancipation from magic' (that is, of rationalisation) that Weber regarded as leading to formal rationality and 'the distinguishing peculiarity of Western culture'.

Was there really no analogue in China? Take the case of rationality in the realm of law. While the view of China as a despotic state implies the absence of a rule of law, in fact the main provisions of the Tang code persisted until 1911. An analysis of the poet and lawyer Po-Chüni's opinion in a case of wife-beating that led to her death shows that in the ninth century we have an example of the application of the principle of *eiusdem generis* (interpreting a general term in a more specific way like other terms in the context), supposed only to have developed in Western common law in the nineteenth century.[71] In accepting Po-Chüni's opinion the emperor relied on a 'general consideration of reasonableness', for the Chinese system of criminal justice insisted upon a scrupulous examination of homicide cases, respect for human life and a concern to identify the correct rule.

In both Weber and his commentators, the insistence on formal 'rationality' is highly selective, concentrating on the contexts in which Europe excelled. Some claims are dubious, if not plain wrong. For example, in administration and the economy the earlier East was in some ways more developed than the medieval West after the collapse of the ancient economy, a period that saw a general decline in systems of knowledge and other cultural manifestations in the West. Part of this falling-off was due to the deliberate choice of a restricted religious literacy and to the consequent canonisation of some texts and the exclusion of others, deemed to be pagan. But even with the Reformation, it is not self-evident that Protestantism was more 'rational', even by Western standards, than Neo-Confucianism or Zen Buddhism. If it was more rational in terms of world mastery, that may be because the context of its appearance was different. It may have tried to exclude 'magic' in favour of a direct approach to God; but 'magic' surely consists of the rites of others, or of practices outside the church. On any more objective count, some magic persisted within the church and some outside. Catholicism continued to dominate Christendom. A change did occur; but was the result as radical as the effects of Confucianism? In any case the whole discussion is slanted by selection; items, areas and periods in which others excelled have been underplayed.

Weber himself tried to avoid the assertion that non-Western cultures failed to display rationality, phrasing the divide between West and East

---

[71] MacCormack 1994.

in another way.[72] He appreciated that substantive rationality, like capitalism, was found in many societies. What interested him was the distinctiveness of Western capitalism, of modern production-oriented capitalism.[73] So he dwelt on the distinctiveness of modern Western rationalism which was 'the rationalism of world mastery'. That formal rationalism was associated not only with the 'disenchantment' of the world, of which secularisation is the extreme case, but with the depersonalisation and bureaucratisation that he connected with the rise of ascetic Protestantism,[74] especially in the seventeenth century when it became a 'turning point of the whole cultural development of the West'.[75]

Weber recognised that Confucianism prescribed a form of rational conduct through sobriety but he saw it as dramatically opposed to the European type, advocating rational adjustment to the world rather than rational mastery of it. Concerned with individual action rather than with total conduct, the latter was said to be norm oriented rather than principle oriented.[76] Moreover, that difference was developmental, evolutionary, part of the general transition over time from a magical ethic to a law ethic, with Confucianism classified under the first head. So that while the Chinese had rationality, they had the wrong kind of rationality to enable them to modernise, that is, to originate if not to adopt modernity.

We may agree that Weber did not see rationalisation as peculiar to the West since it was present in all world religions (that is, in Bronze Age societies) but only in Europe did it lead to a form that established both particular Occidental features as well as general ones, that is, features characteristic of modernity as such.[77] But were these consequences or contributors to the onset of modernity? Did they emerge before (and if so how and when) or did they follow?

According to Habermas, Weber analyses the process of disenchantment in the history of religion which 'fulfilled the necessary internal conditions for the appearance of Occidental rationalism', which develops at a societal level and is intrinsic to modernisation and capitalism, 'the universal-historical emergence of modern structures of consciousness,

---

[72] Weber distinguished between the formal and substantive rational aspects of law in the context of legal procedure and legal purpose, but the distinction between *zweckrationalität* and *wertrationalität* (see Wilson 1977; Tambiah 1990: 144) applied more widely to the instrumental calculation of means and ends and to the absolutist rationality of ultimate ends.

[73] Schluchter 1981: 6–9.

[74] Rothe in Schluchter 1981: xv.   [75] Weber 1952.

[76] Schluchter 1981: 61, 67.   [77] Habermas 1984: 155.

on the one hand, and the embodiment of these rationality structures in social institutions, on the other.'[78] His major point of orientation was 'why, outside of Europe, "neither scientific, nor artistic, nor political, nor economic development entered upon that path of rationalization peculiar to the Occident"'.[79] The 'specific and peculiar achievements of western rationalism' were related to the capitalist economic ethic 'for just as the development of economic rationalism is dependent on rational technique and rational law, so it is also dependent on the ability and the disposition of men to adopt certain types of practically rational conduct'.[80]

One difficulty lies at the level of sub-systems. Both for Weber and for Habermas, the formation of sub-systems for 'rational economics' or for 'rational administration' is regarded as 'a differentiation of spheres of value that represent . . . the core of the cultural and societal rationalization of the modern age'.[81] But whereas this process of the differentiation of sub-systems developed in 'the modern age', it certainly began long before. The Bronze Age saw the differentiation into what Oppenheim called 'the great organisations' which pursued the kind of rational goal specified by these authors. The separation of the 'King's Two Bodies', of the personal and the corporative funds of the ruler, goes even further back, almost to the very notion of an office-holder.[82]

A constant problem in Weber is his view of custom as sheer habituation, the unconsciously functioning compliance with rules, which he contrasts with an instrumental order based on self-interest and the purposive–rational weighing of advantages and disadvantages. Generalised to a societal level, custom lies at the basis of 'traditional' societies in opposition to modern ones. 'In traditional societies . . . new ideas . . . do not arise in the form of regulated argumentation.' The shift is effected by charismatic figures.[83] The difficulty with this characterisation is that custom marks all societies in some degree, as does instrumental rationality. In no society are actors incapable of acting in one way or the other. While differences in degree obviously exist, there is no radical disjunction. Let me return to the argument that the East could copy but not originate modernity, or capitalism, or even industrial production. The claim assigns these concepts a misplaced concreteness, a precision they do not deserve. The process involved in the development of mercantile and industrial capitalism cannot be compared with the

[78] Habermas 1984: 143, 156.   [79] Habermas 1984: 157.
[80] Weber 1958: 26.   [81] Habermas 1984: 72.
[82] See for example the role of treasurer (*Sanaahene*) in the Asante state, west Africa.
[83] Habermas 1984: 189, 192.

invention of the wheel, which could in theory be patented. The claim
represents, in my view, a misunderstanding of the nature of economic
development. It is no more meaningful to talk of who invented capitalism than it is to ask who discovered feudalism. Capitalism must be seen
as the result not of a sudden cataclysm but of a long series of events, some
of which took place outside the confines of western Europe, especially
before the Renaissance. That situation appears to be recurring today,
when new developments in productive systems are taking place in the
East. Societies that are in the vanguard (modernising) at one point give
way to others at another; the pendulum swings. Looked at over the
longer span of time, no one region is solely responsible for the birth of
modern society.

The dichotomising view of rationality, or a kind of rationality,
especially of economic rationality – either you have it or you do not –
sustains the popular notion that the East must lack such a quality. An
alternative hypothesis is that the Age of Reason in the West did not usher
in a different kind of rationality but extended its dominion over human
affairs, as in the work of Descartes. His formula, 'I think, therefore I am',
was put forward as the intellectual foundation of his rationalism, his
attempt to establish truth and avoid error. Rationality became the
dominant aim.[84] Opposing Aristotle's views on physics in a posthumous
volume entitled *Rules for the Direction of the Mind* written in 1628,
Descartes called for the strictest application of the rules of reasoning.
Those rules were:
1. Accept nothing as true that is not self-evident.
2. Divide problems into their simplest parts.
3. Solve problems by proceeding from simple to complex.
4. Recheck the reasoning.
The model was mathematical and his physics, aimed at mastering nature,
was mechanistic. It was the achievement in the mechanical arts and
crafts, such as the construction of automata and of calculating machines,
that provided the practical foundation of the Cartesian approach. His
was an attempt which aimed to set aside the prejudices of others.
Important advances in knowledge systems were clearly being made in the
West at that time but if the scope of rational enquiry was extended, it did
not of course put an end to all 'irrationality'. In any case the notion of
extension presents a rather different claim from that embodied in the
notion of the birth of an Age of Reason because it did not imply that
other cultures lacked the equipment to catch up and surpass. They
simply differed in development and in application.

[84] R. I. Moore, introduction to Gellner 1992.

That is not to assent to the claim that Western rationality had a special relationship to capitalism. We have argued that at a more general level people in all human societies are applying a version of 'logical' means–ends calculations, as in the Azande case. What occurs with writing is the development of particular types of argument and procedure utilised in sequential reasoning. In these situations we are dealing not with the presence or absence of rationality, nor yet with a Western variety, but with the application of rationalising procedures to the accumulation of knowledge. Since such systems are in part cumulative, and therefore part of an inherited tradition, it would be preferable to speak not so much of an intensification of rationality (as if it was some quality we could measure) as of a more extensive use of rationalising procedures. Of this the growth of science (*scientia*, knowledge) was one major result, and at this period was promoted not so much by the presence of writing as such but by the wider and more rapid dissemination of information following the use of printing in the West.

From this more general stance, it seems unnecessary to ask whether particular cultures or even particular people are rational, but only whether they have developed or adopted specific forms of argument or cognitive procedure, such as the formal logic which has been a major focus of our attention. This argument links up with my final point. One feature that often leads the West to conclude that the East either lacks the requisite kind of rationality, or having got it, does not apply it, is its continued use of diviners, astrologers and tellers of the future in various guises. There are historical reasons for this difference. Such activities were roundly rejected early on by official Christianity (and by other monotheistic religions of the Near East) not so much on the grounds of their 'irrationality' but because they depended on forces other than the Supreme Being. Divination was the work of the devil. In fact, both ecclesiastical and popular forms persisted. The latter continued as 'alternative' modes of seeking the truth outside the church. Decision-making by drawing lots was not only a procedure for randomising chance in lotto, it also persisted in some religious contexts, both in the Bible and subsequently, the notion being that God's hand would guide the selection. Others achieved the same result more directly by prayer as in the choosing of a new Pope.[85] But they continued despite the disapproval of the church. In other words, that disapproval meant that it was not the Reformation that originated this partial 'disenchantment', this 'rationalisation', although that movement certainly tried to clear away

[85] Even the final choice of a new Master of St John's College, Cambridge, is made within the chapel.

some accretions that were seen as marking the practices of Catholics. Because, while for some early scholars and scientists 'magic' may have ✓ been irrational, for the religious, and for the bulk of the population, it was sacrilegious.

Disregarding their own popular actions and beliefs, the modern West had no difficulty explaining the apparent economic backwardness of the East in terms of the presence of non-rational forms of decision-making, which were not to be found in the syllabus of the Harvard Business School. But the rise of Japan and of the Four Little Dragons casts doubt upon the correctness of this assumption, as well as threatening the earlier self-confidence of the West. Nevertheless their success raises the analytic problem in a more acute form. In these and other countries such as India, how is it that businessmen are successful when they place decisions in the hands of procedures or persons that to the Western observer are not in a position to assist? For the purpose of the argument I assume the correctness of the position that sets aside the possibility of the astrologer having privileged access to information (though obviously there are many highly 'rational' achievers in business or in academia from the East who would take quite a different position). There are several conceivable answers. First, any decision takes into account not only the soothsayer's advice but a wide range of 'rational' considerations which may swamp any particular suggestions that run in an eccentric direction. The recourse to divination as one among a range of possibilities emerges clearly in the Great Law said to have been promulgated by the Emperor Wu-wang in the twelfth century BCE. This text, which in some ways resembles Indian works on the duties of a king (*rajadharma*), offers the following advice regarding

the examination of doubtful things. It is necessary to select and appoint sooth-sayers to ascertain the truth, some by means of the tortoise shell and some by means of the reeds. When you have doubts on an important affair, discuss it yourself, discuss it with your ministers and officers, consult the people and have the tortoise and the reeds consulted. If your undertaking is approved by yourself, by the tortoise, by the reeds, by your ministers and officers and by the people unanimously it will succeed.[86]

Second, an individual (or collectivity) may consult a number of diviners about any decision, getting advice from one which he or she can play off against another. Third, any advice so obtained may be sufficiently ambiguous, or interpreted as such, as to be capable of a variety of different meanings – as in many pronouncements of the

---

[86] Bagchi [1951] 1971: 179.

Delphic Oracle. Fourth, some business decisions may positively benefit from, or at least not be harmed by, the introduction of a random element, as has been suggested for the divination for game in hunting societies.[87] What may be important is for the individual to make some decision rather than to become paralysed in Hamlet-like inaction. Tossing a coin or seeing a diviner may provide a solution as good as any other. Perhaps better, because it externalises the problem and doesn't throw all the onus on the individual. It relieves him or her of a burden. Similarly when Christians say prayers to help them succeed in a commercial undertaking or in a battle against other Christians, the procedure may be irrational or a-rational but it fortifies the spirit. That is, for the individual it not only reduces uncertainty but has some of the uplifting effects that ceremonial, rituals and performances have collectively. Such a possibility would help to account for the persistence of such procedures among, for example, Parsi businessmen of Bombay who have been making important and successful commercial decisions for centuries;[88] or in the use of *Feng shui* (literally wind-water, hence geomancy) for business in Singapore.[89] But as we have seen any particular procedure is rarely determinative in major matters and especially in new activities which tend to escape old taboos. So they do not appear greatly to impair the outcome, although consulting geomancers did lead to changes in the garden layout of the Singapore Hyatt and in Norman Foster's design of the forty-seven-storey building of the Hong Kong and Shanghai Bank in Hong Kong. Many of the great achievements in Chinese, Japanese, Korean and Indian civilisations have been made by individuals who resorted to such practices. That was, and is, also the case with some scientists and businessmen in the West, as well as with some social anthropologists. They contextualised their beliefs, and applied so-called non-rational ones where they mattered less. When Evans-Pritchard worked among the Azande of the southern Sudan, he kept a supply of the oracle poison (*benge*) to feed to chickens and so, he writes, 'we regulated our affairs in accordance with the oracle's decisions . . . I found this as satisfactory a way of running my home and affairs as any other I know of'.[90] Many of the issues about which diviners are consulted are from an observer's point of view not that important as a decision either way. It does not matter very much what name you give to your child or what date you

---

[87] Moore 1957.
[88] The problem is not dissimilar to that of the persistence of magic discussed by E. B. Tylor (1871).
[89] See the book of this title by Evelyn Lip, Singapore, 1989.
[90] Evans-Pritchard 1937: 270.

marry; perhaps even who. What alternative strategies exist for producing better (more 'rational') results?

The compartmentalised mind is sometimes a matter of criticism in the West. Writing of the comments of a Hong Kong entrepreneur about business morality, an author comments: 'We observe at work here the compartmentalised mind, the mind which can deal elastically with matters of good and evil because it is not trammelled by some ultimate black-and-white sense of right and wrong.'[91] In fact much practical morality that guides action is contingent in this way and 'ultimate black-and-white' moralities are of the decontextualised book rather than the contextualised life of the streets; they are typical of the overgeneralisation of legal and moral phenomenon which the written word encourages, but which does not really stand up to empirical investigation. Weber saw the religious morality of the ascetic Protestant as suffused through economic life; that may have been true of a few but in most cases successful merchants ceased to be truely ascetic across the board, if they ever were. Equally members of those religions that forbad usury did not seem to be inhibited by this prohibition; they either ignored it, or found a way around it, though it is true they may have been attracted by sects such as the Cathars that enabled them to avoid this cognitive contradiction. On the other hand compartmentalisation was always available to them, indeed was necessary to their mode of life.

It is not only at the level of decision-making in the economic sphere that the East has been judged to be lacking in rationality. Though a few writers have expressed doubts about aspects of the Weberian thesis concerning Western rationality, most of the major sociological commentators have accepted his views. These coincide in general with those of scholars in adjacent fields as well as with popular conceptions. One of the main problems is that the argument does not fully take into account the way the human mind can operate compartmentally, that what happens on Sundays does not necessarily control daily behaviour, that even computer operators may believe in the Dao, in Buddha, in the Christian Trinity or in transcendental meditation. Disenchantment is a contextual matter, though Protestants may possibly be seen as farther along this road than Catholics.

The compartmentalisation of the human mind is paralleled by the compartmentalisation of social life. The global, holistic notion of culture (or social structure), so attractive to many social scientists, proves unable to explicate social change. In discussing the nature of business activity among the Chinese, Redding attempts to penetrate to those 'deeper

---

91 Redding 1990: 194.

influences' as they exist in the 'base layer of culture – that layer of mental life where a society's most elemental formulae are worked out'.[92] That claim is as mystical as any we have come across. But one of the particular features discussed by the author is the striking absence of abstracts in the Chinese language which he sees as providing evidence of different thought processes from those normal in Indo-European languages and associated with Western rationality. He goes on to suggest that because the large Western corporation could not have been founded without 'prior imaginings' of abstract concepts like 'the marketing function', that type of organisation may have been unthinkable.

The problem is connected with the Whorf hypothesis about the role of language. Here a supposed feature of Chinese, its greater concreteness which is possibly linked to the nature of the script, is globalised to become an integrated feature of a holistic culture, so that we are asked to consider the possibility that for the Chinese large corporations were not even 'good to think' but indeed unthinkable. The argument is suspect on several grounds, that it overdetermines the role of a particular language and script in thought processes, it fails to allow for the lexical generativeness of language, it gives insufficient recognition to historical developments and is based on too holistic a view of man and his society. Rationality is seen to qualify men and cultures rather than some of their actions some of the time.

That is not to deny the possibility of a more realistic level of argument that links subsequent achievements with possible antecedents in the sphere of formal rationality. Needham compares Greek and Chinese science in their inheritance from the Babylonians. 'Greek mathematics was doubtless on a higher level, if only on account of its more abstract and systematic character, seen in Euclid.'[93] Chinese mathematics adapted to many practical contexts but did not help to achieve the degree of abstraction needed for more theoretical developments (possibly reinforced by the use of the abacus). If this were so, it was a matter of degree, only partly influenced by language and script. Babylonian mathematics, which also used logographic writing, was well advanced and had its own formalised graphic representations of space. These discoveries in geometry paved the way for Euclid, just as the procedures of proof did for Aristotle.[94] The Egyptians too discovered a formula for calculating 'empirically' the volume of a pyramid. Indeed it has been suggested that the notion of demonstration probably first attracted

[92] Redding 1990: 139.
[93] Needham 1959: 150–1.
[94] For a recent account of Babylonian tablets, see Nissen, Damerov and Englund 1990.

attention in connection with geometry, one trend in Greek logic being 'determined in large part by reflection on the problem of presenting geometry as a deductive system'.[95] What the Greeks did was to produce further 'rules' for proof and demonstration, a procedure that the Kneales specifically compare to the grammarian producing the rules of language. Rules of syntax clearly existed before writing but they did so implicitly. They became evident in and through the written word, which also created them in a meaningful sense; in linguistics it was a task that Panini carried out for Sanskrit. In the West it was again not so much logic as logical rules ('logic') that emerged, and these appeared in somewhat less developed forms in other written cultures. In these 'logical procedures', limited as their impact was, the West may have had a competitive advantage of a kind. But it is certainly not one that we can usefully discuss in terms of a special form of rationality, as a holistic, hegemonic concept such as the 'rationality of world mastery' or 'Western rationality', since there were many spheres of knowledge, of 'rational' endeavour, in which the Chinese were not only outstanding but in advance of the West until the Renaissance. 'Rationality' has to be given a more 'historical', less culturally enduring character.

I have been trying to explain how the economy in the East can operate so well in an environment that many Westerners see (less so now) as lacking rationality. What is as important is to understand the particular context in which Europeans could make these judgements and it is important to realise the basis (and its frailness) on which they often did so.

Theoretical parsimony or good housekeeping suggests we have no need to call upon a general notion of logic or rationality when trying to distinguish the different trajectories of the West and the East in the modern world. At one level these activities characterise all human societies. In a more specialist sense, they are features of societies with writing, though alphabetic scripts may make a difference to the abstract nature of the syllogism. And they vary in other, more specific ways. The crucial point is that the potentiality for further development was there in both regions, since all the main societies of the Eurasian continent built on the common achievements of the Bronze Age in terms of wealth (through production, consumption and exchange or trade) and knowledge (through writing). In contrast to Africa, they had these crucial features in common. In subsequent periods, the West triumphed at times, the East at others. There were no deep-structural features such as differences in rationality that prevented such an oscillation, but rather

Eurasia vs Africa

95 Kneale 1962: 2, 6.

more immediate, contingent ones. So the search of much Western social science for reasons for the rise (and possibly decline) of the West needs to be re-examined and aimed at different targets.

One feature that Weber, Schumpeter and others tried to link with the development of Western capitalism was double-entry bookkeeping. Now bookkeeping in all its forms was known as *'ragioneria'* in Italy and account books were *'livres de raison'* in France, linking up with the notion not only of rationality but with that of 'ratio' and computation. That is the subject of the next chapter.

2 Rationality and *ragioneria*: the keeping of books and the economic miracle

Since the idea of rationality has been applied to the economy, it will come as little surprise to find that it is closely bound up with that of book-keeping. In Italy, the technique was known as *ragioneria*.[1] For the French, *un livre de raison* was a book of household accounts, while in Swiss German the Italian-derived term *Ragionenbuch* was current. Such usages may appear to support Weber's association of rationality (at least the rationality of world mastery) with the advent of capitalism and bureaucracy in Europe, which he links with the practice of double-entry bookkeeping (*partita doppia, partie double*). In the first chapter I suggested that, unless one could identify particular features of rationalising procedures as unique to the West which required, for their development, a special form of cognitive operation, to isolate a form of rationality of world mastery and identify it with Europe was an instance of circular not to say ethnocentric reasoning. In this chapter I claim that in the case of double-entry the second of these criteria does not hold, and that there must be considerable doubt about the first.

In his analysis of social and economic organisation, Weber argued that 'capital accounting has arisen as a basic form of economic calculation only in the Western world',[2] that it is a form of monetary accounting which is peculiar to 'rational economic profit-making' and aimed at 'the valuation and verification of opportunities for profit and of the success of profit-making activity'.[3] While he thought of this process as involving double-entry, he recognised that an elementary form of such activity was to be found in the *commenda*, which in turn gave rise to joint-stock companies. The accounting and the association were linked.

---

[1] Reynolds 1951: 37; see F. Melis's comprehensive study, *Storia della ragioneria* (Bologna, 1950), and earlier F. Besta, *La Ragioneria* (Milan 1909). For a full discussion of the use of 'ragione' in Italian accounts and business correspondence see F. Edler, *Glossary of Mediaeval Terms of Business, Italian Series, 1200–1600* (Cambridge, MA, 1934), pp. 236–7.

[2] Weber 1947: 193.

[3] Weber 1947: 191.

In the earliest beginnings of rational profit-making activity capital appears, though not under this name, as a sum of money used in accounting. Thus, in the 'commenda' relationship various types of goods were entrusted to a travelling merchant to sell in a foreign market, and possibly he was also commissioned to purchase other goods wanted for sale at home. The profit or loss was then divided in a particular proportion between the travelling merchant and the entrepreneur who advanced the capital. But for this to take place it was necessary to value the goods in money; that is, to strike balances at the beginning and the conclusion of an enterprise. The 'capital' of the commenda relationship or the *societas maris* was simply this money valuation,which served only the purpose of settling accounts between the parties and no other.

Why then should capital accounting be seen as a basic form only found in the Western world? Is it because the critical feature is taken to be double-entry bookkeeping, which appears to have been a relatively late invention?[4]

It was not only Weber but Sombart, H. M. Robertson and Schumpeter who assigned a fundamental role to what was called 'rational' or 'scientific' bookkeeping in the development of modern capitalism. By this they meant double-entry bookkeeping which they saw as making possible (or at least advancing) the calculation of the profit and the loss, the rationalisation of action and the depersonalisation of business. The attribution of 'scientific' to this form of bookkeeping needs to be questioned on the same grounds that we have already queried the term 'rational'. All trade involves some form of reckoning and in literate societies this takes the form of some kind of keeping of books.[5] Double-entry is one development that in time replaced earlier systems as the major accounting procedure. How important was that change and was it confined to Europe?

While early modern Europe made important contributions both to bookkeeping and to forms of partnership (in particular to double-entry and the joint-stock company), forerunners were to be found much earlier in the Near East and further afield. What appears as the sudden rise of these institutions in Europe at that time has to be seen against the background of the decline of commerce in the north during the Dark Ages. That decline was reversed partly as the result of renewed contacts with the East, especially the Near East and its mercantile practices. Nevertheless a gap had opened up, leaving the way open to new

---

[4] Is it because further qualifications are required, that 'profit-making enterprises with capital accounting' have to be 'doubly orientated to the market in that they both purchase means of production on the market and sell their product there'? (Weber 1947: 201).

[5] See Goody 1986.

developments, just as much earlier the alphabet emerged on the unspecialised and uncluttered periphery of the literate world rather than the institution-bound centre. Let us look at these developments in more detail.

The rise, decline and growth of Mediterranean commerce

European developments in bookkeeping are clearly linked to the history of trade, especially in the early Mediterranean. On this commerce rested the growth and expansion of classical Greece. The basics of the alphabet were acquired from the Semitic trading cultures, probably Phoenician, of the eastern extremities of that inland sea. In its modified form that alphabet encouraged the rapid accumulation of recorded knowledge, as well as the development of poetry and drama, which had earlier been stimulated by contacts with an East that had possessed more complex civilisations. It also assisted trade, the recording of accounts and the reckoning of the profit and the loss.

The earliest recorded imports to classical Greece from the Near East were Syrian rather than Phoenician. These included bronze figures dating from the ninth century of the same kind that have been found in Etruria in northern Italy, and it was this Syrian influence that played 'a weighty part in the formation of the Greek style of the late eighth and seventh centuries'.[6] Syrio-Phoenician traders travelled further westwards in the Mediterranean, as did the Etruscans and later the Greeks. In southern France the late seventh-century trade was largely Etruscan, often relating to the consumption of wine. Then about 600 BCE Ionian Greeks from Phocaea established a colony at Marseilles and also traded in wine, some of which was locally produced like the containers for transport and for drinking, which required the use of the wheel and of controlled-draught kilns.[7] The Greeks also looked to the East from where they received so much. They spread down the coast of Asia and established a colony at Poseidon (the present Al Mina), mentioned by Herodotus; it contained warehouses and lay at the end of the overland routes from Assyria. In earlier Mycenaean times Ugarit (Ras Shamra) farther to the south had been settled, though there is no indication of a continuous Greek presence.[8] The importance of the Eastern connection is of course shown not only by the presence of Ionian Greeks in Asia Minor but by the continuing military struggles that took place, leading in

---

[6] Dunbabin 1957: 37, referring to Homann-Wedeking.
[7] Dietler 1990.   [8] Dunbabin 1957: 24.

the late eighth century to the conquest of the island of Cyprus by Assyria. Not only did Greeks settle in the Near East, following Alexander's conquest they spread as far as northern India. As merchants they may have settled in the coastal cities of south India while others may have acted as mercenaries for local princes or worked as skilled craftsmen.[9] The Roman empire later took over both these occupations and the trade routes with them, exporting to Britain in the west and in the east to India and indirectly to south-east Asia and China.

Roman and hence European commerce with the East eased off drastically after the decline of that empire. The great centres of commerce fell into ruin and the trade routes were impeded by warfare and by restrictive treaties.[10] From the end of the fourth century coins and artefacts of Mediterranean origin disappear from India and become rare in Ceylon. The rise of the Sassanian dynasty in Persia in the early third century led to the control of the land route on the eastern frontier. In the same period a great upsurge in commercial activity took place in central Asia, in the Indian Ocean and in the South China Sea, as is shown by the great quantities of Tang and Song porcelain and stoneware as well as by the wide distribution of Chinese coins. Merchants travelled between India and China, often accompanied by Buddhist monks. Meanwhile colonies of Arabs and Persians were established in south-east Asia and China. In the seventh century south-east Asia saw the rise of the great maritime empire of Srivijaya in Sumatra. Population increased and the exploitation of mineral wealth was expanded. As a result the loss of the Western trade 'did not retard the economic development of the Indian Ocean littoral'.

Pirenne considered the economic decline of Europe had begun before the German invasions of the fifth century, with the slowing down starting at the end of the third.[11] Some trade with the East still continued until the Islamic conquests of the beginning of the eighth century, after which the economy collapsed, virtually extinguishing urban life and leading to the disappearance of merchants and to the substitution of local trade for a more inclusive economy of exchange. Even with the decline of the empire, some commerce in the Mediterranean still took place, bringing spices and manufactures from Asia and sending cereals, wood and metals in return. The merchants in the towns of Gaul, Spain, Italy and north Africa, who were largely Syrians and Jews, continued to trade

---

[9] See the discussion in Raschke 1978: 673; it assumes that Yavšana in the Tamil literature at this period refers to Greeks.

[10] Raschke 1978: 678.

[11] Pirenne 1929: 15; Rostovtzeff 1926. For a recent discussion of the Pirenne thesis in relation to the rise of emporia, see Hodges 1982.

even after the Germanic invasions, so that spices and papyrus travelled as far as the north of the Frankish empire.[12] These Mediterranean merchants had to deal with local traders in the north who needed some education to enable them to participate at the fullest level. Until the eighth century they were able to acquire some skills from the public schools in which the elements of arithmetic and of law were taught. The extent of the use of writing in general is seen by the continuing imports of Egyptian papyrus.[13] But commercial activity as a whole declined until the Islamic conquest of the Mediterranean finally separated north from south and west from east. As a result the fleet of the Byzantine empire could keep open only the Aegean and Adriatic seas, a corridor that later opened the way for the rise of Venice beginning in the tenth century.

The Adriatic region surrounding Venice and the coast of Flanders became the two key areas in the eventual recovery of the European economy. These were the places on which trade was centred, in Venice to the eastern Mediterranean and in particular Constantinople, in Flanders through the production and sale of woollen cloth exported to France and Italy. By the eleventh century considerable fortunes were being built up by the new bourgeoisie, who also required an education – or at least the services of the educated – since the circulation of goods and money was facilitated by both correspondence and accounting, including recording the loans made to landowners. From the thirteenth century the commerce associated with the towns of Flanders, that is, Ghent, Bruges, Ypres, Lille and Arras, as well as that carried out at the fairs of Champagne which acted both as markets and as clearing houses, called for what Pirenne described as 'la collaboration continuelle de la plume'. No businessman was without his chest (or 'huge') of books of commerce, his chirographs and his correspondences (or 'letters').[14]

Instruction for 'clerks' was now available in church schools, their lay equivalents having disappeared by the seventh century. Since the Carolingian period the church had developed its teaching and preserved a reduced and formalised version of classical culture. In Le Goff's words, ecclesiastical culture took over the intellectual equipment that had been established between the third and fifth centuries by the didactic authors who had systematised classical knowledge in a simplified and mediocre

---

[12] Cumont 1906; Pirenne (1928: 184) discusses the commerce of the seventh century between Marseilles and Clermont-Ferrand, which consisted mostly of goods from Africa and Asia (spices and papyrus), but also of Mediterranean oil and candle wax.

[13] Pirenne 1928: 178.

[14] Pirenne 1929: 27.

way. The clerics now had a virtual monopoly of high culture, which had roughly the same structure throughout Western Christendom and was characterised by a strong regression of lay culture as compared with the earlier period.[15] At the same time the clerics employed a minuscule script, adapted to the lettered class, that came to displace the more utilitarian cursive, which only made its reappearance in the first half of the thirteenth century.[16] Neither learning nor script met the demand of merchants which was not for instruction of a literary and scholarly kind but one directed towards the practices of commercial life, reading, writing, arithmetic and the rudiments of Latin. This education the better-off could provide in their own houses by employing a clerk. But that provision alone was insufficient to meet the wider demand and in the middle of the twelfth century the merchants of Ghent attempted to open their own schools. While the Church had no objections to such developments in themselves, it nonetheless rejected 'the insolence of the laity' and insisted that these institutions should be brought under its control. In that the Church was successful, although its instruction also changed to include more practical subjects. At the beginning teaching was entirely in Latin but examples of commercial correspondence were offered and use was made of a cursive, gothic script rather than the Carolingian minuscule which was reserved for more deliberate, scholarly writing. By the second half of the thirteenth century, Latin was no longer the only language used in teaching reading and writing in Flanders; the first charter in French dates from 1204 and the commercial *lettres de foire* turned to the vernacular in the same century.

This development of education was part of a more general revival of learning which was aided by the Gregorian reforms of the Church, one major support of which lay in the study of canon law.[17] In 1179 the third Lateran Council tried to put on a sound economic basis the cathedral schools that supplied literates for the state as well as for the church. It would be wrong to see this revival as too closely tied to commerce in any direct manner. Education had already made advances of a major kind in southern Europe. Out of the cathedral schools arose institutions, *studia*, that attempted to provide instruction of a higher order. Significantly, the first important institution was that of Salerno, south of Naples, which became known as a school of medicine as early as the ninth century and, as a result of the work of Constantine the African (1020–87), its fame spread far and wide. Salerno derived much of its strength in medicine from the Arab conquest of nearby Sicily that lasted from 827 to 1091.

---

[15] Le Goff 1967: 782–3.
[16] Pirenne 1928: 178.   [17] Murray 1978: 216.

Constantine himself came from the Muslim city of Carthage and when he entered the Benedictine monastery of Monte Cassino he organised a centre for the translation from Arabic into Latin of significant works in philosophy and the sciences. In this way Islam's extensive knowledge of Greek medicine was introduced to the West. That foundation and that knowledge heralded the rise of the universities, beginning with Paris, at the end of the twelfth century.

While commerce was not the only factor in the revival of Europe, trade, especially with the East, did play a major part. In the early medieval period Venice was the main focus for the trade between East and West. Around the year 1000 that haven of boatmen engaged in transport and trade up the rivers of the Po delta, turned seawards and developed into the great sea-power of the Mediterranean. The inhabitants of the town were expert shipbuilders, using wood brought down from the hills of north Italy. They built ships for the government in the Arsenal, conscripting or engaging local labour, but the work was mainly carried out by private employers. This private work might be regulated by the government, especially if it was to take delivery. In other words, there was 'no persistent prejudice either for or against the government being the builder' and the role of the state was critical.[18]

The trade with the East itself flourished under Byzantine protection. So Venice became an entrepôt for the import of incense, silks and spices for the courts and monasteries of northern Italy and beyond; in return the town required grain to sustain its population. Later, when increased prosperity in the Po valley led to greater demands for eastern goods, the Venetians turned seawards and took part themselves in the trade in northern slaves and lumber destined for Muslim merchants. Christianity did not object to the enslavement of pagans and infidels (in the beginning Anglo-Saxons, then in the ninth and tenth centuries, Slavs), although at times it objected to their sale to Muslims, as well as to the sale to pagans of Italian timber which was in short supply. However, it was this trade that gave Venice the foreign exchange in gold and silver needed to buy the luxury goods of the East at Constantinople.

The development of trade spurred on that of accounting. The chief officials on a twelfth-century merchant vessel were the sailing master (*nauclerus*) and the ship's scribe (*scribanus*). It was the latter's job to keep a record of wages and freights.[19] Ownership of the ship was often divided

---

[18] Lane 1973: 48.
[19] Lane 1973: 50. Already in the Qur'an one reads: 'And if you are upon a journey and you do not find a scribe . . . ' (2: 283).

into shares among different persons, while the financing of voyages involved a complex network of partnerships and loans. A typical cargo might represent the stakes of a hundred investors, placed in the charge of a group of travelling merchants. By the second half of the twelfth century such investments often took the form of a quasi-partnership known in Venice as the *colleganza*, and elsewhere as the *commenda*.

That was the time of great growth for the economy as well as for East–West trade, with the Crusades further stimulating the demand for eastern luxuries – for sugar, spices, silks and incense. The European exports were now metals, especially from Germany, and textiles, especially the woollen goods produced by specialists in the Low Countries largely from English wool and bought at the fairs of Champagne. In the middle of the thirteenth century this trade was facilitated by what Lane calls the Nautical Revolution of the Middle Ages which involved the development of portolan maps, the first to be drawn to scale, and the use of the compass. A 'Commercial Revolution' followed, commission agents taking over from the *colleganza*, with bookkeeping helping the now stationary merchants (previously they had travelled with their cargoes) to keep track of agents and of partners, with the development of marine insurance against loss or piracy, of bills of lading and bills of exchange and of banking institutions more generally. These activities favoured literate merchants, that is, an educated bourgeoisie who were well rewarded for their work and enterprise.

Its intimate involvement in the rise of European commerce in the Mediterranean after the Islamic invasions led Italy to develop many of the features intrinsic to later capitalism. The Italians were innovators 'in all the domains that touched upon the economy: navigation, trade, commercial law, banking techniques, insurance, etc. Throughout the Middle Ages, they had a considerable advance in these fields on other peoples of the West.' As a result 'for centuries, banking was practically a foreign monopoly, almost entirely in the hands of Italian merchant bankers'.[20] They too were the ones to make the advances in bookkeeping; and double-entry was probably developed by them in the thirteenth century.[21]

Well before the Portuguese discovery of the sea route around Africa, Italians had already made direct contact with the major trading system that had grown up in the East, centring on India, south-east Asia and China. The father of Marco Polo, a Venetian, visited China between

[20] de Roover 1954: 66.
[21] de Roover 1937: 176; Yamey 1949: 101. Spain has also been suggested as its birthplace, largely on the adoption of Arabic numbers.

1260 and 1269. Before the end of that century, the Vivaldi brothers unsuccessfully planned to reach the Indies from the West, drawing up partnership and loan agreements for the voyage. Side by side with trade, the activity of the missions expanded rapidly. The Franciscans established a base at Quanzhou (Zaitun), opposite Taiwan, which during the later Tang became the greatest harbour in China, where already in 1326 'Genoese merchants were not an uncommon sight'.[22] Many Persians and Arabs had settled there much earlier and the building of ocean-going ships gradually enabled the Chinese from Fukien to replace Arabs as the chief carriers of the trade with the Near East, at least until the beginning of the fifteenth century when China withdrew from long-range trade. One of the major imports to Europe, India and the Near East was silk and in 1340 customs records show that this material was being brought into England by the Frescobaldi company of Florence. Much earlier, of course, the Romans had imported silk in large quantities and even during the Dark Ages it continued to be used in Europe for the clothing of priests and for other luxury items.

At roughly the same period, a group of six merchants left Venice for Delhi, probably going by boat to the Crimea since the Sultan of Egypt attempted to control access to the southern routes for India and China. In any case there was a good market for European cloth along the coasts of the Black Sea. A little later overland voyages to China stopped with the disappearance of the Mongol dynasty, so that Chinese silk doubled in price, as did many spices. Trade continued by sea by way of the Persian Gulf. Despite the Egyptian conquest of Lajazzo, the main port of the Christian kingdom of Armenia situated on the mainland north-east of Cyprus, and despite the invasions of Tamurlane, Italians still visited India right up to the arrival of the Portuguese caravels in 1499, exploiting the newly opened sea route round the Cape of Good Hope.[23]

Of course, Italian merchants were not the only ones to use the land routes by which the West traded with the East. Before the conquests of Islam, Nestorian Christians and Persian merchants plied the silk road to Tang China and evidence of their activities is enshrined in the Imperial Shosho-in treasures of Nara, the ancient capital of Japan, that date from the seventh century CE.[24] Persians and Armenians penetrated to south-east Asia and were frequent visitors to south China.[25] Meanwhile the sea route to India and further east had been kept open since Roman times by Semitic merchants, Arabs, Christians and Jews, who sailed their ships between the Red Sea, the Arabian peninsula and the Persian Gulf to

[22] Lopez 1943: 165.   [23] Lopez 1943: 184.
[24] Hayashi 1975.   [25] Colless 1969; Manandian 1965.

Gujarat and the Malabar littoral of south-western India and beyond, leaving settlements of all three religions scattered along the coast.

Accounting for commerce

This brief outline of commerce in the Mediterranean since the rise of Greece makes the point that Europe experienced a radical decline in trade, especially in comparison with the rise in Eastern commerce over the same period. That decline was followed by a revival in the course of the so-called Nautical and Commercial Revolutions of the thirteenth century, together with the parallel expansion of communication by means of the written word.[26]

This growth of the European economy increasingly brought it closer, both physically and in quality, to the more active Asian system. It was accompanied by the development of the literate procedures needed for accounting, for partnerships and for banking. The great historian of medieval business, de Roover, argued that commercial accounting, which differed in its aims from national accounting, had no great part to play in the closed, domainal economy of early feudalism, where exchange transactions were few and credit non-existent. However even in the eleventh and twelfth centuries European trade had reached the point where merchants were seriously disadvantaged if they were altogether illiterate; they had to engage in correspondence with other traders as well as reckoning their own accounts.[27] It was this burgeoning activity that led de Roover to speak of the 'birth' of commercial accounting in Europe at this time. That was needed firstly to maintain a note of credits and debts, that is, to calculate one's own position regarding third parties, and secondly to keep track of the operations of commercial associations. These associations appeared in Italy even before the Crusades as temporary groupings, organised around one voyage, and are described as 'the earliest forms of capitalism'.[28]

The oldest surviving Italian account book dates from 1211 and consists of the fragments of a *libro delle ragione* (of 'reason') of a company of Florentine bankers. The techniques are simple: the entries are given in chronological order, with debts and credits following one another after a space left to record payment. The extension of business encouraged more complex developments. At the end of the thirteenth century, the house of Bonsignori at Siena employed a number of books, including a cash book (*libro del'entrata e dell'uscita*) and a ledger of current accounts,

[26] See Stock 1983 and Clanchy 1979.
[27] Pirenne 1929: 19.   [28] de Roover 1937: 174, 176.

giving debtors and creditors. It seems that the evolution of the latter towards a two-column system showing debts and credits (in a 'bilateral form') probably took place in Venice since the practice was later known as *alla veneziana*. Even before the advent of such a system the use of a plurality of account books, often known by the colours of their bindings (the red book, the blue book), could serve to keep a check on the movement of funds and of goods within and without the enterprises.

The two-column system was then supplemented by the practice of entering each transaction twice, keeping as it were a double account. What this did was to introduce 'the fiction of exchange transactions between the different parts of a single enterprise; or, between different accounts' in order to improve the reckoning of profit and loss.[29] This development may possibly have arisen from the practices of deposit banks, whereby the entry of an amount in a customer's account (a credit) is also shown as a potential debt to the bank, that is, in a different account. There were two advantages to this procedure.[30] The general position of the bank regarding debts was immediately visible: the profit and loss could be calculated at any point. Secondly there was a definite separation of the corporate from the individual accounts. These were important gains.

European manuals on bookkeeping stress this point, emphasizing the value of written records in general as against the reliance on memory. 'The merchant should not rely upon his memory in his business dealings; unless he is like King Cyrus, who knew each one of his numerous soldiers by name.'[31] Later, in an early eighteenth-century text, the merchant was warned that there was a way 'by which we can wrong others, and even ourselves, without doing any wilful Injustice, and that is, by giving our Memory too much Trust, and neglecting to write down every Transaction of our Affairs, or setting them down in so disorderly and confused a Manner, that every Person's Right is not truly distinguished, but they are charged too much or too little'.[32] Not only were credit dealings promoted by bookkeeping but in some circumstances the law recognised account books as evidence of debt.[33] Thus the immediate utility for the

[29] Weber 1947: 193.
[30] *Errata*: In Goody 1977: 89, I referred to double-entry bookkeeping in Babylonia, following Albright (1968: 53). That was an error. So was the reference in the same book to the absence of writing in Central America: that should read South America (p. 83).
[31] B. Cotrugli, *Della mercatura et del mercante perfetto* (Venice, 1573), quoted in Yamey 1949: 103.
[32] A. Malcolm, *A New Treatise on Arithmetick and Book-keeping* (Edinburgh, 1718), quoted in Yamey 1949: 103.
[33] Yamey 1949: 103.

merchant and client was supplemented by the frequent preference of courts of law for a written record.

The growth of European commerce in an international setting required banking institutions to ensure the exchange of one currency for another, to provide credit and to take deposits; it also involved bills of exchange, which again were critically dependent upon writing.[34] The letter or bill of exchange was not simply an order for payment, a cheque which is a simple assignation and has a different origin, but a combined instrument of exchange and credit. It does not emerge from Roman law, which knew no contract of exchange and appeared as a notarial act between 1275 and 1350.[35]

Bills of exchange necessitated having correspondents living in the other towns, and in the other countries, especially if they were not subject to discount. That was the case in continental Europe until the last quarter of the eighteenth century although in England (where bills had been introduced from Italy in the fifteenth century) discounting was introduced a hundred years earlier.[36] Why did this development take place, de Roover asks, in London rather than in the 'more liberal milieu' of Amsterdam? The Dutch city was more closely linked with other continental establishments to whose usage it had to conform. London, on the other hand, was still a place of secondary importance at the beginning of the seventeenth century, suspicious of engaging in (overseas) exchange.[37] As in Europe as a whole, under conditions of expansion earlier backwardness paid off, leaving London more free to innovate.

In this respect of discounting bills, a Protestant country made concessions to the 'spirit of the century' before the Catholic ones. Discounting was condemned by the latter as partaking of 'usury', which was distinguished in subtle ways from 'interest'.[38] The concept of usury derived from the Near East and is found in both Jewish and Muslim law. Nevertheless both were active trading civilizations and it is not clear how far such notions placed any great inhibitions on commerce apart from tending to limit rates of (and sometimes claims for) interest.[39] In Hanafī law, which was based in Iraq and was more sympathetic towards trade,

---

[34] In Europe letters of credit may have originated among the moneychangers in Genoa in the twelfth century.

[35] de Roover 1953: 18.

[36] de Roover 1953: 18.

[37] de Roover 1953: 146.

[38] To discount was to pay the value of a promissory note before it was due, making a deduction equivalent to the interest at a certain percentage for the period it still had to run.

[39] 'Allah has allowed trading and forbidden usury' (Qur'an, 2: 275).

the courts tended to accept the practices of merchants and a whole system of 'casuistry' developed to reconcile the two, namely *ḥiyal*, legal devices which were subsequently incorporated into the body of the law. In Europe de Roover claimed that 'scholastic doctrine in no way hindered the development of banking, but modified its character in condemning loans on interest and in legitimising real exchanges from place to place'.[40] With doctrines on usury in mind he notes that 'the Church has not hampered the march of capitalism, but it has changed the course of its evolution'. As a result of its innovations London became the centre of discounting, whereas in France, for example, no interest could officially be charged on loans until the Revolution.[41] De Ste Croix demonstrated that the Greeks and Romans did not develop double-entry bookkeeping despite the wide range of their trade and empires. In discussing the implications of this absence, Macve asks what they missed as a result. The most familiar products today are the 'profit and loss account' and the 'balance sheet', giving 'income' and 'capital'. But the Romans and the Greeks could work these out in so far as it was necessary. As de Ste Croix remarked, and as is well worth remembering in the Weberian debate, 'we must not belittle the intelligence of the Greeks and Romans because they did not try to do what the nature of their economic system made it unnecessary for them to attempt'.[42]

Written records were especially useful in the case of the partnerships that played so important a part in early trading operations. Whether of a formal or informal nature, of long or short duration, partnerships were very frequent in the early days of European trade, and 'remained an important type of commercial organization until replaced, partly by the limited liability company'.[43] Their records were obviously more complex than those of one-man concerns, so that 'a well-advanced system of agency or factorage accounting existed at an early date'.[44] Nevertheless, as Yamey points out, such accounting required nothing more than 'a record of transactions, analysed, for convenient reference, into accounts of debtors and creditors, and with cash transactions grouped together in one account', requirements which can easily be met by a single-entry system supplemented by a cash-book or 'memorial'.[45]

Indeed, he goes on to claim that 'the vast majority of enterprises used a simple form of record-keeping . . . until well into the nineteenth century'. He later writes that 'the frequency with which merchants and bookkeepers evaded the mathematical discipline of the double-entry

---

[40] de Roover 1953: 146.   [41] de Roover 1954: 74–5, 67.
[42] Macve 1994; de Ste Croix 1956: 34.   [43] Yamey 1949: 104.
[44] Yamey 1949: 103–4.   [45] Yamey 1949: 105.

system does suggest that its special feature was not highly regarded'.[46] That fact brings up another issue for it must cast some doubt upon the critical role allocated to double-entry in the rise of capitalism itself. Even when double-entry was used, the balancing of accounts that it promoted resulted not so much from the 'rationalistic pursuit of profit' as from 'narrow bookkeeping purposes'. The bookkeeping purposes were perhaps narrow in another way. If it was the case that double-entry was at this point unnecessary from a strictly commercial ('rational') point of view, it may have developed under an aesthetic impulse, a pressure towards symmetry, neatness and perfection in the organisation of accounts which drove accountants to elaborate their systems beyond the immediate demands of utility.[47] We also see evidence of an internal progression in the series of accounting developments that took place in China. The system was certainly recognised as being useful for showing the profit and loss on particular lots of goods. But its use was promoted not so much by businessmen as by teachers of accountancy and did not become of great positive benefit until enterprises grew much larger.

If the use of double-entry was uneven in the later period, that was certainly true of the earlier one. In the later Middle Ages, 'the leading business men of Europe were the Italians' and it has been claimed that their organisation was far superior to that of any of their rivals.[48] Only in the sixteenth century did the Spanish and Portuguese begin to catch up. Earlier 'their monopoly was nearly absolute' and Italian banking houses dominated the money markets in London and Bruges. De Roover sees their superior organisation, which included their unique use of double-entry before 1500, as enabling them to put their competitors out of business since 'unsystematic records put severe limitations on the size of a business', for example, on the number of overseas agents. That was especially true in northern Europe where forms of business organisation were less well developed than in the south. 'Unsystematic bookkeeping' prevented 'extensive delegation of powers' entailing increased mobility for the merchant, limiting the size of firms and slowing down economic progress.[49]

Another view is possible. It could be maintained that at this time the nature of the commercial activity in the north did not call for greater expertise, which could after all have been imported from Italy. While accounting methods may have had some effect upon growth, it is more

---

[46] Yamey 1994: 256.
[47] I am indebted for this suggestion to a discussion in the Department of History, University of Illinois, Urbana.
[48] de Roover 1974: 164.
[49] de Roover 1974: 173.

likely that, given the systems of accounting that already existed, growth would have led to the development (by borrowing or by invention) of new methods. In any case, as we have seen, it has been suggested that those methods were perhaps not all that intrinsic to the running of many forms of capitalist enterprise.

However, even if the development of so-called 'scientific', double-entry accounting was not central to parts of the mercantile economy of late medieval Europe, bookkeeping itself was very important, especially in the growth of those mercantile associations whose appearance in Italy has also been considered as critical in the development of capitalism.

The problem for the European thesis is that while double-entry was not known in the earlier Mediterranean, the 'rationality of monetary accounting', on which Weber insists, is clearly present in the Ancient World of the Near East and did not have to wait until Europe was ready. For its existence was directly connected with the application of writing to the incomings and outgoings of mercantile 'firms' and partnerships as well as of the temples and palaces of the region.[50] Whatever important developments in society and particularly in the economy took place at a later period, they included neither the introduction of rationality nor yet of rational accounting.

The recognition of the value of writing in economic activity that we found in Europe is certainly not confined to that continent. Similar injunctions are to be found in the Qur'an. Although in theory written contracts only constituted collaborative evidence, practice was very different. A Qur'anic injunction ran: 'O you who believe, when you deal with each other in contracting a debt for a fixed time, then write it down; and let a scribe write it down between you with fairness; and the scribe should not refuse to write as Allah has taught him.' For 'this is more equitable in the sight of Allah and assures greater accuracy of testimony' and eliminates doubts.[51] A branch of the practical law became devoted to notarial science which recognised 'the indispensability and widespread use of written contracts for extensive commerce'.[52] These advantages accrue from any system of graphic notation and were just as relevant for a merchant in the seventh-century Near East as in thirteenth-century Italy. Indeed, mercantile accounting was one of the important uses of writing from its very beginning in cuneiform Mesopotamia around 3000 BCE.

It was not then the case that earlier systems of written accounts could not present a picture of the profit and the loss, even though this

[50] Goody 1986: chapter 2.
[51] Qur'an, 2: 282.   [52] Udovitch 1970: 88.

calculation was more laborious. Moreover the notion of a corporation in which individuals had shares had long been present.[53] We cannot attribute to double-entry, as some have tried to do, the abstract concepts of profits, the firm and its capital valuation, concepts deemed intrinsic to the development of a modern industrial economy.[54] Some calculations were assisted by the introduction of double-entry but, at least implicitly and often explicitly, these wider notions were intrinsic to the operation of earlier Asian and European commerce. Well before its introduction the keeping of single-entry accounts in Italy and Flanders accompanied a considerable degree of success in business, suggesting that Sombart's claim about the inefficiency of medieval accounting that made use of such methods was exaggerated. Medieval merchants and bankers worked along similar though less complex lines than those used later on, employing procedures that had been in more or less continuing development, despite the decline in medieval Europe, since the early uses of writing in Mesopotamia. The main contrast has to be with those African traders who did not have access to writing and whose scale and organisation of activity was consequently limited; hence part of the attraction of written religions to those traders who were more than itinerant pedlars. The value of writing in computation exists quite apart from the invention of double-entry.

In other words to speak of the 'birth' of such activities in the West during the Middle Ages represents a misunderstanding deriving in part from the relative backwardness of Europe after the fall of the Roman Empire. When he wrote of 'the limitations on the development of capitalism' in the ancient world, Weber realised that activities of a capitalistic kind were carried out long before the existence of the medieval *commenda*, and that those activities were dependent upon accounting procedures of a fairly complex kind. What we witness in the later Middle Ages, as in so many instances of European achievement at this time, was a rebirth (or recovery) rather than a birth. This recovery certainly did not entail a slavish copying, a precise reproduction; the earlier hiatus meant that procedures were not ossified and had to be rethought.[55]

Partnerships

Of the formation of such associations, de Roover writes: 'It is in Italy, where the first forms of capitalism appeared during the Crusades and

[53] Goody 1986.
[54] Chaudhuri 1978b: 418.   [55] See Goody 1986.

even before, that temporary associations were created to carry out long-distance trade. These were generally for the duration of a single voyage and between merchants endowed with the spirit of enterprise, capitalists thirsty at the prospect of large profits.'[56] Such associations were known as *commenda* or *societas maris* depending upon the extent of the partici-pation of the moneymen whose interests, like those of other participants, had to be tracked by periodic inventories and by other forms of accounting. In Europe the first such contract dates from 1157 and de Roover sees such procedures as representing the shift from a domainal to an exchange economy, just as Weber saw the *commenda* as leading to the development of capitalism.

In Europe partnerships were of two main kinds: family partnerships and contractual arrangements between unrelated merchants. In Venice in the late Middle Ages, it was the family partnerships or *fraterna* that predominated. Contrasting the trading networks of Venice, with their employment of commission agents (often kinsmen), to the banking activities of Florence, de Roover remarks that 'Kinship was of extra-ordinary importance in the Middle Ages even in business'.[57] Since these groups were not organised exclusively for business purposes, they did not correspond exactly to the modern corporation. But some enterprises required the use of so much capital that several families banded together to spread the risks and undertake a joint venture, the ownership being divided into shares. Unlike modern corporations they were usually of temporary duration, lasting only for the length of a voyage.

The family partnership obviously had longer-term objectives than the contractual ones. As its name suggests it was based upon fraternal ties. 'Originally *fraterne* derived their existence from the physical fact that brothers often lived together in the same house, shared the same board, and consumed together the produce of their country estates. Under Venetian law members of a family thus living together and doing business as a unit automatically became full partners without any formal contract.'[58] When the family constituted a business partnership, 'all the property inherited from the father – houses, land, furniture, jewelry as well as ships and merchandise – was entered on the books of the *fraterna* unless withdrawn from it by special agreement'.[59]

The assumption that the *fraterna* represents a form of joint household requires some qualification, although it is clearly related to what is often referred to as a *frèreche* in which a number of brothers belong to the same property-holding unit and normally work an undivided farm or other

[56] de Roover 1937: 174.   [57] de Roover 1974: 161.
[58] Lane 1944: 178–9.   [59] Lane 1944: 179.

enterprise. In the first place, each of the brothers could also own his distinct property and carry on commercial operations on his personal account. This separate fund came from the wife's dowry, from a personal legacy or by borrowing from the partnership. The operations an individual carried out might lead to the setting up of other partnerships nested within the main one. In the case of the Pisani brothers, there were three such units, the parent *fraterna*, the London Company and the Syrian Company, each of which acted as agents for the others in buying and shipping or in receiving and selling.[60] Minor subsidiaries appear to have been set up 'to give young men of the family a chance to try their skill', while elsewhere commission houses were employed.

The non-familial partnerships were based on temporary agreements for joint ownership and agency where larger capital or greater risk-spreading was needed. One reason why Venice did not see a major development of such partnerships was that the ships used for trade were built and operated by the Republic who rented them out to local merchants. So there was little need for any private business institution having either the longevity or the large capital and powers of command characteristic of the 'modern' corporation. As a consequence Venice lagged behind in the development of the joint-stock company that emerged elsewhere in Europe in the fifteenth century, and which in the sixteenth century became a regular feature of the mining industry as well as of oceanic commerce and colonisation. But the 'backwardness' of Venice in this respect, compared with Florence or Genoa, gave her merchants considerable flexibility in a 'world market', so that they were more readily able to shift their trade to different points in the Mediterranean and the North Seas as circumstances dictated.

The *commenda*, however, is a more specialised arrangement 'in which an investor or group of investors entrusts capital or merchandise to an agent–manager, who is to trade with it and then return to the investor(s) the principal and a previously agreed-upon share of the profits'.[61] This form of association combines the advantages of partnership and loan, the investor being limited to losing his capital, while the agent has normally no liability for the latter.

Both these institutions, the kin and non-kin associations, were essential in one form or other to most commercial operations of any complexity, and go much further back in history although not necessarily in precisely the same legal form, which in any case represents an attempt to come to grips with commercial practice. What we observe here is the co-existence of economic relations based on kinship and those based on

---

[60] Lane 1944: 185.   [61] Udovitch 1970: 170.

contractual ties. In so far as proprietary partnerships are concerned, the inheritance of undivided property by siblings gives rise automatically to such a relationship, without the individuals having to do anything unless they wish to dissolve the joint fund. In the other cases a contract (and predominantly a written one, since in the case of Islam Udovitch speaks of 'the indispensability of written contracts to commerce') has to be established to set up the other form of partnership or 'agency'.[62] Kin may still be involved but the relationship does not rise directly out of the devolution of property between generations but rather from common, commercial, or in some cases productive, interests with a view to making a profit, or at least a livelihood.

The prophet himself established a *commenda* with his wife Khadija, in which the partners were equal, one furnishing the capital, the other managing the business.[63] This was a form of capital investment, with 'a capitalistic calculation of accounts' whereby the partners drew out profits on an agreed basis. It became more popular in the Near East with the introduction of Indian positional numerals at the beginning of the ninth century by the Islamic mathematician al-Khwarizmi. His book on the subject was compiled to meet the needs of people in solving questions 'of inheritance, wills, purchase and sales agreements, in surveying, in the cleaning and digging of rivers and canals, in measuring goods and in technical matters'.

In discussing the development of Indian accounting methods, Labib notes that after a sale the merchant would enter the profit or the loss in his ledger in such a way as to present the current situation. Indeed he speaks of 'the double entry method' being an important part of a merchant's skill.[64] In the absence of evidence from ledgers, it is difficult to know whether he is referring to double-entry of the Italian kind or of the simpler, bilateral system. However other institutions of a Near Eastern origin were certainly adopted or revived, not only the *commenda* but the *moana* (*ma'una*), a kind of private bank loaning out the state's money. The precursors of the modern bourse were also present in Islam, providing for the activity typical of the modern commodity exchange, namely the trading in goods to be delivered at a later date. However, except in Mughal India, insurance was not well developed, being left rather in the hands of God.

Varieties of fraternal partnership exist in virtually all those societies where brothers farm or own property together; less often the practice is found among sisters, when they are not dispersed by virilocal marriage

[62] Udovitch 1970: 9.
[63] Labib 1969: 91.   [64] Labib 1969: 92.

(for example, in certain types of matrilineal society such as that of the Nayar and the Garo of India). In the simpler societies, non-kin co-operation also takes place but less commonly. However the elements exist. The advent of more complex mercantile economies encourages the extension of such practices and their embodiment in written legal forms, leading eventually to joint-stock companies, to limited liability and to other forms of co-operative activity. These developments represent an increase in economic complexity in the organisation of commerce. In fact they can emerge one from another with relative ease, especially as the joint activity is based on more general human institutions (namely, the co-operation of brothers) which it supplements rather than replaces; it was to 'brothers', not to non-kin, that Biblical prohibitions on lending money at interest were originally applied. Indeed as I shall argue, a major misunderstanding about the nature of capitalism has arisen through a unilineal interpretation of the past which sees new bureaucratic institutions as inevitably eliminating earlier forms, such as family enterprises, as 'modernisation' proceeds.[65]

The problem is that just as forms of 'rational' bookkeeping, though not double-entry, were widespread in the Mediterranean before the revival, so too was the *commenda*. It was known and practised in the Near East since the Babylonians; it was mentioned in the Talmud and is treated in the *Corpus Iuris Civilis* of Justinian.[66] De Roover and others have tended to see these partnerships as a specifically European invention linked with the first shoots of capitalism. The suggestion displays the same kind of historical and sociological myopia that marks the discussions of bookkeeping itself. For what we find in Italy was in essence a rebirth, recovery or re-creation of an institution that had existed in various forms even in the Near East.[67] The *commenda* of the Italian merchants of the twelfth century is comparable to the partnership procedures of the Near Eastern merchants of that period, the *shirka* of Jewish traders and the *muqarada* of the Hanafī school of Muslim law.[68] These institutions in turn reflected Mediterranean provincial usage in later Roman times. And there is a more general sense in which the practice goes back to trading activity in the ancient Near East, in the Persian Gulf and the Indian Ocean, in the form, for example, of the Babylonian *tapputum*.[69]

---

[65] I use 'unilineal' in a special sense to describe a view that sees one form as replacing another (an excluding progression) rather than adding to the human repertoire. A confusion is frequently made in discussing modes of communication and modes of production.

[66] Udovitch 1970: 8.   [67] Goody 1986.

[68] Lopez and Raymond 1955: 174.   [69] Goitein 1954: 195.

Types of company formation associated with complex, commercial operations, and the forms of accounting that were intrinsic to them, were widely available in the Near East before these developments took place in late medieval Europe. Indeed the *commenda* of the Italian seaports of the late tenth and early eleventh centuries, so germinal to the expansion of medieval European trade, may have been a direct introduction from Islamic law.[70] In that law there are two ways of pooling resources for commercial purposes, by means of the partnership and *commenda* contracts. These procedures establish different kinds of associative relationship. In the Hanafī and Mālikī schools the two types of partnership are proprietary and contractual (or commercial). In the first case joint ownership is the only qualification; it arises when two people acquire something together, some interest by inheritance (in compulsory association) or by purchase (in voluntary association). It too exists in principle when two brothers inherit from their father and therefore bears a general resemblance to the *fraterna*.[71]

Bookkeeping, commerce and religion in medieval Cairo

This discussion points to two problems involved in most existing accounts of these critical developments in the European economy. The first is the neglect by some 'modern' historians of the commercial activities of the later Middle Ages. De Roover makes this comment about activities in Genoa and elsewhere in Italy as they emerge, for example, in the account books of the Medicis.[72] Under the influence of works such as those of Tawney (and more generally of Weber), too great an emphasis has been placed on the commercial and banking innovations of the sixteenth century; much had been accomplished in the preceding centuries. The same was true with developments in commercial law, insurance and, as we have seen, with bookkeeping. In de Roover's words: 'The corporate organisation of modern business has its roots in the medieval partnership, our bill of exchange is a direct descendant of exchange contracts of the Middle Ages, and our accounting stems from ways contrived by early fourteenth-century Genoese merchant bankers.'[73] But what these medievalists in turn tend to lose sight of is that, while it is true that accounting gradually became more elaborate, written procedures for establishing the profit and the loss had long been present in the Near East.

That is clear from the situation that existed in the Near East and on

---

[70] Udovitch 1970: 171–2.   [71] Udovitch 1970: 24–5.
[72] de Roover 1953: 65.   [73] Lopez and Raymond 1955: 3.

the African shore of the Mediterranean at the very beginning of the expansion of commerce at Venice. For we find there not only the *commenda* but the associated practices in trade and banking. 'There seems to be a close connection', writes the historian, Goitein, of Cairo, 'between the banking practices reflected in the Geniza documents of the eleventh century and those known to us from Europe two or three hundred years later.'[74] The role of such banking was primarily as a clearing house, weighing, assaying and changing money. As the rich correspondence preserved in the Cairo Geniza shows, Jewish and Muslim merchants of that period engaged in an extensive trade in the Mediterranean and Indian Ocean in which they made use of writing for a wide range of business purposes, for passing on information, for keeping inventories and in legal disputes, including those over 'questions of bookkeeping', and for maintaining contact with their families when travelling.[75] The records of the Jewish community were preserved in the dry soil of Egypt in which they had to be buried because, as in Muslim and Christian usage, 'no writing which may contain the name of God should be destroyed by fire or otherwise'.[76] Much of the material had to do with commerce. 'It seems that everybody was supposed to read Hebrew as well as Arabic, but not everybody at all was fluent in writing', which might be undertaken by a clerk. As elsewhere this bias towards reading reflects the priorities of a system of education dominated by religious considerations and the consultation of a holy book, but on the other hand it did not prevent an extensive trade.

The merchants themselves were often businessmen as well, as were the Patriarchs of Alexander in the sixth century and many *kadis* throughout the region. Like the *kadis*, rabbis were both religious and legal officials, so that the rabbinical courts charged with judging disputes between merchants were often staffed by experts in the field. Religion was an important element in trade; while there was much interdenominational co-operation, co-religionists often travelled together, sought out each other's support in difficulty and at times suffered collective discrimination, as when Islamic rule levied higher customs dues on Christians and Jews.

The connection between religion and business in medieval Cairo is apparent from the fact that this mercantile capitalism was firmly built on the basis of trust in one's fellow men which was in turn guaranteed by the word of God. So too with bookkeeping. It is sometimes thought that it was the Reformation that led to the close link between religious and

---

[74] Goitein 1967: 230.
[75] Goitein 1954: 195.   [76] Goitein 1954: 182.

business accounting. 'Next to being prepared for death, with respect to heaven and his soul', declared Defoe, 'a tradesman should always be in a state of preparation for death, with respect to his books.'[77] The idea is close to Weber's thesis, although it might appear contradictory that rational disenchantment insisted upon invoking the deity in such mundane matters. And it received support from writers like William Temple, who, commenting upon an early exhortation of this kind, remarked that the spirit of the age 'for the first time made the keeping of accounts a religious duty'.[78] But once again historical myopia obscures the vision of the past. The conflicts of Jewish and Islamic merchants had long been resolved by religious courts, while Catholics too called upon God and the Virgin Mary to vouch for the rectitude of their accounts. One of the earliest bankers' books, copied from two accounts dating from 1313 and 1316, begins as follows:

> In nomine domini, amen. Ut Infra
> Reperitur in Cartulario banci quondam
> Lanfranchini de Donato anni de MCCCXIII
> die XII Februarii, quod Incipit in primo
> folio: In nomine domine nostri Jesu Xristi et
> Sanctorum sit.

The activities of Jewish and Arab traders in the Mediterranean and the Middle East were not simply earlier examples of the kind of economy that later reappeared, and was developed, in Italy. There were concrete historical connections between the two since they were part of the same trading network. And those connections went back much further in the region to earlier trading systems that existed as far back as at least 1500 BCE in Mesopotamia. Nor were these features in any way confined to west Asia. We have already seen that as trade in the West was declining, from the third century CE, a complex trading system in the East developed between China, India and south-east Asia, associated *inter alia* with the eastern push of India into that region and with the Han expansion to the south. Both the external and the internal trade in those countries required 'rational accounting' and trading partnerships.

Some (but not all) of these activities in Europe represented growth after an earlier decline and therefore cannot be seen as unique developments in the forward march of the West, as many historical analyses would imply. Thus the establishment of permanent markets in place of the annual fairs as centres of international finance at the end of the thirteenth century and the stages that followed these events, were

[77] Defoe [1745] 1841: 321.   [78] Yamey 1949: 104.

not unique, at least as far as the early phases were concerned.[79] These developments, the disappearance of *commerce caravanier* in favour of a more sedentary type of exchange, had happened before in the Mediterranean. It was the backwardness of Europe in post-Roman times that required this process of catching up, this reinvention of the commercial wheel, although, as we have seen, the very fact of backwardness was perhaps of some advantage in the development of new forms. Economically backward in the sixteenth century in relation to much of Europe, England developed the practice of discounting, trading in, bills of exchange.[80] While the kind of sequence found in the West, in the development of exchequer accounts,[81] of commercial accounts, of market finance from the fairs of Champagne to more stable banking,[82] of commercial documents and of commercial associations such as the *commenda* and joint-stock company, was important to the development of industrial capitalism, it was a sequence that had already taken place in other parts of the world.

Bookkeeping in south and east Asia

It is important for the argument to note that the combination of business activity with supernatural supervision was not confined to Europe and the Near East. In 1987 I visited two *pedhi* (accounting offices) in Ahmadabad, Gujarat: one employed accountants trained in the European tradition, the other used traditional Indian techniques. Although both were Jain enterprises, they were regularly visited by Brahman priests at the annual ceremony of Divali when prayers were said and holy water sprinkled over the new books prepared for the coming financial year, each book being marked with the sign of the swastika. Like the Chinese New Year, Divali is the time when debts have to be paid and when an annual reckoning is made, so that family and other shareholders know the state of their affairs. The office using the Indian techniques dealt with a large and variegated business employing many people. It seemed to have no difficulty in accounting for its activities either to the principals or to the other beneficiaries with which they were dealing. In the early Italian manner, a series of books kept a record of expenditures and receipts, while a further series summarised the transactions. Had they been a public company with shareholders, however, pressure would certainly have been felt to change to a double-entry system which was the standardised way of presenting the accounts of such concerns.

---

[79] de Roover 1953: 38.   [80] de Roover 1953: 67.
[81] Clanchy 1979.   [82] de Roover 1953.

India is a country of bookkeepers and accountants, sitting cross-legged in stores and businesses at low desks of the kind also found in Japan. In the Ahmadabad flower market the accountants sit in the open shop, keeping records of their various transactions with sellers and buyers. With such elementary techniques (or technicians) at their disposal, shop-keeping is an activity in which many Indians participate, even though they do not necessarily come from trading castes. Gujarati 'barbers' run general stores in Africa and in Britain. More complex transactions had to be recorded in more elaborate and formal ways, especially those of the bankers and moneylenders who operated at all levels of the economy, in villages as well as in towns. That was also true of other organisations that dealt in large-scale outgoings and incomings, whether of goods, money or services, where the agents had to 'account' for their actions. A notable case was that of the medieval monasteries in Buddhist Ceylon which had their annual audit as well as regular checks of balances.[83] For the 'church' had been granted large areas of land, which, as in Europe, eventually amounted to about one-third of the total available resources. The accounts of those establishments had to make sense to the monks themselves, to the body of past and potential donors, as well as to the overarching polity, the government who dispensed them from taxation and allocated them a charitable status, although their religious aims made that status difficult if not impossible to refuse.

Evidence from a more recent period provides fuller details of the use of accounts. The system that prevailed among the Chettiar bankers of south India made use of several books, including a *peredu* in which was recorded all payments and receipts. The anthropologist, Rudner, examined in detail one *peredu* that 'seemed to consist of a number of subsidiary ledgers, describing various transactions and listing the associated payments or receipts in two separate columns: one for credit entries (*adhaya*) and one for debit entries (*varavu*)'. In other words, they operated a bilateral system which differed from double-entry in that each transaction was recorded a single time; there was no simultaneous entry crediting or debiting the agency's cash in the same amount.[84] The two columns provided some correlation of income and expenditure, giving a picture of the relationships with each client. But the information was not pulled together into a general ledger and summarised in a balance sheet.

The financial activities governed by this method of bookkeeping were far reaching. Rudner discusses the system of making deposits (many by the bankers' kin including Chettiar women with their dowries), together with the complexities of interest, of written methods of payment (*hundi*,

[83] Gunawardana 1979.   [84] Rudner 1989: 438ff.

a kind of bill of exchange), and the manipulation of long- and short-term loans, all of which made it possible to raise large sums for investment, amounting to some 100 million rupees in 1896. Chettiar bankers gave considerable assistance to one another; theirs was a caste-based, kin-based network adapted to the task of accumulating and distributing reserves of capital, and capable of providing large-scale finance for the purposes of development. It was the Tamil-speaking Chettiars living in a suburb of the Malay town of Malacca who controlled the lucrative trade in nutmeg, mace and cloves with the spice islands of Indonesia. One of their number, Nina Chatu, befriended the early Portuguese and assisted them to get control of the trade.[85] As one resident noted of Singapore in the middle of the nineteenth century the Chitties (a more general category than Chettiar) 'have the command of fabulous sums of money'.[86] While the negotiable financial instruments of the *hundi* and the linked agencies differed in detail from the so-called 'rationalised' versions of the West, they were 'well adapted to take advantage of opportunities for international trade and finance in the colonial society of south and south-east Asia'.[87] Moreover there is no reason to believe that other occupational or caste groups were not engaged in similar practices at a much earlier period, since the long-standing trade in cloth and spices to the East had to be financed by similar means.

Large-scale commercial enterprise could not be managed by simple accounting methods such as a record of income and expenditure; more complex forms were necessary.

The entries made in the different ledgers or account books preserved in the collections of Haribhakti and Mirzamal, Baroda bankers, indicate that, besides maintaining a record of daily receipts and debits (rojnamcha), the firms kept separate accounts for different clients, for cash receipts and debits, and for transactions made through hundis and other letters of credit. The consolidated account was kept in a monthly ledger, and finalised with the closing of the year in October–November. The accounts recorded and carried forward showed income and debits and the balance against each client; these were then tallied against the general ledger following the system of double-entry. In short there prevailed quite sophisticated forms of accountancy.[88]

The procedures used in India were slightly less sophisticated than those that emerged in Europe during the centuries when commerce developed so rapidly. Indeed Western analysts have often argued that such forms could not have appeared in the East. Weber thought that 'rational' bookkeeping failed to emerge among the Chinese because they

---

[85] Hoyt 1993: 32.   [86] Vaughan 1971: 1.   [87] Rudner 1989: 451.
[88] Sharma 1993: 43; see also Robb's comments in the same volume.

lacked a positional notation and depended upon the abacus which hindered tabular reckoning.[89] At the same time he argued that closed family firms, in which family and business were merged, did not need such procedures. On all these features Weber was misinformed. The zero existed. The abacus supplemented rather than replaced bookkeeping (as it does today in highly industrialised Japan). And both in the East and West family firms kept accounts. In the West as in the East those accounts were usually kept in single-entry form which was the most usual method until well into the nineteenth century.

The comment that the abacus would hinder tabular reckoning seems misplaced. It is true that it only provides the result of the calculation whereas with a pencil and paper (or slate or waxed tablet) all the steps are recorded. But the modern Chinese variety, also employed in Russia, does make use of tabular principles. Indeed the early abacus of Greece and Rome was essentially a tabular device, involving the shift of counters between rows and to some extent columns. As I have remarked, it was always an adjunct to forms of written calculation, an invention of literate societies which did not require literacy to operate. In Greece and Rome the name abacus referred to a board or slab, a draught-board, a calculating table. The earliest known counting-board is a Greek marble tablet from the island of Salamis of unknown date but which was probably used in the fifth century BCE. It was this type that was adopted by Rome and spread throughout their dominion. But the Romans also had a hand abacus, of the bead-frame variety, consisting of a bronze tablet with grooves in which small spherical counters could slide, resembling the one that later came into use in the Near and Far East. Such a system is described in the Chinese literature for the second century but did not come into general use until much later, during the thirteenth. This counting-frame type of abacus (*suan-pan*) had an extra counter and was a much faster instrument than the flat table, so that it is still being used today both in Japan and China. In the West other forms existed; in early English the word was also applied to a sand-board on which geometric figures could be traced, or alternatively to a calculating table.[90] The sand-table 'abacus' is mentioned in the tenth century but

---

[89] Following Weber, others have maintained that the absence of a concept of zero promoted the use of beads and meant that the writing of accounts was for memory rather than for analysis (Hirschmeier and Yui 1975: 42).

[90] This usage dates from the second half of the tenth century and continued until the fourteenth; a similar usage from Auxerre dates from *c.* 700 (Murray 1978: 164). The Latin word *abacus* means 'a flat surface', derived from the Greek *abax*, which was possibly related to the Hebrew *abaq*, dust. On this surface little stones (*calculi*) were used as counters.

later in the same century we find references to the abacus board. In Europe that became more widely used following the time of Gerbert of Aurillac, later Pope Sylvester II (d. 1003), who wrote a book on the subject following a visit to Spain. He was a prominent figure in the mathematical revival, which some writers have described as the 'birth of mathematics'. That can be said only in the context of events in Europe. For the table had been widely used in Roman times; many counters have been found but the wooden boards themselves have left no trace.[91] Whether or not the use of this device disappeared from Europe after the fall of Rome, as Murray suggests, it was certainly little used, coming into favour again only with the growth of trade.

The abacus became an important instrument in mathematical calculation, which 'the clumsy notation of the Greek and Roman' numerals made difficult in writing. The Middle Ages acquired much of its grounding in science from the sixth-century writings of Boethius. In his work *Geometrica* he describes a tabular system of reckoning, called the *abacus,* said to have been invented by the Pythagoreans (hence *mensa Pythagorica*). As in board games, the table consisted of a number of rows between which were moved markers representing the value of numbers by position. The nine numbers were named in a special way and took the form of arbitrary characters.[92] The results of the computation were then expressed in Roman numerals.

The abacus continued to be found in Europe until the nineteenth century but its use had already begun to decline late in the twelfth. Earlier in that century knowledge of Arabic (or Indian) numbers, known as *cifrae,* from the Arabic, *al-cifr,* 'the vacant one', were introduced into schools in western Europe. As a result of being able to express position through the use of zero and of having a much simpler way of recording numbers, scholars gradually discarded the columns of the abacus. *Algorismus* became the common name for arithmetic until the sixteenth century. These changes were certainly stimulated by Arabic knowledge from which so much was borrowed in the twelfth century.[93] Nevertheless the name 'abacus' lingered on, to provide a link with bookkeeping. For bookkeeping and arithmetic, using Arabic instead of Roman numerals, were taught in Venice by pedagogues called 'masters of the abacus', referring to written arithmetic.[94] It was these men that gave instruction among other things in double-entry. One of these tutors was Luca Pacioli, author of the earliest treatise to include an account of that system,

---

[91] Pullan 1968: 22.   [92] Wright 1861: ii, 64.
[93] Wright 1861: ii, 70.   [94] Lane 1944: 141.

Summa de Arithmetica, Geometria, Proportioni e Proportionalità (Venice 1494).

Why did the abacus die out in the West and not in the Far East? Was it that Western mathematics, using Arabic numbers, enabled one to work out the sums on a piece of paper (once papermaking had reached the West from China)? Did European schoolmasters insist that their pupils use pencil and paper for computations? Whatever the reason the abacus disappeared in western Europe, whereas in the major countries in the Far East, which lacked an alphabetic script and Arabic numerals, the instrument is used to this day, even in Japan, the contemporary home of 'scientific' electronic calculators themselves.

So too in China, which was in fact the scene of interesting developments in bookkeeping. Accounting of some kind was required by the Chinese economy. Indeed, 'portions of rent ledgers, tax registers, merchant sale books, and temple financial records survive from as early as the Han and T'ang dynasties, along with other evidence of pawnshop registers, shopkeepers' records, and even gambling accounts from the T'ang.'[95] From the individual's point of view one of the basic aims of financial activity was to maintain and extend the family's position in political, social and economic affairs.[96] In the domestic domain there is evidence of wives acting as a 'domestic bursar' since the fifth century.[97] Her duties were incorporated in household manuals, a very late example of which is Mrs Nieh's *Family Governance Study*, based on a Japanese work of 1893. It is written by a member of the élite and therefore cannot be taken as representative of Chinese society as a whole. But her emphasis on the role of women in family budgeting argues that they should be the rulers of 'inside'. They are responsible for drawing up and keeping to a budget, that is, making an estimate of family income and expenditure on a monthly or annual basis. But the family is also a 'saving unit'. Wives should attempt to save half the family income and then invest any savings in property or interest-giving ventures; 'she is therefore potentially not only a land dealer but a money-lender (if only to a bank)'.[98] The author's autobiography describes how her mother-in-law managed the family's wealth according to her own wishes, buying land, making loans, handling bank deposits, drawing up wills and

---

[95] McDermott 1991.
[96] On China, see McDermott 1989, as well as P. B. Ebrey (translated and annotated), *Family and Property in Sung China, Yuan Ts'ai's 'Precepts for Social Life'* (Princeton, NJ, 1984) and R. P. Hymes, *Statesmen and Gentlemen, the Elite of Fu-chou, Chiang-Hsi, in Northern and Southern Sung* (Cambridge, 1986).
[97] McDermott 1990.
[98] McDermott 1990: 19.

investing, 'all without prior consultation with the male members of her household'. Mrs Nieh herself did much the same but since she was not a widow, she did consult others. In the case of the account she had opened in a Hunan bank with her dowry and her inheritance from parents and relatives, it was her brother whom she got to carry out an inspection; for her own funds were kept quite separate from those of her husband. Unlike her mother-in-law, she was educated not only in the Confucian classics but in mathematics and algebra. Her education and her activities show that the pursuit of profit and the Confucian way were by no means 'irreconcilable opposites' in late Imperial China. Nor was this role of women confined to the rich. In the 1940s Niida Noboru found that many poor Hopei peasant women controlled the 'keys' to family savings kept in cases and grain chests; that was clearly a traditional role.[99]

The foundation for commercial calculation lay embedded in household finance and such practices inevitably led to the elaboration of systems of accounting. At the domestic level this reckoning might take the form of keeping lists of property acquired as dowry or as marriage gifts, which we have recently examined both in China and Japan. It was also true that accounting was needed in the management of lineage affairs, largely connected with landed estates, as in the organisation of trade and commerce. Following Weber and Braudel, Faure sees the latter as inhibited by the lack of capital accounting, by which he means double-entry bookkeeping.[100] As we have argued, the role of that system seems to have been exaggerated. Moreover some form of reckoning of the capital goods involved must surely be a characteristic of any enterprise, especially the large-scale trading in which Chinese merchants engaged. In commerce more elaborate procedures were created.[101] One branch of recent Chinese historiography has discerned 'sprouts of capitalism' as present at least from the middle of the Ming dynasty, associated with the use and spread of private commercial bookkeeping. Of course some bookkeeping was present as early as we have merchants with access to literate skills but more importantly in any state system that is collecting taxes (in money or in kind) and supplying resources to the court, the army and to artisans. Chinese officials had employed a basic methodology since the late Song period, which formed a model for private records. It used the 'four-columns system' (*sizhufa*) comprising

[99] See Goody 1990. In discussing gender equality in contemporary China, Whyte noted that women had 'an unusually high degree of control over family funds' (Stockman 1994: 759). That seems to have been a traditional role in many areas.

[100] Faure 1989.

[101] On the growth of rational capital accounting in Chinese business see Rowe 1984; Stockman 1994.

the four categories of balance forwarded, new receipts, outlays and present balance, which were adapted to suit the needs of merchants. A similar system was in operation in Korea in the eleventh or twelfth century.[102] It was in the Ming that the Chinese developed the *Sanjiao Zhang*, 'the Three-legged Account Book', which Guo sees as a single-entry system with some features of double-entry, though still a long way from 'scientific bookkeeping'.[103] That form appears to have been followed by the *Longmen* (Dragon Gate) system which originated in the commercial world of north-west China at the end of the Ming and the beginning of the Qing, although the only extant examples are from the late Qing. While this was not full double-entry, it did have a number of similar features. It was followed in turn by the *Sijiao Zhang* the 'Four-legged Account Book' that was associated with Fujian and Fukien in the south and was developed until it constituted what Hsu Tzu-fen calls 'an indigenous Chinese double-entry methodology, without the influence from Western double-entry bookkeeping techniques'. He designates this the receipt–payment method in contrast to the Western debit–credit one (*shouzhi bujifa*) and describes its workings in the following words: 'The receipt–payment method is used to record and calculate the increase and decrease of every entry involving a firm's assets, capital, liabilities, and profit and loss accounts . . . If a capital account is either increased or decreased, an assets account is correspondingly increased or decreased.'[104] Thus two entries are needed for each transaction. Based on the flow of ready money and used both by the state and in private households, this system was in some ways the reverse of the Western debit–credit method, which was introduced after the Meiji from Japan where 'Dutch learning' had long been strong.[105] However indigenous procedures continued to be used during the late Qing period, for example by the Tai-Yi Hao firm of Chinese merchants living in Nagasaki at the beginning of the twentieth century; in other words for large-scale commercial activities.[106]

Whatever the exact extent of these developments in China, they suggest a reconsideration of certain central assumptions of Western

---

[102] Some Korean historians claimed it as a double-entry system, preceding Europe by two centuries, but the evidence does not altogether warrant such a claim (Gardella 1992).

[103] Guo Daoyang, *Zongguo kuoiji shigao* (A Draft History of Chinese Accounting) (Beijing, 1988), vol. II, pp. 111–13. I am indebted to Victor Mair for his notes on chapters 7 and 8. He comments that the author gives no primary sources and is vague about dates.

[104] Hsu Tzu-fen 1991. Literally 'the receive–pay method', apparently a neologism, according to Mair.

[105] The source he gives is Cai Xiyong, *Lianhuan shang pu* (The Manual of Serialised Account Book), the main terms of which suggest a Japanese origin, according to Mair.

[106] Hsu Tzu-fen 1991.

historians, economists and sociologists. For it is widely held that there is one form of 'scientific' bookkeeping, that this was 'Western' and that its absence was of critical importance in holding back developments in other parts of the world.[107] That is implied by Goethe when he has Werner say, 'It is among the finest inventions of the human mind'.[108]

What does the term 'scientific' mean in this context? It is a word much used in attempts to account for the Rise of the West and it is closely linked to the concepts of 'rationality' and 'logic' discussed in the first chapter. Indeed, in their account of Japanese business Hirschmeier and Yui regard the absence of 'rational' bookkeeping as retarding the evolution of a 'liberal mentality'.[109] Rationality, scientific bookkeeping, even the notion of a civil society, a liberal democracy, form a cluster of features which is thought to characterise the West but not the East. In fact, as far as bookkeeping went, the heart of the Japanese shop was the accountant's desk and his books, together with the abacus. While there was no double-entry system of the kind used in Italy in the thirteenth century, they had elaborate-enough methods to make it possible to run businesses, to organise bank credit and to trade in futures. In other words 'rationality', 'science' and 'liberalism' must have been present in sufficient strength to permit and promote mercantile and industrial activities.[110] In any case neither 'rationality' nor 'liberality' arrived with innovations in bookkeeping, important as these and other techniques may be in elaborating a complex system of production and exchange. Such techniques may be considered more rational, more scientific; they cannot be taken to define such qualities.

By allocating the value-laden epithets 'scientific' or 'rational' to double-entry, the more advanced form of bookkeeping is set off from earlier developments by a kind of quantum jump and its invention then attributed to the special characteristics of a particular culture, people, or even mentality. The argument is valid neither theoretically nor empirically. Theoretically, all forms of bookkeeping can be described as 'rationalising' procedures employing written records. Those procedures are never perfect for the jobs to be done but all of them increase the control of merchants, manufacturers, partners and governments over their operations. Even for complex economic activities, single-entry is adequate for many purposes and was widely used in the West until the nineteenth century. Double-entry represents only a further step in a

---

[107] In his article 'Scientific bookkeeping and the rise of capitalism' (1949), Yamey seeks to modify the closeness of this relationship.

[108] *Wilhelm Meister's Lehrjahre*, i, 10.

[109] Hirschmeier and Yui 1975: 42.   [110] Hirschmeier and Yui 1975: 42.

process we may call rationalisation, not a unique system that can only be attained as the result of a special form of rationality, a Western one. That is where empirical material is relevant, for the history of bookkeeping in China makes it clear that this step could have been taken in other commercial cultures. Where accounting was an important activity, individuals inevitably tried to improve their procedures, just as the Italians had done in the thirteenth century.

It is of course possible that Western double-entry was introduced to China at an earlier stage and influenced the development of the Chinese forms. However, that occurrence seems unlikely since Guo demonstrates the internal, logical development that took place within the framework of Chinese bookkeeping itself. But let us assume that Western double-entry did indeed influence these Chinese forms. It could be argued, and it is an argument often used, that 'we' (the West) invented double-entry (for example), and 'they' only borrowed it, showing that they lacked the rational skills. In Europe the technique was developed in Italy and borrowed by the Dutch and the English. Did they too lack the rational skills? Let me transfer the argument to another 'invention', and assume that the splitting of the atom first occurred in Britain. Should we conclude that American (or Russian) 'backwardness' prevented them from making the advance, giving a moral, possibly genetic, or at least cultural–genetic value to the attributes involved?

The refutation of this argument may seem unnecessary; yet consider how often it occurs, for example, in the accounts of English or European writers on the rise of capitalism. When the Chinese adopted 'rational' or 'scientific' bookkeeping, they surely must have already had the 'rationality' or 'science' to do so. We are only led to think otherwise if we select such a feature as marking the cut-off between the presence and absence of a positive value such as rationality. In this way a significant advance is generalised into a great divide of unjustifiable magnitude and attributed to an abstract mental quality rather than treated as a specific, cognitive achievement. The preferable alternative is to see all book-keeping, beginning with its use in Anatolia in BCE 1500 if not before, as rationalising and to perceive the human agents who invented and used these techniques as being capable of improving upon them, given favourable economic and educational circumstances. In other words there is a developing internal 'logic' or 'rationality' about these processes rather than an external injection of 'science' or of mentality.

3   Indian trade and economy in the medieval and early colonial periods

In the previous chapter I began by looking at bookkeeping in medieval Italy and concluded by discussing the nature of accounting in India and elsewhere in Asia. The developments in bookkeeping, in company law, in banking and in commercial associations have been attributed by some historians to the growth of mercantile activity in medieval and Renaissance Europe. But we have seen that most of these activities were grounded in earlier practices in the Mediterranean. From this particular standpoint, the economic preconditions for the take-off that occurred in Europe existed much further back in time than modern historians have generally allowed. Even the economy of the 'feudal' period, following the decline of Rome, was more diverse than the term itself would suggest and various authors such as Pirenne and de Roover have discerned at least the shoots, if not the very beginnings, of capitalism.

Was this the case not only with Western 'feudalism' but with other contemporary societies elsewhere in the Old World? Marx and Weber thought not, for rather different reasons. Like many other, more recent writers they took as their starting point the Uniqueness of the West with respect to features determining the major transformation of society that could occur in western Europe alone. The reasons they sought partly in 'Asiatic exceptionalism', partly in the economic ethic and partly in other features thought to be present in the one and absent in the other. I have tried to suggest that, with regard to some of the chosen features, rationality or *ragioneria*, trading associations and banking, there is little reason to suppose that these differed critically as between Europe and Asia in the late medieval period, not in such a way as to prevent the development of those changes brought together under the rubric of 'capitalism' (which to Hodgson was machine production), industrialisation or 'modernisation'. As Goitein remarked, a large and powerful merchant class arose all over the Middle East as early as the eighth and ninth centuries when it quickly became the main bearer of Muslim civilization. I want to argue that this was also true of South and East Asia.

In this chapter I want to look very broadly at the role of trade in India and its relation to the local economy and society, concentrating particularly on the region of Gujarat in the west of the country. While European overseas trade later came to surpass that of Asia, at least during the period between 1700 and 1900, that was not the case at the time of the opening of the maritime route from the Atlantic. The initial advantage of the newcomers to the Indian Ocean lay in certain features of ships and guns rather than in the production and exchange of goods, for which they frequently had to provide precious metals in return, as the Romans had done before them, since they had relatively few manufactures or raw materials to offer. Gold they sought with difficulty in west Africa. That region, relatively close to Europe as it was, already had indirect links with the trading system of India and to a lesser extent with China, indicating the great importance of the existing trading network of the East.

Many valuables in the cultural repertoire of west Africa were manufactured outside that continent: Venetian beads, Mediterranean cloth and, later, guns. But three important items of 'material culture' came from yet farther afield. Firstly, there were the cowrie shells that were widely used for marriage payments, for market transactions, for divination and for gambling. Until recently, no single object was more central to the life of the tribal LoDagaa in what is now Ghana. They were used in their millions; for example, LoDagaa weddings involved a transaction of 20,000 cowries that had to be carefully counted out in the presence of the representatives of bride and groom. All of these shells are of Indian Ocean origin and were imported from the Maldives by way of Gujarat; some were used there for small change but the bulk were re-exported to Africa, where they are often described as shell-money and used for decoration and for exchange of many kinds.[1] Large amounts came by way of Europe and played an important part in the purchase of slaves. But while quantities increased, there is little doubt that shells had been used for the purposes of exchange, local and even long-distance, long before the period of European expansion.

Just as these cowries are now being rapidly discarded in favour of minted coins and paper money, so the red-faceted carnelian beads worn round the waists of the better-off women in the nearby kingdom of Gonja are being put aside in favour of coloured plastic. There are no known sources of carnelian in Africa: the beads were imported as cut stones from Cambay (Khanbat) in Gujarat and mined near Baruch (Broach, as it was known) and were remarked upon by early sixteenth-century

[1] On cowries in the area see Johnson 1970; Somda Nurukyor (n.d.); Perlin 1983: 62ff.; and Heimann 1980.

travellers such as Barbosa.[2] Cambay was a major port that was later used by the English and Dutch when their ships began to sail along the coast of south Asia, leading to the construction of a fort by the East India Company.[3] In the workshops of the town, these semi-precious stones were prepared and faceted for export to Africa, as they are to this day.[4] The trade had existed since medieval times and the beads may have already reached the Nile Valley in the days of ancient Egypt. As with cowries, the coming of European merchants and the opening up of the direct route expanded what was already a well-established trade.

The third item of material culture comprises those colourful printed cottons that are often seen as the typical dress for west African women and are known locally as 'mammy cloths'. From the late eighteenth century these were manufactured in Manchester and other European cities, and formed one of the basic export items of the early Industrial Revolution. Before Europe took over their manufacture, the original Indian forms of these cloths, sometimes decorated with elephants, peacocks and other oriental designs, were imported into west Africa from Gujarat by the English East India Company and other commercial concerns. Even before the opening of the sea route to India, they had made their appearance in the West, having been imported through the Near East. Some of these *pintadoes*, painted (or block-printed) cloths, were then taken by the first Portuguese voyagers to west Africa to exchange for gold, ivory and slaves. By the middle of the seventeenth century Guinea cloth had become a specialised product of Gujarat, purchased by European traders for taking to Africa along with cowries and carnelians, just as they took over much of the Arab trade in these commodities to Indonesia and the East.

Cowries and carnelians were used in west Africa before the arrival of the Europeans at the end of the fifteenth century. There is no evidence of Gujarati cloths reaching west Africa before that time, but there was a vigorous pre-European trade from India to Ethiopia and the east coast of Africa which is recorded in the mid-first-century traders' guide to the Indian Ocean, *The Periplus*. These exports included cotton cloth.[5] Indeed east Africa's pre-colonial trading contacts went much wider than

[2] Arkell 1951; Chittick 1971.
[3] Sleen 1967; Arkell 1936.
[4] The account books I was shown on a recent visit (December 1993) listed transactions with Muslim merchants in Kumasi and Bawku in Ghana, as well as with Nigeria during the 1970s. More recently exchange restrictions had put a stop to this trade but the beads were still being prepared for sale elsewhere.
[5] Schoff 1912. The date of the *Periplus* is much disputed (Matthews 1975). Some place it in the second century. I have followed Raschke (1978: 659).

India. The indirect importation of Chinese porcelain dates from the ninth century, though the majority of foreign pottery was Islamic.[6] In the fourteenth century, the Chinese imports began to dominate, leading up to the direct but limited contact of Chinese merchants with the coast in the early fifteenth century.

The wide distribution of the three items, one collected, one shaped and one manufactured, gives some idea of the range of Indian commercial networks before the colonial period, as well as of the importance of large-scale artisanal production, a production that was capable of great expansion in response to overseas markets. Note the broad difference between the exports of Africa, even today, and those of earlier Asia. Basically the former consist of primary products, of the forest, of the mine and of the oil well, as well as some from agriculture, palm oil and the acquired coffee, cocoa, tea and ground nuts; in earlier times, human beings too, as slaves. On the other hand the bulk of exports from India were essentially of manufactured, value-added commodities; if humans came they did so as traders and later as indentured labourers. That was true of other major Asian societies. An export trade in silk from China has been in existence since the opening of the silk route to Europe about 200 BCE. Chinese ceramics have an equally long history as exports, as does bronzeware. These manufactures were produced and exported in great quantities, especially after the opening up of the sea lanes. A vivid example is the recently auctioned cargo of a ship that sank off the coast of Vietnam at the turn of the eighteenth century which consisted of some 20,000 pieces destined for the entrepôt of Batavia in the Dutch East Indies and from there to Europe.[7] Many of those items were especially made for the overseas trade which had begun with Arab dhows from the Near East and ocean-going Chinese junks capable of travelling to India. The arrival of western ships extended the range even farther. Spanish galleons from Manila travelled to Acapulco, and ultimately back to Spain across the Atlantic; Portuguese merchant ships from Macao delivered goods up the River Tagus to the Court in Lisbon, and latterly in the seventeenth century, aggressive merchants from Holland, England, France and even Denmark and Sweden shipped commodities from China to their respective Company headquarters.

This eastern sea trade in commodities linked China to India well before the arrival of the Muslims, let alone the Europeans. The sea route from Ceylon (Sri Lanka) is attested from the early fifth century CE when the monk Fa-hien travelled overland via Khotan, returning by sea after

---

[6] Chittick 1971: 98.
[7] *The Vung Tau Cargo: Chinese export porcelain.* Christie's catalogue, 1992.

meeting a Chinese merchant.[8] Direct Chinese trade with Ceylon may have begun about the beginning of the Christian era;[9] certainly embassies were sent there at the end of the first century. But the big expansion of trade in the South China Sea took place under the Tang (618–907), and with the founding of the Kingdom of Srívijaya in Sumatra in 683 CE, possibly earlier. By Tang times Chinese trade with the countries of the Indian Ocean was considerable.[10] Long before the Chinese voyages to east Africa, led by Muslim merchants and officials, that continent was known as a source of ambergris, thought of as solidified dragon spittle. Other imports from that region were ivory and rhinoceros horn, frankincense and myrrh, all expensive luxuries.

That trade was carried on by independent merchants organised in guilds. Two famous guilds (śreni) flourished in South India from the eighth century. These were the Maṇigrāmam guild of traders and the Ayyācvoḷe association. In the latter Brahmans were well represented together with traders and members of other castes;[11] they became traders by choice not by descent. Such guilds engaged in extensive trade from fortified settlements that employed their own militia. Guild custom maintained order, regulated trade and administered the town, under royal sanction. Trade was wide ranging: the Maṇigrāmam association is mentioned in an inscription from Takuapa (Thailand) while another Tamil inscription has been found in the Red Sea. From the middle of the twelfth century there are definite indications of participation in foreign trade, and in the fourteenth century the increased demand for pepper from Venice was felt at the entrepôts of Alexandria and Beirut. But trade was also significant to Burma, to south-east Asia and to China, and in 1015 the Cōḷa kingdom sent a three-year mission to China that offered pearls, ivory and frankincense to the emperor. Similar associations existed in Sri Lanka and south India at an earlier date.[12]

This trade was not confined to local imports and exports. There is reason to believe that '[F]oreign commodities were brought at rates fixed . . . by the exigencies of supply and demand'.[13] This trade resulted in the influx of precious metals from the East and the West, some of which went into royal treasuries (hence their desire to encourage trade) but most going to individual merchants who built up 'vast funds'. The guilds themselves maintained no reserves though they encouraged members to give to temples.

---

[8] J. Legge (trans.), *A Record of the Buddhistic Kingdoms* (Oxford, 1886).
[9] Perera 1952b: 306.
[10] Wheatley 1975b: 104.   [11] Abrahams 1988: 93.
[12] See Thapar 1992b: 23.   [13] Abrahams 1988: 139.

India was involved even earlier in extensive sea trade. It was in the first century BCE that south India moved from prehistory to history, and we soon find widespread evidence of an active external trade.[14] The Roman site of Arikamedu on the east coast of India appears to have been involved in the export of cloth (muslin), jewels, spices and animals to the Mediterranean, the former presumably to Roman specification.[15] The Romans had also imported silk along the overland route from China from the second century BCE. In Arikamedu we find a warehouse, locally made beads, evidence of the manufacture of muslin cloth, two-handled jars or amphorae characteristic of the Mediterranean wine trade, as well as Roman lamps, coins and glassware. There Wheeler found Samian ware, some of it coming all the way from the extensive potteries of Graufesenque in the interior of southern Gaul; in addition there was glass, another item easier to transport by sea than by land.[16] These goods were not only for the use of the colonists themselves since the red polished ware has been found distributed as far afield as inland Gujarat.[17] Despite these exports, most of the commodities had to be paid for in gold, leading Pliny to complain bitterly of the strain that an annual drain of 55 million sisterces placed on the country's finances, while Tiberius grumbled that 'the ladies and their baubles are transferring our money to foreigners'.[18] These complaints are supported by the fact that Roman gold coins have been found in considerable numbers, especially in Tamil Nadu in the south, together with classical intaglios and seals.[19] As a result of this seaborne trade, carried out largely by Roman citizens, enclaves of

[14] On the trade between India and Rome, see M. P. Charlesworth, *Trade-routes and Commerce of the Roman Empire* (Cambridge, 1926); and E. H. Warmington, *The Commerce between the Roman Empire and India* (Cambridge, 1928).

[15] Thapar 1966: 115; Miller 1969.

[16] Arikamedu appears to have been established in the pre-Roman period, as early as the middle of the third century BCE, with the first evidence of Mediterranean trade, probably through Arab intermediaries, dating from the late second century BCE. Arretine ware is found in the first quarter of the first century CE, amphorae earlier, and rouletted ware yet earlier (in local copies). The amphorae dating from the first half of the first century BCE held wine from Campania, while others contained olive oil from the northern Adriatic while some came from Spain. For recent work on Arikamedu, see Begley 1983 and the following summaries from the *American Journal of Archaeology*, 91 (1987): 292–3: R. D. de Puna, The Roman bronzes from Kolhapur; H. Comfort, Terra sigilata from Arikamedu; E. L. Will, The Roman shipping amphoras from Arikamedu; and V. Begley, Ceramic evidence for pre-*Periplus* trade on the Indian Coasts. For a recent edition of *Periplus*, see Casson 1989.

[17] Sankalia 1987: 145ff.

[18] Pliny 6.101, 12.84; Tacitus, *Annals* 3.53.

[19] Glover 1990: 3; Raschke 1978: 637. In his discussion of Pliny's statement, Raschke accepts that Rome had an adverse balance of trade with the East but regards this as being with India rather than with China, and mainly for spices. Indeed he plays down the importance of the early trade in silk with Europe.

Western merchants established themselves on the shores of the Indian Ocean. Ptolemaic travellers sailed to India in 118–116 BCE; the Western discovery of the south-west monsoon in the late second century and the rise in wealth in the Mediterranean after 30 BCE led to an increase in commerce in the Indian Ocean, especially in spices. Nor was this trade carried out only by marginal merchants; they were often backed by the owners of landed property who, as in the Middle Ages, constituted 'an important source of commercial capital'. Indians too participated. On the spice island of Socotra, to the south of the Arabian peninsula, Greeks, Arabs and Indians had lived together since Ptolemaic times.[20] One report tells of the Ptolemaic coastguards rescuing a shipwrecked Indian sailor. Indians may even have come to Meroe in the reign of Augustus and the influence of their architecture and religion, including Buddhism, has been seen in Axum on the coast of Ethiopia.[21]

That was not India's earliest contribution to the trade. The ancient site in Lothal, Gujarat, included what is probably a large dockyard dating from the third millennium BCE that remained in use until about 1000 BCE, some five hundred years after the end of the main Harappan culture in the Indus Valley itself.[22] Stone blades and beads were manufactured and the town had contacts with both Mesopotamia and Egypt.[23] Evidence of this trade appears in the terracotta sealings which have helped towards understanding the purpose for which the well-known inscribed Indus seals of steatite or copper were prepared; they were meant for sealing documents or packages of goods involved in export. The appearance of Indian seals in Mesopotamia dating from the earlier half of the third millennium BCE shows that 'there existed in the valley of the Indus a high civilization which maintained active communication with Babylonia just at a time when the civilization of that land was also standing at its height; this prosperity cannot have been fostered by anything but trade.'[24] Trade from this area may have been extended to the Mediterranean at the beginning of the first millennium if the reference to Solomon's ships going to Ophir can be taken to refer to that region.[25] The sailors were probably Phoenician and merchants from the

---

[20] Raschke 1978: 645–6; Dihle 1978.

[21] Arkell 1936, though some of his suggestions are distinctly dubious.

[22] For the southernmost extension to Surat see F. R. Allchin and J. P. Joshi, Mālvan – further light on the southern extension of the Indus civilization, *Journal of the Royal Asiatic Society* (1970): 20–8.

[23] On the early trade between Mesopotamia and India see Childe 1939; Gadd 1932; and Mallowan 1970. See also E. Mackay, in J. Marshall (ed.) *Mohenjo-daro and the Indus Civilization* (London, 1931); and Mackay 1931.

[24] Gadd 1932: 206.   [25] I Kings 9: 26–8; Hourani 1951: 8.

Near East continued to trade along those routes during the Graeco-Roman period and long after, though following the decline of those empires, the emphasis shifted to Persia.

Persian Christians were present in the region by the year 650 CE at the latest; there is some archaeological evidence from Oc-eo in the Mekong Delta for Iranian influence in the third and fourth centuries.[26] Already in the sixth century a Byzantine writer, Cosmas, mentions boats and goods going to Ceylon from India, Persia, Ethiopia and China, bringing silk, aloes-wood, cloves and sandalwood. In Tang times Iranian merchants appear in Chinese tales associated with the import of 'strange treasures' from west Asia, especially pearls. Persian boats travelled between Canton (Guangzhou) and the maritime kingdom of Srívijaya. Islam had very rich merchants, especially among the Kārimī of the eleventh century who, with the Franks, came to dominate the East–West trade from the twelfth century, taking over from the Christians and Jews of the Near East. Their *funduqs*, scattered along the trade route which reached to China on the one hand and Mali (for gold) on the other, were 'specialized large-scale commercial institutions and markets which developed into virtual stock exchanges'.[27]

During the Roman period the main items of export from India were cloth and spices. While the cloth was woven in India, some of the spices came from Indonesia, which in turn received cloth from India. Indians traded with south-east Asia from the early centuries CE, settling in Malaysia possibly by the fourth century, then in Indo-China and Indonesia where the archaeological evidence suggests they arrived shortly before the Tang ceramics and stoneware from China. They were probably looking for gold although political expansion has also been suggested.[28] However spices were also important and the Indonesian supplies seem to have been destined for India and the West, since Japan and even China displayed little interest. In other words, centred on India there existed an enormous trade network in the Indian Ocean, a kind of world system, stretching from the Near East to the coast of Vietnam and down to Indonesia, and into the China seas towards the Philippines.[29]

To the west the extent of Gujarati trade in the Indian Ocean before the opening of the direct route to Europe is indicated by the fact that Gujarati pilots were among those who showed the Portuguese the way

[26] Colless 1969: 13.   [27] Habib 1969: 85.
[28] Raschke 1978: 675.
[29] For an imaginative account of the mid-twelfth-century Jewish trade between Egypt and India, see Ghosh 1992, based on Goitein's work on the Genizeh documents from Cairo (Goitein 1973).

from the east African coast.[30] At this time, as Barbosa remarked, the Gujaratis were providing the fine silk and cotton textiles worn by African rulers. From Cambay came 'many cotton cloths, some spotted and others white and blue, also some of silks and many small beads, grey, red and yellow'.[31] In exchange they took back gold and ivory from the Kingdom of Monamatapa in present-day Zimbabwe. Going as far as the Red Sea, especially to Aden, the Gujaratis traded in textiles, beads, gems, rice, sugar and spices for gold, copper, mercury, vermilion, madder, rose-water, woollen textiles, slaves and opium.[32] At Hormuz in the Persian Gulf, goods were sold to be sent overland to central Asia, west Asia and Europe. From that entrepôt in return came not only gold and silver, but silk and horses.

To the south, the Gujaratis traded with the Maldives for cowries, with Ceylon for cinnamon and elephants; to Burma to the east went 'printed Cambaya (and Palecate) cloths and both cotton and silk, which they call Paṭolās. These are coloured with great skill and are here worth much money.'[33] Goods were also taken to Thailand and Indonesia but the great entrepôt was Malacca (in present-day Malaysia), where both coarse and fine textiles were sold and where Cambay currency circulated.[34] That town was described by the Portuguese Tomé Pires in the sixteenth century as including 'Moors from Cairo, Mecca, Aden, Abyssinians, men of Kilwa, Malinda, Ormuz, Parses, Rumes, Turks, Turkomans, Christian Armenians, Gujaratis'.[35] It was precisely these two ports of Hormuz in the Gulf and Malacca in Malaysia that the seaborne firepower of the Portuguese enabled them to take over in 1515 and 1511 respectively.

The seaborne trade between India and China relied upon following the prevailing seasonal winds, since with existing naval technology it was difficult to sail against them. Ships from China sailed south in the north-east monsoon between November and March, while those from India sailed with the south-west monsoon to the Malacca Straits from April to October. The harbours on the west coast were especially favoured for sheltering ships, which could unload their goods in the warehouses of Malacca and wait for the return voyage, leaving their agents to sell the goods they had brought. From there too, merchants took part in the spice

---

[30] Gopal 1975: 1.
[31] Barbosa [1918–21]: 7–8.   [32] Gopal 1975: 3.
[33] Barbosa [1918–21]: ii, 153–4. Paṭolās, a fine silk fabric from Pātan, Gujarat, is still woven in that town.
[34] Before Malacca, other trading ports existed along the western coast of Indo-China.
[35] *The Suma Oriental*, vol. II, p. 268; Colless 1969: 43; de Barros, author of *Da Asia*, writes of 'Gujarati Moors'.

trade. The lucrative indirect journey to the Moluccas, which took almost a year, travelled with Indian cotton to Java, exchanged that for Chinese copper 'cash' and changed this at Sumbawa for rice and cotton, which were then used for buying the spices.

Malacca, on the eastern shore of the straits between present-day Malaysia and Sumatra, was an important centre where Arabs, Indians and Chinese exchanged goods, including spices and incense from Indonesia. The narrow Malaysian peninsula had long provided an overland way of passing from the Indian Ocean to the China Seas, but Malacca became especially important as an entrepôt in the thirteenth century. Except for the famous expedition of Cheng Ho at the beginning of the fifteenth century, which used Malacca as a base (as well as Calicut in south-west India) and some elements of which reached Africa, Chinese merchant ships had ceased to travel to India before 1400.[36]

The rulers of the settlement of Malacca had been converted to Islam when that religion came to the Malaysian peninsula in the thirteenth century, and it was Islam that dominated business transactions, which were 'sealed with a handshake and a glance at heaven'. The entrepôt trade demanded well-to-do and trustworthy merchants because of the need to stockpile an inventory while awaiting traders coming by the next monsoon. The goods were stored in warehouses in a fortress within the city walls, which were surrounded by a palisade with four gates and watchtowers, patrolled at night by watchmen ringing bells.[37] The city was divided in two by the river, joined by a bridge, with the merchants living on the north side and with the court and the aristocracy on the south. Malacca was a city of some sophistication, with the population enjoying 'music, ballads, and poetry', as well as the abundant fruits that grew around the town. As far as trade goods were concerned, silk, camphor and pottery came from China, sugar from the Philippines, and cloves, nutmeg and sandalwood from the Moluccas. From a westerly direction came printed cotton, copper weapons, seeds, grains, incense, tapestries, dyes and opium.

Disagreements exist over the control of the Indian and Far East trade

[36] Mills [1433] 1970: 239.

[37] Hoyt (1993) presents this structure as a Malaccan institution. But the description comes from Ma Huan's account of Cheng Ho's expeditions (Mills [1433] 1970: 113–14) in which the building of the stockade is ascribed to the Chinese themselves. 'The ships which had gone to various countries returned to this place and assembled; they marshalled the foreign goods and loaded them in the ships; [then] waited til the south wind was perfectly favourable.' While this statement refers only to the period of the voyages of Cheng Ho in the early fifteenth century, it is clear that China continued to trade 'throughout all the Oriental countries' as the Dutchman Linschoten observed at the beginning of the following century (Mills [1433] 1970: 4).

in pre-European times. Sergeant and other Arabists considered it was dominated by the Arabs until 1498. Mills asserts that China had the most powerful navy in the Orient, enabling the Chinese to maintain their political control in the Indian Ocean after the Ming expeditions. Meilink-Roelofsz sees a division between Arabs in the western half and Indians in the eastern. All three groups were heavily involved in the sea trade in those areas, but in the early fifteenth century the Chinese certainly displayed their strength.[38] Cheng Ho's expeditions were vast in terms of men and ships, bringing many foreign rulers within the Chinese tributary system. He gathered much information about the sea routes and geography of Asia, as well as collecting many valuables and rarities, just as the Europeans later did to fill their cabinets of curiosities (which were also found in China). As a result, China became 'the first power, with the strongest navy, in Asia, and the principal trading country of the Far East'.[39]

This external trade was based upon a lively internal market, which required commercial institutions as well as links to the political and administrative establishments. While Mughal wealth was largely agricultural, a part derived from trade. The level of public expenditure was supported by customs revenues which supplemented the land tax. 'The high degree of centralization achieved by the Mughals in govern-ment had a strong financial and monetary base, which was fostered by a long tradition of banking and commercial exchange.'[40] That tradition carried out through financial intermediaries was associated with 'an active market mechanism' in, among other things, 'industrial handi-crafts'.[41] These items fed into the trade routes that covered the sub-continent of India. Many smaller towns were heavily involved and some, like the Jain centre of Mount Abu in Gujarat, participated in the movement of goods and people through pilgrimage. The dispersal of urban centres away from the sea coast has been seen as a proof of 'the thriving internal commerce, of interdependence of town and country-side, of the penetration of the money economy'.[42] An active interregional commerce, supported by a system of credits and bills of exchange, sustained 'a fairly advanced form of economic specialisation'.[43]

The state of the economy impressed many Europeans on their arrival. They found a number of towns as big or bigger than London or Paris. One of the local merchants, with branches in a number of towns, chartered European ships and was reported to be the richest in the

[38] Mills [1433] 1970: 4.   [39] Mills [1433] 1970: 33.
[40] Chaudhuri 1979: 144.   [41] Chaudhuri 1979: 144; Steensgaard 1972: 144.
[42] Pavlov 1964: 151.   [43] Chaudhuri 1979: 143.

known world.[44] Mercantile capitalism, the money economy, production for the market, all were well developed, as was a thriving range of craft industries. The notion of the growth of the economy at this period can only be interpreted as 'expansion' of existing activities. For example, while sales of land undoubtedly increased, they had existed long before; it was not the Europeans who introduced them. So too with the other features of the economy. It was the scale that expanded. The basic institutions of capitalist enterprise were already present.

The main exports of Gujarat in the fifteenth century were based upon the manufacture of cotton cloths of a great variety, especially in Ahmadabad, Surat, Pattan, Baroda and Broach. The method of production can be largely constructed from early seventeenth-century records of the Dutch and English, and a similar system can be found on a smaller scale today. The cloth was produced by artisans working at home. They were advanced money by 'capitalists', to use the term for persons controlling capital (rather than for entrepreneurs in a 'free enterprise' economy), so that they could support themselves while they worked.[45] Some brokers supplied the materials for production while others offered advances. Although Steensgaard does not consider these transactions to constitute a putting-out system in the European sense, they did support those producers who could not afford to buy the materials and the system appears to be related to the Islamic *sillim*, 'a contract invoking prompt payment in return for a distant delivery'.[46] This indigenous practice was later adapted by the Dutch and English who exercised increasing quality control over the productive process, though clearly the supervision was not as direct as if wage-labour had been employed.

The 'capitalists' were called 'shroffs' by the English, a corruption of the Arabic *sarraf*, a banker. Although few in number, they played a major role in the economy, making use of *hundis* either as letters of credit to distant places or as short-term capital. 'They lent money on longer terms to officials and others. They financed the production on which Gujarat's prosperity was based, and its petty traders.'[47] And they changed money, for even if rural Gujaratis made little use of cash at this time, the trading community employed it widely.

The merchants themselves were either resident Muslims, some from abroad, or Hindus and Jains of the Bania castes, those traditionally in the

---

[44] Chandra 1982: 164.
[45] Pearson 1976: 21.   [46] Steensgaard 1972: 159.
[47] Pearson 1976: 21. The word 'shroff' is today used in Hong Kong for a collector of money, for example for parking.

business of lending money. Records of rich Jains go back to the twelfth century at least and in the sixteenth there were numerous Jain 'millionaires'. Mughal India possessed many merchants and money-lenders, especially in Gujarat and Rajputana among the Jains and Marawaris (of Jodhpur) for they were situated on the trade route to the capital at Delhi. These men also acted as tax collectors, army purveyors (*modi*) and moneychangers (*sarraf*) – in other words in any activity connected with money and its accounts. Accounting was of great importance and the *pedhi* was already the heart of business concerns. For reasons discussed later, the great merchants were often jewellers as well as bankers, providing the ruling class with varied luxuries. As far as taxes went, they often paid the treasury in advance (Akbar had introduced a money tax) and collected from it later, just as they might lend money for a campaign. For their distant transactions they employed bills of exchange.[48] One reason why these circulated so successfully was that they often did so between members of the same caste or descent group between whom there was a fiduciary relationship of a more inclusive kind.

Indian traders as well as trade spread far and wide. The Marawari had a colony in Astrakhan and in the middle of the sixteenth century, Muslim traders from Bengal sent three ships with silk destined for Russia through the Persian Gulf. In the seventeenth and early eighteenth century Indian merchants, who were engaged in trade on the Volga, were frequent guests in Moscow. At the beginning of the sixteenth century the Portuguese author, Pires, likened these Banias to Italian merchants. The wealth they accumulated was not always safe, especially for the Hindu. It was sometimes confiscated and often taxed by the Muslim authorities, so Hindu merchants tended to dress simply and to keep their wealth in movables such as jewels and money that were easy to hide rather than to invest in land. In Mysore in the south, they could seek a guarantee of their goods from the local rulers whom they in turn supported against colonial intrusion, but in the north they were more easily reconciled with the invaders, possibly again to safeguard their wealth. Of their importance there can be no doubt, whatever the Brahman ideology had to say. The contrary view about early trade and markets found among European writers arose largely because they were more concerned with differences than with similarities, and because, with the often unspoken aim of accounting for the later pre-eminence of western Europe, they widened the earlier gap between the economies of East and West to such an extent that they played down the presence of market activities in the former. A similar approach pervaded the analysis of the rural economy.

Estimates of the extent of Gujarati exports at this period are difficult to make, but they spread throughout the Old World. Merchants from this region, both Hindu and Muslim, traded between Aden (for the Mediterranean) and Malacca (for China and Indonesia), as well as to east Africa. Overland, Indian cottons found their way to Poland and the Mediterranean. As we have seen, when the Portuguese first opened up their trade to west Africa, one of their most important trade goods consisted of the painted or block-printed cotton of India, probably from Gujarat.[49] The extent of this trade was vast. Pearson estimates the value through the ports as 1,00,00,000 rupees, but since the goods were locally produced, we have to consider much more than the revenues from 'ports of trade'.

As for production the manufacture of cloth meant not only the cultivation of cotton, but its weaving, its dyeing, its printing and its sale. The extent of the trade required large-scale merchants, as well as a system of putting-out, of advances and of buyers-up; in other words, much proto-industrial activity. Such activities in their turn affected the production of food crops. Gujarat had to supplement her own grains to meet local requirements: firstly, because a sizeable portion of land and labour was diverted to cash crops such as cotton and indigo; and secondly, because the ships leaving the ports needed stores of provisions. A demand was created which had to be met by imports from neighbouring territories, that is, rice from the Deccan in the south and wheat from Malwa to the north.[50]

Given the need for internal routes to transport this produce from farm to consumer, it was important for the region that Akbar, who took over Gujarat in 1573, started a vigorous road-building programme to improve the infrastructure. Gujarat was already famous for the fine quality of its bullocks, camels and horses. Camels, bred in the dry region of Kutch, were used to transport goods and, in the case of horses, men. But most goods were moved by two- and four-wheeled carts drawn by bullocks which were much prized and said to travel 120 miles in twenty-four hours.[51] They were much in demand, especially when increased trade with Europe entailed the transport of larger quantities of goods to the sea ports. According to one Englishman, 200 loaded wagons left

[49] Steensgaard 1974.
[50] Gopal 1975: 125.
[51] See Garcin de Tassy 1847: ii, 321–3, giving an extract from the *Araïsch-i Mahfil*.

Ahmadabad for the port of Cambay every day, a journey of 100 kilo-metres;[52] others give this as the figure for ten days.

The extent of the trade, the interests of the government and the increasing demands of external commerce meant that there was also a measure of co-operation on the part of the producers and the merchants. An early commentator remarked that 'when the Europeans entered India, they found at Surat one of the greatest marts in the world'.[53] 'Arabia, Persia, and China, were from hence supplied with cloths, and all other productions of the kingdom. Later we have known a merchant of that city the sole proprietor of twenty ships, none of less burthen than five hundred tons.' Some suffered from the exactions of princes but trade is 'better encouraged than it usually is in a despotic state'.[54] In the south of India in the seventeenth century Hindu merchants who became tax farmers took large areas in lease in a manner that suggests 'a certain measure of governmental authority devolved on the revenue farmers'.[55] That also happened in England with custom dues. Some traders operated on a large scale. Virji Vora in Surat established a monopoly over certain imports and was described as the biggest broker in the world. In the last quarter of the seventeenth century, when business was poor in Gujarat, much of the trading and moneylending was concentrated in the hands of three families, Virji Vora, Abdul Gafur (a Bohra) and Khoja Zahid, that is, of two Muslims and an Armenian Christian who was also known as Haji Zahid.[56] The extent of trade in cloth encouraged production. Indeed on the Coromandel coast and in Bengal 'it is difficult to find a village in which every man, woman, and child, is not employed in making a piece of cloth'.[57]

So, contrary to Polanyi's supposition, Mughal India was certainly not marketless, however 'imperfect', in Steensgaard's view, the mechanism. Moreover, the traders involved were not simply pedlars (as van Leur has suggested) but included important wholesale merchants. One study of the development of trade with early south-east Asia has been subtitled 'from reciprocity to redistribution'.[58] These categories of exchange are much used in anthropology and in cultural history. They were given wide currency by the works of Polanyi whose substantive approach to the economy represents on the one hand a rejection of classical economics and on the other a modification of Marxist and similar stage theories. Without accepting the advisability of applying classical economic theory

52 Purchas 1905–7: iv, 63; Gopal 1975: 149.
53 Orme [1792] 1805: 415.   54 Orme [1792] 1805: 411.
55 Raychaudhuri 1962: 9.   56 Gopal 1975: 179–81.
57 Orme [1792] 1805: 409.   58 Wheatley 1975a.

to non-industrial economies, one might wonder whether the commercial activities of the Christian Europeans in the Indian Ocean were really so very different, at least in the initial stages, from those of the Muslim Arabs and the Hindu Indians that preceded them. Were they different enough, that is to say, to exclude one from the category of 'trade' and the other from that of 'redistribution'?

The *jajmani* system, the village community and production for the market

The antiquity and the extent, both geographical and quantitative, of Indian trade inside and outside the country, stand out in contrast to earlier notions of the self-sufficiency of the Indian village community discussed by Maine and Marx. These notions appear under another guise in interpretations of the *jajmani* system of organising village labour and exchange. The extent of that trade also bears upon the nature of craft production and its relation to the market, which was posed by Polanyi and others in attempting to characterise pre-capitalist economies. That again raises the more general question of India's readiness for further economic growth, which is not simply a matter of the past but very much of the present. Before looking at the overall problem, let us turn to the specific question of *jajmani*.

As described in the classic text of Wiser, this system was one where the direct or delayed exchange of crops for goods and services occurred within the Indian village, thus obviating the need to use 'money', currency. He sees the system as a natural economy in opposition to a monetary one and as having two major characteristics: 'it articulates the division of labour by means of hereditary personal relations, with each family using for each special task a family of specialists'. On the other hand it regulates in a customary fashion prestations and counter-prestations. As Dumont remarks in his commentary, Wiser viewed the system, idealistically, as more or less symmetric, each family working for others, an expression of the closed village community. Many have taken it to represent an earlier stage in the Indian economy, indeed of human society as a whole, fitting in not only with many nineteenth-century schemes of long-term development but also with those of distinguished Indianists of the present day who want to draw a radical distinction with Europe and capitalism. While wanting to modify Orenstein's functional explanation of *jajmani* that was put forward in opposition to the notion of exploitation, Dumont nevertheless excludes the system from the 'economic' domain altogether, placing it firmly in that of the 'religious'. *Jajmani* relations are not of the market where the individual pursues his own gain, but belong to 'the hierarchical collectivity'.[59] This particular concept derives from his tripartite division of ideologies in their relation to social formations which takes the following form:

1. hierarchical collectivity: resources distributed more or less consciously;
2. anarchic individualities: external and automatic regulation;
3. regulated individualities (or) egalitarian collectivities: deliberate regulation.

The first is represented by the caste system, the second by capitalism, the third by socialism.[60] Only in the second are found money and markets, or individualism and class (or even stratification). Their absence elsewhere is linked to widespread dualist approaches to 'primitive' and 'advanced' economies, as well as to the more graduated stage theories of the nineteenth century, so that it is not surprising that Dumont calls on the support of Weber and Marx.[61] Weber distinguished between the market situation (which is both autocephalous and autonomous) where the agent acts of himself and in his own interest, and that existing in the Indian village where the elements are autocephalous but heteronomous, providing for the needs of members of the group. This latter situation is described by Marx as one where production is for the immediate consumption of the community and does not become merchandised.

Dumont's characterisation occurs at the level of the ideology, of what the actors may think they are doing. Even at this level it presents only a partial account (as all ideologies do). Which actors are involved? Are their notions distinguished by hierarchical position, by political persuasion or by religious affiliation? In any case ideological statements exercise different normative pulls in particular situations, and have to be interpreted contextually. Let us turn to the 'systems' that represent abstracted ideologies. As many have noted, the kind of 'moneyless' transactions involved in *jajmani* are still characteristic (though increasingly less so) of aspects of the rural economy, even on the outskirts of a great industrial town like Ahmadabad where the ideology is certainly of a more differentiated kind from that envisaged in the categories of the tripartite division. In 1977 in the village of Nandol (*c.* 3,000 inhabitants) occasional exchanges of vegetables for grain took place, in addition to the longer-term arrangements between specialists and farmers whereby Brahmans, craftsmen and others provided services in return for annual or more frequent 'payments' of one kind or another.

Some of those involved, for example the barbers, also ran shops in the

[59] Orenstein 1962; Harper 1959; Dumont 1970: 105 (1966: 139).
[60] Dumont 1970: 105(1966: 139).   [61] Dumont 1970: 294–5 (1966: 138).

nearby town of Degham; others from the same *jati* kept stores in central Africa while yet others were working in the woollen manufactories of the English Midlands. Close relatives could be found in each of these three activities. Since a Labour government was in power in England, and since the Gujaratis benefited in various ways from the redistributional efforts of the welfare state, it would not be a great exaggeration to say that members of this *jati* (or caste section) participated equally in all three of Dumont's systems, that is, in the developmental stages or modes of production of other writers. It would be an error to see this overlapping simply as the result of recent events. It is essential to consider the way local activities 'articulate' or operate concurrently, not simply on an abstract basis of distinct systems or stages but among the members of one and the same *jati* who continue to interact with one another, who move between one type of operation and another. We need to see this, in other words, not only at the level of social system or of modes of production but of articulation at the cognitive level (personal and interpersonal). Even in the West today, a person participates in one type of transaction within the family, the church or the friendly society and quite another in the market-place. An articulation of barter, gift-exchange and trade has been reported in India in the earliest records. The *Periplus* refers to merchants 'who must have bartered at times and at times purchased', even at the same ports, whether in Africa, Arabia or India.[62] That situation is confirmed for south India by the analysis of local records.[63] It is true that at the societal level, one 'ideology' may dominate, despite the diversity of economic activities, but it would be an error to think that such diversity did not have its cognitive counterparts of a normative kind. They flourished for that very reason.

As far as India is concerned, there are three analytical possibilities for explaining this complex, interactive situation. Firstly, we could assume that whatever had been the effects of colonialism and capitalism in Bombay and Calcutta, there remained many 'pockets' of 'pre-capitalist' activity. There is some validity in this position, to which those analysing the radical changes of the sixteenth century and later have sometimes failed to give sufficient attention. Anthropologists have been made more sympathetic to arguments about the 'articulation' of modes of production or of socio-cultural systems partly by the nature of their own field experience in a changing world and partly by the work of recent Marxist writers. Secondly, the period in which Wiser was working could be looked upon as one of 'de-development', either through a reversion to an earlier system, or, preferably, as a newly created combination in which

---

[62] Casson 1989: 30.   [63] Thapar 1992a: 15.

some elements of the old had been removed by imperial rule and foreign capitalism. This second process is what the economic historian Perlin claims happened at the local level not only in Maharashtra but in other parts of India and Africa in 'late pre-colonial society'.[64] A study of eighteenth-century Maratha documents reveals 'a remarkable involvement in monetary relationships by humble people, not only to service the revenue demand but to pay rents, to exchange products in local markets and, through their receipt of day and monthly wages for soldiering, household service, agricultural labour, and craft production, all in money forms'.[65] However, the occupation of the area by the English East India Company led to 'the displacement of local elites from the countryside, the more ruthless and efficient exploitation of peasant populations and the large scale export of taxed wealth' which left the villages suffering 'a relative demonetization of the local economy and a contraction (or withering away) of those social, political and economic conditions characteristic of the old order, in which monetary exchanges could flourish'.[66] He argues, against Habib, that earlier monetisation was not simply 'parasitic' on the central organisation of the Mughal state, declining when that state declined, because 'monetized tax demands could only occur in wider contexts of monetary relationships'.[67] The latter point is not all that clear; certainly in Africa the demands of both colonial and independent states promoted the use of the currency in which tax demands were made. However he is right to argue that the use of exchange media, including cowries and copper, had long been accepted in the context of production, of commerce as well as of administration.

So there is a 'progressive' model whereby existing evidence of *jajmani* is a survival of earlier modes, and a 'regressive' model whereby it represents a reversion to that mode. But there is a third possibility. In certain contexts of contemporary village life such activities are not in any general sense incompatible with the operation of extensive trade and markets, even on an international scale. Indeed for centuries past these differing forms of exchange had existed side by side; it is only a misapplication of evolutionary notions and of categorical divisions (the notion of what I have called 'an excluding progression') that has led observers to overlook this fact. Wiser was an American missionary working in the small village of Karimpur in the upper Paychi valley in the Doab (Uttar Pradesh) during the 1930s and his account claims to be a field study. How could such a system continue to operate alone and

---

[64] Perlin 1984: 100.   [65] Perlin 1984: 100.
[66] Perlin 1984: 100.   [67] Perlin 1984: 101.

undisturbed in a continent that, disregarding earlier differentiation, had been so strongly influenced by European contact since the sixteenth century, both by being subject to British imperialism and by incorporation in a world system? This point raises a fundamental question for anthropological research, since its practitioners often assume that they are dealing not only with a non-European subject in a geographical sense (that goes without saying) but also in a social or psychological one, that is, with a subject characterised by otherness or beforeness (anteriority). Indeed such assumptions are often crucial to their implicit or explicit comparisons. But there are great dangers in focusing upon a persisting set of 'non-market' transactions, then looking at contemporary commercial activity either as a later introduction from abroad or as operating on quite different principles of exchange, and finally concluding that one total system is replacing another. It is true that *jajmani* transactions are inappropriate to many urban situations and increasingly to rural ones. But earlier there was no inherent incompatibility between the different modes of transaction co-existing in the same society. It is widely true that exchanges within the 'domestic group' differ in their nature from those outside. That makes them 'incompatible' only for those who opt for an oversimplified account and overlook the problem of contextuality. Such an approach represents the misapplication of developmental thinking.

The *jajmani* system can gather under its umbrella craft production within the village, in which the potter and other artisans get their share of grain at the end of the farming season. But how can such a model be reconciled with the extent of regional and international trade in cloth and other products that the Europeans found on their arrival? In *Homo Hierarchicus* Dumont is even led to pose the question of whether one can apply to traditional India the very category of economics, or profitably discuss the connected problem of the place of wealth in movables and chattels, money and commerce, in Indian society.[68] He claims it was only at the end of the eighteenth century that economics appeared as a distinct category, independent of politics, and a footnote refers us to the words of Karl Polanyi: 'A self-regulatory market demands nothing less than the institutional separation of society into an economic and a political sphere, which one did not find under tribal, nor under feudal, nor under mercantile conditions.'[69] That split was 'a singular departure' of the nineteenth century.

The question of institutional separation needs to be kept distinct from that of analytical distinctions, though substantivists tend to conflate the two. Strongly influenced by Polanyi, the classicist Finley also queried

[68] Dumont 1970: 154 (1966: 209).   [69] Polanyi 1945: 76–7.

the applicability of the notion of the economy to ancient society. However in his specific analyses of economic operations a tension remained between notions of the great transformation, the quantum jump, and the perception of developmental continuities between the 'ancient' and 'feudal' modes.

In Dumont's case he sees the transformation of India from a traditional to a modern régime as having begun under the English domination. That event led to 'a distinct sphere of economic activity in the proper sense'. The English transformed the land into merchandise and assured the security of possessions. The question of the purchase of land has two aspects, one general, the other particular. At a general level, it is sometimes assumed that in the 'ancient economy' land was *extra commercium*; this is one of the central tenets of the Polanyi school and other protagonists of the Great Divide. Empirically, it is plainly wrong. Some of the earliest written records from Mesopotamia refer to transactions in land and those were well established in ancient Egypt. So the particular question is how far was this true of India? While British legislation had a definite effect in promoting commercial transactions, there is plenty of evidence to show that pre-colonial India was in a similar position to China, Japan and the rest of Asia with regard to the sale of land. Alienation was certainly possible, even if restrictions (such as *le retrait lignagère*) existed.

Regarding the earlier state of insecurity, Dumont relies on quotations from expatriate sources (such as Bernier, Dubois and Elphinstone) to demonstrate 'the subordination of merchants and the insecurity of riches'.[70] But occasional, even widespread, insecurity in a large continent, like piracy at sea, certainly did not prevent, though it may have inhibited, the build-up of riches and the activity of merchants. On the other hand, as we have seen, the depredations of rulers may have influenced what they did with their gains, putting these into movables rather than immovables.

The problem is not only a matter of empirical facts but of a 'theoretical' approach that sees India, like 'many other traditional societies', as conforming to a particular type in which 'religion in a way encompasses politics, so politics encompasses economics within itself'.[71] So the politico-economic domain is subordinate to religion and Hindu texts speak of royalty but not of the merchant. 'The ideology is silent on the question', he claims, that is to say, Hindu texts make no mention; ideology and the text are identified and exclusion from the text is taken to be an exclusion not only from that ideology but from ideology in a

---

[70] Dumont 1970: 165 (1966: 210–11).   [71] Dumont 1970: 165 (1966: 211).

wider sense. Hence the precariousness of the merchant's position. It explains why there were fluctuations in merchant activity depending upon the extent to which the merchants' wealth was guaranteed by royal power. 'The main economic implication of the caste system is . . . the very uncertainty.' Merchants are not absent from the scene but they are the playthings of royal power.

It is true that in most societies before the eighteenth century merchants were at times harassed by political authorities as well as by lawless elements. Habib quickly dispenses of the notion that insecurity seriously blocked trade by examining rates of interest.[72] There were here as elsewhere some ideological declarations that played down their activities. But in India as throughout Eurasia commercial exchanges were extensive and essential to the working of the society, intrinsic to the culture in the wider sense. The alternative view depends on the imposition of a radical dichotomy that does violence to our present knowledge. In a significant footnote, Dumont draws attention to the fact that he has neglected to deal with the 'brilliant historical reconstruction' of Max Weber which brought out the protracted conflict between the patrimonial power supported by the priests and the wealthy class of merchants or 'bourgeois' in the process of making good. He claims to lack the competence to deal with Weber's interpretation, partly because the latter has produced 'une oeuvre d'imagination' ('a piece of fiction') and 'more precisely because Weber interprets the data within the framework of general ideas taken from the West and especially from the European Middle Ages . . . in the end he shows profound differences but by presupposing similar dynamics'.[73] Whereas Dumont regards himself as having sketched out 'a more radical approach'. Both statements are true; both writers attempt to draw sharp distinctions but from different points of view. The anomalies are apparent.

Whatever the model, the radical opposition between *jajmani* and mercantile transactions tends to lead to their assignment to different types of social system. As a result existing examples in the contemporary Indian context become survivals (in the progressive model) or regressions (in the alternative one). The evidence suggests that these two forms of transaction characterised the Indian economy over the long rather than the short run, and that institutionally and cognitively, people had to accommodate them both. That seems particularly clear in the way that craft production provided a link between the village and the long-distance trade, rather than being an aspect of self-sufficiency. Equally the transformation of crops from their natural form into peasant-produced

---

[72] Habib 1969: 70.   [73] Dumont 1970: 314 (1966: 212).

commodities might involve not only collective work on the part of the peasants but also the intervention of merchant capital. That was certainly the case with cotton as well as with other items, for example, the processing of sugarcane (an Indian cultigen) into *gur*, a brown form of sugar which was a major commercial product until the 1930s.

Capitalism and crafts

The dichotomy posed by many earlier European theories would deny to India even the potentiality for the development of capitalism. It has been modified in recent years, partly at the hands of nationalist politicians and writers. The most drastic type of modification is that suggested by Nehru in *The Discovery of India*, where he maintains that by the time of the British conquest 'India was a highly developed manufacturing country exporting her manufactured products to Europe and other countries'.[74] The implication was that had it not been for the European conquest capitalism would have developed there, if it was not already present.

A less radical modification is embodied in the work of a group of Soviet scholars of India who took up the argument in the post-Independence period with different eyes than Marx. Following the lead of I. M. Reisner in the 1950s, they examined 'the embryonic capitalist relations on the threshold of the nineteenth century'. Even those like K. A. Antonova, who first denied their existence, have moved closer to this position and the controversy is now about the degree and timing of these develop-ments. The argument turns partly around the role of craftsmen as distinct from traders, partly around the nature and level of craft production and partly in the way this was affected by the coming of the West.

The discussion of the role of traders and craftsmen often refers back to a statement by Marx who perceived two ways of making the transition to capitalism. First there was 'the really revolutionary way' whereby small producers developed from craftsmen into industrial entrepreneurs. That was, he claimed, the pattern in England, whereas elsewhere, in Asia and Eastern Europe, merchants were the prime movers in establishing direct sway over production. For Marx, only the English way would lead to radical change. 'However much this [the merchant path] serves historically as a stepping-stone – witness the English seventeenth-century clothier who brings the weavers, independent as they are, under his control by selling their wool to them and buying their cloth – it does not by itself lead to the overthrow of the old mode of production.'[75] While

[74] Nehru 1951: 262.   [75] Marx, *Capital* III: 336–7.

England (and, according to Pavlov, Russia) followed the first course, Asia followed the second.

That statement sounds very much like a *post facto* reading rather than a reasoned prediction; England was the first industrial nation, therefore what it did was the way forward. But it has given rise to much discussion among Soviet historians. Pavlov sees India as excluded from the 'really revolutionary' path partly because the independent producer was destroyed through the advent of the British factory, but also because the buyers-up oppressed the craftspeople. In other words the latter did not have the capital to invest in the technical developments (especially in the machines driven by steam and no longer worked by hand) which could have turned them into capitalists. Pavlov therefore dismisses the contentions of Alaev and Reisner that, while handicrafts declined during the first half of the nineteenth century, other profound changes were going on. Regarding self-sufficiency, scholars like Alaev argued that the weavers did become separate from the village community, not being part of the service system. But how separate did they become? The development of weaving saw the poorer weavers taking their clients' yarn, the richer ones buying their own, a process which led to an exchange between town and country, establishing the pre-conditions for capitalist development. He found evidence of the emergence of the 'feudal' village landowner and the moneylender as well as of petty commodity production which could have led to a capitalist mode including manufacture. One such change was seen as taking place among the weavers in Dacca, an important centre of muslin production which turned to making coarse cloth, reorienting petty commodity production to the growing home market, towards the peasant consumer. Increasing, too, was the practice of advancing yarn to the weavers. While Pavlov recognised 'the first nuclei of capitalist production' as arising 'in the bowels of feudal society', for him this development was retarded and distorted by colonial rule. Instead, the development of capitalism in the middle of the nineteenth century saw the large industrialists coming not from the ranks of craftsmen but from representatives of big trading and moneylending capital; that was not the 'really revolutionary' way.

Others perceived the barriers to further development as internal. The problem relates to that of the self-sufficiency of the village. Pavlov saw the Indian economy as developing well beyond the stage posited by Marx. According to the latter, the Indian village community was based on possession of land in common, on the blending of agriculture and handicrafts and on an unalterable division of labour,[76] that is to say,

---

[76] Marx, *Capital* I: 357.

'spinning and weaving were carried on in each family as subsidiary industries'. The beginning of the shift to private property in land, which some Soviet scholars saw starting as early as the second to fourth centuries CE, provided the countries of the East with the possibility to transform feudal private property into capitalist private property.[77] It was a transformation that began before the European penetration stopped the process from fully developing. However Pavlov did not see that process as having gone very far, for he claims that Akbar's money tax of the seventeenth century did not lead to commodity production and so failed to affect the 'natural self-sufficiency' of the village.[78] Surendra Gopal, an Indian student of Antonova, sees the inability to develop further as due to the dominant position of the Muslim political élite, some of whom were themselves traders. The American historian, M. N. Pearson, on the other hand, gives more weight to the lack of power wielded by traders: in his view it was this internal constraint that prevented the growth of capitalist entrepreneurship. Economic, social and educational factors also militated against such a development, which could therefore not have taken place in Gujarat, even with European stimulus.[79]

In his work on craft production, Chicherov attempts to go more deeply into the question of what he sees as the transition from the organisation of 'traditional village crafts'. Despite the paucity of evidence for the pre-European period, particularly at the village level, he tries to reconstruct 'the village community crafts' and 'traditional forms of economic structure' by eliminating everything in early European reports that has to do with wider, more inclusive socio-economic action and concentrating upon subsistence activity within the village. So the fact that in nineteenth-century Maharashtra a 'peasant' still produced cloth for his own consumption is taken to be evidence of an earlier state of affairs when everybody wove cloth for their own use and for no one else's. In a more sophisticated manner, the economic historian, Habib, uses a similar approach. He views the earlier India as an example of the 'pure' peasant economy, a stable self-contained community, which was thrust into trade and commodity production 'virtually as a consequence of [the Mughal] revenue systems'.[80] Since the village was the unit of tax assessment, the community was partly the construct of the central administration.

There is a certain plausibility to the 'idea of the village community' in that it conforms not only to our folk views of the distant past, but also to

[77] Pavlov 1964: 8–9; *Great Soviet Encyclopedia* 1970: 10, 18.
[78] Pavlov 1964: 11.
[79] Gopal 1975: 244.   [80] Habib 1969: 42.

the practice and sometimes the conclusions of those anthropologists who see life from the village level and, in their attempt to reconstruct the 'traditional' culture, subtract all manifestations of local life, policemen, politicians and plastic flowers that appear to emanate from outside. Plausible, yes, but mistaken, at least as far as weaving goes. The production of cloth was rarely confined to the village, let alone to the domestic level. Such limitations were not true of Mesopotamia from early times. The contrary notion arises from a retrospective and primitive discounting of trade and commercial activities in line with prevailing notions of social evolution.

In 1900 BCE, the caravan trade from Assur to Kanish in Anatolia took cloth (woollen goods in all probability) and tin northwards and brought back rare metals in return. For this purpose the woollen goods were produced 'domestically' as well as by putting-out, but at other times they were manufactured in workshops ('factories' to some) by paid and slave labour in much the same way that, for example, high-quality silk goods were produced in the royal *kharkhanas* of Mughal India.[81] Those imperial workshops consisted of large halls to which workers went for the whole day. One ruler employed 400 weavers of silk and 500 of golden tissues, each group under a head. These were imperial 'workshops', but export weavers often worked in communities.[82] We find a history of 'factories', corporations and both free and slave workers through the Ptolemaic and Roman periods (not necessarily continuous) to the Byzantine manufacture of silk in which women were employed and protected from 'corruption'.[83] Lopez contrasts the organisation of state factories where work was concentrated with that of workshops which prevailed 'in the industrial organisation or the private guilds'; it is held to have increased the efficiency and yield of production and it existed in the provinces as well as the capital, at least until the seventh century, after which they suffered from the conquests of Arabs and Germans.

In Mughal India there was 'extensive commodity production', together with a large volume of merchant capital. Roads were relatively secure and commerce included not only manufacture but also 'a large drain of food grains and other agricultural produce from the countryside

---

[81] Commissariat 1938: ii, 297; Singer 1968: 239–40; Gopal 1975: 196. In Ottoman Turkey masters of several looms would install them in workshops (Kārhāne). These were also state workshops. Inalcik describes the silk industry of Bursa as 'capitalist production' since it was aimed mainly for the external market and was dependent on merchants engaged in interregional trade, who exported the goods (rather than the master weavers). But the production of cotton cloth was also organised by merchants by means of a putting-out system (Inalcik 1969: 116).

[82] Habib 1972.

[83] Lopez 1945: 6.

to the towns'.[84] The size of the capital involved was huge, one seventeenth-century merchant conducting trade equal to that of the whole of the East India Company. Trade was facilitated by a banking system that comprised a *schroff* (moneylender) in every sizeable village who acted as a banker to make remittances and issue letters of exchange. In the Ahmadabad market, merchants made payments 'almost entirely through transfer of paper'. It is noticeable, remarks Habib, that Europeans in the seventeenth century make no serious criticism of the Indian credit system; they note the differences, but not unfavourably.

In India in historical times production too was never limited to village craftsmen. We have seen that whole villages were devoted to weaving[85] and in Gujarat, for example, a village of weavers and spinners is already reported by Salbancke, the first Englishman to travel there, in 1609.[86] It is hardly conceivable that such a specialist form of production should have arisen in response to European demand within 100 years of the arrival of the Portuguese, since the great period of increased European exports only came later with the English and Dutch.

Chicherov sees the 'traditional' system as already being followed by a 'new' form of economic organisation of crafts in the precolonial period, in which 'non-community artisans' respond to the orders of customers. Petty commodity production was carried out either by peasants working partly on the land, partly for the market, or by professional artisans.[87] This 'change' was already in evidence from inscriptions from the fourteenth to the sixteenth centuries, when weavers' settlements were often found around temples which they supplied with cloth and taxes. He concludes that in the seventeenth and eighteenth centuries we have evidence of 'capitalist domestic industries', for example, in textiles, as well as 'capitalist manufactures' (enterprises with a division of labour employing wage-workers), for example, in shipbuilding, iron-working and diamond-mining, although they continued to retain features of the old (feudal) mode of production. If India was approaching the manufacturing stage in the development of capitalism, it was largely through her own efforts. European trade was only one factor; capitalist relations were established with Indian and other Asian capital rather than European.[88] Indeed it was the coming of the Industrial Revolution in England that set back the Indian economy and prevented it developing further. Chicherov's hypothetical reconstruction of a pseudo-historical sequence falls into the same error as that made by those Western

---

[84] Habib 1969: 71, 72, 73, 74.   [85] Ramaswamy 1985b.
[86] Gopal 1975: 192, quoting Purchas 1905–7: iii, 82.
[87] Chicherov 1971: 44.   [88] Chicherov 1971: 234.

scholars who, like Polanyi, claim to stratify systems of exchange in a similar, exclusive way. But it is quite impossible to reconstruct a 'primitive society' retrospectively from a complex one in which all the concrete evidence points not to self-sufficiency but to the articulation of village and town.

Leaving aside the question of what inhibited the shift from craftsman to capitalist in later India (whether it was the unspecified effects of British rule or the sheer amount of capital required by industry at that point), let us turn to the question of who took major roles in the transition to a manufacturing and industrial society. In the next chapter we will discuss the role of merchants and bankers. But there is plenty of evidence to suggest that some weavers had already made the transition to merchant in the great days of the export trade of India cottons.[89]

We get a better idea of how the process of production lay behind this earlier export trade by examining the material from inscriptions and early travellers to southern India, recently analysed by Ramaswamy. What we find is a complex system of production with poor weavers taking in the thread of clients to weave while others buy yarn.[90] The handing out of thread, while not amounting to a fully fledged, putting-out system, embodied similar principles; given the advent of a wider market it could be easily expanded in that direction and indeed may at times have already done so in the pre-Portuguese export trade to south-east Asia.

For a putting-out system, which has been seen as 'an innovation in social organisation' in the proto-industrial West, was widely used in India. While the first evidence for their existence comes from a later period, the earliest medieval records show that 'guilds' (usually castes) of weavers and merchant corporations played important roles.[91] One major corporation was known as 'the five hundred of the thousand directions', referring to the great range of their commerce. Although these groups did not hold monopolies, they exercised a considerable measure of control over the raw materials such as cotton and dyes as well as over the finished products. They also maintained their own armed regiments to ensure the safe conduct of their wares just as did the European companies at a later period. From an inscription of 1538, these merchants appear to have wielded great influence over the productive process, indicating types of yarn to be used and of weave to be followed.[92] This degree of control seems to suggest that 'some form of putting-out system existed

[89] Ramaswamy 1985b.
[90] In Mysore, for example: see Buchanan 1807: i, 217–18.
[91] People made investments in guilds for charitable purposes, for example, to supply monks with cloth (Thapar 1992b: 257–8).
[92] Ramaswamy 1985b: 67.

because such authority can be explained only in terms of a system of advances'.[93]

It is significant that some weavers were prosperous enough to function as merchants; they lent money and acquired land, by purchase and gift, as well as making gifts, corporate and individual, to the temples who also acted as their clients. In this way they succeeded in improving their ritual status (by the process known as 'Sanskritisation') although at the same time they gave their support to movements such as the *lingayats* that circumvented the caste hierarchy in other ways. It was a classical case of mobility and protest.

The rise of individual weavers to the status of merchant indicates the internal differentiation that was taking place. A fifteenth-century record shows that a master-weaver, employing artisans for several looms at a single weaving site, was also a merchant; other records of the same period reveal large numbers of looms in a few hands.[94] It was this level of craft production that set the stage for the staggering success of the exports of Indian textiles in the seventeenth century. By 1684 the East India Company was importing into England more than a million and a half pieces a year, purchased at up to half a pound a piece and sold at a profit of 300–500 per cent,[95] partly for internal consumption but partly too for re-export to Europe, Africa and the Americas.

The control of the local trade shifted increasingly into the hands of European companies to the vicinity of whose 'factories' weavers were drawn in larger and larger numbers. While the guilds survived, they were no longer the same privileged groups, having weakened their ties of royal and temple patronage (formerly they were often located next to the temple) in favour of external commerce and so began to lose their bargaining power.

To summarise, readings of the Indian economy have been highly 'ideological'. Western scholars have tended to see the situation as having been transformed by the coming of European traders along the maritime route. Others have seen their arrival as marking the beginning of a shift away from a non-market or hierarchical system which prevented the development of capitalism. It is nationalist writers who have most resolutely pursued the question of the earlier status of the Indian economy. Western and Soviet authors have had more difficulty in throwing off the implicit or explicit assumptions built into their models. Pavlov has no doubt that India saw the beginnings of capitalist manu-

---

93 Ramaswamy 1985b: 81.
94 Ramaswamy 1985b: 84.   95 Ramaswamy 1985b: 137–8.

facture before European rule. However he cannot altogether break with
the notion that India could not have developed capitalist production,
even though he recognises important steps were made. 'It is quite certain
that a differentiation process was taking place among the weavers and
that simple capitalist manufacture existed in the weaving industry.'[96] For
here we find merchants lending money to weavers, some of whom had
several looms and employed 'loomless' men. Similar differentiation
occurred in the iron foundries in Mysore, in the Bengal sugar industry
and in Surat shipbuilding. These capitalist relations 'did not yet amount
to a capitalist structure of society';[97] rather society displayed signs of
a transition to late feudalism. In his view Nehru was wrong in claiming that the economy had reached the highest possible peak prior to
the Industrial Revolution because it had not developed capitalist
manufacture which is a basic requirement of the transition to factory
production.

Nehru of course was not alone in making this claim. Dutt states
that India was 'the hub of this world commerce prior to the period of
the Industrial Revolution'.[98] It was her 'craft' products and other
merchandise that attracted such a large percentage of the gold and silver
that the Spanish and other European powers looted from South
America, so great was the superiority of its manufactures. It is an
argument diametrically opposed to those who rest their analysis on *le
régime de caste*.

It is important not to primitivise the precolonial Indian economy; there
was much more than shoots of mercantile 'capitalism'. Extensive
mercantile activity did not come into being only at the beginning of the
seventeenth century, imposing itself on a system of village communities,
or one of a more hierarchical character. While stimulated by the
European trade it had existed long before, probably since Harappan
times, though more extensively from the first century CE.

Whatever went on at the different levels of the social system, each had
in a very broad sense to be 'consistent' with one another; for example,
wage labour had to live with service (*jajmani*) arrangements. For we are
not dealing with a short transitional period but with one that stretched
back to the beginnings of 'civilisation', of written cultures themselves;
stretched back, but developing over time, as it was doing when the direct
sea route was opened to western Europe. Certainly the arrival of the
Europeans led to the decline of Indian sea-power. But it also meant an

[96] Pavlov 1964: 38.
[97] Pavlov 1964: 42.   [98] Dutt 1962: xvii.

increased demand for exports which could now be sent to the West more cheaply and in greater volume to satisfy the rising middle-class demands. And the contact through trade and conquest led in turn to a growth in Indian business.

4 The growth of Indian commerce and industry

There is then little doubt about the state of craft production and trade in India by the time the Europeans arrived. The newcomers were amazed at what they saw, amazed at the extent of cloth production and at the riches of the country, quite overshadowing their own. While there are many disagreements about the comparative standards of living in Europe and India, it was not the case that luxury was confined to the palaces of the Maharajas while the rest lived in poverty. On entering Murshidabad, the old capital of Bengal in 1757, Clive wrote: 'The city is as extensive, populous and rich as the city of London, with this difference that there were individuals in the first possessing infinitely greater property than in the last city.' Similar words were used of Agra, Fatechpore, Lahore and many other Indian towns. At this time the percentage of the population living in cities was higher than in the countries of Europe and America before the middle of the nineteenth century.[1]

By comparison with some of India's great merchants, the English were by no means rich nor yet remarkable in other ways. For merchants from Cambay and later Surat already traded in cotton, cloth, indigo, opium and hides, plying the sea routes from Aden to Malacca, where Pires claims to have met 1,000 Gujarati merchants plus some 4–5,000 seamen. When the British arrived on the coast of Gujarat, houses in Surat already had windows of Venetian glass imported through the Ottoman empire. Nor did their trade include only luxuries or trade goods in the usual sense, at least internally, for as we have seen grain was imported into Gujarat to feed the population, many of whom were involved in textile production and other activities.[2] There it was mainly Muslims (Bohra and Khoja) who were engaged in the foreign and maritime trade, while Jains and Hindus (Bania and Bhatta) predominated in banking, money and internal trade. Later on it was these same merchants who often acted as links between the Europeans and the Indian rulers, and who gave financial support to both. In the seventeenth century the richest of these

[1] Morris 1963.   [2] Pavlov 1964: 77.

113

merchants in Ahmadabad was made Nager Seth, Head of the Town, a title which still persists in an honorary way.

While trade was extensive, it was also risky; the failure of one ship to arrive might affect the market in a radical way. Most pre-modern commerce was relatively small scale, subject to large price fluctuations that increased the speculative element, and was more or less directly dependent upon the flow of bullion. Such uncertainty brought great changes of fortune. While pedlars existed side by side with big merchants, some of the former would make it into the wealthier class. That happened especially among foreigners from other Asian countries. Weber's thesis led him to write of 'der stationäre Character der persischen Staatswirtschaft',[3] a statement which the distinguished historian of Armenia, Manandian, describes as 'highly dubious'. The latter goes on to show the critical role of Armenians in the trade of the Persian Empire, including with India and China. After 1258, one of the important towns in the caravan trade to the East, before the opening up of the sea route, was Tabriz in present-day Iraq, whose importance was recognised by the Genoese. One visitor from Europe estimated the revenue received from that town at the beginning of the fifteenth century to be larger than that of the greatest Christian monarch.

After their mass deportation to the outskirts of Isphahan following their defeat in 1603–5, Armenian merchants were particularly active. For many centuries they had inhabited an area that was central to East–West commerce and they now had further incentives to engage in the Indian trade in which they had been long established. Involved in the export of Persian silk and of jewellery to Europe, and of European cloth and manufactures eastwards, they traded in many other goods as well, for example, selling Madras cottons in the Philippines for gold and silver. In Asia it was largely silk, Indian cloth, dyes, precious stones, medicinal plants, musk and spices. These merchants practised all types of commerce, often simultaneously: 'le colportage, le commerce caravanier . . . , le petit et le haut négoce'. They even adapted themselves from the caravan to the seaborne trade, some becoming shipowners themselves. They were small merchants as well as big, and there was movement between the two.

While early trade between India and Europe concentrated on spices and the cheaper pepper, mostly imported by the Portuguese and Dutch, it was not long before manufactured goods in the shape of textiles took

---

[3] Weber, 'Agrarverhältnisse im Altertum', in *Gessamelte Aufsätze zur Social -und Wirtschaftsgeschichte* (Tübingen, 1924), quoted in Manandian 1965: 17, 203.

over. Initially Europeans had to purchase Indian manufactures to exchange for spices. 'From trading Coromandel and Gujarat piece-goods to the Indonesian archipelago, the European Companies found it an easy step to extend their import into Europe itself.'[4] First of all small samples were brought back to London; then in 1613 calico appeared as a regular item in the auction sales of the East India Company, the fine white fabrics being considered suitable for the 'Moorish' market and the painted calicos for fine quilts and wall hangings at home. These goods were able to compete because they were cheaper than local linen cloth, but other advantages of the material and design were important in the rapid increase of the sales to western Europe. Cotton was a particularly good material for taking dyes, in which India had great expertise, and the bright, vivid colours of the cloth made an immediate impact on the middle-class market, giving them designs hitherto obtainable only on much more expensive fabrics. By 1684 the number of pieces of cloth imported by the English Company amounted to more than 1.5 million. So great were the quantities that this weight of imports eventually led to the imposition of heavy protectionist duties in many countries.

The impact of Indian printed cloth on European culture was enormous, both in its immediate effect and its later consequences. When these gaily coloured materials reached Europe they created a sensation, 'a consumer craze that overrode the opposition of governments, vested interests (the existing wool and silk industries) and, above all, the centuries old vernacular traditions in dress'.[5] Cotton cloth had been a major export of India to south-east Asia probably from the beginning of the Common Era, but it seems to have been largely the higher-valued silk materials and delicate muslins that were then exported to the West. The eastern route had the advantage for the large-scale consumption of less-expensive goods in that the goods could be sent more easily by sea, whereas to the West, at least for part of the way, caravans often had to be organised to transport the commodities by land. In any case one problem about the western route was the aggressive nature of its commerce that led to settlements of Romans in Arikamedu, of Syrian Christians in Kerala and of Jews in Cochin.

What was remarkable about Indian commerce and manufacture was its flexibility, not only in terms of quality but of design for the market. Just as the Chinese adopted decorative themes from abroad, incorporated them into porcelain designs and then modified these for the export market, so too did the Indians with their cotton cloth.[6] The

---

[4] Chaudhuri 1982: 400.
[5] Chapman and Chassagne 1981: 5–6.   [6] Rawson 1984.

attractions of printed cotton or *chintz* for the European market were such that British and Dutch merchants fed back to their agents information about designs that would be popular, thus altering the content as well as the volume of that segment of the export industry and at the same time having some influence on local taste.[7]

The success of the English and Dutch traders has been partly attributed, by the historian Chaudhuri, to the structure of their joint-stock companies. These institutions put 'all their corporate efforts into the creation of an organizational system which was independent of both time and personnel. As a result, economic decisions were taken on the basis of definite operating rules which covered practically every aspect of trade – the coordination of a complicated shipping schedule, the levels of buying and selling prices, future market trends, the ordering and delivery of goods, and not least the incidence of carefully planned political relations with indigenous Indian rulers.'[8] In many ways, the East India companies were the precursors of the modern multinational, multi-product business corporations, with worldwide trade, centralised distribution and wholesale marketing, which paid special attention to the standardisation of the import goods produced by artisan enterprise. But if they were forerunners of multinationals they were also successors to the earlier forms of partnership such as the *commenda* found throughout Eurasia. Indeed the first joint-stock companies 'were certainly familiar with Italian precedent in the financing and management of collective colonial enterprises'.[9] There was thus a measure of continuity with both earlier and later developments, and we certainly need to modify the view that we are in the presence of a unique Western invention which others could not have achieved.

Indian merchants had already had to face problems of organisation in exporting textiles to Indonesia, south-east Asia and the Middle East. But it was the scale of European purchases for their growing middle classes and the insistence on long-term contractual responsibility of a precise, economic kind that made the difference. The companies ensured a regular supply of standard goods by means of the 'muster' system. Contracts were usually given out to Indian merchants some eight to ten months before the arrival of the ships from Europe. This contract listed the precise quality, dimensions and prices of the textiles together with the delivery dates and names of the merchants. When the cloth was brought to the warehouse, the pieces were sorted according to the samples that had been provided at the earlier stage and those that did not meet

---

[7] Irwin and Brett 1970; Irwin and Hall 1971.
[8] Chaudhuri 1982: 404.   [9] de Roover 1963: 58.

the specifications were either rejected or purchased at a lower price. The large contracts, plus the lack of alternative local markets for goods made to these specifications, placed a constraint on the Indian merchants but they in turn could exercise some control over the timing of their deliveries.

How did this trade affect the general standard of living? The question of the comparative level of *per capita* income at the time is necessarily difficult to answer. Morris, who stresses the improved standard that obtained in the nineteenth century under British rule, declares that it was low compared with early modern Europe, corresponding in fact to a late medieval level.[10] Others have seen it, at the peak, as being equivalent to that of Elizabethan England. But it is difficult to tell what is being measured since demands are different, depending on climate and culture. For example, Jones remarks that Europe ate more meat and livestock products but this is hardly a recommendation for a community where vegetarianism carries high status.[11] Moreover, the raising of large numbers of livestock often implies a less heavily populated region, peripheral to the main areas of civilisation. What is clear is that we are dealing with a highly successful economy if we think about the proliferation of crafts, the development of the arts, including a refined cuisine not confined to the upper groups alone, and the capacity to produce and sustain a dense population.

These achievements, as we have seen, were associated with the extensive networks of overseas trade in manufactured as well as in primary goods. Exports of this scale necessarily entailed long-standing continental, regional and local trade, including the existence of markets where these goods and services could be transferred. It was these mercantile and commercial institutions of Hindu India that laid the basis for further developments in the economic sphere.

If those economic achievements were not always directly associated with advances in knowledge, the reasons are not hard to seek. As in medieval Europe, literacy was largely under the control of the priesthood. But more than that: while it had its own glories, the advent of Islam proved a great setback to Hindu culture. When Islam first came to the north, some major centres of Hindu religion shifted farther down the peninsula. Even there they were later threatened by the Muslim penetration, but in the north suppression was often much more determined. Aurangzeb, the great reformer who ruled from 1658 to 1707, attempted to enforce the practices of an Islamic state. He forbade the building of new temples and the repair of old ones, issuing orders to

[10] Morris 1963.   [11] Jones 1981: 4.

demolish all schools and temples of the Hindus and to put down their teaching and religious practices.

The economic ethic

What is the evidence that such economic activities were inhibited by religious factors? Many Western commentators, and even some Eastern ones, try to explain the process of development that took place in western Europe after 1500 by assuming that not only a series of events but a set of practices and beliefs, unique to that continent, were responsible. As we have seen, that argument takes many forms but it was Weber in particular who insisted upon the role of religious attitudes in economic affairs. In a series of classic contributions he saw ascetic Protestantism as playing a positive role in the development of capitalism, contrasting its economic ethic with that marking the other major world religions. For India, Hinduism was seen as inhibiting economic growth partly because of the caste system. However Indian society supported both mercantile and banking activity and it is not clear that the Hindu religion was necessarily a major deterrent. In any case, high Hinduism was not the only important local creed. Since the thirteenth century Islam played a major role in India and, in Gujarat for example, that permitted a rough division of labour. Muslims had none of the prohibitions on travelling overseas that marked some Indian castes; the Hindus and Jains had few of the problems about dealing with interest (usury) that marked some Muslims. The Muslims predominated in overseas trade, the others in banking at home. Moreover, internal criticism of the Brahman ideology goes back to its very emergence in written form. Buddhism and Jainism were doctrines of that kind: they tried to counter not only its religious practices but the caste hierarchy itself. Islam had a similar effect from outside, as did Sikhism from within. Even inside Hinduism itself, the ideology did not go unchallenged.

The growth of those alternative religions was not unconnected with the political economy. The Mauryan period (c. 335–150 BCE) saw the emergence of empire under the leadership of Aśoka (c. 250 BCE), who was a strong supporter of Buddhism. Edicts and inscriptions provide evidence of regular assessments for the purpose of land revenues. Rents were collected on land, taxes paid on produce, in addition to which there were irrigation and water taxes.[12] At this time there is evidence of the personnel involved in the administrative economy, such as the Treasurer and Chief Collector, of the accounts recording their transactions, as well

[12] Thapar 1966: 77.

as of expenditure in the form of gifts to Buddhist monasteries. Religious support and political reorganisation went hand in hand.

Both Buddhism and Jainism had emerged in the sixth century BCE as heterodox, puritanical sects that stood opposed to Brahman orthodoxy. Both stood against the animal sacrifices of the Vedas and in favour of a monastic life whereby the few achieved perfection on the basis of the support of the wider community. Their orientation was largely urban, attracting merchant groups, while the monks themselves were actively engaged in seeking alms as well as in missionary and educational activity. These were in essence 'democratic', non-caste movements which flourished particularly during the period from *c.* 200 BCE to CE 300 when through all India the merchant community prospered, as we see from many inscriptions, especially those relating to their donations to charity.[13] In India as distinct from south-east and east Asia, the rise of Buddhism was followed by a decline in its congregation which the historian Thapar associates with the decline in the prosperity of the merchants who supported it.

The growth of sects opposed to orthodox Brahmanism was a recurrent process. In the later thirteenth century the Mahānubhāva sect, part of the general Bhakti movements, 'proclaimed a God not bound to the stone of temples and their images, nor restricted by the rules of ritual purity'.[14] Such a God was to be addressed in the vernacular rather than in Sanskrit, and by members of all castes and of both sexes. It was monotheistic, transcending all other sects and religions, both Muslim and Hindu. Its literature was written in cipher and kept secret until the present century, not so much because of Muslim persecution but because of Brahman orthodoxy. Many merchants were attracted to what were heresies from the standpoint of orthodox Hinduism, and which gave them more encouragement, or less discouragement, than some Brahman writings. Indeed Dumont has stated that 'economic history is tributary to the history of heresies';[15] the connection is often close, though we may not wish to phrase the dependency in precisely that way. However, Hinduism was perfectly compatible with these mercantile activities at many levels. Although somewhat devalued in Brahman texts, the role of merchants, of the Banias, was of special importance in those regions where temple establishments participated in the economy and where the merchants endowed the temples. A close connection between trade and religion emerges in the peninsula of south-east Asia where early trading activity led to subsequent 'brahmanisation' of the region. In the

[13] Thapar 1966: 109. See also Thapar 1992b.
[14] Feldhaus 1984: 4.   [15] Dumont 1966: 212.

course of Indian domination of the area, trade and religion went hand in hand.

Nor do these Indic religions appear to have inhibited entrepreneurs, at least not to a greater extent than other creeds. Discussions about the rise of capitalism often stress the importance of a class of vigorous entrepreneurs, whose presence has sometimes been seen as related to the existence of a particular ethic which promoted the growth of that intangible quality, 'individualism'. In the case of Japan this development has been linked to a change in social attitudes after 1870, in contrast to what happened in China.[16] The English 'take-off' to industrial production after 1780 required very few entrepreneurs and a modest outlay of money.[17] There is therefore no need for the whole society to display these characteristics, only some of its members. At the same time there seems to have been no shortage of the skill, since entrepreneurship was widespread in mercantile operations. Even the inhabitants of many countries often seen as relatively 'backward', that is, India, Greece, China and the Levant, display great entrepreneurial activity overseas. That is just as true of individualism. However, such economic activity is usually connected with either the prior existence or the subsequent development of wide family ties.[18] Entrepreneurial activity is rarely completely individualistic but often occurs within a wider collectivity.

A revisionist view of Max Weber has been associated with Tenbruck (1984) and applied to India by Kantowsky (1984). It rejects the idea that his studies of the religions of India and China were attempts to test the thesis about the relation between Protestant inner-worldly asceticism and the spirit of capitalism but rather about the much wider question of rationality, how one religion could foster a matter-of-fact orientation to, and a practical concern with, the world, and why was this not the case with other religions?[19] If such an approach put the accent in a different place, it still assumed 'the problem of rationality in the West' and saw this in the context of modernisation as the continuation and intensification of the processes of rationalisation and disenchantment.

What is at issue here is whether those processes were absent elsewhere. I have argued that a measure of scepticism, which can be considered a form of disenchantment, is present in oral cultures. So too is rationality or rationalisation. That aspects of those processes are made more explicit and developed in written cultures is undoubtedly true. Traditions of dissent are constructed which build on earlier scepticism, which includes a measure of disenchantment of the world, both in the sense of personal

---

[16] Nakamura 1964: 24.   [17] Berrill 1964: 243.
[18] For the former see Cohen 1976 on Taiwan.   [19] Tenbruck 1984: 329.

disillusion and the acceptance of less 'magical' beliefs. Scepticism is not only a product of our own belated vision, nor can we accept Lucien Febvre's denial, in *Le Problème de l'incroyance*, of the possibility of atheism in early modern France.[20]

Markets

In fact economic activity in Asia in the seventeenth and eighteenth centuries does not seem to have differed greatly in its nature from that in the West. In his detailed analysis of Asian markets and merchants at this period, Chaudhuri takes a very different view than many European historians. For he sees this activity as using 'the same basic commercial methods' as in Europe, operating according to similar principles and similar price mechanisms.[21] The extensive commerce was associated with three types of market.[22] Firstly, seaport markets such as Surat dealt with places as far away as Mocha in the Red Sea and Canton (Guangzhou) in China. Secondly, there were the regional entrepôts such as Benares, which was also a major centre of pilgrimage and learning, and so visited on many accounts. Thirdly, there were the markets of a group of neighbouring villages producing a single export commodity. For example, the villages around Sarkhej, near Ahmadabad in Gujarat, grew indigo on a large scale, so that in 1620 Dutch merchants established a factory there for its purchase. At this time indigo (*indigofera sp.*), which had long been important in Asia, was being imported into Europe on a large scale, it having earlier been used by the Egyptians and Romans.

Each of the three types of market included three types of market activity, namely, local transactions, a wholesale spot market (supplying retail, bazaar and interregional commerce) and a wholesale forward market.[23] Part of the forward dealing consisted in merchants making advances to agents who then passed them on to producers. One of the most sophisticated markets in India was to be found in the town of Ahmadabad in Gujarat, which as we have seen was also an important centre for production. Forward dealings, the selling of futures, was widely practised and is reported as a regular feature of the financial operations that existed there. These activities were of long standing and provided a local basis for the take-off into an industrial economy.

The town of Ahmadabad, founded in 1411, had been the centre for the production of arms, swords, daggers and other high quality metalwork. In the following century the wider region of Gujarat, which had come

---

[20] A. Patterson, *Between the Lines*, forthcoming.   [21] Chaudhuri 1979: 160.
[22] Chaudhuri 1979: 160.   [23] Chaudhuri 1979: 156.

under Muslim domination in 1298, had many other skilled craftsmen working in ivory, precious metals and stones (including the carnelian mined near Broach), gold thread, wood and other material. But already in the sixteenth century the major activity was the production of cotton and silk goods. Pires counted twenty different varieties of cotton textiles at Cambay, whose abundance of craftsmen reminded Barbosa of France,[24] while J. H. van Linschoten thought the textiles not only cheap but excelling 'any Dutch cloth'.[25] Trade and processing were not only regional but international; camphor from Borneo was refined and sold.[26] Jewellery and silver were imported from Turkey and Iraq; imitations of Turkish, European and Persian materials were prepared. In the seventeenth century Ahmadabad became the centre for the production of silk textiles, including luxury varieties with gold and silver threads. But cotton remained at the core. One of the most recent historians of the Asian trade, K. N. Chaudhuri, remarked:

Before the discovery of machine spinning and weaving in Britain in the second half of the eighteenth century, the Indian subcontinent was probably the world's greatest producer of cotton textiles. The overseas markets in Asia and Africa were of course long dominated by Indian products, and to the demands of those two continents Europe added its own in the seventeenth and eighteenth centuries.[27]

There were three major production areas for the export trade: western India, that is, largely Gujarat; southern India, mainly Madras; and lastly Bengal, Bihar and Orissa, mainly Dacca. How was this trade affected by the coming of the Europeans? Their advent undoubtedly led to the expansion of Gujarati trade and production, though the control which the newcomers eventually exercised partly reduced the Indian role in sea transport. When the Portuguese entered the Asian trade, they attempted to control not only the spice and cloth trade with Indonesia but also the trade between Africa and India. For they needed the gold and ivory that Africa produced in order to finance their own purchases.[28] As a consequence, towards the end of the sixteenth century Gujarati ships were barred from visiting parts of east Africa by these new competitors, although they never entirely succeeded in excluding them either from the African or from the Asian trade. It was largely the Portuguese who now

---

[24] Pires [1944]: i, 43; Barbosa [1918–21]: i, 14.
[25] Linschoten [1598] 1974: i, 60. Van Linschoten was a Dutchman who worked six years with the Portuguese in Goa and then became an important figure for the Dutch when they turned their attention to Gujarati cloth in an attempt to pay for spices from Indonesia.
[26] Linschoten [1598] 1974; i, 113; Gopal 1975: 129.
[27] Chaudhuri 1978b: 237.   [28] Gopal 1975: 10.

transported much of their production, including carnelians, taking Gujarati goods as far as Brazil. When the Dutch (and later the English) came to dominate the trade route to Europe at the beginning of the seventeenth century, they encountered similar problems: they possessed insufficient silver to purchase the spices they sought on the Malabar coast. It has been said that 'it is inconceivable that the European trade with India – or with Asia in general for that matter – could have been sustained on a large scale for any length of time without the discovery of American silver-mines'.[29] Nevertheless that source was not inexhaustible and the Dutch and English made efforts to cut down the export of bullion. That was discouraged by mercantilist theory, a fact that led the Dutch to look for other goods to exchange for spices. 'There was . . . one commodity which was readily acceptable to the producers of spice . . . throughout the East people were clad in Indian cloth and would buy it "no matter what it cost".'[30] The main sources were Gujarat on the west and Coromandel and Bengal on the east and the Dutch simply followed 'the long-established trade in "coast cloth"' for the inter-Asian trade, a step which the Portuguese had already taken when they established colonies at Malacca in south-east Asia, in Colombo (Ceylon) and at Goa and Cochin in the west. The Dutch and English also exploited the potentialities of the trade in Indian textiles to south-east Asia, eventually setting up their main trading stations on the Coromandel coast, in particular at Golconda. When they lacked the money to buy fabrics, they had to borrow from merchants and rulers, paying up to 40 per cent interest a year.[31] To avoid such rates the Dutch and English increased the tempo of their search for textiles and indigo. For the Europeans Gujarat was the source of farm produce such as indigo and opium as well as other medicinal herbs, vegetable dyes, re-exported spices and cowries; among manufactured items were carnelians, but the basis was textiles. And in return came bullion, as the 'Gujarati economy was never in need of foreign articles of everyday use for the common masses'.[32]

The appearance of these western European merchants in the seventeenth century brought a new dimension to commercial practice. They were organised on the basis of 'a bureaucratic institution acting as a central distribution agency in the selling markets of Europe'; that is to say, the goods were auctioned by the joint-stock company. That procedure is said to have imposed some form of unified decision-making

[29] Chaudhuri 1978b: 195.
[30] Raychaudhuri 1962: 2, quoting Admiral Cornelius Matalief in 1607.
[31] Chicherov 1971: 115.
[32] Gopal 1975: 8–9. For later and more detailed references on pre-colonial Gujarat, see Gokhale 1969, 1979 and Das Gupta 1979.

on markets that were traditionally 'decentralized and fragmented';[33] for at the buying end large numbers of individual merchants took part in the markets. But in India too merchants were by no means isolated individuals. We have seen that the notion of merchant associations and of caste co-operation in banking was far from foreign to local practice; and there was also co-operation in production, for the Europeans were often dealing with villages of weavers.

To begin with the newcomers traded on the coast. Then, in the seventeenth century, they journeyed inland, especially the Dutch and English looking for textiles and indigo. The rise in demand brought weavers down from Sindh. Specialisation developed. Broach had water that was especially good for washing and bleaching clothes; so Ahmadabad and Baroda sent textiles there for bleaching as the English later did from north India.

Many of the textiles of Broach were made expressly for south-east Asia ('Priaman' and 'Teese'); the chintz of Ahmadabad was sold in Japan, as were the 'chader' of Surat; Japan became an important source of silver for the Dutch and English in the purchase of Indian goods. Nevertheless it was trade with Europe that altered the scale of commerce and production. For example, in 1630 the Surat factory was asked to send 900,000 pieces of one type of cloth and 300,000 of another.[34] These included cloth for west Africa which had become an important market,[35] especially for tapseils, a mixed fabric.[36] Of the twenty-three types of cloth listed as being made in Gujarat in the post-European period, ten had been developed for the west African trade, a market to which they adapted very rapidly; these were boralchowder (striped), brawle (blue and white striped), cheilos (striped), chintz (block printed), Guinea stuff (plain dyed, checks and striped), nicannees (striped), pantkeys (plain white and dyed), tapseil (striped), bejutapant (striped and checks) and negapant (striped).[37] By and large the finer quality goods went to England as did the white cloth, some of it to be used for block printing. In France such printed cottons became known as 'indiennes', which were defined as 'Etoffe de coton peinte ou imprimée, fabriquée primitivement en Inde, puis imitée par les manufacturiers européens'. They were 'indian' even when printed in Europe, just as porcelain was china.

The organisation of cloth production on this scale meant a dramatic increase in the numbers of local workers involved. In Bengal in the early

---

[33] Steensgaard 1972: 145.
[34] The extent of the trade can be seen from the fact that the English at Baroda were dealing with 800 weavers at a time.
[35] Gopal 1975: 205.
[36] Irwin and Schwartz 1966: 24.   [37] See also the list in Raychaudhuri 1962.

eighteenth century employment was provided for a sizeable section of the population while the income from taxes on merchants and weavers was considerable. Production was organised on the basis of a putting-out system but one which was usually worked not by the supply of materials to the artisans but by the provision of cash advances which the merchants in turn obtained from the trading companies and which were regarded as a deposit on the orders. When the European companies arrived they organised the trade after their own fashion, once they had established shore-based 'factories'. The companies gave money to merchants who handed it to 'retail traders' who travelled around the weavers, although some weavers were not dependent upon advances.[38] In other crafts, such as jewellery and smithying, materials were handed out in advance, as in many other parts of the world now or within living memory.

The extent of the trade with Europe brought problems as well as benefits to both areas. The organisation of trade and production ran up against several problems. To increase their incomes, the rulers tried to interfere with commerce beyond collecting 'normal' taxes. Such interference continued long after the coming of Europeans. When the British constructed a refinery for saltpetre at Ahmadabad, royal requirements had to take precedence and the venture failed. Then the shift to cash crops took its toll. Originally an American cultigen, tobacco soon spread and entered the export trade. The area under indigo expanded.[39] Such expansion with its consequent specialisation increased the likelihood of famine in bad years, as in 1630–2; weavers, dyers and washers dispersed; those who remained required to be paid in grain.[40] That famine had terrible consequences for both people and commerce, leading the English to transfer many of their interests from Gujarat to the Coromandel coast on the south-east of the sub-continent. The production of indigo, which had been so important, never recovered, since in future the British drew upon West Indian supplies, so that while Gujarat was one of the most precociously industrialised regions in the seventeenth century, its position later declined.[41]

This changing activity gave rise to labour problems. In 1622 a group of porters went on strike, refusing to work for less than a mahmudi a bundle.[42] In Broach and Surat English purchasers of yarn raised the prices so that local weavers refused to sell them cloth. The weavers of Broach temporarily abandoned the town in protest against the governor's

---

[38] Pavlov 1964: 30–31.   [39] Gopal 1975: 163.
[40] Gopal 1975: 203.   [41] Perlin 1983: 47.
[42] Gopal 1975: 163, 167. A mahmudi was a silver coin and money of account in Persia, but in India a gold coin.

tyranny. Traders also left the towns when Aurangzeb pursued anti-Hindu policies. Some of the protest was religious, but the general economic position also created great hardships. Goods became more difficult to transport because of robbery, so that as in earlier times some caravans were accompanied by Brahmans and by Bhattas, whom the thieves were thought to respect. Famines were frequent. In 1685 the Momnas and the Matias, mostly weavers, rose in revolt and were suppressed with difficulty. However, by the end of the century the Gujarati textile trade did recover at the time of the rise of the Parsis as middlemen and big traders and with the growth of Bombay.[43]

In some ways the effects on Europe were as striking as those on India as it adapted its 'proto-industrial' system of artisanal cloth production to a large-scale export trade. At first bullion had to be exported in large quantities to pay for the imports since its manufactures were not wanted by the Indian market. Then widespread protectionism developed.

The extent of the trade with Europe was such that it led to protests from local producers of cloth in that continent, resulting in bans on Indian imports being imposed by various countries at the end of the seventeenth century. These were never very effective and handloom products continued to be imported into England on a large scale. In 1681 London's silk weavers sent a petition to Parliament protesting against the population wearing Indian fabrics, but it was declined. Import duties were raised first to 10 per cent in 1685, then to 20 per cent five years later. Nevertheless the imports continued to increase, leading the silk weavers to attempt to destroy the premises of the East India Company. In 1701 the import of Bengal silk fabrics was banned, a fine imposed for wearing them and an additional 15 per cent duty levied on white calicoes.[44] Even the manufacture of 'indiennes', printed cotton made with blocks copied from India, was forbidden in the silk centre of Lyons so that production moved over the border to Geneva, to the benefit of Swiss manufacturers.[45]

Europe was by no means the only outlet for Indian goods. In the middle of the eighteenth century Bombay had profited from the fact that Ahmadabad had been partly cut off from the coastal trade by the advancing Maratha power. In the hands of merchants, especially English and Parsis often in partnership, Bombay flourished and firms sprouted.[46]

---

[43] 'They were the first artisan community, who transformed themselves into a trading group in the 17th century' (Gopal 1975: 184).

[44] Chicherov 1971: 125.   [45] Lüthy 1961: i, 50.

[46] Of those firms registered at the beginning of the nineteenth century, sixteen were Parsi, fifteen Hindu, nine European, four Muslim, four American, three Portuguese and two Parsi–Chinese.

At this time many more of the exports from Bombay were going eastwards to China (especially cotton and opium) than to England. Even so, Britain had a constant trade deficit with India. During the period 1710 to 1759 the East India Company imported goods worth £9,240,000 and exported bullion to the value of £26,833,000.[47] Of course there were additional 'invisible' earnings in the shape of salaries and booty but the trading account showed the same kind of deficit in gold and silver that Pliny had objected to some 1,700 years earlier. Much of this deficit was incurred from the purchase of cloth which continued to be exported in large quantities despite protectionist measures. Indeed these measures were ones taken by the home rather than the colonial government. The latter encouraged the Indian handloom manufacture throughout the eighteenth century. Working through intermediaries, merchants imported silk and cotton, made loans and collected the finished products.

It was not only cloth that was in demand from overseas. Europe's own production of cotton cloth began long before industrialisation and required the import of the raw materials. Cotton was an Indian cultigen that had constituted the major fibre for making cloth for many centuries. However Indian short-staple raw cotton was little used for the export trade before the middle of the eighteenth century.[48] Some was exported to China but the great suppliers of the British mills had been long-staple varieties from the southern states of America, where production had spread and had been greatly improved by the use of Whitney's saw-gin (1780). But with the outbreak of the American Civil War, that source became endangered; as a result the external demand for Indian raw cotton grew very suddenly and the price rises between 1859 and 1866 were enormous.

Linked to the manufacture of cotton was the extensive use of indigo and that too was imported in large quantities when Europe came into direct trading contact with India, although it had been grown in Egypt, used in Rome and was brought into Italy by Jewish traders. There it began to replace the woad (French: pastel, voude, *isatio tinctoria*) that had been widely grown in Germany (especially around Erfurt in Thuringia), France and England, although that too originally came from China and Arabia, reaching Italy and Germany about the tenth century, France and Spain about the twelfth century and the British Isles in 1582.

---

[47] Pavlov 1964: 92.
[48] Herodotus (III: 106) mentions 'wool growing on wild trees' in India while cotton cloth has been found in the Western Cemetery at Meroe dating from the Graeco-Roman period (Arkell 1951: 32).

For a long time efforts were made to keep indigo out of Europe, where it could not be grown. In 1799 the dyers of Nuremberg took an oath to use nothing but woad, while Henri IV of France ordered the death penalty for all those who used the pernicious substance. Only in 1737 were French dyers able to use indigo freely. As we have seen, the growth of indigo in India had been much encouraged by the Dutch and British in Gujarat in the vicinity of Sarkhej, but it suffered under the famine conditions that obtained in the early seventeenth century when Europe had to seek its supplies in the West Indies.

In summary then, when the Europeans first came to the Indian Ocean in the sixteenth century, they made a relatively small initial impact. The immense network of international commerce stretching between east Africa, Arabia, the Persian Gulf, India, south-east Asia, Indonesia and China was not at first greatly changed by their presence. While the Portuguese were interested in taking control of the spice trade away from the Arabs, much of the Asian trade remained in the hands of Gujarati merchants who carried not only their own cloth, indigo and opium but also the goods produced by others, especially spices.[49] European ships were smaller and less capitalised. The English employed an average capital of 200,000 rupees even at the beginning of the seventeenth century, while some Gujarati vessels trading to the Red Sea were worth five times this amount. The largest of the Chinese 'treasure ships' involved in the famous expeditions of Cheng Ho to the Indian Ocean in the early fifteenth century displaced about 3,100 tons whereas none of Vasco da Gama's ships exceeded 300 and in 1588 the largest English merchant ship was less than 400.[50] 'The Europeans were poor relations. Nor, in the seventeenth century, were they capable of teaching new commercial or manufacturing techniques to the locals. The two seem to have been on much the same level of development.'[51] In other words at this point in time there can be little sense in characterising one economy as capitalist and the other as feudal, stagnant or Asiatic. The European miracle had yet to happen and the data adduced by writers on India, not to speak of China or the Near East, even suggest that it might have happened elsewhere.

The point is reinforced by Gough's analysis of the southern Indian kingdom of Thanjavur in which she commented on Marx's notion of the Asiatic Mode of Production. Up to a point she accepts the existence of

[49] Pearson 1976: 10.
[50] Mills [1433] 1970: 31. However the Portuguese carrack *Madre de Dios* captured by the English in 1592 displaced 2,000 tons.
[51] Pearson 1976: 10.

the local 'self-subsistence community' and speaks of 'village communes', although the idea sits a little uncomfortably with the other evidence she gives. For there was also extensive trade and a state bureaucracy. Despite communes, she claims, 'there seems to have been nothing inherent in this system that would prevent the expansion of empires, the increasing division of labour and the growth of specialised urban populations, of manufactures, and of trade'.[52] From the economic standpoint, the preconditions of capitalism were almost complete. The one exception in her view was that the state kept a firm control over manufacturing, trading and private wealth, 'so that it seems doubtful that capitalism would have developed without European intervention and eventual conquest'.[53] The gap must certainly have been small. For India was not without its independent entrepreneurs. Some emerged later on as factory owners in mid-nineteenth-century Gujarat, where they were often associated with earlier trading families and castes. Meanwhile state control existed elsewhere too. Indeed a measure of state intervention has often been seen as critical in the mercantile activity of Venice, in France's manufactures in the seventeenth century, and later in Japan's industrialisation. The balance between the individual activities of the entrepreneur and the intervention of the state is always difficult to measure and their respective contributions hard to assess. Both contributions are needed, possibly in different degrees at different times and places. The analysis cannot proceed far on the basis of a forced choice between the individual and the state.

In Gujarat at this time we are not dealing with state-organised trade or manufacture, though that could be found in south India. Nor are we dealing with a servile labour force, although the extent of the 'freedom' of weavers, whether untouchables, caste Hindus or Muslims, is a matter for debate. The critical question is whether that labour force could have provided the urban workers needed for radical developments in the manufacturing sphere, and that is a question to which I return in chapter six.

What really changed matters, first in Europe and then in India, was the competitive reaction to imports. As Chaudhuri points out 'it is perhaps not entirely by chance, that the large-scale application of machinery to production occurred in the textile industry in Europe, in which the Indian imports probably served to map demand conditions for English entrepreneurs'.[54] Over the long run the response to mass cotton imports and to local demand was to develop mechanised forms of production,

---

[52] Gough 1979: 5–6.
[53] Gough 1979: 6.   [54] Chaudhuri 1982: 397.

culminating in factory production around 1780. Fibres other than cotton were also the subject of factory production: the East India Company encouraged sericulture during the Napoleonic Wars when there was no access to Italian silk.

The process of manufacture spread rapidly in Europe. For example the opening phase of the Industrial Revolution in Saxony began between 1800 and 1830. By the latter date in Chemnitz (for a while Karl Marx Stadt) there were eighty-four spinning factories (with 361,200 spindles), sixty-five water driven and four steam. As in India, the factory-spun yarn was fed into handlooms at home, though further processing took place in the factories; moreover they were still producing according to the statutes of the guilds.[55]

Indian merchants and their partners responded in a similar way some fifty years later. By the middle of that century they had started purchasing the older machinery from Europe to provide yarn, then cloth, for local market demand and sometime later they entered the competition for overseas markets. If one applies the same line of argument to India that is widely used for Europe, such rapid changes could not have taken place unless the economy and the society (at least the relevant segments) were ready for this development.

When it came, the shift in the direction of the trade in cloth was dramatic. It took place over the years 1814–21, immediately after the end of the Napoleonic wars, as we see in Table 4.1. As for the internal market, many authors followed Marx in assuming that it collapsed with the development of the Industrial Revolution in Europe: 'the bones of the cotton-weavers are bleaching the plains of India' he wrote.[56] However that does not seem to have been altogether the case. While cloth prices fell with Manchester competition, the advent of machine-made yarn strengthened the position of the indigenous handloom as distinct from hand-spinning;[57] moreover demand for cotton cloth seems to have increased, partly because there were more people, partly because they used more cloth (e.g. in the bodice) and partly because they shifted to cotton from other materials. Nevertheless the industry was affected, especially with the spread of railroads which did much to hasten the decline of some Indian handicraft industries since trains could now bring cheap manufactures from England. Entire craft villages lost their markets, increasing the number of agricultural labourers at the end of the century. However the handloom industry continued to be important in India and experienced a revival in Bengal and elsewhere under the

[55] Stützner and Szöllösi 1985: 69.
[56] Marx, *Capital* I: 4.   [57] Morris 1963: 612.

Table 4.1 *The trade in cloth between India and Great Britain, 1814–28*

	Indian exports to Great Britain (pieces)	British exports to India (yards)
1814	1,266,608	818,208
1828	422,504	42,822,077

Swadeshi movement which encouraged the use of country-made cloth. This was part of the resistance to the occupying power as well as a return to local tradition, and it achieved its high point in Gandhi's attachment not only to the handloom but to handspun (*khadi*). The production of 'non-factory made' cloth still retains a considerable share of the Indian market, partly because of the quality of handicrafts, partly because of government support, partly for ideological reasons and partly for aesthetic reasons.

The growth of Indian industry

Machine-made yarn and textiles were introduced into Ahmadabad in 1818, the year the British took over the town. The local factory treatment of cotton in India got going with the founding of the Bombay Spinning and Weaving Company by Davar in 1851, the first mill being started in 1854, with both the equipment and the coal being imported from Britain. That was within a short time of the complete freeing of the prohibitions on the export of machinery. For not only Britain but France, Germany and Belgium prohibited the export of textile machinery as a protectionist measure, until the trade in machine tools became an industry of its own;[58] in 1843 Robert Peel lifted the prohibition.

Two other mills followed in the next three years, all founded by members of wealthy families. Bombay's profits from cotton, opium and shipbuilding, which largely ceased with the coming of steam, were now being funnelled into industry. The first Bombay mill was soon followed by a mill at Broach (Baruch) started in 1855 by a British cotton grower, Landon, who had earlier set up American machines for cleaning and pressing cotton; he had spent seventeen years working in the cotton industry in America and was engaged in introducing the long-staple variety. In fact this mill had been set up following the collapse of a joint venture with Ranchhodlal Chhotalal of Ahmadabad who had long dreamed of introducing industrial methods to India. When a dispute

[58] Mehta 1982: 38.

arose with the Baroda bankers investing in the firm, Landon decided to go ahead alone and was very successful.

The examples of Bombay and Broach were not lost on the merchants of Ahmadabad. Even before that, in the 1840s there were efforts to improve production, leading to the establishment of a steam gin and to discussions about floating a joint-stock company.[59] One person contemplating the introduction of machinery at that time was Ranchhodlal, a government servant who belonged to a Brahman family involved in administration rather than commerce. He had thought of founding a mill about 1847 and tried two years later.[60] But he was unable to raise the capital and it was not until 1861, ten years after the successful Davar mill in Bombay, that the first spinning factory opened in Ahmadabad, supported by the most important members of the town's financial élite. In describing the credit nexus in Gujarat from the middle of the eighteenth century, Sharma has stressed the importance of the farming of rural and urban (trade) taxes by bankers and traders who used much of this income for commercial purposes. Payments were made in towns by clearing-house methods, that is, without money actually changing hands.[61] That expertise continued to be important in the rise of industry.

This was only the first of Ranchhodlal's enterprises and he built a larger mill, part of the great expansion in that town. Some years later, in 1893, he participated in the Indian National Congress, an episode in the long association of the Gujarati businessmen with the independence movement, which culminated in Gandhi's residence in the town. Ahmadabad later came to be known as the Indian Manchester, and recently advertised itself as 'The City of Entrepreneurs'. It was the beginning of the growth of Gujarati industry, initially founded on cotton. However, none of the first three mills in Ahmadabad was founded by members of the commercial groups, although the latter invested in these companies. They preferred to stick to trading and banking, their traditional activities, in which the returns were higher. Moreover Jain participation in manufacture was at first inhibited by the view that insect life was lost in the manufacturing process.[62] Eventually this reluctance was overcome and a Jain mill started to operate in 1878. From then on Jains and Vaishnavas dominated the industry, often using caste ties to gain support and select members of the managing agencies.

The later achievements of Ahmadabad were not the result of the activities of a single entrepreneur nor yet of a small band. As Mehta remarks, the establishment of the first mill in Ahmadabad in 1861 took

---

[59] Mehta 1982: 20.   [60] Pavlov 1964: 281.
[61] Sharma 1993.   [62] Mehta 1982: 86–7.

place against a whole climate of enterprise. When the British arrived in 1818 they found a city suffering from the struggle between Marathas and Mughals, but one which had long been associated with industry, banking and commerce, especially in the domain of cotton production.

In discussing these problems, Timberg points to the fact that the founding of new Indian industries involved entrepreneurship of a different sort from that embodied in the first textile mills in England. 'The technical problems had already been overcome elsewhere. What was necessary in India was the "coordination of the factors of production", to produce efficiently enough to meet the constant foreign competition.'[63] In that case what was crucial to the first as distinct from the 'follower industrialisers' was, apart from a market, capital and so on, the technological know-how which was a question of relevant knowledge of a developing technology. That is obviously related to an existing tradition of craftwork. Clearly if one is working at the growing point of technological achievement one is going to have greater entrepreneurial opportunities. But that growing point has little to do with social, psychological or cultural variables of a deep-seated kind, since leadership in those fields can change relatively easily, at least under conditions of 'self-sustaining growth'.

The first weaving, as distinct from spinning, mill in India was the 'Oriental', built in Bombay in 1860. It was founded by the Sassoons, a Sephardic family that had come from Toledo via Baghdad, later to establish themselves in Hong Kong and England. In 1860 a 10 per cent customs duty was levied on imports in order to clear the debts incurred by the Indian Mutiny (1857–9) and it brought a demand from British members of Parliament for a tariff on Indian cloth equivalent to Indian customs duties. Once again Indian production was seen as a threat. The power of Lancashire was such that they forced the Government of India to impose an 'equalising' excise tax of 5 per cent on Indian-manufactured cloth, to compensate for the import tax levied in 1894, thus convincing many Indian mill owners to support the Indian National Congress which from its founding in 1885 helped to propagate the virtues of Swadeshi, part of the reaction to the import of manufactured goods from Europe.[64]

At first much of the production, especially of yarn, was exported to the East. A great opportunity presented itself in China where merchants had long been involved in the trade in opium as well as in indigo and hand-woven cloth. To this constellation was added yarn for local use. As a result it was the spinning industry that first developed in India. At the

[63] Timberg 1978: 3.   [64] Mehta 1982: 116–17.

outset this move was not opposed by the English manufacturers of Lancashire but by the middle of the 1880s India had started to oust their products from the market. With the gradual dominance of Japan in the China trade (though the Tatas of Bombay also exported cotton to Japan) by the end of the 1880s, there was a swing in orientation to the internal market, both in terms of yarn and of cloth. The Indian mills, until then spinning thread for the handlooms, turned to weaving, hitherto dominated by Lancashire.[65] By the end of the century this swing had led to a dramatic drop in the British exports of cloth to India from 1,932 million yards in 1896–1900, to 1,166 million yards in 1918–22, while the Indian exports to Europe rose rapidly. After 1918, Japan began to make inroads even into the Indian market, increasing the level of competition.

Whereas Gujarati and Marawari merchants had been somewhat unwilling to invest in land, and hence were cautiously prepared to shift to factory production when the chance came, in Bengal that was not altogether the case. Local merchants did purchase land and it was the British that took over much mercantile activity. However Bengalis themselves invested in these foreign firms, in which they expected to get jobs, as well as eventually starting some enterprises of their own. Of 546 registered firms in Calcutta before the First World War, 179 were still European owned, but 367 were Indian. The Indian businesses, largely private, belonged mainly to members of the Kayastha caste (scribes), to Brahmans and to a lesser extent to Sikhs and Marawaris.

The jute industry followed a similar pattern to cotton. Until 1830 jute manufacture had been monopolised by the Bengal handloom. Then a processing factory was built in the Scottish town of Dundee leading to the import of raw jute. The Crimean war (1853–6) cut off the Russian supply to the Scottish mills and stimulated the export of raw jute from Bengal. That was followed in 1854 by the construction of mills in Bengal, with the first power loom coming four years later. These enterprises were largely in European hands, but they were transferred to Indian soil and encouraged local investment and eventually local ownership. By 1908 India's jute production was greater than Dundee's.

Europeans in India made some efforts to start other factories but without much success. On the other hand there was a considerable build-up of financial services, with the establishment of banks and insurance companies as early as 1780 (and in some cases even before), life insurance in 1797, then later the Calcutta agency system. From the 1820s the demand for coal grew with the advent of steamships. Opportunities for local entrepreneurs increased from 1833 with the

---

[65] Timberg 1978.

abolition of the East India Company's monopoly and the partial, then the complete, freeing of the export of machinery to India in 1825 and 1843 respectively.[66] The steamship was followed by the steam train and while the railways were largely financed and equipped from England, they made use of the coal from local mines whose exploitation had been encouraged. Efficient transport, as Marx pointed out, transformed the country.[67] It was the railways that helped to transport the machinery from the coast to Ahmadabad, though the machinery for the first mill was transported by bullock cart from the port of Cambay.[68] Marx saw the railways as breaking through the caste system founded on a hereditary division of labour. This did not happen as rapidly as he predicted, because, as Dumont notes, 'les changements se sont cantonnés dans la sorte de "poche" politico-economique'.[69] But neither has that system prevented industrialisation taking place.

One basic reason why a measure of industrialisation could occur is that the relevant differences in the pre-industrial economy between Europe and Asia were not as radical as Marx, Weber, Dumont and the majority of social theorists have allowed. The point is well made by the economic historian, Perlin, who insists on the world dimensions of the Indian economy in the late precolonial period. Like Europe, India 'was affected by profound and rapid changes in the character of its societies and economies, and state-forms, from at least the sixteenth century. A fundamental aspect of that development was a local merchant capitalism which emerged *independently of that in Europe*, but within a common international theatre of societal and commercial changes'.[70] Those changes were related to a process of monetisation that involved world-wide trade:

silver from Mexico and Peru percolating from Europe overland in fairly substantial amounts throughout most of the sixteenth and early seventeenth centuries, and carried in increasing quantities by ship round the Cape of Good Hope; copper, firstly from Europe, then shipped from Japan in massive amounts by the Dutch East India Company, as well as by way of more indirect routes used by Chinese merchants, and later, in the eighteenth century, increasingly from European sources once more; cowries from their only major source in the Maldives, being part of an extraordinary distribution network that ultimately joined up the Atlantic and the Indian Ocean trades in a complex relationship of interdependency; *bodam*, an inedible bitter almond, imported from Persia into the ports of the west coast of India. All these media . . . were used as circulating currency.

[66] Hobson 1902.
[67] Rungta 1970.   [68] Mehta 1982: 53.
[69] Dumont 1966: 276.   [70] Perlin 1983: 33 (my italics).

Perlin sees this expansion as related to the significant increase in population growth and agricultural settlement taking place about the fifteenth century, as well as to the accelerated urban growth (closely linked to textile production) and new taxation systems, implying the development of extensive commodity production in the countryside and of the markets involved in its distribution.[71] In other words parallel processes were happening on the economic front in both Asia and Europe.

According to Perlin, the reason that India did not industrialise at the same time turns on the problem of shifting from commercial to industrial capital. This the colonial penetration did much to discourage through promoting production in Europe and 'underdevelopment' elsewhere. The redirection of capital was certainly important; but other countries in Europe had to shift capital to new enterprises for industrialisation. In Saxony this process began twenty years after Britain and took a further twenty years to get fully established. Within a further twenty years mills were being constructed in India, not long after the lifting of restrictions on the export of machinery made this possible and even before the advent of railways. This delay hardly looks like the result of deep-structural impediments but rather of more specific difficulties. Indeed for some time the economies of India and the West had been running in parallel courses, one excelling in one sphere, the other in another. For a long time India had lain at the centre of a trading network stretching from the Near East to China in which her manufactured cloth was the most important commodity.

I have argued that we need to look back to earlier commercial networks, based ultimately on Bronze Age developments, that flourished in the Indian Ocean and the China Seas on the one hand and in the Mediterranean on the other, as well as the overland routes represented in their most dramatic form by the Silk Road.[72] Other aspects of the social systems of East and West have often been seen in terms of the contrasts, and the differences are important. But these differences have too often been viewed as preventing the 'modernisation' of Eastern societies and as encouraging 'their relatively unchanging character or stagnation'.[73]

---

[71] Perlin 1983: 63, 69.

[72] See for example the collection of papers, *The Significance of the Silk Roads in the History of Human Civilizations*, the proceedings of an independent seminar held in Osaka in October 1988, in association with the UNESCO project, 'Integral Study of the Silk Roads: roads of dialogue'. For further references, see the project's Newsletter, No. 3, April 1993.

[73] Raychaudhuri 1962: vii.

Current developments, past history and theoretical parsimony suggest we should look again at some of these claims, especially, for example, those about kinship and the family, impeding development in the one case and encouraging it in the other.

5   Family and business in the East

Given the extent of mercantile and manufacturing activity in India, how was this managed? We have seen that already in the ancient Near East merchants created a number of partnership arrangements in the course of running their affairs, anticipating the later *commenda* and *fraterna* of the Mediterranean. From the early records (at least from 1900 BCE), two kinds of joint endeavour existed in business. The first was the family enterprise consisting of kinsfolk; this is often called a firm although strictly that involves a partnership based on contract. The second is a partnership of interested parties, based on just such a contract. Since co-operation with kin or kith, with family or friends, is a general feature in pre-industrial society, it is hardly surprising to find similar arrangements in south and east Asia. Some scholars, including Weber, have argued that the importance given to caste in India and to clan in China placed inhibitions on the development of 'capitalist' activity which was said to depend upon bureaucratic (that is, essentially non-familial, non-nepotic) organisation allied with an individualistic approach to entrepreneurship. In this theory, not simply the extended group but the family itself was a hindrance to development. A common European view runs as follows. 'When western traders first came to India in numbers, they found her people organised in a rigid economic and social system, the unit of which was the agricultural village . . . The villagers were divided into castes and within the castes were "joint families" – grown brothers and their families – who often owned property in common.'[1] 'Simple' tools in agriculture and crafts meant a village-based economy, apart from the few cities and courts. Certain factors held back economic advance, as in other 'oriental countries', namely 'the religious interpretation of life, the attitude toward women and early marriage, the family and caste systems'.[2] Take the family: the ownership of property by a large group gives protection in hard times when famine is brought about by

[1] Buchanan 1934: 13.   [2] Buchanan 1934: 16.

138

population pressure but is a deterrent to economic progress; on the other hand individualism, which encourages experimentation, is 'a great advantage'. I will return to those points later. However in the major Eurasian societies there is no categorical separation between these modes of recruitment, rather one of emphasis. Both principles of attachment are present.

Although it may be true that in some simple hunting and gathering communities, all men were literally brothers and all women sisters (or anyhow kin), in the Bronze Age societies of the East and West economic activities were not confined to kin alone. Even in simple agricultural groups like the LoDagaa of west Africa, people act together as friends (*ba*) or as neighbours in situations where kinship is not the primary tie, perhaps not even relevant at all; one of these spheres is economic co-operation in the fields. On the other hand kinship has continued to be of central significance to economic activity in India, not only in the rural sector and in merchant activity but in the development of industrial firms.

Family and business in India

The 'joint' family

The part played by kin in commercial and other enterprises is often seen as linked to the presence of the joint family or what is known in law as the HUF, the Hindu Undivided Family. Since that is usually associated with the European extended family and opposed to the nuclear unit of the modern industrial world, we need to examine the notion in some detail. What are its main features?

Two main branches of Hindu law dealt with the 'joint family', namely the *Mitakshara* and the *Dayabhaga*. According to the first, it was not mandatory for persons to live in a residential joint family in order to maintain coparcenery rights, rights to share in the family property, but they had to have a common ancestor at the fourteenth ascending generation. Under the second branch of law, which originated in Bengal, a son was unable to exercise those coparcenery rights during his father's lifetime; fission was not allowed between adjacent generations.

A joint family of this kind included men, sons, unmarried daughters and wives. A married daughter would already have received the *stridhana* which included jewellery and other valuables, and which could not, in principle, be alienated from her without the consent of her kin. The 1937 Woman's Right to Property Act further conferred upon a wife the right of enjoyment of her husband's share in the coparcenery, or jointly inherited property, during her lifetime without giving her a right of alienation.

In Hindu law, as transmuted by contact with the British and with British concepts, co-ownership relates to the joint owners of common property, holding a co-ordinate and equal interest. The shares may be fixed (among co-sharers) or indeterminate (among coparceners). Hindu joint family properties are of the latter kind. There are in fact three recognised forms of co-ownership, namely:

1. a joint tenancy
2. a tenancy-in-common
3. coparcenership.

Under British law there was also:

4. tenancy by entireties, as when a husband and wife are regarded as one and the property passes between them; since 1925 this particular form of co-ownership has merged with the first.

In a joint tenancy, the parties are equal and there is a unity of interest. Shares cannot be willed because of the survivorship rule: the share of any member who dies goes automatically to the coparceners until the last one dies or until the estate is partitioned. A share can be disposed of *inter vivos* if all agree, in which case the giver and receiver cease to be joint tenants. However it is always possible to give property to a daughter at or after marriage, as well as to others for pious purposes. In addition, under the Hindu Gains of Learning Act of 1930, property acquired through a training that has been funded by the 'joint family' is no longer considered to be joint property.

Under traditional Hindu law of the *Mitakshara* variety, a joint family consists of the descendants of a common ancestor in an unbroken male line, including daughters before marriage and wives afterwards, as well as adopted sons; in the three highest castes, illegitimate sons get only maintenance. In principle such a family is bound together by ties of agnation, affinity or adoption as well as by its common fund of property, but it may also have a common mess, common worship and common residence, although in fact none of these latter are essential. It comes to an end when members formally separate, not when someone dies. However, it cannot end while one is able to add a member, that is, while it contains a potential mother. While a family may cease to be joint in respect of food, worship and residence, only when the estate is divided does separation finally take place. For it to be divided (rather than just end), no documentation is necessary if it is formally agreed. Agreement may be presumed to have taken place not only through separate possession or enjoyment but when a partial separation has taken place; indeed even if the shares are formally defined, there may be a presumption of division.

The joint family in business

A joint family business belongs to the undivided unit and devolves on the coparceners, including those who come later, though the absence of a contract means that it is not formally a firm. It is the *karta* or head that has complete control until partition takes place and can even use the funds to start a new business. The existence of joint interests does not prevent individual members from operating on their own. For example, one major joint-family firm in Ahmadabad is structured around the number of children. There are seven mills, each one looked after by an offspring of which there are five sons and two daughters. If they work in their enterprises they are paid a salary; otherwise they draw dividends or acquire shares. At the same time most members attempt to set up their own businesses, especially as the original group may eventually become too large, leading to a final split. So family members often hold two jobs, a situation of which the founding fathers would certainly have disapproved since the second employment would have been seen as working privately in company time.

The 'joint family' persists in these industrial enterprises not just because of tradition or inertia, but also because of advantages that are appreciated by the actors. Kapadia notes that 'Although the younger generation often complains of the suffocating atmosphere of the joint family, at the same time it appears to be conscious of certain benefits derived from joint living: economic help, refuge in many crisis situations, proper upbringing of young children, restraining influence of clashes between husband and wife'.[3] Such mutual assistance occurs whether or not people are living in a common residence; often to ease tensions, to give more room for individuality, they will not. This aspect continues to be a cause of misunderstanding, especially for demographers who are dependent upon household censuses. When the joint family came under discussion during British rule, and often today, 'the reference was to the joint household or to those living jointly in a house'.[4] This is precisely the information that appears in census reports which rarely if ever trace the relations between those living in adjacent, let alone distant, houses. Yet these ties are always important at the local level where they could be the basis of 'joint families'. In the Hindu village of Nandol in Gujarat, the large majority of the inhabitants lived in conjugal households. One would

---

[3] Kapadia 1966: 291.   [4] Desai 1964: 25.

often find relatives living nearby, sometimes next door. Where the neighbours consisted of two brothers, they might still co-operate in farming or
in other activities and so constitute a unit from the standpoint of production or consumption. Units of this larger kind are characteristic not
only of Hindu groups. In discussing Muslim 'households' in Pakistan,
Korson gives figures for co-residence, a category in which he includes
close residence (that is, co-operating units). The figures are given in
Table 5.1.

The pattern of distribution shown in Table 5.1 is common enough in
European as well as in Asian societies, implying social and economic
co-operation within the larger residential groups as well as between some
adjacent households. In India, the Hindu joint family may well persist
irrespective of subsequent co-residence, for that legal corporation turns
on the division of common property and remains of the greatest
importance for propertied families, including business ones. Arrangements for living and working together vary greatly, and vary *inter alia* on
a 'class' basis. The more restricted the space, the greater the potential
problems. Even where common residence did not continue, a common
purse might be maintained with the income going into a common fund,
at least from the joint enterprise. Epstein remarked that a brother who
had secured a job in the city often retained an interest in his village and
might continue to belong to a 'share family' or an 'undivided family'.
While poorer families rarely share this ideal explicitly, they are likely to
practice it as they get wealthier, indicating an acceptance either of
'higher' norms or of management advantages. In less formal ways, too,
family influence may be strong, especially in the choice of mates. Such
influences are strongest when the elements of the joint family live nearby,
although internal tensions may inhibit co-operation. For example, in the
upper middle class urban families a number of adjacent households may
be established on one piece of land, so that people live in one place but
not in one house. A variety of 'interactions' may again exist between the
constituent units, from minimal to maximal, partly determined by
genealogical distance. One of the most common co-operative arrangements is for the older generation to eat, regularly but not continually,
with the younger, even when they maintain separate dwellings.

Such joint families played a very prominent part in business. A major
role in India's industrial development was undertaken by the Marawaris
who were Rajasthani Banias (merchants) and included Jains as well as
Hindus.[5] Unlike the Bengalis, the Marawaris were not a very progressive,
educated group. But for industrialisation one needs both the educated

---

[5] Timberg 1978.

Table 5.1. *Mean size of 'households' in West Pakistan*

'Households'	Size
Extended	17.3
Expanded	15.1
Other	7.6
Elementary	60.0

Source: Korson, 1975

to run the administration and advance knowledge in the scientific–technical fields, as well as the 'businessmen' to make things go. And as businessmen Marawaris were certainly not illiterate. They traded in grain and textiles as well as being involved in moneylending. One commentator notes, as others have done, how 'Their business was organised around the joint family system'.[6] The Marawari merchants used the extended family as a base in their travels. As they moved they got support from their 'communal fellows'; they often stayed in 'collective messes' which have been described as a particularly effective part of their trading system.[7] They worked together until a family row broke out and then separated. Such a process suggests a limit to the growth of family firms and their eventual replacement by managerial corporations. In other words there appears to exist not only a process of internal, cyclical development but also an evolutionary one whereby family firms are replaced by those organised on a bureaucratic basis. Many commentators who have seen bureaucracy as taking over from kinship confuse such internal development with evolutionary change. That error gives rise to one of the contradictions we have noted earlier. While there has certainly been a growth of such corporations over time, the family firm has mechanisms for containing the effects of rows, and even allows for a degree of separation. But more importantly, new family firms are constantly being generated both within existing ones (using inherited capital) and by new entrepreneurs (often with borrowed capital).

One major advantage of the Hindu undivided family, like the *commenda* among kin to which it is clearly related, is that it provides the longer-term continuity of investment and organisation that companies may need. Its existence does not depend upon the life and death of individual members, though obviously it disappears if all descendants die out. But that is unlikely to happen in south and east

[6] Rungta 1970: 165.
[7] Timberg 1978: 6, referring also to Papanek's work on the Memons of Pakistan.

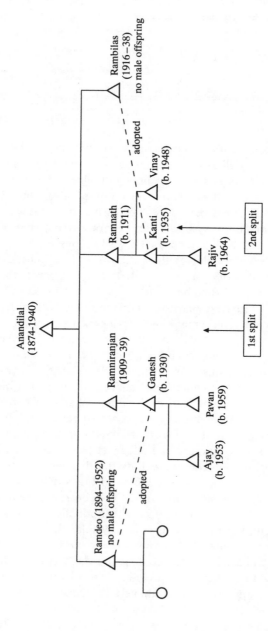

Figure 5.1 The decline of the Podars (*Source: Business India*, 4–17 November 1985)

Asia, as distinct from Europe and the Near East, since in the former if there were no heirs they could be created by the practice of adoption. As a result these family corporations need never die. At the very least, their existence is prolonged a generation and of this the historical record is full of examples at all levels.[8]

Let me take one from India at the present day. In November 1985, *Business India* printed an article headed 'The Decline of the Podars' which presented an account of the problems of a family textile firm in Bombay. The founder, Anandilal (1874–1940), had four sons. When the second (B) died, leaving one son of his own, his elder brother (A, Ramdeo) who had no male offspring, adopted him. The third brother (C) thereupon gave his only son in adoption to the youngest (D), who also had no male offspring. As a result the two grandsons were each eligible to inherit the property of both their 'natural' and adopted fathers. However C had another son, thirteen years after the first, and the symmetry was upset. In 1966 that led to a provisional parting between the two main groups, followed by a definite split two years later that aroused a good deal of bitterness. Although the branches are no longer talking to each other, they still have offices in the same building. That is an important aspect of joint families; common interests may persist even when the talking stops, leading to the possibility of revival at a later time or by the next generation. Meanwhile the second son of C, who is only entitled to a half share of his father's property, broke off from his better-endowed brother in 1983 and is thought to be moving closer to the segment consisting of the descendants of A and B.

This kind of history is not uncommon. Indeed it is predictable demographically. Since a proportion of conjugal families will have no male heirs, the probability of continuity is clearly much greater if male offspring can be redistributed in this way. The alternative can adversely affect long-term planning and encourage the kind of short-term interest in a firm that public shareholders may display. Let me take another

---

[8] I give one example from China. At the beginning of this century the memoirs of a district officer of the British-occupied territory of Weihaiwei provided a striking case. A certain man came before his court saying, 'My rights to the property of Sung Lien-têng are being contested by my distant cousin. I am the rightful owner. I buried Sung Lien-têng and have charge of his soul tablet and carry out the annual ceremonies' (Johnston 1910: 140). It turned out that the man in question, whose property was in dispute, had died childless in 1701 and that the plaintiff's ancestor had in that year defrayed the funeral expenses and acted as chief mourner. By family agreement he was installed as the adopted son to the deceased and heir to his property. The incident demonstrates not only the close link between funerals, property and ancestor worship, but also the 'fictional' continuity that adoption provides and the strong sense of that continuity in the minds of the actors.

example from a textile mill in Ahmadabad. In this case a senior member
of the family had two daughters but did not adopt any sons. Instead he
had two in-marrying sons-in-law who had little taste for business. You
can choose whom to adopt but today it is not always so easy to choose
one's sons-in-law. The subsequent policy of the family firm was strongly
influenced by that man's lack of concern for continuity. Indeed the desire
to sell produced a similar kind of 'close-residence-but-no-talking' split
that occurred among the Podars.

In other words the extended family was not confined to agriculture or
crafts; it was no stranger to complex financial transactions either in the
past or in the present, and its operations continued over the generations.
We have seen the way that craftsmen might transform themselves into
merchants while other merchants inherited long-standing financial
interests. Both categories became leaders in the modern Indian business
class but the latter were especially important during the British colonial
period. For example Kasturbhai Lalbhai, who built up one of the major
mill-owning (and now diversified) businesses in Ahmadabad earlier this
century, was a descendant of the famous Shantidas, jeweller to the
Mughal emperors, Jehangir and Shah Jehan.[9]

On moving into modern industrial production such enterprises
continued to operate as family firms. Nor was this feature in any sense
confined to Gujarat. A study carried out in Madras found that except for
the public-sector industry and one private-sector company, all the
enterprises in the sample consisted of family firms.[10] Once again, the fact
that members of these firms usually lived in 'nuclear' households did not
necessarily indicate a breakdown in the 'joint-family' system because
they continued to maintain many 'joint-family obligations' and constituted 'modified joint households' which arranged marriages, joined
together in domestic worship and sometimes organised the consumption
of food in separate male and female groups.

The same feature seems to be found in Indian families in Africa. In a
comparison of the business family in Kenya, it was found that African
entrepreneurs rarely work with kin whereas Asians frequently do,
although in other ways African societies are dominated by kinship.
The indigenous Africans have land as their principal security while the
immigrant Asians depend upon money and kin. Family finance is a
necessity partly because of the initial lack of long-term banking facilities.
With the establishment of banks the difference is still observable.
What stands out is that Indian business based on kin ties is the more
successful.

[9] Tripatni 1981; Markowits 1985.   [10] Singer 1968: 440.

In India, contemporary family firms are often more complex in structure than the term suggests. Some have gone public, with the family owning only a fraction of the stock. Nevertheless they have maintained control by various devices, of which the most widespread was the managing agency. One of the problems in India was that since banks, both Indian and British, were largely geared to short-term financing, virtually only those Indians capable of raising funds from family or caste circles could undertake industrial development which needed longer-term investment.[11]

That was true of other traders in India, for the family firm was not confined to local inhabitants. At least from the seventeenth century, Armenian traders in Asia, who apparently employed double-entry book-keeping probably learned from the Italians for whom they had acted as intermediaries in the Asian trade, formed companies with limited or mixed liabilities (*commandités*, a limited partnership). As with the *commenda*, these societies were established among kin as well as with outsiders. Indeed kinship was often essential to their continuing activities, which were capitalistic in nature, especially when they had little or no state support. 'This world of traders, geographically dispersed but socially integrated and built without the direct support of any state, gave birth to a commercial capitalism founded largely on the family. Ties of kinship and marriage, as well as of dependence, created relationships of trust. They formed real merchant dynasties, in which the transmission of goods was often guaranteed by marriages between the great families.'[12] Here as elsewhere in the major states of Europe and Asia, daughters as well as sons were entitled to part of the conjugal property, as dowry, as inheritance or as both. Hence their marriages were often of great importance in the process of control and transmission. These also played their part in raising capital and providing personnel; ties of both kinship and marriage supplied the trust that was essential for long-term collaboration.

The Armenians used the same trade routes from the Near East on which many Indian merchants relied, particularly the Muslims and Parsis (Zoroastrian refugees from Persia) who had none of the restraints that some Indian castes placed upon their members. The latter were not meant to travel outside the country, so that when Gandhi came to England for the first time to study law, a special rite had to be performed to release him from this prohibition. As in many other cases, it did not prevent him leaving.

Other merchant houses, using those same routes, were organised in a

[11] Streefkerk 1985: 33.   [12] Aghassian and Kévonian 1985.

similar way. The story of the 'House of Chinoy' is described in the autobiography of Sultan Chinoy (1962). His father, a Muslim Khoja from Kutch, had been found a place by his parents in a firm that did an extensive import–export business with China on the one hand (in opium and hessian) and with Muscat on the other (in pomegranates and kharak). One son, Sultan, was sent off to study while his brother went directly to work – the two activities were seen as going hand in hand. 'My hopes are centered on him', the father wrote, 'for developing our business and enhancing our family.' In 1904, through the good offices of his brother, Sultan was offered the Shell petrol agency by a family friend, a Briton. His father 'decided I should seize it', saying, 'Sultan, now that I'm putting you in business'. No success story, for so it turned out to be, could be farther from that of the independent entrepreneur.

A similar tale is recounted in the biography of Vasantro Dempo who was born in 1916 into a Brahman family in Goa, already one of the largest landowners, who were concerned with the mining of iron ore. Dempo succeeded in building up the shipping interests on an international scale. He came from a Hindu undivided family ruled over by his father's uncle who told him who to marry. This restriction of individual decision-making in certain spheres did not inhibit his entrepreneurial endeavours; indeed the family was the starting point of his whole career. Both Chinoy and Dempo were members of established merchant dynasties who attained individual success as businessmen with the help of their families, though this help often meant submitting to their wishes in terms of career and of marriage.

Managing agencies

We have seen that Indian family firms in the broader sense are not necessarily private. When they go public the family may keep a larger or smaller part of the stock, but even so it can still maintain effective control. Until recently the favoured method was through the 'managing agency' which acted as a subsidiary of a 'parent' company under the family's aegis. The agency then appointed some family members on the board of directors and even in a managing capacity.

The 'managing agency' was an invention of the Indian sub-continent, although it had many parallels elsewhere. These agency houses first arose in Calcutta in the 1830s. European intermediaries collected capital from military and civil officers in India in order to promote trade and make a profit. At first there were many failures but in 1833 the system was regulated by a charter which defined an agency as 'a person, firm or company entitled to the management of the whole affairs of a company, by virtue of an agreement with the company'. In other words, to protect their investments, the agency undertook the management, carrying out research, promoting joint stock, employing funds, raising finance (by acting as guarantors), marketing the produce, buying machinery and stores and running the business. Remuneration for these services came in the form of a fixed sum plus a commission on sales.[13]

While these agencies were first owned and staffed by British personnel, they were later taken over by Indians and membership was generally hereditary.[14] So there was a concentration of power with interlocking directorships in the various enterprises, a species of trust usually created by the expansion of a successful enterprise.

Another major form of joint-stock company came into existence early on in the course of European contact with South India. The joint-stock company was the way in which merchant companies of England and the Netherlands were organised in a development of the earlier types of company found in Italy and the Mediterranean. These European companies fostered the same form of organisation among Indian merchants in order to avoid having to deal with numerous small traders and it was the small traders that favoured the idea rather than the larger merchants of Surat.[15] Such companies, which generally consisted of some five to ten merchants each subscribing between 10,000 and 150,000 pagodas, involved partnerships between two or more joint-family businesses rather than two or more individuals.[16]

The methods of indirect control practised by later managing agencies are familiar in Europe. They emerge in the attempt to deal with the tension that easily arises between financial power and technical expertise. While that problem is already significant for the founders of an enterprise, particularly when it reaches a threshold in growth or in technical complexity, it may be yet more troublesome for those who follow. Modern business corporations separate ownership from control by vesting the former in the shareholders and the latter in the directors. Shareholders may still include the family of the original founder, as well as private individuals and increasingly the 'institutions', especially insurance companies and pension funds. Even a private company may require a degree of of separation between ownership and control for technical reasons. Or some separation may arise because the firm has to go public and offer shares in order to raise additional capital. In either case the Indian managing agency offered a possible solution since it

---

[13] Jha 1963: 153ff.
[14] Jha 1963: 157.   [15] Rungta 1970: 1–2.
[16] A pagoda was a coin usually made of gold, formerly current in south India.

allowed both for a separation of powers and for the retention of an interest by the founding family.

'Collective capitalism'

There is nothing surprising in the involvement of the family in Indian firms, except to some Europeans who have been raised on the Crusoe myth of capitalism being the preserve of the individual entrepreneur. Caste and kinship continue to be important in Indian communities both at home and abroad. If they had been sufficient to prevent or even inhibit the development of capitalism, how is it that so many (Gujarati) shopkeepers, merchants and industrialists have established businesses in east Africa and in many other parts of the world, including present-day England and America? Mercantile capitalism was clearly as important in the East as it was in the West. Europe subsequently developed forms of industrial production, although proto-industrial activities were certainly carried out in India, often by merchants. But whether we are dealing with adaptation or invention, Indian success in these activities has often been achieved with the aid of and not despite these wider ties. While co-operation has mainly taken place at the domestic level, it has not been confined to the nuclear family. More extensive ties of caste or *jati* have also played their part, as among the Marawaris, the Chettiars and the Jains. One example of a caste-like sort comes from the Ismaili community in the English Midlands town of Leicester. When Indians from this Muslim group arrived following their expulsion from east Africa, the sect sent two businessmen from Canada to set up activities, including a petrol station, in which their co-religionists could be employed. The Ismailis are a religious community in which the obligation to help other members is particularly strong. But on a less ambitious scale co-operation takes place among many other groups in that city.

The Indian evidence suggests we need to query the thesis of sociologists and others that the presence of wider kinship ties inhibits 'modernisation'. For extended ties, of family, kin, caste or class, have obvious advantages for certain types of merchant activity. That has been particularly true of bankers in Gujarat, Rajputana and among the Chettiars. In these cases the existence of wide networks of information, hospitality and trust were advantageous, if not intrinsic, to the nature of their activities. As I have suggested, one of the problems in India was that since banks, both Indian and British, were largely geared to short-term financing (even then they sometimes failed, as in Madras in 1906), Indian entrepreneurs were often dependent on raising funds from family or caste circles. I have discussed the support given by joint families but the important operations of Chettiar bankers depended directly upon their caste ties as well as ties among narrower kin. Their banking has given rise to a discussion of the role of joint and nuclear families in financial activities, which led to the wider question of the opposition between collective and individual action. The Japanese sociologist, Shoji Ito, claimed that pre-industrial Nakarattar banking was based on autonomous decision-making powers vested in the conjugal unit or *palli* in a Western-like way; only after the 1930s did the increased scale of industrial investment involve pooling resources in joint families. Another observer, Madhevan, saw a shift as taking place from intra-caste to caste organisation. Rudner on the other hand considers that Chettiar banking has always been carried out by joint-family units, at least among the successful firms. So he denies the validity of the Western comparison, seeing south India as displaying a 'collectivist spirit of capitalism' rather than the individualistic spirit held to obtain in the West.[17]

He is almost certainly correct about the earlier activity of Chettiar bankers. But to characterize societies as individualistic or collectivist, as marked by conjugal or joint families, is too exclusive a way to describe this situation. We are presented with unrealistic alternatives. Both simple and complex family structures exist in all societies, since they are part of the developmental cycle of domestic groups. Their proportions differ in ways that are related among other things to the political economy. In India consumption groups, households, are on average little if any larger than in other parts of Eurasia. In comparison with the West the extended family, the offspring of common grandparents, plays a greater part in everyday interaction, sometimes as a HUF, normally in less formal ways. Beyond that lie the wider kinship ties of lineage or *jati* which tend to lose some of their importance in new urban situations. Contrary to the hypothesis of many Western writers, the 'extended' domestic units and the wider caste or kinship groups, far from inhibiting the growth of the economy, often play a critical role in commercial and industrial activities. Nor was this phenomenon confined to India.

Family and business in China and Japan

A similar dependency on kin exists in businesses throughout the East. In the Ming and Qing periods Faure sees the Chinese lineage and the family as providing 'some basic structures for business operations'. However it was the family that was involved in commercial operations,

---

[17] Rudner 1992.

following the pattern of family farming, though if the scale increased they might hire professional managers or go into partnership, which were especially prominent in salt- and coal-mining. This is exactly what we find in the Mediterranean *commenda* or in earlier Babylonian partnerships, which were not necessarily confined to kin, though these generally formed the basis of such units especially where trust was at a premium. Lineage members might cluster around a successful merchant, these ties being recognised as 'the most fundamental relationships in economic organization, not only for consumption but also for production and trade'.[18] Faure points to the commonly acknowledged difference between lineage and family, that one is lasting and solidary, the other temporary and divisive; one focuses on ancestors, the other on the domestic group. However he also recognises that if family land remained undivided it could act as a peg for establishing a branch of the lineage. As a business enterprise the lineage in Canton did not engage directly in commerce but did aim to realise a regular profit on its corporate estate, which consisted largely of land but could also include rural markets, shop premises, kilns and foundries, as well as ferries and uncultivated land. The lineage did not farm these lands directly but rented them out to members of the lineage as tenants. The profits were shared in ancestral sacrifices only between those members of the lineage who had contributed to setting up the estate.

Following Weber and Braudel, Faure suggests that Chinese businesses did not keep capital accounts. That he argues on the basis of sixteenth-century sources; and in the 1930s a survey of Cantonese practices noted that shops did not record the movement of goods in as great detail as cash transactions, relying on rules of thumb for the distribution of profits. He sees this absence as being connected with the absence of corporate, property-holding structures in family mercantile operations and with the personal nature of business undertakings. Following this Weberian argument, he goes on to point out the link that sociologists have made between family enterprise, personal connections and traditional methods of accounting on the one hand and joint-stock ownership, limited liability and capital accounting on the other, suggesting that 'much of the development of Western business from the sixteenth century to the nineteenth century can be written in the framework of the growth of the latter set of relationships from the former'.[19] The contrast seems too heavily drawn. The 'family' that conducted commercial operations might well have as its core a minor lineage, with an extended family including even cousins and their sons, though management was devolved on one

---

[18] Faure 1989.   [19] Faure 1989: 360.

man. This unit was eventually bound to split, involving the separation of ownership from management. Faure calls attention to 'the uncertainty of investment when the business could not transcend the person of the merchant and the resultant identification of the family (*chia*) with the business operations of its head'.[20] Of course partnerships, whether with kin or outsiders, obviated this problem to some extent since they entailed a measure of continuity even if one partner disappeared. Indeed Faure seems to exaggerate the ephemeral nature of family business, which may persist over several generations, quite long enough to give an ample return on an investment.

However this may be, Faure recognises the potentiality of the Chinese economy in other ways. It was perfectly capable of developing a futures market even before the establishment of England's 'equally speculative' stock market, but Faure sees a move in this direction as destroyed by the trend towards the imperial grants of monopoly, for example in the salt trade.[21] Nevertheless the underlying potentiality is obviously realised in the active capitalist markets of Taiwan and Hong Kong which are heavily dependent on family ties that do not seem to inhibit development. On the contrary, in Taiwan, apart from government enterprises and foreign-owned corporations, an estimated 97 per cent of all firms are familial in form; even of the largest 100 business groups, 82 were dominated by familial kin groups.[22] These family enterprises are sometimes run by rural joint families that have one wing in the country and one in the town. Family firms are also dominant in the financially based concerns of Hong Kong. A characteristic of overseas Chinese enterprise has been this family component. Some have seen this element as linked to Confucianism which holds 'familism' as a central tenet, just as Weber and his followers have seen ascetic Protestantism as doing a similar job for individualism in the West.[23] In other words the specific content of the economic ethic may be less important than its validation by the prevailing religious or ideological system, whatever that may be. However the Indian evidence makes this whole argument seem questionable. Moreover, adjacent parts of mainland China, not notably Confucian since the victory of Communism forty years ago, have seen very rapid rates of growth. Since Deng Xiaoping's reforms of 1979, the southern Chinese province of Guangdong has experienced a real growth of 12.5 per cent a year, compared with 7.5 per cent in Thailand. This development centres upon the Special Economic Zone of Shenzhen, a city that has increased in size over the same period from less than

---

[20] Faure 1989: 356. [21] Faure 1989: 365.
[22] Greenhalgh 1987. [23] Redding 1990: 2.

100,000 to 2 million inhabitants, with an average gross domestic product per person of near $2,000 per year and an average annual increase in individual output, trade and foreign investment of 40 per cent. Nor is the growth confined to the privileged zone; it covers a large part of Guangdong. Everywhere much is owed to the 'neighbourhood effect', the transfer of capital and know-how from Hong Kong, often to distant family members, but it is local entrepreneurs who make the going.[24] The same use of family ties is very much a feature of the rapid take-off in Hong Kong, Taiwan and elsewhere among overseas Chinese communities. But long before these modern developments lineage funds in south China were used for mercantile and other investments.[25]

The role of the lineage in China is connected with the significance of ancestor worship. Neither are hang-overs from primitive society. It is in part a consequence of the deliberate rejection of the world religions, especially Buddhism (though Buddhist temples like Taoist ones continued to be repositories for the memories if not the remains of the dead). The threatened dominance of the Buddhist 'church' over the state and over the economy, which actually occurred in Tibet, was counter-acted by a return to Confucianism with its stress on family, lineage and ancestors. That stress persists today, when the deposition in the grave and the memorial in the temple continue to play a highly significant role in many families in Hong Kong that are vigorously engaged in the commercial economy. In other words ancestor worship involves not simply a survival from earlier forms of social organisation but a deliberate rejection of the accumulative church which tried to take so much in so short a time.

In many cases these enterprises in the Chinese diaspora are often small and family based. It is sometimes argued that they *have* to remain small. The reasons given are partly organisational, partly because of the tensions within families which lead them to split and partly because over the longer term direct family lines die out owing to the absence of heirs or to their lack of interest. Examples have already been given of how this last possibility can be avoided by adopting one of the possible mechanisms of continuity. In pre-industrial societies about 20 per cent of couples will end up with no heir and another 20 per cent with daughters but no sons. If males are thought to be necessary for continuity (for example, for the continuity of the enterprise), then plural marriage is one possibility for producing additional children when the first wife has not succeeded. Otherwise the problem in 20 per cent of the cases can

---

[24] 'The South China Miracle', *The Economist*, 5 October 1991.
[25] Rudner 1992; Faure 1989.

be solved by bringing in a son-in-law to marry a daughter. In the other 20 per cent, where there are no children at all, another strategy is adoption. That mechanism has only recently been available in Europe and has been little used for the purposes of continuity since it was rejected under early Christianity. Its virtual absence forms one of the characteristic differences between Eastern and Western family firms; such enterprises in India and Japan have a greater continuity because they adopt kin rather than relying on the lottery of procreation alone.[26]

Regarding family tensions, these have been prominent in some of the examples discussed. But they are of course the reverse side of family solidarity and trust, which is one of the major advantages of the family firm. Moreover while the family may split and the split may signal the end of one joint family, it is also the beginning of two others; fission changes the existing structure but it does not necessarily destroy continuity. The overarching kinship framework can be put in abeyance but not easily erased. In any case tensions occur between unrelated partners and these may be more difficult to overcome.

Thirdly, when family enterprises become large scale, organisational difficulties certainly arise. But when such firms get larger, they normally mix kin and professional managers, as in the Indian agency system. That is also the case with the well-known Japanese conglomerates. The development of business in Japan from 1880 took place in a country where banking and mercantile activity was already well advanced long before the Meiji Restoration of 1868. Already in Tokugawa times, Japan had a complex credit system for dealing in rice, including 'futures'. A rice exchange as well as a sort of clearing market was operating in Osaka in 1730, some forty-three years before the founding of the stock exchange in London.[27] Forms of paper transaction including cheques and bills of exchange were to be found in Japan.[28] The motivation too was in place. A seventeenth-century source announces that 'We are merchants motivated by a spirit of independence and self-reliance'.[29] Trade opened up the possibility of increasing one's social status. Merchants displayed a high regard for frugality and diligence, and the term *shimatsu* is translated by Takenaka as 'economic rationalism'. For this end the calculation (*san'nyō*) of the profit and loss was essential. Indeed he claims that book-keeping methods, which reached 'a high level', included 'double-entry bookkeeping by which property accounts were discriminated from profit

---

[26] See Goody 1976, 1983 and 1990 for a more detailed discussion of these mechanisms.

[27] Takenaka 1969: 149.

[28] Takenaka speaks of cheques (1969: 148). They also existed in the Ottoman Empire as well as in India.

[29] Takenaka 1969: 152. See the teachings of Ishida Baigan (1685–1744).

and loss accounts'.[30] It was an activity that, based on monetisation, inevitably encouraged equality and liberty in transactions.

After the Restoration the lower Samurai who carried it out provided much of the steam behind the process of modernisation. By 1884 every fifth Japanese household belonged to the 'business sector'.[31] Factories sprang up everywhere in the countryside. Encouraged by the government and sometimes being started centrally, they were later sold off to the private sector. The manufacture of cotton yarn was a strong focus of attention because it constituted 30 per cent of all imports. A mechanical mill, using water power, had already been established before the Restoration and by 1884 there were some twenty spinning mills. At that time the Osaka mill was founded to employ steam power and the latest technology to work over 10,000 spindles. With this break-through 'Japan first entered the world market as equal competitive partner'.[32]

Earlier merchant activity had largely been carried out in kinship units, that is, in the *ie*, a term that referred to the house, to the family as well as the business. In the West, too, reference is made to business houses, to *les grandes maisons*. But in London, for example, there appear to have been more rapid changes of the name and ownership of firms.[33] The family firms of Tokugawa Japan on the other hand displayed remarkable continuity for the reasons just discussed. While in theory primogeniture prevailed, in practice succession had to be flexible if it was to be successful. In the first place a capable manager might become the son-in-law of the boss (a phenomenon that is common enough throughout the world of affairs on a less formal basis). In the second, if neither a son nor a daughter were available, then 'a manager or some capable guild member could be adopted to continue the business'; such ties might come second to 'blood' but they were nevertheless transformed into kinship by a 'legal fiction'.

As in India, merchants in Tokugawa Japan have been compared to those of Renaissance Italy. Others have argued that they were too conservative and lacked the 'liberal' mentality, which made it more difficult for them to lead the take-off to industrial growth. That such a take-off was assisted by the intervention of foreigners and the overthrow of the Shogunate is correct; but its basis had already been laid by these (mainly) family enterprises. When industrialisation developed, the

---

[30] Takenaka 1969: 153. I know of no other evidence for double-entry in Japan, unless among the Dutch, but we have seen that a form existed in China.

[31] Hirschmeier and Yui 1975: 103.

[32] Hirschmeier and Yui 1975: 109.   [33] Hirschmeier and Yui 1975: 38.

family continued to play a very important role, even in large firms such as the *zaibatsu*.

Japanese business consisted of three main types of firm:

1. the *zaibatsu*, a group of diversified businesses owned *exclusively* by a single family or extended family;
2. the joint stock company;
3. the small business under owner-management, which was especially prominent in the fields of building, civil engineering, publishing, retailing, medicine and cosmetics.

A major role in modernisation was played by the *zaibatsu* which were largely family firms in origin which spread into a variety of different fields, financing this expansion themselves and so keeping ownership concentrated. Some of these groups had long been established at the time of the Meiji Restoration. Some had made a fortune as government contractors and it was these funds that in the 1880s were invested in the new enterprises. Many of the families moved from finance and mining to shipping, shipbuilding and metal-making, some forming trading companies and establishing banks. These mutually supporting multi-business concerns recruited salaried managers and supplied capital for new ventures. The original family sometimes retired from active management, but retained ultimate ownership and control.[34] Indeed some of these family firms were more concerned to recruit talented salaried managers than other firms, either in Japan or in other countries. While ownership was concentrated, and central control maintained, they encouraged flexibility and independent management in the constituent enterprises.

Some Houses, such as Mitsui, divided in such a way as to give owner-ship but not management to the sons. But the customary procedure was to divide the *noren*, the dark blue cloth which hung in front of the entrance and bore the name of the store. That cloth was synonymous with the House itself, so that its division was equivalent to setting up branch Houses (*bunke*) according to the rule of thumb practised in Osaka whereby six parts went to the elder and four parts to the younger.[35]

The Mitsui *zaibatsu* had formerly been government purveyors. Like many larger firms, it deliberately incorporated 'familism' into business as a means of combating socialist ideas. Around 1900 the House Consti-tution was rewritten and their meeting was described in the following terms: 'All members of the eleven joint families assembled, prostrated themselves before the ancestral tablets, and took the oath to keep to the teachings of the ancestors day and night, and to work so that the glory of

[34] Morikawa 1992.   [35] Hirschmeier and Yui 1975: 39.

the Mitsui House be handed over to the next generations.'[36] While the various Mitsui companies were joint-stock companies with unlimited partnership (*gōmei*), they were owned by the family through a holding company, members of which held the ceremonial position of president. So, whereas management was in professional hands, ownership remained in the family.

Because of the role of the company in politics, the family largely withdrew, selling part of the stock. After the war it was American policy to dissolve these large corporations, which were seen as supporting the military establishment. In 1946, twenty-eight such holding companies with family control were disbanded. Mitsui's assets were frozen and its securities sold. That split led to a polarisation between the bigger firms and the smaller, unregulated ones carrying out subcontracting and often organised on a family basis. However, even after these firms had been divided, their managers still maintained close contact with one another; the ties that had existed within the earlier House did not entirely disappear, although they were no longer family ties in the strict sense.

If the importance of wider ties diminished in time, the family, sometimes the extended family, continued to be important. As we have seen the notion that these institutions inhibited or prevented modernisation is associated with the name of Max Weber, though it is widespread in sociological circles. It has been remarked that 'his main interest is in the family as an important obstacle to the development of rationalised capitalism'.[37] In his comparative study of China and of India he emphasised that 'the family structure, especially the corporate kin group ("sib"), throttled capitalist development'. 'The great achievement of the ethical religions', Weber declares, 'above all of the ethical and ascetical sects of Protestantism, was to shatter the fetters of the sib.'[38] That shattering certainly occurred in the West, less so in other world religions, but it happened under Catholicism centuries before the Reformation.

However, while he was wrong about the role of lineage and caste, he did recognise that of the family in early entrepreneurial activity. In fact he remarked that the 'family is everywhere the oldest unit of supporting continuous trading activity, in China and Babylonia, in India and in the early Middle Ages. The son of a trading family was the confidential clerk and later the partner of the father'. Theoretically he never reconciled this recognition of the contribution of the family with his insistence on individualism and bureaucracy. He might have referred to the distinction between political and mercantile capitalism on the one hand and modern

---

[36] Hirschmeier and Yui 1975: 208.
[37] Collins 1986: 267.   [38] Weber [1916] 1951: 237.

industrial capitalism on the other. For he claimed the latter required 'rational' performance (e.g. in accounting) and universalistic criteria for recruitment to the firm, including, others have maintained, the joint-stock company. Not only does that assertion raise problems of definition and periodisation that continue to hamper the analysis, but the family is prominent both in ancient and in modern capitalism.

It was American versions of modernisation theory, pursuing the Crusoe myth, that overlooked the earlier qualification about the family and went yet further in a 'logical' analysis, opposing the role of achievement (under capitalism) to that of ascription (under previous régimes); the first was characterised by bureaucratic recruitment, the second by eligibility based on kinship. Moreover many sociologists, demographers and social historians have seen an 'affinity' between the small elementary family, the stress on achievement and industrialisation. That is a constant theme. Take one example of a view of the process of modernisation in the East based on Weberian and Parsonian theory. In discussing China Levy concluded that 'modern industry and the "traditional" Chinese family are mutually subversive'. Why? Because 'the "traditional" Chinese family was a highly particularistic structure and it dominated all training in the society save that for the bureaucracy, the one sphere in Chinese society of institutionalized universalism'.[39] Within the firm, particularism means nepotism in recruitment, whereas in capitalist enterprise one has to recruit steam-shovel operators on the basis of their capacity or achievement. In the same way the purchase and sale of commodities have to be open, maximising activities, not part of reciprocal gift-giving.

Such assertions fit the ideological bias of the West. But they do not accord either with the empirical facts or with indigenous models of the East. How did this contradiction arise? How did this myth originate? Levy's account gives some idea. Under factory production the workers are 'on their own'; they need to be mobile to meet varying labour demands. What about the owners? We need to radically distinguish the family needs of the two groups. Levy is again overinfluenced by Weberian notions of bureaucracy which stress achievement, objectively assessed, as well as by the notion of an overall development, an excluding progression, of family firms into impersonal joint-stock companies. The emergence of this form of organisation constituted an important development, especially for large firms who wanted to raise capital from the public in general. But it did not exclude the participation of the family. In any case, most new enterprises have to start off on an

[39] Levy [1949] 1963: 354.

individual or family basis; even at the beginning it is often difficult to disentangle parental and conjugal capital, while in the process of time the individual enterprise will usually become a family one. That is part of the developmental cycle in businesses.

The joint-stock company has been defined as the motivating power behind economic development in the West.[40] That is the orthodoxy of business theory, of the Harvard Business School model. In fact the kind of joint-stock company that engaged in the east India trade was susceptible to important criticisms both in England and in Holland with the result that after the collapse of the South Sea Bubble they were prohibited, just as *zaibatsu* were prohibited by the Americans after the Second World War, and in another way just as family businesses were recently suppressed by nationalisation in many European countries. Secondly they seem to have served not so much as a centralised company (the centralised personnel were few) but as an umbrella for a series of merchants working on a more familial basis.

Familial recruitment and participation may have its disadvantages but it also has its positive features, not only in raising private capital, but in maximising trust, loyalty and in long-term planning over the generations, as well as in motivating the entrepreneur. That is the reason why inheritance tax for small businesses has been limited in Britain and elsewhere, while a confiscatory taxation on egalitarian grounds may have led to the lack of motivation to accumulate in some former socialist countries.

The accepted opposition between the closed (family) systems of the East and the open (joint-stock) systems of the West lies behind Morikawa's study of the Japanese *zaibatsu*. 'The closed system, featuring family ownership, has in the West been associated with a lack of innovation and entrepreneurship and has in fact been regarded as a hindrance to economic development',[41] whereas in Japan a particular type of family enterprise, the *zaibatsu*, provided much of the impetus for the country's modern economic development. It is this opposition that leads Chandler in introducing Morikawa's book to talk of a different form of capitalism, a common theme among business historians. Undoubtedly there are as many differences of organisation as of social context. It is not part of my intention to minimise these but only to point to some common features in commercial and industrial development, and to warn against the attempt to define different 'capitalisms' holistically and by means of binary opposition. To regard the East's development as having been impeded by the family is fundamentally

---

40 Morikawa 1992: xvi.   41 Morikawa 1992: xvii.

wrong. There one of the most significant motivations in creating and especially in managing and continuing a business has been dynastic. While there has been a directional move towards 'open' firms, that is in no way an excluding development.

If Western theorists have been so wrong about the role of family, caste and kinship in the development of commerce and industry in the East, is it not time to look once again at the empirical roots of these statements in their own political economy? How far were these based on folk beliefs about 'the other'? Was there an ethnocentric overvaluation of their own achievements leading the West to insist on revolutionary systemic differences and upon categorical distinctions in a situation where the East was much closer to their own practices than they were ready to acknowledge? How far did the prejudiced perception of oriental society distort Western social theory in general? In the next chapter I pursue this argument for the history and sociology of the family.

In the previous chapter we have seen the major contributions that the family, the extended family and even the wider caste or lineage made to social and economic development in the East. That was the case not only with mercantile activity but also with the development of industrial capitalism, certainly in its early phases. Maintaining the belief that the growth of Western capitalism was marked by individualism, some have discerned in the East a different form of capitalism, based on a collectivist spirit or else upon Confucianism with its emphasis on family ties.

Without wishing to underestimate the differences in the systems of kinship, marriage and the family in the major Eurasian societies, I have earlier (1990) tried to suggest that at the domestic level these are less dramatic than is conveyed by contrasting 'elementary' with 'complex' (Lévi-Strauss), hierarchical with 'individualistic' or egalitarian (Dumont), or yet by the contrasts drawn by many demographic historians, less dramatic that is from the standpoint of contemporary developments in the economy which are not inhibited but often promoted by prevailing family forms.

How is it then that in Europe we have made the opposite assumptions, both about the barriers that the Eastern family has offered to economic advance and about the unimportance of the family in the economic sphere under capitalism? To answer these questions we need to turn to the history and historiography of the family in the West.

Family and kinship

The phrase 'history of the family' is used mainly by historians of Europe studying the modern period – and it roughly corresponds to the field of the sociology of the family. Anthropologists looking at other societies have usually referred to the study of kinship and marriage. I want to suggest that much is lost intellectually by this implied division, the acceptance of which means that neither field becomes truly comparative. Moreover that separation inhibits not only our comprehension of past,

162

and of distant, societies, but important aspects of the present. It was responsible for some of the difficulties encountered in the previous chapter and hampers the understanding of the role of the family and kinship in contemporary developments in the rest of the world, not only in the economy, but in social life more generally and in population control in particular.

The common division between family (sociology) and kinship (anthropology) is not simply a separation of academic fields, it also involves concealed judgements that tend to distort what we are doing and thinking. If this was only a matter of arbitrary academic disciplines, it would be bad enough, especially given the vested interest in the labels that overshadow the softer forms of knowledge as they are taught in universities, even in those places where deliberate attempts have been made to break through what in intellectual terms is often an archaic classification. It is not difficult to show how the fact that history and sociology had usually phrased its problems in terms of the family and anthropology in terms of kinship has weakened the conceptual apparatus of both fields; but that is not my immediate concern.

For what is more important is the way it has distorted the understanding of domestic groups, both in terms of static comparison and of historical analysis. At one level the reason is obvious enough. Sociologists, specialists in industrial cultures, study the family; anthropologists, who deal in 'other cultures', study kinship. That implies that the family is what we have, kinship is what others have. The family, specifically the nuclear family, is what marks industrial societies; kinship, extended kinship, is what marks the other. Indeed, a recent analysis of household structure by world-system theorists has claimed that 'households', though defined in a special way, only exist under capitalism.[1]

This notion of the separation between kinship and the family was not generated by the development of the academic disciplines of sociology and anthropology alone. It was there in much earlier periods and goes back, in its essentials, to the we–they situation, and in particular to the amazement which has struck all human groups when face to face with the practices of others different from their own. Among the LoDagaa, a group in northern Ghana with whom I lived, it was the duty of the brother of a dead man to inherit (i.e. marry) his widow and to breed children in his name, an aspect of the solidarity of siblings and of collective responsibilities. It is a practice known to anthropologists as the levirate, found in the Bible (in both the Old and the New Testaments), practised by Jewish communities in eastern Europe until recently, but

---

[1] Smith *et al.* 1984.

forbidden under canon law, in whatever form. It was this prohibition from which the Pope dispensed Henry VIII so that shortly after his accession in 1509 he could marry Catherine of Aragon, the widow of his dead brother, Arthur; and it was upon the question of whether the Pope had the power to give a dispensation for what Henry claimed was a divine injunction that his quarrel with the Church centred. That contributed to England becoming a Protestant country with specific marriage rules which lasted until the nineteenth century. I make this comment to show that we are not dealing with some practice characterising 'primitive' societies alone which has to be explained in the context of barbarism or savagery, to use the terms made current by L. H. Morgan, but one that is relevant to some of the major societies of the modern world.

Returning to northern Ghana, the group in question encouraged this form of marriage. So too did their neighbours, the Dagaba. But the latter also permitted a man to inherit, that is, marry a widow of his father's, providing she was not his biological mother. This my local friends regarded as horrifying, using the same phrase (*be sogna pɔɔ*) as they would for adultery or other sexual offences like incest, since it involved sleeping with a mother, that is, a 'classificatory' mother (as indeed she was terminologically to both groups). But to my friends it was incest, *incasta*, unchaste, just as widow inheritance itself was viewed under the prohibited degrees of the Church of England that appeared in every Book of Common Prayer, and just as it had earlier been in canon law.

Similar attitudes to the permitted practices of other people occurred in the ancient and classical Near East where the Bible's condemnation of the abominations of the Egyptians referred to customs (including marriage to sisters) which the Israelites no longer practised, though they once had done so. And it was feelings not so much of horror but of strangeness that European observers often felt when they came into contact with the Indians of America, their first real colonial subjects. They were struck, for example, by their 'classificatory' terminologies (as in the works of the Jesuit Father, Lafitau, among the Iroquois) which they took as characterising not only a type of wider kin group, the clan or lineage, but as a form of society in which all clansmen were 'brothers', and the mothers of all brothers were 'mothers', and their wives, 'wives'; that is, 'wives' and 'brothers' not simply terminologically, not only in specific contexts of co-operation, like brotherhood among fellow members of a trade union, but in many other ways. So the academic world was presented with reconstructions drawn up by intelligent men like McLennan and L. H. Morgan, lawyers mostly, of primitive forms of marriage, including group marriage, which supposedly stood at the opposite pole from Victorian monogamy. Between the two poles, a number of transitional forms of marriage, polygyny and polyandry, were visualised in a unilineal sequence, one giving way to the other. And these collective forms of marriage possessed their own terminologies, 'classificatory' as distinct from the 'individualising' ones of the contemporary West, just as they had larger domestic groups (extended families, living in long-houses in the case of the Iroquois) compared with the smaller ones (nuclear families) of our own society.[2] As is well known, the version of this sequence propounded by the American lawyer, L. H. Morgan, in *Ancient Society* had its influence on Marx and Engels. But the ideas have also influenced and at the same time reflected the thinking of a large number of other historians and sociologists down to the present.

Individual and collective

The Whiggish notion of an overall move from collective to individualising forms, whether of marriage, kin terms, lineages or households, is not only reminiscent of but is part and parcel of a much wider view of the development of human society which is embodied, for example, in the idea of a shift from communal systems of land tenure to freehold, or from what Marx spoke of as primitive communism to the individual maximisation of the entrepreneur under capitalism. These supposed movements have their affinities with other dichotomising views of cultural history, involving the long-term change from *Gemeinschaft* to *Gesellschaft*, from status to contract, from ascription to achievement.

Most of these dichotomies had a vectorial element about them. They were accounting for where we had got to, with our knowledge systems, our economy, our polity and in some cases our religion. They had a basis in popular perceptions that were not merely egocentric or ethnocentric, for in the nineteenth century they had some limited basis in historical reality.

But not much. Or rather the nature of the dichotomies, firstly as simplifying devices and secondly as ego-based (Western) ones, led to analytic problems of considerable dimensions. Nowhere have these problems been more apparent than in the historiography of the English, and, to some extent, the American family. Why? Because as members of the first industrial nation, the leading spirits in world capitalism, not only the English themselves but writers like Marx and Weber, wanted to know

---

[2] This rough formulation does not do complete justice to Morgan's concept of a classificatory terminology but it approximates to it.

why they were first and what the consequences were, in this instance in terms of family relations.

Given the praise paid to the entrepreneur, the self-made man who is the hero of countless novels, it is not surprising that one of the features that were thought both to moderate and to accompany capitalism was a stress on the individual as distinct from the collectivity. The family was clearly a collectivity of sorts and had functions at the domestic level. But the smaller it was and the less relevant to the macrostructure of society the better. Hence the opposition between kinship and family.

Objections to such statements have nothing necessarily to do with the relativistic or universalistic arguments adopted by many anthropologists. Many important changes in systems of kinship, marriage and the family have taken place over time, just as such changes have obviously occurred in the political economy; indeed at times the two are related. The basic problem lies in the understanding of kinship and in the way that these changes have been conceptualised, explicitly by social scientists, implicitly (and hence perhaps more insidiously) by historians, at two interlinked levels. Firstly, the polarities are often seen as opposites, communal versus individual, extended versus nuclear, kinship versus family. These oppositions are often inappropriate and the types of formation which they are held to characterise are rarely if ever exclusive or stable: that is to say, there is a developmental cycle through which domestic groups pass over the years. We would generally be better off talking of more of this and less of that, in other words of variables rather than dichotomies. While changes are obviously qualitative, they have to be measured and assessed, not simply seen as a shift from A to B, from black to white.

Secondly, the shift from one state to the other is too often seen not as a gradient but a 'revolution', as Sir Henry Maine called the general change he perceived from status to contract. In its aphoristic simplicity his statement neglected the fact that even though we can discern an important difference, some contractual relations exist in all human societies, however simple, some status relations in all advanced ones. If a revolution of this kind occurred (as distinct from a more gradual but stepped evolution), it involved a change of degree. The seed of change had already been sown. However, a more serious objection is that such 'revolutions' are too often associated with the transformation that only *we* (not *they*) have undergone, the transformation (possibly in the plural) that is variously referred to as industrialisation (versus pre-industrial), capitalism (versus pre-capitalist), modernisation (versus traditional).

When that transformation is seen as occurring in one particular part of the world, namely in that of the writer, it is often allocated a historical inevitability by an appeal to preceding conditions. Only in Europe, specifically in western Europe (or was it in England?), did the right preconditions exist for such a development. On the most general level of analysis the contention is redundant, superfluous and circular, especially when it is claimed that the right cluster of (unweighted, unmeasured) variables were to be found nowhere else. That is necessarily true. All groups are 'unique' in certain ways, as are all individuals. But, like individuals, they have features in common. The problem comes in specifying and measuring particular features or variables that are relevant to change. One difficulty is that too often these factors are seen as attached to moral values or to primordial characteristics of our personal, social or religious life, that other nations could not hope to emulate, though that is problematic only if they are seen as preconditions.

The nuclear family and the small household: consequences or prerequisites?

Here we come to a parting of the analytic ways, of the path of analysis, both in history and in sociology. For there is profound disagreement about whether certain features associated with capitalism (again I use the word as shorthand) were preconditions or consequences. Take the case of the 'nuclear family'. In this context what is usually meant is a small household based on one conjugal pair, one couple (married or mated). A long tradition in sociology has seen this type of family (or more usually its 'dominance') as the consequence of the Industrial Revolution, associated with the need for a mobile labour force (or less frequently with the individualising effect of different wage packets received by one man or woman as against another). It used to be suggested that this revolution led to a shift from an extended family to a nuclear or elementary one, again meaning a co-residential group or household. Indeed, as we have seen, in the nineteenth century there was even an argument about whether or not earlier 'primitive' peoples had a family at all. Not preindustrial Europe of course; so-called peasant societies were recognised as having families around which the farming economy revolved. But the first book by Bronislaw Malinowski, one of the founders of modern social anthropology, was entitled *The Family among the Australian Aborigines*. Written in 1913, it aimed to show, contrary to much contemporary thinking, that even these hunters and gatherers had 'families' as well as those more inclusive groups known as 'clans' and 'hordes', and treated as kinship.

The 'virtual universality of the family' became accepted dogma. Nevertheless *extended* families were still thought to be characteristic of pre-industrial societies in contrast to those of the contemporary world. However in the 1960s the historical demographic work on England carried out by Laslett and the Cambridge Group showed that, since evidence became available at the beginning of the sixteenth century, households had always been 'small'. And they were even presumed to have been so in the medieval period. In a well-known paper, revised in 1972, Laslett wrote: 'There is no sign of the large, extended co-residential family group of the traditional peasant world giving way to the small nuclear, conjugal household of modern industrial society.'[3] In England the former had never existed. Note that he is speaking of residence rather than relationships.

So that what others had regarded as one of the consequences of capitalism was now seen to be part of earlier English society; the country that first experienced the Industrial Revolution did not have to reorganise this aspect of its family life. Indeed the assumption was made that this and other features of family and marriage in England, what Hajnal referred to as the European marriage pattern, meaning the western European one, actively contributed to this process. For example, the small elementary family (often described by the scientists' term 'nuclear') was thought to provide for closer, more affectionate, more loving interactions between parents and children, while the late age of marriage for both men and women, and the associated presence of large numbers of unmarried 'life-cycle' servants who worked for a period before marrying, encouraged mobility as well as enabling women to accumulate towards a dowry. Love, mobility and accumulation were all considered to be important features in the development of the modern family and of economic relations.

There are too many threads in this tapestry to unravel in a short space, especially as I want to treat other features seen as linked to this process of modernisation. The facts have been challenged by Razi as far as the earlier period is concerned.[4] What he tried to show was that between the thirteenth and fifteenth centuries, the central part of England (central southern, midland and northern) was marked by extended families until three decades after the plague, which changed the land–human ratios. After that families became nuclearised, as had earlier been the case in East Anglia where the process began in the thirteenth century. The land–human bond was loosened by the number of serfs who were moving from the manor to gain their freedom (unlike Languedoc and Tuscany where they were already free).[5] In both areas most households

---

[3] Laslett 1972: 126.
[4] Razi 1993.   [5] Razi 1993: 38.

Table 6.1. *Mean size of households*

India	5.2
Africa	3.5–5.2 (according to country)
China (Guangdong)	3.5
Japan	4.9[6]

Source: United Nations' census and Nakane 1972.

were conjugal (nuclear). What the nuclearisation of the family means to Razi is lacking kin in the same manor with whom one could co-operate. However the change was not unilinear because in the sixteenth century population growth and land shortage must, he argues, have led to an increase in kin density.

Let me first turn to the question of the size of household, since this can be subjected to numerical analysis. In an article in the first composite publication of the Cambridge Group in 1972 I tried to show that it was not simply England that had small households. Laslett showed that the average figure for that country between the sixteenth and the nineteenth centuries was 4.75. But average figures for other parts of the contemporary world from recent UN census material are not very different, as Table 6.1 shows.

It is true that in some parts of the world, Africa for example, households were sometimes larger. One of the largest averages I have found was among the LoWiili of west Africa where my census showed an average of 16.45 for the dwelling group (compound or 'houseful') in 1950, a time that was experiencing very rapid growth in population. However these households were subdivided into smaller domestic groups, often into smaller productive and consumption groups, with farming groups (the equivalent of 'household') having an average of 10.21, consisting of roughly two males and 0.5 young men who actually did the major farming tasks.[7] Conjugal groups ('families' in one sense) were obviously smaller but in any case all such groups followed a developmental cycle and could easily split. Leaving such extremes aside, until the twentieth century England was not substantially different from other European countries, designated as 'peasant', nor yet from other parts of the world variously designated 'Asiatic', Third World or even 'primitive'.

Change happened rapidly in England at the turn of the twentieth

[6] Between the seventeenth century and 1955, Nakane 1972.
[7] Goody 1956: 31, 43.

century. The mean household size was 4.60 in 1891, fell to 4.49 in 1901 and then decreased further until it was 3.04 in 1961.[8] Note that France had already reached 3.7 by 1880–1, while the USA remained at 5.00. Since the former was often considered less economically developed than England, the latter becoming more so, both figures appear to contradict the major hypothesis. In England the later changes were largely due to falling fertility and mortality. But it is interesting to observe how late they took place in relation to the industrial changes. Indeed the proportion of servants in the population shows a more dramatic drop, somewhat earlier and closer in time to the advent of industrialisation: the proportion of servants in the British population was 6.60 per cent in 1870 (an increase from 1831), 4.7 per cent in 1881 and 0.4 per cent in 1951.[9] How far was the absence of servants linked with falling fertility, at least in the middle classes?

What is of most relevance to our present argument is the negligible difference in household size between the USA in 1880 and India at the present time. If we are thinking of the conditions needed to promote capitalism (and they are of course multiple), there is little to differentiate a large number and variety of societies in terms of the mean size of their households. England and indeed the West were hardly unique.

Extended ties of kinship

Where there is a difference between East and West is in the rarity in Europe of clans and lineages of the kind widespread in the East. Not only were these descent groups rare but there was a difference in the degree of the extension and elaboration of wider (kinship) ties, variables which are more difficult to measure because they concern content as well as form, quality as well as quantity. Of course extra-household, extra-'familial' ties of kinship exist in all societies. Few are nowadays so blind as to imagine that, even in America, such relationships stop at the boundaries of the household or the conjugal family, although the myth of the log cabin may define the entrepreneur as a loner battling against the forces of wild nature or of established culture. Ties of siblinghood, parenthood and filiation relate men and women in different households, though they may not be living in the same dwelling or even neighbourhood. Some attention has recently been given to the reunions of American kin on an even wider basis.[10] Of course such wider ties exist in association with

---

[8] Laslett 1972: 138.
[9] Laslett 1972: 157.
[10] Ayoub 1966; Lindahl and Back 1987; Neville 1984; Taylor 1982; Dumont 1976.

so-called nuclear or elementary families (increasingly non-co-residential). Certainly in earlier Europe we clearly cannot talk of 'isolated' nuclear families in any absolute sense (unless we are simply referring to households which are 'isolated' by definition); kin (not only parents and children) were undoubtedly more dependent one on another than they are today. But even today extra-household ties of kinship are undoubtedly important in the lives of the majority of people and we must not assume absolute categorical differences. If the differences are a matter of emphasis, of percentages, then both nuclear families and extended kin ties are always present and there is no sudden break between individualised and collective social formations.

Some of the significance of the wider ties of kinship in earlier Europe may be hidden by the data used in most historical enquiries. That is also true of the contemporary West because of the nature of sociological censuses and questionnaires. In writing on the European family, Delille and Rizzi contrast the tradition of historical demography, as represented among others by the Cambridge Group, which places its faith in quantitative and only to a lesser extent in qualitative measurement, and the approach of Ariès in France and Stone in England who give preference to the study of psychological aspects of the family, which they regard as being richer and more productive. It is because of the interest in '*comptage*', they suggest, that the first group tend to confine their attention to the units of census recordings, to those living under the same roof, eating from the same pot or cooking at the same hearth. Restriction to the domestic domain inevitably neglects the wider 'anthropological' dimensions of kinship, alliance and 'lignage' that relate to ties beyond the confines of the household. These wider ties require attention, they argue, in order to determine the extent to which we are dealing with isolated 'nuclear' families in any particular part of Europe. The same argument has been put forward by other writers who have studied specific communities rather than aggregate data, which as Levine points out has the advantage of producing comparable results but only at the cost of some very real shortcomings.[11] A number of intensive enquiries about societies in the recent past are beginning to show much denser networks of kin ties than is often assumed, although a caveat should be added that some of these results may be a function of computer processing (and of genetic relationships) rather than ties recognised by the actors themselves (i.e. kinship in the sociological sense).[12] I should add 'normally

---

[11] Levine 1977: 2–3.
[12] Such studies are numerous, but I draw particular attention to Segalen 1991, and to Claverie and Lamaison 1982.

recognised' because a recognition of relationships may follow rather than precede an exceptional event encouraging the tracing back of interconnections, even where those were not directly relevant to the individual at the particular time the event took place. Such a search is characteristic of the work of genealogists and anthropologists, folk and professional.

While such wider kinship ties were important in western Europe, they were certainly less extensive in most respects than in many other societies, not only in the simpler societies of Africa but in China too, in India, perhaps in Japan, and in the Near East, including many of those groups (the Jews, Arabs, Armenians) that took the lead in organising the mercantile activity (capitalist by one definition) between Europe and Asia. What then is the connection between narrower kin ties and industrial capitalism?

I have argued that certain features of the European pattern of kinship and marriage were heavily influenced by the ideology and interests of the Catholic Church, which attempted to substitute its own spiritual kinship for the wider bonds of so-called 'natural kinship'.[13] The Church was against ancestors (at least against their worship, though not necessarily their commemoration) and against clans; the brotherhood of the Church was encouraged in preference to that of the family, and brotherhood meant economic interest as well as sentiment and theology. It is unnecessary to pursue this argument here. But the Church was not the only factor influencing the shape of the European family. At the popular level, the peasant and artisan systems of production and reproduction were in many respects not unique. Some aspects, especially the strategies of heirship and continuity adopted by families or individuals, were to be found among the major societies of Asia, differently distributed but recognisably drawn from a similar repertoire of social mechanisms.

Kin ties were especially important for the economy when the dominant forms of production turned around agriculture and craft manufacture. Under the 'domestic mode of production', kin, especially nuclear kin, often co-operated together in the same enterprise so that continuity, inheritance of land rights and tools and help on the farm or in the shop were all significantly provided by close kin. The reproduction of the individual couple was seen as essential both to inheritance and management, to passing on as well as to working the enterprise.

With industrial production that was no longer the case. Workers were mainly employed as individuals with their own pay packets. The replacement of the workforce no longer depended on family continuity (except

[13] Goody 1983.

for the owners) but on wider societal continuity; that was not a matter of any single individual worker having progeny because recruitment to the factory was open to others, including migrants from elsewhere. The firm will not collapse through individual infertility; its reproduction is promiscuous. The pressure on procreation is relieved.

Nevertheless even for the workers in industrial society kin ties often remain important for general social support, providing a wider frame for continuing amity. Economic support is often confined to the direct line, parents to children, with children making some arrangements for aged parents. However wider kin ties are still significant, even though dispersed, providing general moral support and company in crises as well as on ritual occasions. The massive movements of people at Thanksgiving in the USA and at Christmas throughout Europe are largely of kin. Family visitors fill buses, trains and aeroplanes, even at seasonally inflated prices. While strangers are occasionally admitted to these festivals, they are essentially gatherings of relatives with no particular instrumental aim but which constitute the main form of 'family reunion'.

As a large, mobile and immigrant society, the USA might be expected to play down the familial and to stress the individual. That is what is often seen to be the case at an ideological level, including that of many social scientists. In fact we find a wide variety of family reunion, which are by no means confined to the household. Ayoub sees three main kinds: 'the sibling reunion', the cognate reunion and the name reunion. The first is straightforward. It consists of a group of descendants of a woman or married couple, who get together, usually in a private home, often after the death of the mother. It is a continuation of the group of brothers, sisters and their children that earlier met on ritual occasions, such as Thanksgiving. The cognate reunion extends that group yet further down both lines, but it is likely to split after a few generations as it grows larger and the members more distant one from another. However reunions of even wider kin also take place, sometimes based on a particular name, such as Peacock. Rather like recent name reunions in Scotland, of the McDonalds for example, these 'artificial' creations are characteristic of a dispersed, mobile society where distant kin do not ordinarily meet one another; the organisers try to bring together not only those with whom kin ties can be traced but all those having the same name.

In the Mid-West of the USA family reunions are essentially opportunities for relatives to get together, eat a meal, and introduce their children to one another. Such occasions also occur in the South. Speaking of a reunion on the mother's side of the family in Georgia, one man told me that, although he had not attended for the past few years, he was definitely going that summer because his wife had given birth to a daughter whom he wanted his kin to get to know (and her to get to know his kin).

That declaration illustrates one major purpose of these meetings as well as indicating the cyclical aspect of family and kinship sentiments in the West. For many people outside the agricultural sector, becoming an adult involves leaving home for college, for military service, for work, in another town or possibly abroad. Such dispersal does not extinguish genealogical ties, nor yet the memories of earlier interaction. Indeed it provides the basis for getting together, for offering each other a measure of mutual support, or for building up dependencies, now or in the future. Name and cognate reunions offer other such opportunities, where in a threatening world people may seek solidarity with a wider range of kin than close relatives alone. It may serve a similar purpose as joining a friendly society such as the Masons.

While today these wider family ties have little significance in the sphere of production, they were, and in some ways still are, economically important in one major context in the West, both in the past and the present. That context is at the level of capital (and management) rather than the worker. At the beginning of the expansion of mercantile capitalism in London, dowries brought in by wives were used to help establish entrepreneurial activities, as was the inherited wealth of men. Domestic ties were important to the economy partly because, whatever wider changes took place, most property including industrial property continues to pass, as it has always done, within the restricted family (at present firstly between spouses). So family property lies behind many a capitalist (though not behind every entrepreneur). Effective ties may well extend more widely than the elementary family. Like the later Rothschilds and the owners of other banks and trading concerns, early Italian bankers in London and elsewhere made use of cousins to set up branches in different countries. This role of kin in the economy was not confined to the early days of capitalism. Later too they were a ready source of capital as well as of help in taking on responsible jobs. You could trust those who had interests in the same family circle just as they could trust you; hence you could borrow at lower risk and at lower interest. You in turn had some general obligation to help.

If such wider ties are still significant in the contemporary USA, they are likely to have been yet more so in earlier Europe. In America their importance has been generally underplayed by scholars, and that is also the case with earlier Europe. The result has been to exaggerate the differences on this score between the West and the East.

Continuity and change in sentiments: individualism

In his study of Ghent in the fourteenth century, Nicholas discusses the protagonists of the numerical and the psychological approaches to the history of the family in the context of the argument about continuity and change. In our earlier comment about the relation of family variables to the growth of capitalism Laslett and Macfarlane (for continuity) stood opposed to Ariès, Stone and Shorter (for discontinuity). Certainly discontinuity is an intrinsic part of Ariès' idea about the radical changes in the notions of childhood in the sixteenth century, and of Stone's parallel argument about changes of sentiment towards children in the seventeenth century (as well as about the shift from lineage to patriarchal family to nuclear family, that is, a progression from 'social' to 'individual'), and of Shorter's espousal of a similar thesis about the nineteenth.

Apart from the disagreements about continuity and discontinuity, and among the partisans of discontinuity about the very dates of the major transformations, one feature these discussions have in common is that both sets of writers see differences (in one case) and changes (in the other) as related to the socio-economic developments in modern Europe, particularly in England, the first as causes (or predisposing factors), the second as consequences (or as elective affinities). In each case it is a question of emphasising the discontinuity of family forms, either discontinuity with *our* neighbours, narrowly or broadly defined, or with *our* past in the other.

Even if it were possible effectively to measure (that is, to assess) these psychological variables more adequately, to make reasonably precise statements about 'mentalities', the question of determining continuity or discontinuity would still present many analytic difficulties. For example, in discussing the landed élite in England, Stone has stressed the presence (running against his main discontinuity theme) of 'an amazing family continuity',[14] which was rendered possible, among other things, by a psychological attitude consisting of the strong attachment to the principle of preferential male primogeniture, together with a growing concern for the adequate provision for younger sons and daughters.[15] The latter looks more like a tendency to division between all the children rather than to unigeniture, but whether here, in Japan or elsewhere in Eurasia, any form of primogeniture had always to be modified in real life.[16] Stone sees this continuity as threatened not by the economy or

[14] Stone 1986: 267.
[15] Stone 1986: 26.   [16] See Goody 1962.

polity, but by biology (that is, by demography) and by 'sentiment'. The shift in sentiment that occurred in the late seventeenth and eighteenth centuries was from 'an authoritarian and patriarchal attitude' to 'affective individualism' which manifested itself in a greater willingness to let people make their own choices in life, and in particular to allow children to marry whom they wished, 'free from the coercive paternal economic and moral pressures'. For 'it is generally agreed', he claims, 'that during the eighteenth century courtship, marriage and marital fidelity tended to pass from social to individual control. Marriage based on prior affection tended to replace marriage determined by the interest – whether social, economic, or political – of the family as a whole, spouses being selected by parents, "friends" and kin.' At the same time there was 'a growing concern for the well-being of children', manifesting itself in the desire to limit their number in the interests of quality.

Stone's analysis of the mechanisms of continuity is interesting. What may be questioned are, firstly, the long-term implications of the postulated shift from social to individual, especially as far as the choice of marriage partner is concerned. Many simple societies allow the very choice which he sees as lacking in earlier England, but which the Catholic Church, as illustrated fictionally in *Romeo and Juliet*, attempted to promote. Secondly, the formulation suffers from the same problems of conceptualisation as those we discussed earlier. It is not only in the Durkheimian sense of the internalisation of the social that we insist that social factors are still present in contemporary marital choice (and certainly so in the eighteenth century). Moreover 'individual' factors of choice were hardly absent in earlier periods, as readers of Shakespeare, Boccacio, Dante or Chaucer will know. That a change has taken place over time is clear; the doubts have to do with the general terms in which change is presented (from social to individual), and the further, half-implicit assumption that this is a new (evolutionary) development in human history. Historians often reject the need for general hypotheses, but these are inevitably subsumed in the terms they use, in the problems they perceive. The adequacy or inadequacy of any particular set of assumptions may only emerge when we look at other times and other places. Comparative history or comparative sociology, carefully carried out, can offer a way of assessing a hypothesis about a particular sequence of events.

The point would not need to be pressed if it did not lead to misleading notions about our own society as well as about those of others. Take individualism, often seen as the *sine qua non* of Western society – by some even before capitalism. Individualism is viewed as part of the 'Uniqueness of the West', in contrast for example to the 'hierarchy' of Indian society. The concept needs some sharper definition with its application confined to specific contexts before we can take the dangerous step of using it to distinguish one society as against another. We all think of ourselves as more individualistic than the next man or woman; we easily extend that attribute to the society in which we live, so that English individualism becomes a critical factor in the development of the Industrial Revolution. Or American individualism in the settlement of Massachusetts, in the westward extension of the frontier or in entrepreneurial activity. Asiatics or 'primitives' on the other hand tend to be treated as scarcely undifferentiated masses. However few anthropologists have not, like Evans-Pritchard for the Nuer, insisted on the individuality of the people with whom they have lived and worked.[17] Where the Western claim has some validity turns out to lie in particular contexts, such as the choice of partners. Phrased in a more specific way of this kind, the notion can be subjected to close analysis and one situation contrasted with other contexts in the same or another society. For many people, the 'dark satanic mills' of the Industrial Revolution brought some benefits but hardly a more individualising work environment; on those grounds the farm had more to be said in its favour.

My own experience, both in traditional and transitional groups, confirms the view that at the broad level of individualism there is little valid distinction to be made. In the changing environment of Africa people adjust relatively easily to a wider range of work opportunities, while the actual conditions of work are often more collective, more restrictive, than before. As for the continuing importance of social factors, even external ones, it is worth recalling the comment of the sociological historian, Stephen Mennell, on the general development of formalised modes of social intercourse in nineteenth-century England along with the growth of urban 'society'.

Membership was confined (and marriages contracted among) those deemed to possess the attributes of a 'lady' or 'gentleman'. With the growing number of individuals involved, the required outward manifestations of gentle status became more and more formalised and elaborate. Throughout the middle part of the century, admission rituals and etiquette – introductions, the exchange of cards and formal visits, of who 'knew' whom (in a very specific sense of 'knowing'), and of 'correct' behaviour in every situation (including dining and the giving of dinners) – became ever more defined.[18]

Large numbers of people were involved; large numbers demanded social recognition and thus 'threatened to overwhelm the style of life itself'.[19]

---

[17] Evans-Pritchard 1940.
[18] Mennell 1985: 208.   [19] Mennell 1985: 209.

This description applied to the very heyday of English capitalism and to those who were its leading spirits; 'choice' of companion was heavily restricted: marriages and friendships may not have been 'arranged' in the highly specific way of some societies but they can hardly be looked upon as the result of 'free choice' in any absolute sense. It was a question of loving thy neighbour rather than the world at large. As with individualism in others, we tend not to see our own actions as formal, ritual or even social. Nor has the problem disappeared. We find it difficult to appreciate that our tastes in food, music and partners should be conditioned by social factors since we are choice-making individuals. Nevertheless they obviously are. Nobody constrains us to eat hamburgers every other day, but we do.

Leaving aside the matter of the general way change is formulated there is the further question of its location in time. That historical question would be less important if the supposed growth of individualism in England was not often associated with that country becoming the first industrial nation and taking the lead over continental Europe. Recognising that England shared many features with western Europe as a whole, Stone suggests it was 'the high development of the market economy in England that made possible, and necessary, the theory of economic individualism'.[20] That statement may be correct for developments in economic theory. But more is being implied regarding the strength of the market and the quality of individualism. The towns of Italy, of Lower Saxony and of the Low Countries, all had seen a high development of the market and individualism was not absent. Yet market and individualism are associated by Stone with features seen as specific to England. For example, the Puritan legacy of respect for the individual conscience made possible 'the wide and early diffusion of new familial ideals and practices'.[21] But from another point of view the Puritans sought to regulate family life in ways that allowed individuals little choice.

Others have seen individualism as more deeply rooted in a specifically English tradition going back to earlier times. In an argument that runs parallel to Laslett's attempt to push back the presence of the nuclear household in England, Macfarlane sees individualism as indigenous to that country in contrast to the continent more generally, in spite of the fact that he traces its origins back to the German woods. 'In fact, within the recorded period covered by our documents', he writes, 'it is not possible to find a time when an Englishman did not stand alone. Symbolised and shaped by his ego-orientated kinship system, he stood in

[20] Stone [1977] 1979: 179.   [21] Stone [1977] 1979: 179–80.

the centre of his world.'[22] In that he is almost certainly correct. But the phenomenon was not confined to England. As I have argued elsewhere, the 'ego-orientated kinship systems' have a wide distribution in Europe (and indeed elsewhere).[23] So too does individualism, as the reference to the German woods suggests. However the author goes on to see this indigenous feature as the motor behind later events. Hence individualism was not shaped by Protestantism, population change or a market economy. 'Individualism . . . can be said to shape them all.'[24] And lined up with individualism we find those other English attributes (to which the French were later to lay claim), equality and liberty.

The argument brings out very clearly the difference between the continuity and the discontinuity schools, one claiming individualism as a product of later socio-economic changes, the other as a long-standing feature opening the way to those very changes. However both these sets of writers have one thing in common: they attribute such developments to England and interpret them in the light of that country as the first industrial nation; in other words they practise one form of the teleological history and social science, designated Whiggish by some, that is so prevalent in the Western world. Such Anglocentricism is not always easy to understand. If new family practices first made their appearance in England, how was it that family size first fell in Catholic France? While the Englishness of Puritanism must be dubious in view of its role in Bohemia, Germany, Switzerland, Huguenot France and Holland. It can be argued that this element was only one in a combination of factors. But that contention places the discussion beyond the realm of falsifiability whereas the negative cases must query the positive contribution that specific element is supposed to make to the final result.

Continuity and change in sentiments: parents and children

Let me turn to the attempt to assess intra-family sentiments, seen as so significant in demographic change. As we have seen, the notion of the 'surge of sentiment' takes the double form of sentiment for children and sentiment for partner. But apparently that surge does not apply to more distant kin, even one's own parents, who in theory are sloughed off early and definitively; in other words there seems to be less familial sentiment available for some very close kinsfolk. The concern of parents for the well-being of children has been central to the work of many historians of

[22] Macfarlane 1978: 196.
[23] Goody 1983.   [24] Macfarlane 1978: 196.

the 'psychological' school as well as being related to modern versions of theories about the demographic transition.[25] Caldwell's influential thesis on this topic proposed that the limitation of family size will not set in until the intergenerational transfers of wealth cease to flow from children to parents. At that time the traditional, open-commitment family structure is superseded, children are no longer seen as an investment but as objects of affection (why not burdens?), providing only psychological benefits for the elderly.[26] In her review of the economic value of children, which follows up the demographic work of Caldwell in Africa and Asia, Ware states bluntly of such traditional societies that 'parents have children, by and large, because they profit thereby'.[27] It is true that in most economies based upon a domestic order of production, the maintenance and continuity of the enterprise depends upon each family having children. That is no longer the case under industrial production; under that dispensation no single family needs to reproduce itself and the children that are born contribute little or nothing of financial value to the parents who may be left only with their psychological value, although support is often provided in old age. However, such a shift does not mean that previously children were valued only instrumentally, although that is implied in the work of many modern historians and demographers. Nor does it mean that, at least for the major societies of Europe, the number of heirs (as distinct from children) did not remain a matter of considerable significance, since property, even when it no longer consisted of the means of production, was still inherited within the family.

Let us look at the assertion about sentiments in more detail. The well-known medieval historian, Herlihy, who worked extensively on the Florentine *cadasto*, has remarked that Stone's thesis about the earlier absence of sentiment has been attacked from so many quarters that 'today it has little life left in it'.[28] Yet the general notion behind the thesis remains strongly embedded not only in popular beliefs but in historical and other academic discussions.[29]

The original thesis tried to take into account both positive and negative factors in the parent–child relationship. The negative side had to do with the rate of mortality. It was argued that the high incidence of infant deaths in medieval Europe and other cultures meant that parents were emotionally unable to lavish too much affection on any individual child, who might be here today and gone tomorrow. There is certainly

[25] Caldwell 1976; Ware 1978.   [26] Ware 1978: 25.
[27] Ware 1978: 2.   [28] Herlihy 1985: 207.
[29] For example, in the interesting discussion of Oppong and Bleek 1982.

no absolute bar against introducing cost–benefit calculations into the analysis of kinship and the family. If the efforts of economists of the Chicago school seem reductionist in a 'vulgar' way, that should not inhibit more subtle attempts. In the present context some might object to such an approach on general grounds, thinking that this conception of the economy of sentiments smacks of a capitalist rather than a pre-capitalist orientation to life. But the real objections are more empirically based. If it is possible to make any rough assessment of how human beings react to what until the recent past all have had to face very directly (i.e. the frequency of death in the family), then this view has little or no validity. My own observations on the behaviour of individuals at funerals in a society in Ghana, west Africa, where death was a very common occurrence gave no indication that emotions were any the less deeply engaged; quite the contrary, for the close bereaved had to be comforted and watched so that they did not attempt suicide. Any LoDagaa would be amazed at the apparent 'carelessness' of people about the death of others in urban Western society.[30] I use the word 'careless' literally, with regard to the death even of our nearest and dearest. Of course in Africa and Europe both individuals and the society put up defences against mortality, one of which is the idea that death does not entail the ending of existence, certainly not of the 'soul'. The idea behind T. S. Eliot's line, 'in my end is my beginning', was not foreign to LoDagaa funerals. Some manifest a nonchalance, a bravado in the face of death. But these large-scale occasions, however firmly programmed, were never simply 'formal' manifestations of grief, sorrow, regret or respect. Indeed the notion that others, such as Jews at the Western Wall, display formal, ritualised grief, while only we manifest true, unvarnished sentiments, is a typical product of the ethnocentricism that dogs this whole debate. They have customs (*moeurs*), we have sentiments (feelings). While those LoDagaa less closely involved would conduct themselves calmly, particularly at the funeral of an unweaned child (for theological reasons rather than in order to economise on sentiment), the childbearer herself was always distraught, always particularised within the classificatory category of 'mothers'. Not only had she endured a long pregnancy, a hard birth and all the many chores of new motherhood, but a strong attachment between carer (usually mother) and child is an intrinsic component of the make-up of human beings; at its most instrumental level a heavy, usually parental, investment in children is required in order to reproduce socialised beings and to perpetuate

[30] Goody 1962.

'culture' (even though the investment itself may be 'natural'). For even in the simplest societies, the new-born infant has a great deal to acquire that is learned rather than genetically transmitted.

The extent to which the maternal drive and the attachment to a mother-figure is genetically programmed, or present in animal species, is an important topic but not one to be discussed here. While reports of societies show differences in the mother–child relationship, only in rather peculiar circumstances do we find anything resembling the so-called 'traditional' society that forms the background to much pseudo-historical reconstruction – only perhaps in the kind of circumstances surrounding Turnbull's Ik dramatised by Peter Brook. So observation does little to confirm the conclusions about the single-minded instru-mental character of parental–child relations in pre-industrial society. Moreover the picture of medieval England or Europe painted by modern historians has been firmly rejected by medievalists as well as by classical scholars.[31] If this were not so, one would have to conclude that the realm of sentiment is one in which a study based on documentary materials alone is inadequate for the purposes of making an evaluation (threatening all historical procedures for this purpose). Or alternatively that pre-industrial England (or western Europe) must have been a very unusual place, not in terms of features that might pave the way for the new world to come, but of features that would appear to place grave obstacles in the way of any shift to modernity. On general theoretical grounds, the first alternative is to be preferred.

That is the negative side of the thesis. The positive runs as follows. Not only did earlier societies (or anyhow earlier England) fail to make the same investment in children, but England (specifically England for these authors, except of course for Ariès and other French scholars) devoted more care to children than did other neighbouring societies. There are times in the course of this argument when 'care' is specifically identified with pre-school education, school education and with preparation for the future. Of the 'wealthy entrepreneurial bourgeoisie', Stone writes that 'they care for their children and are anxious to give them the benefits of an élite education which they themselves have lacked'.[32] It was they who, deeply religious, were strongly affected by the stress on holy matrimony and marital affection current in the seventeenth century. 'They are there-fore the first to shed the ties to their own kin (although they use marriage ties to cement business connections), to stress merit and the sanctity of contracts, to develop close affective ties within the home, and to lavish

---

[31] Shahar 1990; Veyne 1978; Hopkins 1980.   [32] Stone [1977] 1979: 174.

care and attention upon their children.'[33] His thesis that English children were being treated 'in an extraordinary affectionate manner', at first in the middle levels of society, then spreading to others, he sees as supported by the observations of a French writer as early as 1697. However it is not clear that, for example, education was more widespread in England than in contemporary Holland or Sweden. Protestants everywhere made moves in this direction, accompanying the extensive use of writing, print and picture by reformers such as Luther and Cranach in Wittenberg which became a major centre of German publishing. As for more subtle measures, these are equally difficult to substantiate, especially, as we have seen, a change that can be characterised positively was so often accompanied by others that can be judged as negative, at least from the standpoint of the child. For this so-called 'maternal, child-orientated, affectionate and permissive mode' also saw the adoption of contraception on the grounds that quality was preferable to quantity. To describe contraception as child-orientated is curious from one standpoint. It also involved the despatch of bourgeois children away from home to boarding schools (though not among the highest nobility), a liberal use of the cane (*le vice anglais*), and the encasing of young women in stays 'pushed in England to an inconceivable point', according to Rousseau. It is possible to interpret these actions, like the binding of Chinese feet, as child-orientated behaviour; as with school, adults are preparing them for their future in society. But the opposite view is equally plausible from the standpoint of the 'other', whether that be the child or the other culture. Certainly many foreigners did not regard everything in the English garden as worthy of praise, nor as signposts to the future.

It is hardly surprising to find French historians take a different view of the development of the family than the English. As we have seen, the smaller family appears to have begun there in modern times, not necessarily a smaller existential family, but with fewer births and deaths. Ariès sees new sentiments towards children emerging in the sixteenth century not only in England but throughout western Europe while J.-L. Flandrin finds more general changes beginning at the same time. The latter's thesis is most succinctly laid out in the following passage: 'between the sixteenth century and the end of the eighteenth century, the family changed in character and a new morality of family relations was adumbrated'. Leaving aside the question of whether whatever changes took place can best be described in so general a way, the notions of

---

[33] Stone [1977] 1979: 174; that is to say, you tend to shed kin ruthlessly when you do not need them.

French historians clearly run counter to the stress on the Englishness of things modern. But, apart from the question of a new morality and whether what happened can best be conveyed in this way, the wider claim that Europeans invented childhood is one of those ethnocentric notions that an inadequately comparative history allows to pass. For anyone who has looked at Chinese paintings of children at play, or who has seen the inventiveness of African children in creating toys and 'games' finds great difficulty in accepting the idea that the West 'discovered childhood as a distinct phase of life'. Ariès claimed there was 'no place for childhood in the medieval world'.[34] Elsewhere he does recognise that the idea of *paideia* existed in classical times but it had been forgotten, so the seventeenth century was experiencing a 'revival' rather than a 'discovery'. He does so without realising how such a recognition threatens the general argument. Once again, the way modern historians reconstruct medieval life makes it seem a very strange place, not at all one that was to lead the world. That is also true of their account of attitudes to death and love.

Husbands and wives

Let me now return to the second aspect of the 'surge of sentiment', that to do with love and conjugal relations. As far as the role of 'affection' ('love') in the selection of sexual partner or mate, contemporary choices are certainly more often those of the partners themselves than in earlier Europe, despite the late marriage age that then prevailed. Parents were inevitably more concerned when marriage involved the handing over of family property in the shape of dowry to women or the endowment of sons, sometimes with the farm itself; or when it was a question of having another couple (the newly married) in the same house (as was often the case in southern France) or working part of the same land. Parental choice was sometimes less marked in earlier societies without the same invest-ment in land and the means of production where property arrangements at marriage were of a different character, although clearly other factors were involved in making these alliances. But in any case affection is not simply a matter of romanticised sexual attraction, especially of the young (love 1): the role of continuing conjugal affection (love 2) is clearly of a different character, as is the love between parents and children (love 3).

The nature of the sentiments in these two relationships, conjugal and parental, are not always positively correlated. Consider the influence upon the divorce rate, and hence on the care of children, of the notion of

[34] Ariès 1962: 33, 412.

free choice. Freedom for parents may be a cost for children and for the parent–child relationship. Since complete freedom of choice is part of what is often described as 'romantic love', it can result not only in the selection but in the reselection of partners. Romantic love is sometimes seen as a specifically European phenomenon, as going back to the Troubadours of southern France, who were much influenced in their poetic discourse by Muslim Spain. Certainly it was not limited to England or even to western Europe. A number of Eurasian societies have seen such love as more appropriate for relations with mistresses rather than wives, where 'choice' as distinct from constraint, the internal 'freedom' against the external 'duty', is all important. Others have associated it with conjugal relations or courting behaviour. In one guise or another it fills the literature of major Asian societies, the Sanskrit love poems translated by Brough, the Chinese poems rendered by Waley, the early Japanese novels, or the even earlier love letters of ancient Egypt referred to by Hopkins, not to mention the Biblical Song of Songs. Of course, each tradition displays its own modalities, but there is no reason to deny the existence of either romantic love or companionate marriage to other, non-European societies.

Nor is there any reason to suppose that these features were altogether absent in earlier Europe. I have referred in passing to the work of late medieval, early Renaissance writers in Italy and England, as well as to the attitudes of the church about 'consensus' unions. Writing of the papal marriage decretals in England in the twelfth century in a book entitled *Love and Marriage in the Twelfth Century*, Duggan remarks:

We should not expect to find a general disquisition on love and marriage in papal decretals, yet there is ample evidence of the importance attached by the popes to marital affection, to mutual responsibilities, to care for children, to a fair solution of alienation crises, and at least to discretion in potentially scandalous situations.[35]

This comment of Duggan's is devastating to aspects of both continuity and discontinuity arguments about England. It provides earlier (Catholic) continental evidence of features that partisans of the surge of sentiment see as late appearances and that others of the continuity school perceive as preparing the way for later developments in England. For many medievalists these features existed earlier and more widely than either hypothesis allows, throughout the Catholic world and well beyond the bounds of western Europe.

Like the care of children, conjugal love, which Shorter attributes to the nineteenth century, Stone to the seventeenth and Macfarlane to

[35] Duggan 1981: 72.

much-earlier England, must be seen as more widely distributed both in
time and in space than these accounts allow. The extensive literature on
Asian societies to which I have referred brings out the ethnocentric
character of these ideas about the existence of conjugal and romantic
love. Yet the notions penetrate so many sociological and historical
discussions. One reason is the perceived connection with the modern
'nuclear' family. The argument runs that 'in England and elsewhere in
Northern and Western Europe the standard situation was one where
each domestic group consisted of a simple family living in its own
house'.[36] The demographic evidence is seen as extending this 'simple'
structure to adjacent parts of northern Europe, not as limiting its
existence entirely to the offshore islands. In each case demography
implies family sentiment. The dominance of the nuclear family reflects
the nature of the relations between husband and wife in companionate
marriage, caring for their children in their own separate household. As
our earlier figures showed, many couples in many other societies live
under similar conditions, although in the absence of high migration, their
neighbours are more often kin. But domestic relationships in an analytic
sense are not limited to such a simple family. Old parents may be outside
the household at one point of time and inside at another: living-in is not
the only criterion of close kinship. We have to take account of the
developmental cycle of such groups and of the relations not only between
neighbouring houses but between dispersed siblings held together by
property and other common interests. The notion of an isolated nuclear
family may have been approximately appropriate for migrating factory
workers of the nineteenth century who had lost even a partial ownership
of the means of production in the process of industrialisation. It was not
at all typical of the industrialists, tradesmen and bankers themselves, nor
did it in fact apply when any relatively scarce resources were being
distributed over time by inheritance or by gifts between the living.

Undoubtedly, important changes have taken place in the family over
time. What we find in recent European societies is that conjugal couples
are often thrown more on their own since there is greater mobility and
since continuity in the family enterprise no longer plays a major part in
the life of most people. At the same time their children are more
independent in making a choice of partner and a job, and increasingly in
leaving them; indeed the forms of independence are not unrelated.
Equally there have been some continuities. But one has to be very
precise about claiming continuities and discontinuities or implying
uniqueness and similarity. It is dangerous to try to specify either change

[36] Laslett 1972: 40.

or continuities in the intuitive, ethnocentric way that some of these discussions have tended to do, especially if one is implying causal connections or consequences, without being exact about the elements involved. The same caveat applies to the claim of uniqueness, which requires a thoroughgoing comparative enquiry to validate.

'Progress'

Even taking these wider perspectives into consideration, there are two other points that need to be made. Firstly, many of these accounts of the development of the family and marriage have a strong element not only of evolution but of 'progress' attached to them. The underlying logic is not always obvious, even in the notion that fewer children means greater child-orientation or care. The number of children born should not be confused with the number of surviving children, the existential family, which is what is most significant from the standpoint of household structure as well as of population growth. The Industrial Revolution was initially accompanied by a heavy increase in population (that is, in the size of existential families) due to decreasing mortality. It produced more not less surviving offspring. At the same time social reformers like Engels were constantly decrying the effects of those events on the family life of the working class, for example in taking both parents into a work situation outside the home, indeed in taking the children themselves into those dismal surroundings. While the middle class could afford increasing numbers of domestic servants to help with the care of children, the working class were affected in quite adverse ways: it was they who supplied the labour in other people's homes and in other people's factories.

It is possible to modify this argument to conclude that Victorian England was only a transitional phase in this development, and only today (the words are Stone's) are we faced with 'the end product of affective individualism', the 'child-orientated family type' of our contemporary world. Once again any social reformer who looks at increasing divorce rates, increasing numbers of lone-parent families or households, increasing child-minding by non-kin (or children not minded at all), possibly increasing abuse and increasing use of illegal drugs, might want to question some of these assumptions.

'Uniqueness'

The second point concerns the claim to uniqueness, since this has wide implications for our understanding of the present as well as of the past, that is the present of others, especially the East, as well as of ourselves. In considering the English or even the European family, those writers who perceive continuity and those who see change, those who see causes and those who see effects (as well as those who prefer different mixes of the various ingredients) proceed largely on the assumption of the uniqueness of these domestic ingredients as they relate to social change. That in turn corresponds to the belief in the Uniqueness of the West which lies at the core of the work not only of many distinguished nineteenth-century writers such as Marx and Weber, but of many contemporary sociologists, as well as of the myriad historians of Europe, teaching what is almost by definition an ethnocentric subject. Of course, all societies, all groups and all individuals are unique in certain of their features. What is at stake here is, firstly, the attempt to determine whether the selected features are indeed unique in the context of the development of the particular features of modern life that one is trying to explain, explicitly or implicitly (the dependent variables). If we regard features of the English family as promoting or inhibiting the development of mercantile or industrial activity, we need to isolate the particular aspects of those changes we regard as relevant and then examine what differences are to be found in other societies, France, for example, certainly the Mediterranean, even more certainly eastern Europe and especially Oriental civilisation, that supposedly prevented them from taking the first step, the great step, forward (though the precise nature of that step is something we have already had occasion to query).

Even within Europe, internal differences throw doubt on these assumptions of relevant uniqueness. Take the contribution of the 'European marriage pattern' with its late age of marriage and large numbers of life-cycle servants. We can readily agree that the medieval Flemish inhabitants of Ghent were equally as 'European' in this respect as the English (indeed equally English in the not always hidden agendas of English historians). But the Catholic Irish who had a much later age of marriage and a profusion of servants, registered few advances in the process of modernisation, only partly perhaps because of English dominance. And is it not churlish to overlook the fundamental contributions to the growth of capitalism and the development of banking, accountancy and trade made in the Italian city states, the inhabitants of which did not always conform to northern European patterns, whether in terms of lateness of marriage or of the absence of extended-kin relations?

The problem takes on greater importance outside Europe. Marx's notion of the stagnant Oriental society (or mode of production) and Weber's idea of traditional society and his treatment of world religions, are all part of a general approach attempting to single out unique features of the West that are not only unique in themselves but contributed to capitalism, to the Industrial Revolution and to modern society. In other words the cluster of features is causally unique. But it is obvious today that since societies of the East have made a successful adaptation, the analysis needs to be modified in one of two ways. Like much dependency theory, the history of the family has failed to take into account the advent of the newly industrialised countries. Either the Japanese family, for example, is similar in potential to that in the West or there is a difference between the conditions required for the original development of a state of affairs and its subsequent adoption in another area.

The second of these alternative propositions is used by many faced with explaining this change in the balance of powers. While it may be possible to argue the case with a particular technique, to espouse such an argument about the development of capitalism is to take a very curious view of its underlying nature.

The West and the East

The first alternative has received a good deal of attention. Already in the first collective volume produced by the Cambridge Group, the parallel between family and development in Japan and England is touched upon. It has been popular, partly as the result of the kind of comparison habitually being drawn by ambassadors of the two island countries that find themselves at the extremities of Europe and Asia respectively. But it has been more seriously extended to Asia by other scholars. Hanley and Wolf have suggested that the contrast drawn between western and eastern Europe with regard to marriage patterns and family size may have an east Asian parallel in the contrast between Japan and China, especially in regard to the presence of stem families as against grand families (here households), of late as against early marriage (at about twenty-four years as against seventeen) and of preventive population checks as against a pro-natalist policy (for males). They take up the point made by Hajnal that is critical to much thinking on this subject. That author asked if delayed marriage might not, like income inequality but in a more widespread manner, stimulate the diversion of resources to ends other than minimum subsistence, and so lay the groundwork for 'the uniquely European "take-off" into modern economic growth'.[37] Hanley and Wolf comment:

[37] Hajnal 1965: 132.

Having seen that the European marriage pattern is not unique, we are led to wonder about the source of Japan's economic take-off. Could it be that similar marriage patterns explain why northwestern Europe and Japan led these regions in economic development? And if this is so, might it not be that one of the preconditions for modern economic development is a stem family system.[38]

By their use of comparative material, Hanley and Wolf have opened up the history of the family in an interesting way, pointing out the similarities between Europe and east Asia. But the perspective needs to be opened up yet more radically. We might then begin by examining cases where these very features were present in societies that were 'unsuccessful' in relation to the take-off, both in Europe and in Asia. Tibet, for example, seems to display a number of the family features pointed out by demographic historians for Europe, including late marriage, life-cycle servants and a kind of stem family. That might lead us to question whether in fact these features have had a necessary part to play in the development of capitalism in any of its forms. On the other side, a number of groups in Europe practised equal division, for example, Ghent in the fourteenth century as well as parts of England. These groups sometimes had stem households, even without primogeniture.[39]

The role of early marriage in inhibiting, and of late marriage in encouraging, development was anticipated by Malthus, who maintained that, in western Europe, varying the age of marriage in relation to economic conditions (the worse, the later) led to 'profound differences between the economic character of Europe and of other parts of the world'.[40] This model of reproductive control was contrasted with the 'Chinese case' which promoted early marriage and high fertility, with the mass of society being accustomed to live on a pittance.[41] China often continues to have this image in the West, but leaving aside the unresolved question of comparative standards of living, the demographic assumptions need some radical qualification. In the first place, 'regular' marriage was not all that early. Nor is later marriage the only way of keeping a population in check. Another tool was infanticide, largely of females. A further, unintentional factor was the increased infant mortality brought

---

[38] Hanley and Wolf 1985: 12.
[39] The Cambridge Group does not find stem *households* in England, whereas in southern France they are often seen as 'traditional' and are claimed to be something of an impediment to change (Rogers 1991, referring to French Government sources). The phrase 'stem *families*' on the other hand presumably refers to the situation where property is handed over to one child, a process that may not involve living in the same household, or even any limitation in the size of the family. The necessary distinction is rarely drawn in any clear fashion.
[40] Wrigley 1988: 22.
[41] Wrigley 1988: 20.

about by famine conditions; some very early 'marriages' also resulted from just such conditions, when poorer families would dispose of infant daughters to prospective in-laws as a way of reducing the demands on the household.[42] That was by no means the only reason for 'in-coming daughter-in-law marriage', as Wolf and Huang point out.[43] But they go on to demonstrate that such early marriages were less fertile than later ones.

There seems little reason to suggest, as others have done, that control was deliberately aimed at in this case. But there were other possibilities of control at the disposal of Asian families, such as forms of 'contraception', coitus interruptus (or reservatus), abortion and even simple abstention, the ethical value of which is certainly part of Indian thinking. The practice of prostitution and concubinage also tend to reduce not only marital fertility but the fertility of women in general, as is the case with polygyny in Africa. Whatever the available procedures, it is scarcely conceivable that a human population, especially a 'civilised' population like the Chinese, should have been unable to come up with ways of relating resources to population. Is the fact that they have been the only country to attempt to operate a one-child policy so completely out of tune with earlier attitudes? It is certainly significant that nothing of the kind has happened in Africa.[44]

The problem of China's millions is not necessarily the result of uncontrolled growth, for according to Malthus those numbers should have reached an earlier plateau had the population really been 'living on a pittance'. In fact China, at least southern China, was and is generally well fed, even if susceptible to famine. Whereas Malthus put the level of consumption below that of the Scots, others like the plant hunter, Fortune, himself a Scotsman, saw the situation very differently.[45] From one standpoint a high population may equally be an index of the past success of the economy, as much as a confession of failure. That could also have been the case in India. However, in the end the growth of towns and the rising number of rural landless in both areas meant that there was poverty as well as increase.

The analysis should also be extended in the other direction, by considering those societies, supposedly ruled out of the game by their family structure or other factors, that have now made a significant transition. Taiwan, Hong Kong and Singapore, not to speak of China

---

[42] Fei 1939.
[43] Wolf and Huang 1980.
[44] On the problem of the relevant differences between Africa and Asia, see Goody et al. 1981a, 1981b.
[45] Fortune 1857: 42–3.

itself, were clearly capable of making the shift to industrial production and of participating in the economic take-off. That was so without their having to adopt a stem family, contraception or most of the other variables involved. As newly industrialised countries, they have made many important advances without taking these particular steps. They have proceeded by adapting their existing families, including 'grand families', to the demands of socio-economic change. Indeed those families have often promoted commercial and industrial development.

Rethinking the West

Those facts about the East should make us rethink the history of the West. In Italy or England, in Japan or today in Taiwan, was it really the isolated, individual Robinson Crusoe (with a whitish wife, of course, rather than a black Man Friday) that led the take-off in its various forms? We have already examined the role of kin in the development of mercantile and industrial régimes in Asia. But the case of the Italian bankers of western Europe, those of Geneva and Alsace, the cotton manufacturers of Lille and Roubaix, all show that the family, often the extended family, of entrepreneurs and capitalists played a large part in creating and running an enterprise.

Let us start with Italian banking, which began with the family. Family businesses were of course common in late medieval Europe. De Roover (1974) contrasted the older form of partnership in which members of the family predominated with the partnerships entered into by fourteenth-century Medicis with non-family members. The growth of non-family partnerships is a recurrent theme of studies of Renaissance Venice and Florence.[46] Undoubtedly the growth of the size and complexity of business enterprises, especially in manufacture, led to an increase in the proportion of firms with non-family members. But there is a cyclical aspect about this apparent move. Family firms may grow into bureaucratic organisations. But they do not disappear since new ones are constantly being set up. Indeed around 1386 the Medicis themselves reverted to family partnerships. As we have seen the alternative forms of partnership, kin and non-kin, existed throughout historic times.

Family business seems to have been particularly significant in banking. Attention has been drawn to the continuing importance in Tudor England of Italian family banks, despite the emphasis placed by English historians on the English merchant and the English regulated and

---

[46] Lane 1973; Goldthwaite 1980.

joint-stock companies of the seventeenth century.[47] But many banks, whether English or foreign, continued to be organised around a core of kinsfolk, as did other businesses.

The sixteenth-century merchant 'might be expected to equip his sons with the rudiments of a business education', usually in his own firm given there was no relevant educational system.[48] It meant a large measure of occupational stability and much more, namely, family continuity. Secondly, brothers often acted together in one 'society', so all writings, bills of exchange and transactions were done in common, while goods were owned together. For brothers tended to 'keep their patrimony undivided for some years after the death of their father' and continued to do so long after if business demanded.[49] Not only brothers but more-extended kin acted together. The Frescobaldis of Florence were one of the two foremost financial powers in Europe between the fall of the Medicis and the rise of the Fuggers. At the beginning of the sixteenth century they had representatives of the family in Bruges, London and Venice. The Bonvisi of Lucca were distributed in a similar fashion between Antwerp, London, Genoa, Venice and Plaisance; at Lyons the six Bonvisi companies formed between 1575 and 1609 consisted of family members.[50] The suggestion has been made that the economic recession in Italy in the sixteenth century may even have led to a greater stress on the family as an economic unit, since efforts were made to reduce costs by living under one roof and by pooling assets as well as by restricting marriage. But that could hardly have been the case with dispersed branches of bankers and was no more necessary for co-operation than co-residence in the 'Hindu undivided family'. Then as now most family businesses seldom survived a second and third generation, although some, such as the Rothschilds, did manage to continue over time. In any case old enterprises gave birth to new. In Lüthy's magisterial work on banking (1961), he treats Swiss and Huguenot bankers as a community united not only by faith and a common history of persecution but even more by kinship and inter-marriage over a region stretching from Copenhagen to Cadiz. Despite the long-term fragility of many family firms, they continued to serve as the core of capitalist enterprise, even for industrial capitalism.

Modern industrialisation first developed on a massive scale in the textile trade, beginning in England about 1780, and involved families

---

[47] Bratchel 1978: 6. More than 50 per cent of English cloth exports were in alien hands by the early 1540s.

[48] Bratchel 1978: 8.

[49] Herlihy 1977: 147.   [50] Bratchel 1978: 16.

other than those of traditional bankers. Industry soon spread to northern France where life and work among the Catholic cotton manufacturers took place around the family as well as in the factory. Only later, according to Bergeron, did 'la famille close' come into its own, part of the evolution of a way of life among the leisured classes produced by industrialisation itself.[51] Austerity and family support were both needed in the earlier phases of capital accumulation when the industrialists distinguished themselves not only from the big spenders among the nobility but also from the great financiers, the big armateurs (ship-suppliers) and merchants involved in the colonial trade who became millionaires following the end of the Ancien Régime. However, with the change in the scale of industrial fortunes in the second half of the nineteenth century, with the great rise in profits in coal, steel and heavy engineering, the lifestyles of industrialists made a move towards greater luxury and patronage.

What is remarkable about many of these industrial families of nineteenth-century France is the strongly familial character of their daily life, which gave little time or inclination for a *vie mondaine*. Their day was regulated by the factory clock, which prevented them from taking more than a short holiday by the sea. Social life was confined to dinners within a particular local circle which was also a marriage circle. Industrialists in Roubaix did not want their daughters to marry outside the town, even with those of neighbouring Tourcoing and Lille. The preference was maintained even at the risk of making a financially less-advantageous union, for there was resistance to marriage 'outside one's place of birth, outside the clothing industry, outside the traditional milieu'.[52] At this time 'the foundation of social life and the main distraction was the Sunday reunion of the wider family'.[53] So strong was the family that the industrialists of Lille were described as living 'dans un véritable ghetto social'.[54] The same word is used of the Protestant communities of Alsace, although one of their number, the author Jean Schlumberger of the famous industrial family, employs an Indian rather than a Jewish analogy. 'C'est peu de dire que la caste est fermée; elle est encore scindée en familles.' The Mulhouse community consisted of refugees at the time of the Thirty Years War, 'practising with few exceptions a strict endogamy, cultivating from the end of the nineteenth century the cult of their own genealogies', which remains a marked feature of the Huguenot minority.[55] He goes on to recount how the men met once a week at the

[51] Bergeron 1978.
[52] Bergeron 1978: 199.   [53] Bergeron 1978: 197.
[54] Bergeron 1978: 198.   [55] Bergeron 1978: 202.

stock exchange in Mulhouse, 'but life of society is limited to "diners de famille", at which, with no attention to personal affinities, to tastes or to friendships, attendance was a matter of consanguinity alone'. His parents went each week to two of these 'rites', at one of which were gathered the descendants of great-grandfather Nicholas, divided into five branches (a whole 'tribe', he comments), while the second took place at the house of his grandparents.[56] Work among this male élite was governed by exact attention to time. The women too met regularly at their 'mercredi des pauvres' to make clothes for the particular Catholic section of the town for which they had taken on responsibility.

It was not only that social activities took place largely around the family but that the family was intrinsic to industry. Nor was its contribution confined to the early days of capital accumulation, for there was a strong tendency to hand over managerial responsibility as well as ownership to family members. Eugene Motte, whose father had also been a dyer at Roubaix under the Second Empire, wrote about the need to avoid becoming a *fonctionnaire* or *rentier*, and to engage in work under a system 'where one left one's children no other inheritance except factories, plant, raw materials and contracts'.[57] His father had expressed to him very clearly both the ideology and the practice of continuity of business in the family. 'Our family, my dear son, has always known work. Our grandparents . . . were always in business.'[58]

Nor was it only the sons. Especially in the early days of industrial-isation, a wife played an important role. The spouse of Jean-Abraham Poupart, the celebrated *drapier* of Sedan, herself belonged to the high bourgeoisie. She actively helped her husband in running his business (indeed what was in some ways their joint business): 'It was she who always took charge of the wallet and the cash-box.'[59] She paid the *fileurs à la main* at the same time as controlling their work. When a husband died, a widow often remained in charge of the business until passing it over to a son.

Among the typical factory owners of the 'first industrial revolution', like the textile owners of Lille–Roubaix–Tourcoing, or of Mulhouse and its surroundings, the outstanding solidarity of the family may have been both a means of cultivating the qualities needed for the success and consolidation of the firm, and a way of asserting their identity as against other élites. However other *groupes familiaux* adopted different strategies and made alliances beyond their own milieux, thus creating networks of kinship of a wider kind. These closed communities changed over time,

---

[56] Schlumberger 1934: 270; Bergeron 1978: 201–2.   [57] Bergeron 1978: 192.
[58] Bergeron 1978: 192.   [59] Bergeron 1978: 193–4.

moving away from 'ghetto life' into the wider world, but the family continued to play a central part in work and in public life as it did in the private sphere.

The industrial patricians of Mulhouse moved more slowly than others but just after 1830 they began to leave the old town and in the second half of the century built new houses in a vineyard or in the outskirts of the town, with some even buying castles after 1870. In Lille the same thing happened. Industrialists moved away from town and factory in other ways too, giving more time to travel, sport and social life. Following the lead of the bankers, some of them took over the roles of collectors and patrons of art from the nobility of earlier times. The Musée Guimet at Paris was the result of one such gift by an industrialist from Lyons whose father had in 1823 invented a method of making an ultramarine dye.

All this is equally true of Britain. We cannot pick up a novel of the nineteenth century, which it has been remarked often chronicled the details of social history more convincingly than the politically orientated historians of the time, without realising the continuing importance of the family among capitalist entrepreneurs. Even among workers, divided as they were by separate jobs and pay-packets, Dickens and others emphasise the continuing support (including small legacies) that the family provides.

Students of the 'managerial revolution' often see the family firm as 'the first stage of organizational evolution'.[60] The use of the terms 'stage' and 'evolution' implies that in higher forms of organisation they will be superseded by bureaucratic structures. It was the importance of these structures which Weber stressed in his account of the rise of capitalism; and it is these that form the theoretical focus of many discussions about 'the Rise of the West'.[61]

Joint-stock companies experienced a remarkable growth under later capitalism. In earlier forms non-familial partnerships played a part in trade throughout the Eurasian continent but they came into particular prominence in the early modern period, for example with the founding of the East India Company in 1600 and the Dutch United East Indies Company (VOC) two years later. Such a form of bureaucratic organisation was particularly appropriate for larger firms where much capital needed to be raised, risks spread and the management diversified. So the central feature of industrial capitalism is taken to be the large business corporation and all major economic activities are seen as taking place

---

[60] Redding 1990: 3.   [61] See for example Berle and Means 1932.

within big joint-stock companies associated with large-scale production of goods or services.

Much of sociology has been built around the contrast between traditional, agrarian societies and urban, industrial ones. The latter are marked by the application of rationality and the scientific spirit to production, including 'rational habits which run counter to immemorial custom'.[62] Whether we adopt this sociological account of industrial society or the Marxist one of the development of capitalism, the shift from earlier structures is portrayed in absolute terms. The sociological account finds a radical opposition between traditional agrarian and modern industrial in which the internal development of capitalism leads to the separation of ownership and control. Marxist theory too sees monopoly capitalism as coming to dominate all others.

The separation of management and control in industry goes together with the bureaucratic differentiation and technical specialisation of management; the particularistic, ascription-orientated role structure of traditional societies gives way to the universalistic, achievement-orientated one of modern régimes. However the extent of separation between ownership (dispersed and therefore weak) and control (by management), emphasised in a well-known study by Berle and Means, has been exaggerated. These authors saw the traditional capitalist forms of private and majority ownership as disappearing over time, though the process was not yet complete.[63] But when Birch reanalysed their material, he showed that in 1929 between 37 per cent and 45 per cent of the top 200 non-financial companies were family controlled, even though many were classified as 'managerial' by Berle and Means. Moreover in 1937 roughly the same proportions existed. Single families held control in 20 per cent of the companies, but the family intervened in more complex ways and their control was in fact present in some two-fifths of the companies.[64] The trend was much less exclusive than had been maintained, and that remains true today.

The Berle–Means model of capitalism was essentially an American one based on the notion of the American public company, typified by strong managers and weak fragmented owners, none owning more than a small proportion of the firm's shares. In this way capital for large firms required by economies of scale and technological change could be provided by selling shares to many dispersed investors. In Japan, on the other hand,

---

[62] Scott 1979: 18, referring to the work of Dahrendorf, Kerr, Aron, Galbraith and others.
[63] Berle and Means 1932; Scott 1979: 51. The same point has been made for Boston by Farrell (1993: 164).
[64] Data from Goldsmith and Parmalee (1940), for which see Scott 1979: 52.

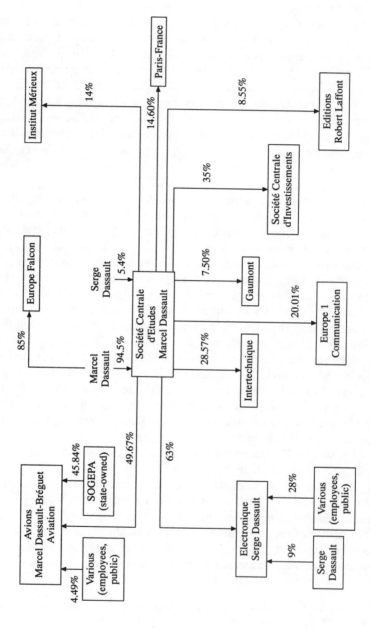

Figure 6.1 The Dassault organisation (*Source: Echo de la Bourse*)

groups of firms and banks are bound together through complex webs of cross-shareholdings, while in Germany banks oversee companies in a dual role as shareholder and lender.

It has recently been suggested that the American corporation owed its existence to the popular mistrust of concentrated financial power, though the situation has been subsequently modified by the emergence of big shareholders in the shape of pension and mutual funds.[65] The notion of the dispersed character of American (and other) ownership is further compromised by the fact that ownership is rarely as widely dispersed as most assume and some shareholders may have bought large holdings with a view to attaining the privilege of placing directors on the board. Above all, in most smaller firms and in many large ones relatives of the founder(s) are inevitably major shareholders by virtue of the laws of inheritance.

The aspect of the managerial approach that sees the evolutionary replacement of the family firm by impersonal forms of economic organisation has little empirical justification and neglects the continuing role of the family not only in smaller enterprises but also in many larger ones. Firstly it gives insufficient weight to the growth of new businesses that are bound to become centred on the family. Even the lone Crusoe marries and leaves his enterprise to his offspring. Secondly, even where control may be transmitted in a bureaucratic way, the property people possess at death normally passes to family members, whether this consists of jewellery, a house or shares. And even in major multinational concerns such as IBM, top managerial positions may pass from father to son. Consequently, despite the dominant ideological model, the role of the family in industrial activity did not disappear with early capitalism. The family firm does not vanish but is renewed with almost every new enterprise that is started. In later industrialisation, some become major public corporations, the development of which represents a process of social evolution, a move to greater complexity, based on the earlier forms of partnership we have examined. When this happens, the original family may relinquish its holdings and invest in a new enterprise. But it may also continue to play a part in management as well as in ownership. Take for example the striking case of the great French enterprise founded by the aeronautical engineer, Marcel Dassault (1892–1986).[66] The complex structure of his operation at the time of his death is given in Figure 6.1.

Serge Dassault was his son and, in keeping with the Gujarati example mentioned earlier, the father appears to have established an electronics

---

[65] Roe 1994.   [66] Reported in his obituary, *Le Monde*, 20–1 April 1986.

business specifically on his account (or so the name would imply) although this branch remained under the control of the parent company. When he died the main headline in a business daily read: 'M Dassault a réussi sa vie et peut-être sa succession.' And on an inside page: 'La succession reglée sauf grain de sable.' The implication was that the entrepreneur made his own testament and decreed his own succession. And he did so in a company that had been nationalised and was no longer even in the private sector. Moreover the succession involved other family members: 'le grain de sable' was the family, since he died leaving two sons. When the succession was resolved, the basic problem was to find 'a new point of equilibrium . . . with the separation of power from capital', the capital remaining with the family, power going to the technical managers. But that division was never clear cut, since Serge Dassault had his own unit and was being considered for the wider succession. In the circumstances provision had been made in the will for both the family and the firm.

Given that most entrepreneurs recruit their successors from their kin, indeed are often running their business with, if not for, their offspring, how is it that the notion of achieved rather than ascribed status was so significant a part of liberal values? In matters to do with government, the army and many aspects of management, it is important to get the best-qualified persons: hence recruitment by impersonal criteria is favoured. But, firstly, that advantage was specific to those sectors of social life, not for the business world in which property is inherited. Nepotism may have been a sin for popes, who had no progeny and in a sense had renounced the bonds of family; it was never an ideal for princes nor yet for any property owner, for to certain offices and to property the family was seen as having a 'natural' right. Secondly, impersonal recruitment was never confined to the West; elsewhere too armies and administrators were often forced to look for 'the best person for the job'. In China since the twelfth century the extensive examination system provided candidates for government posts. While literate administrations have adopted relatively open recruitment of this kind, whether through the temple schools of the ancient world or through medieval European universities, China developed a bureaucracy in a much more radical and extensive way than other major societies before the nineteenth century.

Non-bureaucratic recruitment prevailed in many fields during the rise of capitalism in western Europe. In England senior posts in the civil service and the army were virtually the prerogative of the élite until the middle of the nineteenth century. Only then did the sale of commissions in the army cease; only then were public examinations, standard in China for many centuries, adopted as a means of recruitment. In other words the dominance of 'rational–legal' methods in the government bureaucracy followed rather than preceded the establishment of the industrial system. But although such methods came to be largely accepted in public employment, the private sector continued to utilise kin as well as non-kin at the highest levels, because of the frequent overlap between family and firm. Nor can this be seen only in small firms. The members of many business families were related to one another and where they were not recruiting on the basis of ties of acquaintance (the old-boy network), it was often through kinship. Writing of Boston at the beginning of the twentieth century, Farrell remarks that 'the capacity of sons, sons-in-law, nephews, cousins, and grandsons of Boston Brahman families to gain a foothold in the new corporate economy was greater than has generally been conceded'.[67]

In business the example of Dassault cannot be dismissed as rare or as nationally specific. Industry in England had a similar history and the role of the family in the rise of capitalism emerges in many industrial stories. I take an example from Bradford since, as in the instances from Ahmadabad and Toulouse, here too the structure of the enterprise tended to duplicate the structure of the family. Close to Bradford stands the company village of Saltaire, built by an industrialist, one Titus Salt, who had already made a considerable fortune in the worsted trade. He owned six mills in Bradford and intended to retire to lead the life of a country gentleman. Instead, he created Saltaire, partly that 'I might provide occupation for my sons', and partly because 'outside my business I am nothing – in it, I have considerable influence'.

This association between family and business was not limited to the earlier days of capitalism. A recent article in *The Economist* declares that: 'More than three-quarters of British companies are still at least half-owned by the families that have started them'.[68] It is true that many of these are small firms that have a short life-span. Only 24 per cent of family businesses reach the second generation and a mere 14 per cent survive to the third. But those that go under are constantly being replaced by new firms of the same kind, some of them started with the funds that have been generated by earlier business activity. Of those that survive, some sell shares on the stock market, retaining a measure of control. One such firm is J. Sainsbury, the large supermarket chain, in which the family has a 44 per cent stake. Like other similar, publicly quoted, family firms, public but family, this is a very successful enterprise. Indeed between 1985 and 1989 firms of this kind did better than either wholly

---

[67] Farrell 1993: 164.   [68] 31 October 1992.

public or wholly private companies.[69] The most efficient firms of the British High Street, not only Sainsbury but Marks and Spencer, Tesco and Forte, all have a similar structure. Formerly, those other giants, Woolworths and Boots, belonged to the same species, as did the many stores whose personal names indicate the nature of their early organisation. But in the case of the many highly efficient, high-street firms, the family have retained an element not only of financial but of managerial control.

These features are in no sense characteristic only of Europe. The world's major capitalist power, the USA, displays similar characteristics and the reasons are again associated with the continuity of the family over time, with the transfer of property and the desire to establish junior generations, that is, with the essential constituents of dynasties. In his account of the role of generation-skipping trusts in creating American business dynasties, Marcus writes of 'the late nineteenth-century period of family capitalism and the expansion of the American economy'.[70] These trusts, which were limited to about three generations or a hundred years, favour 'lineal and future relatives over collateral living ones';[71] they comprised some 50 percent of estates by the middle of this century and they led to the creation of dynasties out of middle-class families 'by their associations with complex organizations of wealth'.[72] These estates provided a focus for co-activity, varying in intensity, over a three-generational span. The reference to the period of family capitalism again creates a categorical stage out of a continuing process. While larger multinational firms have become more corporate in character, nevertheless businesses grow up on a family basis and make use of similar but more complex versions of these trusts, since public policy seeks to place bounds on their operation. One result is that founders of potential dynasties are increasingly thrown into the hands of professional managers.

Despite this development, the family continues to play a part in some of the world's largest corporations. A report on the succession in the House of Seagram explains how Edgar Bronfman, Sr, had succeeded his father who had bought the company in 1928. The son grew up 'knowing he had no choice' but to take over the concern, described as 'a publicly held family business', with the family controlling 38.5 per cent of the stock. He in turn decided that his younger son should take over, although

---

[69] A separate study showed that these firms outperformed the stock market average by 30 per cent over the period from 1971 to 1991.

[70] Marcus 1986: 5.

[71] Marcus 1986: 51.   [72] Marcus 1986: 55.

the latter had only worked in the business for three years.[73] Once again, this is not an exceptional case. Indeed the figures (which should not be taken as exact) for the USA are even higher than Britain or Taiwan. For about 95 per cent of American businesses are said to be at least in part family owned. From Dupont to Campbell Soups, small and large firms are in some degree controlled or influenced by the founders or their descendants. That control may well influence recruitment at the top level. Lee Iaccoca left General Motors to join Chrysler when he found that Henry Ford wanted to 'keep it in the family'.[74] A similar situation occurred in other giants of the car industry. It was recently reported that 'the Agnelli family, owners of Fiat and Italy's most powerful dynasty, yesterday selected an heir apparent to chairman Gianni Agnelli with the appointment of his 29-year-old nephew Giovanni to the company's main board'.[75] At the highest level of such régimes, the bureaucratic succession of an outsider stands little chance.

The families involved in business are often larger than elementary families but they are not lineages of any extent. In my experience in contemporary Europe and Asia they are virtually limited to first cousins; beyond that the extended families tend to split into different property-centred units. That does not mean that the firm disappears but it is located in one branch of the family rather than another; and the other may well invest its proceeds in a new concern, often of a different type. So we are still talking about relatively limited kin connections, although wider ones may be mobilised in different contexts.

In this chapter I have tried to review some of the work on the way that aspects of the family in Europe may have predisposed that continent towards modernisation, and especially towards the economic structures we refer to as capitalist or industrial. I suggested that the analysis had been overinfluenced by ethnocentric notions about the Uniqueness of the West, and especially by the overgeneralised idea that it had seen an overall shift from the social to the individual, related to the emergence of the small elementary family of the active entrepreneur.

The vague features that a number of writers had associated with this small family were much more widely distributed than in western Europe alone. Notions that love of partner and love of children were to be seen as its unique attributes appeared mistaken, both historically and comparatively. But the fundamental problem, reflecting the bias towards

[73] *Fortune*, 17 March 1986: 26–9.
[74] Haas, A., 'Treating the Family Business', *Amtrak Express* (1990) February–March: 37–40.
[75] *Daily Telegraph*, 16 November 1993: 24.

an illusory individualism, the attribute of a mythical Crusoe, is the misunderstanding and undervaluing of the role of the family, even in public, 'bureaucratic' companies. That misunderstanding had encouraged the idea that one reason why, at a certain point in time, the East was unable to match developments in the West had something to do with family structure. It is true that widely extended groups such as clans and castes are not characteristic institutions of the West. But there is little evidence that they were more of a hindrance to modernisation than, for example, guilds, which in fact provided a limited kind of commercial law, as did castes in India. Indeed, these groups contributed to the growth of mercantile capitalism in both India and China. In these countries, modern businesses are often run by somewhat smaller kin groups though often larger than the elementary family.

A realisation that the Western notions were inappropriate has led to the argument that the East developed a collectivist form of capitalism. Though there are certainly differences of emphasis, especially in the role of the family and more particularly the lineage: in Europe the latter contradicted the church's notion of ritual kinship and its build-up of resources; whereas in China the lineage and its accompanying worship of ancestors had been deliberately encouraged partly in order to prevent Buddhism doing likewise. Hence that institution was available to promote certain business activities and did little to inhibit them. The validity of this radical distinction between East and West is thrown in doubt when we take another look at the past and present of European business life. Historians today often speak of the early form of industrialisation as one of 'family capitalism', the critical form for the take-off and one that was not radically incompatible with the existence of joint-stock companies. It is certainly true that some of those companies developed into more bureaucratically organised concerns as they became larger and even more multinational. But in the West as in the East the family necessarily remained heavily involved in running commerce and business wherever those activities depended upon private enterprise. In the longer term neither the differences in wider kinship ties nor in domestic groups appear to have greatly inhibited developments in the economies of the major Eurasian societies.

Labour

Family labour was critical to the working of the land in all peasant societies and, as in India, was central to the management of many enterprises in the mercantile, manufacturing and later the industrial spheres. In industry the system made different demands on employees and employers, on workers and owners. Employers often co-operate in a 'joint family' whereas workers may be rewarded for their individual labour, rarely sharing their wages with anyone outside the conjugal family. The entrepreneurs and employers may exercise some individual choice in economic affairs, while their labour force had to accept a work discipline and a subjugation of independence much greater than that required in peasant life. And sometimes they needed to be prepared to be mobile, whereas the owners are often linked to stationary resources around which they establish family seats.

The family was not of course the only source of available labour. In India the caste and guilds systems provided for a whole variety of specialised tasks for the local community as well as for wider, market-orientated trade and commerce. Some of this labour was based upon the internal exchanges of the *jajmani* system, some hired over the short or the long term. Is there any evidence that the existence of these forms of labour inhibited or prevented the shift to new forms of production?

While political economies are often characterised by a dominant form of labour, the notion that the dominance of one particular relationship could be an absolute bar to the adoption of others, or even of industrial modes of production, as Weber and others have suggested, seems highly questionable. Of course the presence of caste might temporarily discourage such developments. The same has been asserted of guilds. But even the simpler agricultural economies make use of a variety of forms of labour so that in time there is no overwhelming difficulty in shifting the weight (even the dominance) from one type to another. From this standpoint such an economy already contains the seeds of others within itself. Even the largely domestic production of Africa, a continent marked by hoe agriculture, was not based on family labour alone. It is true that before 1900 in northern Ghana, which consisted of simple state systems interspersed with acephalous or 'tribal' peoples, there was effectively no free labour market approximating to the ideal type of the classical economists. Nevertheless different forms of labour were utilised at certain times of the year, and individuals themselves would engage in different ones at different seasons.

Among the tribal peoples in the early part of the twentieth century, kinsfolk, friends and neighbours were invited to help clear or weed a farm, largely though not entirely on a reciprocal basis; but they were rewarded with food and drink, the ingredients of which the farmer might have to purchase with cowries in the local market. Such work parties have been described by many observers, including Saul (1983) for the Bisa village of Bentenga in Upper Volta. 'In most farming communities in Africa where the basic production unit is based on primary kinship ties, farmers must also rely on labour associations grounded in relationships of friendship, self-interest, or political dominance.' Among most peoples in northern Ghana, such help groups for farming include kin as well as kith and do not constitute distinct associations.

Such 'hiring' of farm labour, as it is called in west African English, was also found in the states, though it was not so prominent because of the existence of alternative occupations and the lesser interest in agriculture displayed by the chiefs.[1] Some of the inhabitants were concerned more with war, trade and the Islamic religion, all three of which made reciprocity in farm labour less practical and less valued. When such a chief called for farming help, there was a different kind of obligation to assist, a hierarchical one that was certainly not reciprocated in the same manner. It is arguable that the value of the labour was returned in other ways, in providing defence, in sharing booty from war, in the provision of justice and ritual protection in peace and in help and advice at other times. Part of the additional production that such farm labour allowed was retained by the ruler and enabled him to lead a life that was generous to himself as well as to others. He invariably had more wives than his subjects, and his larger holding required gifts, tribute, taxes, booty or, more usually, labour to establish and sustain. The line between exploitation and reciprocity is a shadowy one. Furthermore, at the beginning of the century, there was slave labour, considerable in the case

---

[1] The word is so used in west African English: see the translation of the Second Bagre, Goody and Gandah 1981: 98, line 470.

of the states, minimal in the tribal areas which provided rather than received booty.[2]

It was this model of 'hiring' that the actors transferred to the recruitment of workers by the colonial administration for road-making and similar tasks under the colonial government, that is, for wage labour. As in the adjacent francophone territories, 'forced' labour was initially used on the analogy of the work commoners did for the chief, government services being visualised as provided in exchange. Both forms of 'chiefly' labour were backed up by the sanction of physical force. At the same time 'forced' labour could be seen as a variation of sons farming for their father, just as 'hired' labour was assimilated to the employment of outside help on the farm. All were recognised to be possible transformations of household labour under particular socio-economic conditions. Nor was there any enduring difficulty with getting people to work as wage labour in private mines and factories, which was often seen by the local population as government work. Initially, cheap labour for these enterprises was difficult to find as northerners did not want to make the journey south for a variety of reasons, while southerners had other ways of making money, through growing cash crops. So that in the beginning strong pressures were used by some district commissioners to recruit for the mines (as well as for the army, especially in time of war). But individuals were very soon making their own decisions to go and work in the south, in mines for expatriate firms, on farms for Asante cocoa-planters and in a variety of other occupations, including domestic service. In the early 1950s migrant labour had become so much a part of the experience of each young man that the trek to Kumasi was played out at many a funeral as part of the process of separating the dead from the living ('taking out the dream', they would say).[3] Such labour was seasonal for some, on a longer-term basis for others. But after only forty years of colonial presence it had bitten deep into LoDagaa social life. I vividly remember the incident where a distinguished elder, Bonyiri, half-jokingly gave up his stool to one of his sons, turning to me to say, 'If I don't, he will run away to Kumasi'. That is, he would join other young men and become a wage labourer in the south, the stimulus for which was partly 'freedom', partly novelty, partly savings, but mostly the acquisition of consumer goods such as bicycles.

Such new forms of work were not seen by the actors as constituting in themselves a radical break with existing labour practices within the community. Clearly communal farm labour is not the kind of 'hiring' practised on farms in nineteenth-century England or in twentieth-

[2] Goody 1979.   [3] Goody 1962: 130.

century India.[4] However one can easily see how it can be (and is being) transformed into such a relationship. But the inhabitants were also well acquainted with slavery, either as givers or takers, and this too contributed to the way they viewed European practices. After the British defeat of the Asante in 1874 the roads to the interior were opened up and expeditions were dispatched to the market town of Salaga, the 'Timbuktu of the South'. Knowing that caravans were coming to that town from Hausaland, what is now northern Nigeria, the British sent army officers to recruit soldiers from among the porters who headloaded the merchandise. For they had concluded that the Hausa were a military nation on the north Indian model and, given the medical problems experienced by European soldiers, had established a 'Hausa force' of native troops. However they had difficulty in finding enough recruits in the south of Nigeria among the 'Lagos Hausas' involved in the trade in kola and cloth, so they extended their search to the north of what was then the colony of the Gold Coast. In order to recruit men for the army a bounty was offered, usually to an intermediary. The Gonja, in whose territory Salaga lies, were convinced then, as many of them are today, that in offering such a bounty the British were 'buying slaves' for their army. Indeed most of the porters did fall into that category, many not being Hausa at all but rather captives impressed into the caravan trade.[5]

The second example is more recent. In 1952, the year of the coronation of Queen Elizabeth, the Colonial Office arranged for a number of representatives from the Commonwealth to attend the public celebrations. Among these (largely at his own expense) was the newly appointed Chief of Birifu in the north of the Gold Coast, Namantuo Gandaa. Since I had worked in his area I naturally acted as host when he visited Britain and I tried to show him around the local activities in Cambridge as his brothers had shown me around in Africa. One visit we made was to Pye's factory (now Phillips) which, before the migration of the electronics industry to the countries of the Far East, made radio sets. We went there one morning and were taken into the large workshop where rows of women were piecing together the parts of radio sets according to the latest production techniques. We were shown too another machine, the 'clock' which recorded the times of their comings and goings. Looking first at these women and then at the 'clock' by the entrance, Namantuo turned round to me and asked in all seriousness, '*Gbangbaa*? Are they slaves?'.

---

[4] Dasgupta 1993: 9, where the model of the peasant household is essentially Eurasian.
[5] Braimah and Goody 1967: 106–7.

The examples are more complex than they appear. In one case money was being paid for recruiting labour for the army, the labour of existing slaves, which looked very different to the locals than it did to the British who had 'abolished slavery'. In the other case it was the organisation of labour that was the relevant feature. My friend was amazed that human beings would work under these conditions unless they were literally forced to do so by slavery. It was mainly people of servile status that did the unpleasant work of mining in west Africa: free men who were not bound would not do such fearsome work which resembled that of the gravedigger. I am not suggesting that the actor's perception of the situation should be our sole criteria for the analysis of labour relations.[6] But it is a significant factor, especially when one is considering the relative ease with which individuals move between different forms. That is not surprising because although different economies privilege particular forms of labour, which can then be looked upon as dominant, these are rarely if ever exclusive. That is also true for Europe today, where individuals may engage in different forms of labour not only consecutively but contemporaneously. In contemporary France I have encountered households where members are at the same time share-croppers and wage-labourers, owners and tenants. In pre-Revolutionary China there were also constant switches between different forms.[7]

This flexibility in forms of labour was also found in the ancient world, even in the field of manufacture on the large scale. Up to the Muslim Middle Ages, Oppenheim claims, 'industrial production' was exclusively concerned with the weaving of textiles and related activities, carried out mainly in the workshops of the 'great organizations'.[8] The labour seems to have been partly slave, partly free. In the classical world of Greece and Rome, workshops were initially manned by slaves. In the Italy of Augustus, the flourishing potteries of Arezzo, producing the new *terra sigillata*, employed only slaves, the largest number known in a single establishment being fifty-eight.[9] But when the production of such ware was taken up in southern Gaul, it was carried on by independent craftsmen working in smaller enterprises. In the later Roman Empire, the state factories that now engaged in the direct production of items such as the uniforms and weapons required by the armies, employed a workforce that was servile in a more general sense, the distinction between slavery and other forms of involuntary labour having almost disappeared. In

---

[6] The contention that the notions of the actors should predominate in some but not in all levels of analysis is one that some social scientists, especially anthropologists, have difficulty in accepting.

[7] Chao 1984.

[8] Oppenheim 1964: 84.   [9] Finley 1973: 74.

other words similar activities were carried out by different kinds of labour at different times.

In India different forms of labour were also found side by side.[10] While servile castes of untouchables took part in the production of cloth, so did non-servile groups such as Shudras. In Gujarat the former produced rough clothes for local use, often on a 'service' basis, while the shudras or 'cultivators' wove and also printed and painted finer cloth for the temples, the rich and for the export market which flourished with Asia, Africa and Europe. In Gujarat the untouchable caste of Vankar, who were weavers as well as scavengers, had accounts with individual Bania households, borrowing money to buy cotton and therefore committed to sell part of their cloth production. But they could also travel from village to village to sell the rest or to make over a part to a dyer. In some villages they had arrangements with landowners from whom they received cotton and grain in exchange for a short loincloth, a covering for a bullock cart and a coarsely woven sheet annually.[11] Untouchable castes were also subject to corvée or forced labour (*veth*) for the local ruler, for which some small counter-payment was usually made; at the same time, they might work as wage-labourers on the lands of their patrons (*gharāh*) in the dominant caste.

With the advent of machinery from Europe in the middle of the nineteenth century, Indian entrepreneurs from merchant groups took up industrial production. Their labour force was often subject to caste restrictions; some were reluctant to work in units where leather was used or with groups of a different status. But industrial production developed effectively enough to allow the export of yarn and cloth not only to the Far East but to the very centres in Europe where these forms of production had first originated. So that it has yet to be demonstrated that the presence of other forms of labour relation seriously inhibited the adoption of industrial modes of production. Indeed one might go further and ask if it has been conclusively demonstrated that industrial production works only with 'free labour' (which has sometimes been characterised as 'wage-slavery'). Is it clear that a free labour force, able to bargain for its wages, is essential for the running of an industrial system? That is surely not how some economies in post-war eastern Europe have operated. Nor yet Germany nor other countries during the period of the Second World War, where various degrees of restraint were

---

[10] On the co-existence of different types of labour contract, see Dasgupta 1993: 233, which in the case of Bengal he describes as 'a theorist's nightmare' (but only if he is 'weak-kneed').

[11] Randeria 1992: 80–98.

universal. Is it clear that the Japanese factory system, with its paternalistic practices, works entirely in that way? While members of the largely hereditary occupations in the mines and docks of Britain are free to bargain for wages, are these workers entirely free to seek 'alternatives'? What about the immigrant labour on which so much industrial production of the contemporary West is based? A free labour force, free in practice as well as in law, is hardly a *sine qua non* of an industrial mode of production, although widely found in capitalist systems. Indeed Mintz has forcefully argued that the plantation system of the Americas, based on slave labour, constituted a case of capitalism before capitalism.[12] It is true that most modern production systems tend to encourage greater freedom of the employers to sack their employees and of the employees to seek other jobs (if there are any available alternatives). But those freedoms are not absolutely essential and can emerge out of a number of earlier forms.

I am not maintaining that these forms of work do not differ under different economic (or indeed cultural) systems. But at the broad level at which they have been defined comparatively we frequently find them distributed across types of system (for example, modes of production), not confined to one. So new forms do not need to be 'invented' but existing ones have to be maximised.

Production

The remarks about labour, combined with Mintz's comment on capitalism in the West Indies, raise in acute form the whole question of modes of production in the context of the West and the East. Marx was in no doubt about the radical difference posed by the 'Asiatic mode of production' and Weber was equally firm about the different forms of socio-economic relationship that existed there. So too have been many authors like Polanyi. But if such a different political economy prevailed, how did those countries achieve a cultural superiority over Europe during the early medieval period or make such startling advances at the present day? The first it was possible to overlook, the second impossible to set aside.

There is an obvious answer. In respect of the development of industrialisation the categorical differences were not of the order that both scholars and laity in the West have imagined. Speaking of the period of China's early modern history, Mote remarks that by the end of the Ming period in 1644 China was already part of world history, of the growing

12 Mintz 1985: 58.

'world system'. 'In the consciousness of the peoples, whether Chinese, Europeans, or others, the national entities of Eurasia were worlds apart and would remain so until very recent times. Yet in many ways which strongly influenced such things as their food-products, production, technology, distribution – the civilizations and national entities of Eurasia were becoming mutually responsive.'[13] A recent attempt to face this problem has been made by Eric Wolf who has deliberately tried to look at the world from a non-European point of view. The aim of his enquiry was to provide a history of the encounter of Europe with the rest of the world (not only with the 'peoples without history'). For this purpose he needed some general concepts to work with and he chose the mode of production as a way of indicating the basic changes that were taking place in human history over time. Like Althusser and his followers, he concentrates on relations of production as seen from a special angle, that of the control of 'social labour'. Such control permits the extraction of surplus, a factor that is also prominent in the work of Brenner (1976) and Hilton (1985) on the transition from feudalism to capitalism, as well as of scholars working in the Althusserian tradition.[14] As a consequence modes of production are stripped down to a threefold distinction between kinship, tributary and capitalist.

The basic difference between these three is that under capitalism, labourers have no independent access to the means of production, which are firmly in the hands of the owners of capital. As a result they have to sell their labour power. Under the tributary mode, which obtained in 'the major agricultural areas' prior to 1400, the primary producer had access to land but tribute was extracted by political or military means. In the kin-ordered mode, which takes in the remainder of human societies, kinship is the means of committing social labour to the transformation of nature through appeals to filiation and marriage. In contrast to French writers like Rey who see the kin-ordered mode as stratified by age or gender (and hence as class based), only the first two modes 'divide the population under their command into a class of surplus producers and a class of surplus takers'.[15]

Wolf adopts a pragmatic attitude to this tripartite division. The modes are put forward not as ultimate verities but as tools to analyse 'the spread of the capitalist mode and its impact on world areas where social labor was allocated differently'.[16] He disclaims any intention to regard them as

---

[13] Mote 1977: 195.

[14] For anthropology, see the commentary by Geschiere and Raatgever 1985, on Meillassoux, Godelier, Terray and Rey; for an extreme case, see Hindess and Hirst 1975.

[15] Wolf 1982: 99.   [16] Wolf 1982: 76.

exhaustive, as evolutionary stages, or yet as types of social systems; they serve only 'to underline the strategic relationships involved in the deployment of social labor'. These relationships may 'characterize only a part of the total range of interaction in a society; they may comprehend all of a society; or they may transcend particular, historically constituted systems of social interaction'.[17] While the author allows for much latitude in the notion of the distribution of strategic relationships, he nevertheless talks about 'the spread of the capitalist mode' in a more concrete way. It is difficult to see this development as being critically defined by the control of social labour, especially as these forms of labour are found in a subdominant position in so many societies. In which case 'strategic relationships' are not 'spread'; they are encouraged or emphasised under certain circumstances.

The starting point of the analysis turns on selecting a single aspect of the productive system, namely control over labour, linked to the relations of production. There are both costs and gains in utilising the concept of mode of production in a way that is so limited in the criteria employed and hence highly generalised in its application. The tendency of much recent writing to stress these relations of production as the defining features of the modes tends to lead to a very parsimonious set. In Wolf's case the first, the kinship mode, is similar to what some authors, basing themselves on a more restricted French usage, have called the lineage mode; that in turn has been identified with the domestic mode.[18]

Wolf's schema eliminates the need for the notion of a feudal mode. Feudalism is seen as essential to developments in the West, where its contradictions were critical to what happened later. The question of whether feudal institutions existed elsewhere has much exercised comparative historians, sociologists and anthropologists. Some have found examples in Asia, others have described African kingdoms ('simple states' in Kaberry's phrase) by the same term.[19] On the other hand Anderson sees the political system that defines feudalism as being confined to the West, while Mukhia denies its existence in India or anywhere without labour services.

One attempt to widen the concept of a 'feudal mode of production' (often equated with 'feudalism') is that made by Wickham.[20] Modes of production are defined exclusively in terms of one aspect of relationships of production, their method of surplus production, of which there are few basic types. The distinguishing feature of feudalism he sees as coercive

---

[17] Wolf 1982: 76–7.
[18] For example in van Binsbergen and Geschiere 1985.
[19] For a general discussion see Goody 1971.   [20] Wickham 1985.

rent-taking. Such a basic type is found much more widely, in the late Roman Empire, the Ancien Régime, Song China and Qajar Iran. That extension involves sweeping away notions of the Asiatic mode as being 'too politically and legally specific'.[21] As an alternative to the latter he prefers Amin's 'tributary mode of production' in which a state class extracts tax from the peasantry. Although it often co-exists with local landownership, it nevertheless does so as a distinct mode of production. The Uniqueness of the East consisted in maintaining the dominance of the state which the West lost with the fall of Rome. That empire was already less centralised from the standpoint of tax-raising, which devolved onto local bodies, the nominally independent cities of the Empire that inherited the tradition of the city state; it was this characteristic that makes the ancient mode of production 'an identifiable subtype'.[22] Following Hindess and Hirst, Wickham rejects Anderson's point about the emphasis on the political system as leading analysis outside the economic; otherwise criteria were 'too restrictive', thereby excluding much of Europe.[23] His answer to the uniqueness (or primacy) problem is that the West is one of the few areas where feudalism has *dominated*.[24] Wolf extends this argument yet further, seeing pre-industrial societies in both the East and West as characterised by the 'tributary mode', with the West having a less centralised form than the East.

How does this argument affect views of the rise of capitalism? Feudalism opened the way partly because people were less able 'to control and ideologically englobe merchants and the artisanate than the Asian states'.[25] It was more open to mercantile enterprise. That claim suggests that in a wider perspective the Western variety is hardly essential to the emergence of mercantile capitalism, though it may have encouraged what it seems logical to regard as the necessary forerunner of industrial production.

The role of state control runs up firstly against the recurrent problem of what you are trying to explain. If it is the growth of merchants and the artisanate in the sixteenth century, then there is some justification. But can one really talk more generally about the lack of state control in England at a time when the monasteries were being dissolved and the religion changed, to a significant degree from the top down? If one is referring to industrialisation, capitalism in that sense, then it has been argued that no take-off to continuous growth has been effected without strong government support. Japan certainly provides one example.

---

[21] Wickham 1985: 170.
[22] Wickham 1985: 188.   [23] Wickham 1985: 168.
[24] Wickham 1985: 169.   [25] Wickham 1985: 193.

Berrill also points to the way that the successful military campaigns of Britain in the eighteenth century, organised by the government, created an overseas market for its products.[26] The same might be said for the Civil War in the USA.

What tend to get neglected in this argument are the similarities and differences in the *means* rather than in the *relations* of production. From the broad perspective of pre-historians these major societies of Europe and Asia have all experienced the 'civilising' process, originating in the Urban Revolution of the Bronze Age, as described by Childe and many others since his time. The immediate result of recognising the similar basis of their achievement (instead of pursuing the sociologists' view of 'Asiatic exceptionalism') is the same since Wolf's approach also overcomes the radical East–West divide, encouraging one to look at the Occidental and Oriental precursors of modern developments in the same frame of reference, as co-ordinate with one another. In this way he eliminates the ethnocentric element in much grand theory which, like Marx, treats feudalism as an essentially (Western) 'progressive' element in the march to capitalism, as an advance beyond both the ancient world of the West and the recently backward world of the East. At the same time Wolf allows for an alternation between central and decentralised forms of polity without having to characterise them as different 'modes'. So the approach overcomes the constant tendency of Westerners to see their own world as always having been ahead of the East as if programmed in some semi-genetic, deep-cultural way. By treating the 'feudal' and the 'Asiatic' as variants of a tributary mode of production, Wolf abandons a sequence that both overprivileges Europe's experience and promotes the search for facilitating factors of a more specific kind.

But when did the great shift occur? The question of timing is closely related to one's perception of capitalism. Of the three types of definition analysed by Dobb, the first isolates its 'geist' as a synthesis of the spirit of enterprise or adventure with that of calculation and rationality, a definition associated with the names of Sombart and Weber.[27] The second (adopted by many historians) virtually identifies capitalism with the organisation of production for a distant market. Finally, according to Marx, capitalism was a particular mode of commodity production for a market where labour power had itself become a commodity, in other words, had become wage labour. Its presence roughly corresponds to the distinction between mercantile and industrial capitalism.

When did this form of production emerge, not simply in its first manifestation but as dominating the socio-economic system? For

[26] Berrill 1964.   [27] Dobb 1947.

economic historians it was on Werner Sombart that discussion of the periodisation of capitalism centred. Indeed he was the first to employ the term as fundamental in economic thought to indicate a system dominated by 'capital'; in so doing he was attempting to employ in a neutral way a term that had acquired a distinctly pejorative significance for socialists at least since the time of Marx. He regarded this system, for which he consciously constructed an 'ideal type', as having a particular 'spirit' dominated by (unlimited) acquisition, by competition and by rationality. Economic rationality, in contrast to the traditionalistic organisation of earlier times, takes the form of long-range planning, the strict adaptation of means to ends and exact calculation in order to assess the profit and the loss; it is linked to 'economic freedom', to specialisation, and to a form of enterprise that is independent of the constituent individuals. Indeed it is at the level of the enterprise rather than the individual that the spirit of capitalism operates in its search for profit;[28] it is the 'locus' of economic rationality which is quite independent of the personality of the staff. However that search for rationality is not unqualified. For while 'individual action under capitalism is informed by the ideal of highest rationality, the capitalistic system as a whole remains irrational' because unrestrained acquisition means uncoordinated action. Well nigh perfect rationality exists side by side with the greatest irrationality, giving rise to the strains in the economy.[29]

Sombart claimed that the European Middle Ages constituted a non-capitalist or pre-capitalist epoch, which contrasted in every detail with 'the rational and acquisitive system of modern capitalism'.[30] In his early formulation he argued that only agricultural rents could provide the basis for capital accumulation for investment in trade, which was essentially 'traditional in method and non-acquisitive in motive', a proposition he was later to modify. The thesis did not find much favour with scholars of the medieval period. Pirenne took a broader view of capitalism, while Brentano related medieval trade to the Italian maritime republics and the development of a modern economy.

In a little pamphlet entitled *Les Périodes de l'histoire social du capitalisme* (1914) Pirenne had rejected the contention of Bücher (1893), taken up by Sombart, that capitalism began with the Renaissance and did not mark any aspect of the economy of the Middle Ages.[31] He regarded the essential features of this system, the individual nature of the enterprise,

---

[28] It is a 'happy coincidence' if individual motivation coincides with 'the immanent spirit of capitalism' of which it is a necessary realisation.

[29] Sombart 1930: 198.

[30] Postan 1932–4: 212.   [31] Pirenne 1914: 3.

credit advances, commercial profit and speculation, as being already present in the twelfth century. He sees little evidence of commerce, except in commodities like salt and wine that were unevenly distributed, previous to the eleventh century when towns were formed. The *negociatores* he compares with contemporary Arab merchants coming to the Belgian Congo, half trafficker, half pirate, who established settlements (but not walled towns) at places like Marseilles where transhipment took place. Only after the invasions of the Normans from the north and the Arabic disruption in the Mediterranean to the south did European economic activity begin to take off, especially in Italy and the Low Countries, leading in 1127 to the meeting of merchants from these countries in the fairs of Flanders. They operated in guilds, in hansa, in *carités*, partly for protection but no doubt to spread other risks. And Pirenne sees this activity as leading to the later developments of trade and industry that took place before the Renaissance, which gave rise to 'une différence quantitative, non une différence qualitative, une différence d'intensité et non une différence de nature'.[32]

In rejecting the Sombart thesis, Pirenne does what de Roover later did to the theses of Weber and Tawney: he claims that he has exaggerated the significance of changes to create a categorical gap where none existed and that they were in error in attempting to restrict to the later period the term 'capitalism' and the notions it implies. Confining his attention to western Europe, Pirenne, like de Roover, insists that such features characterised the growth of the economy in the later Middle Ages. The earlier Middle Ages on the other hand display none of these characteristics, bearing a greater resemblance to the kind of activity carried out by Arab traders in black Africa.

This notion of African trade as conducted illicitly by alien robbers does not stand up to serious examination. Legitimate trade carried out according to accepted principles has long been present in Africa and some writers have seen it as characterising an 'African mode of production'.[33] The error is significant theoretically because not only does Pirenne 'primitivise' early medieval trade, he also primitivises the non-European. If the trade of that period in Europe was similar to that in Africa at the end of the nineteenth century, then it was more complicated than he suggests. If it did not reach that level, then the post-Roman decline had indeed been catastrophic, back not just to 'barbarism' in Morgan's terms but virtually to 'savagery'.

For other scholars such as Passow (1918) it was quite inappropriate to use the term 'capitalism' for activities that pre-dated the nineteenth

[32] Pirenne 1914: 5.   [33] Coquery-Vidrovitch 1978; Meillassoux 1964.

century. In other words the term should refer to 'industrial capitalism' and not to 'mercantile capitalism', that is, to what Sombart calls 'full capitalism' which he dates from 1750–1914, and that was followed in its turn by late capitalism.[34] However he does allow, at least in his later work, for the idea of an early capitalism which operated from the thirteenth to the middle of the eighteenth century and continued to be marked by many of the earlier features including 'patriarchal industrial relations'.

In his discussion of the problem, Dobb looks not for the appearance of large-scale trading and of a merchant class (mercantile capitalism) but for evidence of the 'direct subordination of the producer to a capitalist', which he sees as happening in the later sixteenth and early seventeenth centuries.[35] For him this is the period when capitalists became the dominant class in organising production. That conclusion obviously leads him to reject the thesis, associated with Pirenne, that locates the birth of capitalism in the twelfth-century Netherlands, or with the fourteenth-century development of urban trade in Italy. He argues it was only by the late sixteenth century that capital had begun to penetrate production on a large scale either through wage labour or by the 'putting-out' system. While these forms of labour had existed previously, they were sufficiently widespread to be able to speak of a new mode of production. So Dobb distinguishes between adolescent capitalism before the late sixteenth century, a time when the feudal system had broken down and capitalism was not yet born, which was followed by early capitalism and finally by mature or industrial capitalism at the end of the eighteenth century.

Wolf comes down resolutely in favour of the latter, deliberately setting himself apart from Frank and Wallenstein for whom capitalism is a 'system of production for the market, propelled by the search for profit realized by non-producing entrepreneurs who pocket the surplus of the direct producer'.[36] In concentrating on the 'process of surplus transfers', they take the Weberian position that capitalism is oriented to profits from exchange. For them the world system of capitalism came into existence with the expansion of mercantile activity in the sixteenth century, a notion Wolf sees as collapsing the concept of the mode of production into that of the world market.

The problem about taking the earlier period in Europe for the birth of capitalism, whether these are developments in late medieval Italy or the Netherlands, or the emergence of far-flung, European mercantile

---

[34] Sombart 1930: 203.
[35] Dobb 1947: 17.   [36] Dobb 1947: 297.

activity beginning in the sixteenth century, is that in global terms there was less of an economic breakthrough at these periods than is often supposed, except perhaps in the range of action (the sea link between East and West) and, some have argued, in its organisation. Braudel has put the case for differentiating between the economy of the tradesman and that of the merchant (*negotiant*), the first being involved in the economy of the primary or public market, the second (that of the capitalists) in the private market of large-scale commerce. Such commerce existed well before the advent of the European 'world-system' both in the West and the East, where the commerce of the Indian Ocean and South China Sea had become very active by the time of the Tang dynasty (618–907) and the founding of the Kingdom of Srívijaya in Sumatra in 683 CE or earlier; even in Europe it had developed in the Mediterranean long before the rise of the north-west of that continent. About this Braudel's comment is incisive: 'Les pays du Nord n'ont fait que prendre la place occupée longtemps et brillamment avant eux par les vieux centres capitalistes de la Mediterranée. Ils n'ont rien inventé, ni dans la technique, ni dans le maniement des affairs. Amsterdam copie Venise, comme Londres copiera Amsterdam, comme New York copiera Londres.'[37] If we accept this wide view of mercantile capitalism, then the Mediterranean takes us back further to the activities of merchants in early Mesopotamia, where they acted sometimes for the state, sometimes independently. It includes the development of that mercantile economy in the ancient East, in the Harappan civilisation in India, in early China, as well as along the silk, cotton and spice routes by land and by sea. Of course there were great changes in volume and range, but this process was never confined to the Western economies even though it was those that saw the greatest development of the market for imports and where exports came to play a dominating role.

Others see capitalism as coming into being at a significantly later point in time, though stimulated by that earlier merchant activity. Wolf's interpretation of Marx is that capital differs from mercantile wealth in its combination with other elements, with machinery, raw materials and labour power; when wealth can purchase human energy and tools, it becomes capital. In his view that conjunction did not take place until much later than Dobb supposes, only at the end of the eighteenth century in Britain with the advent of the factory production of cotton textiles. The factory developed when the limits of the putting-out system had been reached. That dispersed organisation of labour was difficult to supervise (both for time and for quality) as well as being difficult to

[37] Braudel 1985: 69–70.

sustain and expand. Of course from the standpoint of labour discipline the factory was not an entirely 'new' form of organisation. It existed in an elementary form in Elizabethan Britain, yet earlier in the *karkhanas* of Mughal India, much earlier still in the weaving establishments found in many parts of Eurasia and going back to the 'workshops' of the ancient Near East. However, apart from problems of the volume and quality of output for the expanded market, aspects of the new technology of mass production *required* factory organisation and the capital investment in complex machinery, especially with the introduction of steam which cannot operate at a domestic level as easily as water power, largely because of engineering factors. Later, with the advent of yet newer forms of energy, dispersion again became possible and parts of complex machines could be produced in the home, as we see in the contemporary electronics industry of Kerala and Taiwan; while the organisation costs may be greater, these may be offset by the lower wages demanded by home working, which in a sense represents a reversion to a form of putting-out. In developing countries such consideration may continue to give the edge to rural production, to work in the house, particularly to the work of women. Working on their own, or even in small co-operatives, the marketing difficulties may be overwhelming. But that is not the case if they are working for a firm which is primarily oriented towards the market.

In Wolf's view the advent of capitalism as a mode of production (that is, 'capitalism-in-production') is effectively identified with the Industrial Revolution, with what economists have discussed in terms of the take-off to (more or less) continuous growth. It is not the development of the market nor wage labour in themselves that testify to the advent of capitalism, but large-scale factory production with its concomitant, agricultural capitalism. 'Not until large-scale industry, based on machinery owners, does there arise a permanent foundation for capitalist agriculture.' This argument runs counter to that of many historians, mainly medievalists, who stress the role of agriculture in the transition from feudalism to capitalism, an argument that has been rehearsed in the debate that followed a controversial article by Brenner. For him European economic development 'can only be fully understood as the outcome of the emergence of new class relations more favourable to new organizations of production, technical innovations, and increasing levels of productive investment'.[38] The breakthrough from a 'traditional economy' to relatively self-sustaining economic development is 'predicated upon the emergence of a specific set of class or social–property

[38] Brenner [1976] 1985: 18.

relations in the countryside – that is, capitalist class relations'.[39] These relations failed to develop in France, he claims, because of the predominance of petty proprietors with relatively powerful property rights as compared to England.

But what does capitalism signify in agricultural terms? According to Brenner it means 'large, consolidated holdings formed on the basis of capital improvement with wage labour';[40] not just production for the market which had gone on around most large towns since an early period to provide the inhabitants with vegetables. Around Paris in the thirteenth century that work was carried out by free peasants and serfs.[41] However, for agricultural capitalism the essential was large, consolidated holdings, improved by capital investment and employing wage labour.

That situation was found (and still is) in many plantation economies. That was the basis of Mintz's notion of 'capitalism before capitalism' in the sugar production of the Caribbean, earlier yet in Brazil and other 'slave economies'. Slavery was not simply a particular method of surplus extraction favoured by the owners as a means of gaining a greater amount from the workers, but a way of obtaining labour when there was no alternative supply. It was a form of labour that depended not so much on internal class relations as on the ability of a dominant group to acquire slaves indirectly through commerce or directly through military conquest.

The phrase 'capitalism before capitalism' again throws the emphasis on industrial capitalism. That emphasis, together with Wolf's identification of Eastern and Western pre-capitalist formations as 'tributary', overcomes one general problem in explaining the rise of modern society, since it no longer uniquely privileges the Western sequence of development through feudalism, mercantile expansion and proto-industrial activity. Implicitly at least, it allows room for the possibility of these processes in other parts of the Old World. That concession is essential, because if south and east Asia did not provide the same bases for a world system of trade and domination as emerged from the European ships and guns of the sixteenth century, they constituted more than the limited 'économies-mondes' of which Braudel writes.[42] The extensive trading systems of India and China in the Indian Ocean and the China Seas involved a corresponding elaboration of their manufacturing organisation for cloth, beads, china and bronze, which go back in embryonic but significant forms to the ancient Near East but emerged to dominate the Eastern oceans.

[39] Brenner [1976] 1985: 30.   [40] Brenner [1976] 1985: 28.
[41] Brenner [1976] 1985: 25.   [42] Braudel 1985: 87.

If we see capitalism as linked to the extensive use of capital in commerce, then this long existed in the East with the development of the caravan trade but especially with water-borne exchange. In western Europe, such activity goes back to the late Middle Ages but earlier in the Italian cities. If we see capitalism as coming into its own 'as soon as capital has established the sway over production' rather than distribution,[43] then the problem of its origin is clarified, because that only became dominant with the advent of industrialisation in Europe, first in England in the late eighteenth century. In this latter case any explanation of why capitalism developed in Europe bears little relation to the previous existence of mercantile capitalism itself nor yet to proto-industrial activities or to particular forms of labour, since these were found throughout the major societies of Eurasia. In all such societies we find wealthy merchants as well as state enterprises engaged in external as well as internal trade based upon local products.

The qualities that we associate with commercial activities, risk-taking, entrepreneurial skills, the search for foreign markets, the mobility, the 'individualism' and the desire to accumulate and reinvest, these qualities were widely distributed and cannot be looked upon in the framework of European developments alone. The 'spirit of capitalism' was found in much of the Eurasian continent, though its development was hindered at times by too much political or ecclesiastical interference. At other times, however, both state and church were supportive of such developments, contributing to the investment, the innovation and the search for the markets that were required.

We find a broad spectrum of comparable activities throughout the major societies of Eurasia at a more profound level than is indicated by the word 'tributary'. What is important for the kind of rapid economic growth that we see in those societies today lies in the kind of advanced artisanal and manufacturing processes and the urban centres that enabled them to produce for export from an early period and to adapt to new types of mass production when they came; they had access to the appropriate economic ethic, entrepreneurial skills and labour practices. These achievements were in turn linked to the development of knowledge systems which writing rendered possible.

The question still remains of why the final phase of industrialisation took place in Europe. Wolf sees that continent as enjoying 'locational and technological advantages' over other merchants, although the latter were presumably not available earlier than the fifteenth century, and only in limited respects.[44] That technology included ships, guns and maps,

---

[43] Marx, *Capital* III.   [44] Wolf 1982: 85.

which joined in helping take over and develop new trading areas. However he rejects the notion of Weber, Wallenstein and Frank that these mercantile activities were 'the direct ancestors of capitalism', and denies that the change from merchant wealth to capital is 'continuous, linear and quantitative'; capitalism cannot be seen merely as 'an expansion of processes already at work in the tributary mode'.

The argument turns on the word 'merely'. Clearly mercantile capitalism was an essential preliminary of the decisive change that took place with the advent of industrialisation. Most historians of Europe consider the previous three centuries as constituting not only a necessary lead into those developments but as manifesting the 'uniqueness' that permitted the Rise of the West. Wolf too sees a critical factor for England as lying in the growth of the rural production of woollens in the fifteenth century which permitted four interconnected developments: the commercial transformation of agriculture, the wide involvement in trade, the development of a rural population in need of part-time or full-time employment, and the relative freedom of merchants and landowners. But as we have argued the medieval West also suffered from a measure of backwardness compared with the contemporary East as well as with the ancient world of the West. And this situation added some vigour and some openness to the rebirth.

Whether or not these factors represent an adequate framework for considering the Rise of the West, we are well beyond any uniqueness hypothesis which attributes some special 'dynamism' to Christian Europe,[45] requiring a 'miraculous' concatenation of circumstances to produce the modern world;[46] beyond, too, any notion that such change was rooted in the moral qualities of its entrepreneurs. By concentrating on the role of industrial capitalism and the factory system of the West, and by seeing the earlier mercantile capitalism as a variant of a more widespread phenomenon, more attention can be placed on features that represent specific aspects of knowledge systems, including the 'technological', that made them possible. One of the restricting features of analyses that take modes of production as central to modern development is their failure to integrate developments in the economy with those in the (partially autonomous) expansion and distribution of knowledge, discussed by many historians of science, technology and the intellect, which in their turn rest heavily on changes in the mode of communication outlined by Eisenstein and others.[47] These changes effectively began with the vigorous rebirth of European knowledge systems at the

[45] Trevor-Roper 1966; Hall 1985b.
[46] Hall 1985a: iii.   [47] Eisenstein 1979.

time of the Italian Renaissance. At the end of the fifteenth century that process was greatly stimulated by the adaptation of movable print to an alphabetic script, originally a feature of the vigorous culture of German merchant towns. The growth of education, the Scientific Revolution, the Enlightenment, all benefited from this development and in turn made a contribution to the major economic changes which depended both upon earlier mercantile activity and upon the existence of an educated bourgeoisie prepared to contribute to and apply the inventions leading to mass production in the factory. The 'Uniqueness' of the West depended on the great burst forward in knowledge, partly a consequence of catching up and then surpassing earlier backwardness and partly of changes in the mode of communication. The application of that knowledge, and indeed its development, was greatly stimulated by the overseas exploration, based on the superiority of guns, ships and maps, which brought back curiosities as well as booty, developed trade and led to the expansion of knowledge at home and to subsequent colonisation abroad.[48]

In the perspective of modes of production, the contribution of knowledge systems tends to be given a peripheral status with regard to major transformations, yet they were central to that expansion. That is true of other 'cultural' factors that helped create the demands, eventually the mass demands, which stimulated change in the economy in the widest sense. 'Consumerism' was intrinsic to the factory production of cloth and china that dominated early industrial capitalism in England, just as the demand side continues to promote capitalist production in the East.

Discussion of these changes in terms of modes of production, of capitalism, of modernisation and even of industrialisation, tends to place the problem of explanation on so general a level that it encourages the search for broad, structural factors unique to the culture of the West. If we no longer overprivilege the historical sequence that occurred in western Europe, which was in some respects a matter of rise, fall and recovery before take-off, then we can look at the question of the modernisation of the East in a different light. Throughout the Eurasian continent, the Bronze Age gave birth to cultures based on intensive agriculture and commerce. These cultures saw the invention or utilis-ation of writing, making possible the developments in mathematics, astronomy, botany and many other branches of knowledge that began in Mesopotamia and were developed in Egypt and in other literate cultures, both in the East and in the West. Other developments took place in

[48] See Lach 1965.

literature, which in the literal sense were dependent on the written word. Yet others occurred in artistic activities that were linked, less closely perhaps, not only to changes in the modes of communication (of which in a sense they were a part) but also to the patronage of the court and above all of merchants and the wider bourgeoisie who could create a mass demand in a way that courts could not. The most significant threshold for modernisation seems to have been a developed, literate, merchant culture and that existed both in the East and the West. The British adaptation of steam to driving machinery, developed especially for the factory production of cotton and the concomitant development of coal and steel, was clearly a major contribution of the West, and the process was then applied to other commodities. But given the existence of literate mercantile cultures elsewhere it did not take long to spread to other parts of the world.

8   Revaluations

We can look at the history of the landmass of Europe and Asia in two ways. We can lay stress upon the division into two continents with two substantially different traditions, the Occidental and the Oriental. The Occidental derives from the classical tradition of the Mediterranean societies of Greece and Rome, culminating in the Renaissance, the Reformation, the Enlightenment and the Industrial Revolution of western Europe; while the Oriental comes from quite 'other' sources. Alternatively, we can place the emphasis on the common heritage of both parts of Eurasia from the urban revolution of the Bronze Age, with its introduction of new means of communication (the written word), of new means of production (of advanced agriculture and crafts, including metallurgy, the plough, the wheel, etc.) and of new forms of knowledge. The account that is embodied in much Western sociological theory, history and humanities stresses the first and the resulting division of the continents into West and East. Without wishing to deny the specificity of cultural traditions, including that of Europe, it is easy to exaggerate these claims, especially when our own society (very successful in these latter centuries) is involved. That is what I maintain has happened in much of Western thought and scholarship. The distinctiveness has been puffed up at the expense of the other, distorting not only the understanding of the Orient but of the Occident too.

Let me insist (because I have often been misunderstood on this point) that I am not trying to make all the world the same but simply to state that the major societies of Eurasia were fired in the same crucible and that their differences must be seen as diverging from a common base. Moreover these differences are rarely if ever of the deep-seated kind that would prevent 'modernisation', or even its onset. Of course we have to explain why certain important events took place in the West rather than the East and led to differentiation. But the reverse is also true. It is impossible to explain this *temporary* advance by allocating *permanent* advantages to one team or the other. Moreover, many of the general advantages that most Westerners have seen as charac-

226

teristic of their country or continent can reasonably be shown to be illusory.

Our discussion has turned on Western explanations of its superiority to the East in these matters of economic and social development that are referred to as capitalism or industrialisation. We have concentrated on the views of European sociologists and historians, though these vary more than we have allowed for. Many have been concerned with the very general ways, in areas such as the family, politics, religious dissent and so on, the Uniqueness of the West has contributed to the advances made there in the late eighteenth and nineteenth centuries. Economic historians on the other hand have often paid little attention to these broad features, dwelling on more specific variables such as technological advance, the rate of capital formation, an increase in world trade and even agricultural change. Indeed reading their work one is struck by the gap between the two sets of explanations: the particular provides a complete alternative to the general, the one has no apparent need of the other. Indeed nowadays the very extent of the 'revolution' is queried: 'less happened, less dramatically than was once thought'.[1] In this perspective one might have no need for any hypothesis of Uniqueness.

Leaving aside the extent and rapidity of the changes, they were clearly important and we have no desire to play that down. What we are concerned to modify are the accounts that suggest the East could not have made it for just those general reasons, such as a lack of the right type of rationality or family. Any answer has to take into account the temporary nature of the comparative advantage, despite the strong belief of humanists that this goes back to Greece and Rome or to the tribal roots. The right level to pitch the discussion seems to be the more particularistic approach of much economic history rather than the profoundly cultural way preferred by others. Some of those economic historians have seen the Industrial Revolution in Britain as 'a flash in the pan', with the country later reverting to a new feudalism. That seems too exaggerated, but it supports the notion that comparative advantage was in many respects a temporary phenomenon.

This is a theme that has been essential to my research on the family. In *Production and Reproduction* I attempted to show that the kinds of advanced agriculture associated with the Bronze Age led to a hierarchical distribution of landholding in the core societies, a system of classes in which access to the means of production was highly differentiated in broad contrast to the relative egality of the shifting, slash-and-burn

---

[1] D. Cannadine, 'British History; past, present, and future', *Past and Present*, 116 (1987) 183, quoted Hudson 1992: 1.

agriculture of most of sub-Saharan Africa. The differentiation affected styles of life, leading to the development of sub-cultures that encourage endogamy and other ways of preserving the position of one's offspring in social life. As a result a similar range of strategies of heirship were to be found in those societies. In *The Oriental, the Ancient and the Primitive*, I present this analysis in a more detailed, ethnographic fashion in order to show that the structure and organisation of domestic groups (households etc.) had a greater similarity across the continent than many social and demographic theories allowed, because they faced similar problems to do with the organisation of production and the management of resources. That is a theme I have pursued on the 'cultural' level in looking at some other topics, namely, literacy, food and flowers.

The process of modernisation in the West has been seen by European scholars as being linked to the emergence of the city, of its corporate political body, guaranteeing certain freedoms for its inhabitants and separating the private from the public. Intellectually, it is seen as fostering the primacy of rationality, both in legal procedures and in the economic focus on the capacity to calculate returns on investment. In Weber's words, the medieval urbanite was well 'on the way to becoming an economic man (*homo oeconomicus*), laying the groundwork for early capitalism'.[2] In other words, Europe was well prepared for subsequent events.

This particular development of the city was seen as having taken shape in the form of the *commune* in the northern Italy of the eleventh century, from where it spread through western Europe. That was the thesis of Henri Pirenne in his work on *Medieval Cities* (1925) and of Max Weber in his influential essay on *The City* (*Die Stadt*). Both Pirenne, by implication, and Weber, quite explicitly, excluded the towns of Asia from this category of city. The reasons need not detain us for they are in need of drastic revision following the work of recent historians of the East. For India, Gillion's analysis of the Gujarati city of Ahmadabad shows it as having had many if not all of the features thought to be exclusively European.[3] For China, Rowe's detailed study of Hankow demonstrates that contractual guarantees were provided by the administration and that Chinese firms used 'principles of rational capital accounting' in 'a rational, orderly market'. He shows the importance of guilds as 'proto-capitalist corporations' as well as that of other voluntary associations which helped Hankow to escape 'heavy-handed

---

[2] This account is derived from Rowe's book on the Chinese city of Hankow in the nineteenth century (1984: 3).
[3] Gillion 1968.

bureaucratic domination'.[4] In other words, at least some of the Indian and Chinese cities were not as monolithic as had been supposed, leaving ample opportunity for trade–commercial relations as well as providing a window for the later adoption of factory production and knowledge from the West.[5]

While this situation is well known to specialists, it has rarely been incorporated in the approaches of those historians, sociologists and anthropologists of the West who continue to 'primitivise' the East, not always explicitly but by implication in their assumptions about the process of modernisation. Those approaches need a thorough revision of the kind that art historians have given to Chinese painting and that Joseph Needham and his collaborators have done for the natural sciences. The reason has little to do with sentimental relativism or an emotional concern with an undifferentiated 'other' but is essentially derived from the fact that the major societies of the East are heirs to the same urban revolution of the Bronze Age as the West and so their literate, mercantile sectors retained much the same potential for commercial and cultural development. What is important to note, as Adams has argued, is that the societies that went through this process did so in ways that had a good deal in common, despite the unlikelihood in many cases of direct influences of a significant kind (although some of these are discussed in the Appendix).[6] Indeed from a proto-industrial standpoint, parts of the vast Chinese empire were distinctly more advanced in the late Middle Ages than Europe. When Marco Polo visited the southern capital in the thirteenth century, he thought Hangzhou the greatest city in the world, one whose economy and social life surpassed anything in Europe at that time. These developments were held back neither by the kinship system, nor by the polity ('Asiatic society'), nor yet by the absence of an appropriate economic ethic. Indeed they were hardly held back at all. For, as one commentator notes, 'the masses of the Chinese people were basically well fed, well clothed, and well housed throughout most of their history . . . they ate well enough and had enough of a sense of security about survival to think beyond that primary problem'.[7] Part of the reason for their prosperity lay in the fact that Chinese peasants were relatively lightly taxed by their government, presumably because 'defence' expenditure was limited, as were the amounts required for the support of other 'great organisations'

---

[4] Rowe 1984: 10.
[5] The same point was made by Gillion about the Indian city of Ahmadabad, which transformed itself into a modern industrial centre (1968: 5).
[6] Adams 1965; Curtin 1984: 61.
[7] Mote 1977: 199.

such as the religious ones. Their horticulture was advanced, and rites, performance and other arts well developed, as were many of their scientific enquiries and technological practices. Even if they limited their participation in the sea trade after the great voyages of the fifteenth century, they had an extensive internal market, larger than Europe itself.

Cloth provides some indication of this state of affairs. Textile production was extensive, mainly rural based, employing both domestic and wage labour. Merchants were motivated by the profit and the loss. In many respects peasants acted along lines familiar from other areas of Asia and Europe. In making this claim I am not trying to overlook differences (of which there were many) nor to introduce a Euro-centred view into China. Rather I am arguing for the reverse, for the necessity of looking at developments in Europe from a wider perspective, of taking a global point of departure.

So, far from being marked by the stagnating features of Asiatic production, a centralised régime imposed some limited restrictions on its inhabitants but left freedom of choice in most competitive market situations.

During nearly two thousand years, an individual could sell his labour on the free market or sell himself, or a member of his family, on the slave-market. A slave could end his servitude by buying himself out. A person could obtain land by purchase or other means, renting it out or working it himself. Those who had capital could invest it in a variety of ways.[8]

Peasants engaged in non-agricultural work, including work for the market. Workshops and factories, often organised by the state, existed well before the fifteenth century. The Office of Weaving and Dyeing had twenty-five large works producing different kinds of silk cloth. During the Tang (618–907) and Song (960–1279) even the government recruited workers on the free market. While some industries, especially the production of arms, were in the hands of the state, others such as mining and iron-working were often private. In the production of other objects, both public and private industry were engaged, with the state gradually giving way to the latter, especially after the fifteenth century when the private sector became more capable of supplying sufficient goods.[9]

Textile manufacture in China, especially of silk, was a secondary seasonal activity for more than 2,000 years, and that seasonality was related to its base in the country. Nevertheless it served not only local

8 Chao 1984: 961.   9 Chao 1984: 863.

needs but for the greater part of its history the government demanded taxes in the form of textiles, which were used as gifts, for exchange and in trade, internal and external. However silk of the better quality was also produced by artisans and factories in the town.

The alternative to silk was 'grass cloth'. Cotton was introduced as a commercial crop at the end of the twelfth century but spinning and weaving did not spread until the fifteenth, the period of great population growth. At this time latifundia disappeared in favour of tenant farming which left the peasants free to organise their family labour. Cotton was taken up as a domestic industry and production was adapted to part-time work, using one's own materials. Of Guangdong in the 1850s it was said, 'Of all the countries in the world, it is perhaps unique to China that you find a loom in every household', although in fact the same could be claimed for parts of India. Some areas produced less, others more, and there was an active market in cotton cloth, much of it emanating from Shanghai and distributed to distant parts of the country by means of local agents and itinerant merchants who had access to considerable capital. By 1730 the exports extended to Europe and to North and South America, but they dropped off drastically by 1833 under the impact of European industrial production.

Looking at a wider front, the knowledge systems and the arts of China and Japan were in the same league as the West, at least until roughly the fifteenth century. Indeed in certain important ways the East had been more 'developed'. It was not the case that the achievements made by the West in the classical period saw them comfortably through to modern times, providing a comparative advantage for the later take-off: the decline in the early medieval period was only too apparent. During the intervening millennium after the classical period Europe in many respects lagged behind in knowledge, the arts and the economy. Looked at over the *longue durée*, there was an alternation in achievement based on the common attainments of the Bronze Age. Over the centuries we find a swing of the pendulum with one advancing on one front at one time, another at a different stage. At other periods similar developments were taking place in both regions, partly in parallel (they were building from similar bases), partly by adoption (that too made possible by the similar backgrounds). The alternation was due to hold-ups on the one hand and to rapid advances on the other. Hold-ups could be caused by invasion from the outside, by unrest within, by 'a high-level equilibrium trap', by the interference of church or state, or simply by inertia. The advances could be promoted by new means of production or communication, new advances in knowledge and in practice, new resources, or by other contingent features. And it is a pendular movement that continues today, with the East now beginning to dominate the West in matters of the economy.

To take a specific field, in botany China produced many species of ornamental plants that later came to the West, plants that had been developed on the basis of its techniques of intensive horticulture which over the centuries had been applied to 'aesthetic' (ornamental) as well as to utilitarian products. That intensive production was accompanied by the development in the fourth century BCE of a botany that Needham sees as roughly equal, certainly in the number of identified species, to that of Aristotle's pupil, Theophrastus. In the medieval period knowledge in the West stagnated, indeed declined, and only recovered to catch up the East with the advent of the German botanists of the fifteenth century (whose work was assisted by woodblock printing, even in the period before the development of movable type) and later extended by the increasing number of plant species coming from the overseas voyages beginning at the end of that century. Symbolic elaboration went along with productive success. Eastern and Western practices were not of course identical nor can they even be seen as transformations in any immediate processual sense but nevertheless they were homologues of one another, representing alternative paths of parallel development.

A similar falling off to the one that took place in botany occurred in the sphere of mathematics. Looking at the subsequent development of mathematics in the later Middle Ages, some European writers are led to talk about the birth of this science. For example, the medieval historian, Murray, discusses critically the theory that it was in the counting-houses of Europe that 'the art of mathematics was born'.[10] He did of course recognise that the practical art of algorism was named after the great emporium on the Caspian (Kwarazm or Khiva) where Arabs had learned the Indian art of arithmetic. Nevertheless he verbally confounds the particular and the general, so that the specifically European development is described as a birth, a birth that was brought on by the growing needs of commerce. The confusion of frames becomes apparent when the author speaks of 'the evolution of a mathematical sense' in Europe. At another point, he plots the increasing concern with numbers in the medieval period under the heading of 'the emergence of the arithmetical mentality'. The chronology of this development is unclear for he also looks further back in English history and writes of the six and a half centuries since Bede's calculations of Easter as seeing 'the evolution of what is virtually a new intellectual faculty'.[11] Murray is well aware not only of the Arabic roots of the numerals but also of the Roman origin of

[10] Murray 1978: 190–1.   [11] Murray 1978: 186.

the abacus, the two main technical contributions of the thirteenth century on which he concentrates. But those considerations do not prevent him making more ethnocentric claims.

Aside from chronology, his emphasis suffers from two problems. The first is geographical, in overemphasising the European contribution at the same time as minimising (or neglecting) that of others. The second is a matter of 'mental levels', in placing the change at the level of 'mentalities' rather than of cognitive operations. Thus the achievements of the West are overgeneralised in two ways, each to the detriment of the 'others'. Those 'others' are implicitly assumed not to have witnessed the birth because they did not possess the mentality. In fact, if we accept the statement about the algorism and bear in mind the contributions of Mesopotamia, India and China to the growth of mathematics we must assume that the birth and the mentality were general features of these literate societies. So that what happened in medieval Europe was a regeneration following a decline, a notion which modifies excessively nationalistic claims, especially those based on mentalities and on evolution, at least in any strict sense of these loaded words. That is to say, all these societies participated, differentially at different times, in parallel traditions that were sometimes being cross-fertilised. To make this point in this way may appear to be taking phraseology too seriously. At one level such writers are well aware that Europe is not the only place in which these developments have taken place. Nevertheless the recourse to an account in terms of mentalities (precisely the term used by Lévy Bruhl in his account of 'primitives') is based on the assumption of 'uniqueness' at quite the wrong level of cognitive structure, as we have attempted to show regarding logic.

There is another cause for concern about the chronology. The period when the medievalist Murray sees these cognitive developments as emerging is much earlier than those given by historians of the Scientific Revolution of the sixteenth and seventeenth centuries. A similar debate occurs about the history of banking. In an article subtitled 'the primitive bank of deposit, 1200–1600', Usher writes of 'the origins of banking' in the medieval period. He knows that banking existed in the Roman empire and had he taken more care he might have entitled the article 'The origins of modern European banking'. As it is, the title implies an unsustainable claim to global priorities. From one point of view the problem is again a matter of expression. But expression matters; it sets the frame. In discussing 'New Interpretations of the History of Banking' (1954), de Roover too begins by saying 'The first references to banking are found in the Genoese notarial records of the twelfth and thirteenth centuries'. Again the statement is carelessly phrased. In its present form it applies only to western Europe in the Middle Ages, after the virtual collapse of the earlier economy. The rebirth is presented as if it were the birth.

As we have seen, there is no fixed view of the timing of that rebirth. While de Roover insists on the relevance of the radical changes of the thirteenth century, Tawney and others emphasise the revolutionary significance of developments in the later period based on the general stimulus given by the Renaissance and the Reformation. The early modern historians tend to place more weight on external (socio-cultural) features; the medievalist tends to stress the European mind, or changes in mentality.

Mathematics was one of the fields in which parallel but not identical developments took place in the East and the West and it was, as is often asserted, the key to growth in many branches of science. We have already dismissed the claim that the birth of the subject occurred in Europe. With geometry, the early development took place in Mesopotamia and Egypt, and only later was the subject taken up and further systematised by the Greeks. In China attempts were made by the followers of the philosopher Mozi towards formulating axioms and presenting proofs by means of step-by-step deduction. However these notions were never as systematically pursued, so early Chinese geometry remained less developed than the Greek. The proof of Pythagoras' theorem, for instance, was virtually confined to a numerical demonstration. By the third century BCE that had been generalised into an algebraic proof (also found in India) which is simpler than Euclid but without the 'deductive rigor'.[12] That difference may be related to the character of logographic writing, which did not provide the same pool of abstract, non-numeric symbols as the alphabet. In certain aspects of mathematics that situation may have given the Chinese a possible advantage. For example, their abacus was not in general use until about the fourteenth century but it had earlier played an important part intellectually (as it still does in daily operations throughout the East). Zeros were first represented by blanks in the relevant column and by about the year 1000 the space was filled with an open circle, the zero. Quite complicated problems in multiplication and long division could be tackled without using any symbolic notation as operators, though knowledge of the multiplication table (which came early on with writing) was essential.[13] Indeed it is possible that the procedure of long division, developed in the third or fourth centuries, was transmitted from there to Europe to become part of schoolroom method. As Blunden and Elvin remark, in the High Middle

[12] Blunden and Elvin 1983: 194.   [13] Needham 1959.

Ages Chinese mathematics was the most advanced in the world and its subsequent decline is one of the puzzles of intellectual history.[14] That falling away has to be set against the contemporary advance of the West, just as that advance has in turn to be set against Europe's earlier decline and the achievements of the East. Apart from any positive reasons for the West's advances in mathematical knowledge, there were some problems of a technical order that held back the East. One perhaps lay in the fact that the abacus, unlike paper and ink, left no record for checking or for contemplation. Lack of an explicit formal symbolism meant there was 'an in-built limit on how far they could go' as well as inhibiting the exploration of some less 'realistic' problems. On the other hand, Chinese accountancy did develop a special range of numbers aimed at trying to prevent fraud; business does not seem to have been negatively affected.

A major problem lies in the way that such developments are phrased. Blotz sees a major feature in the West's achievement as being 'a unique scientific outlook', that is, not even a tradition, but an 'outlook', perhaps a mentality. In his work on the Asian trade (1978), Chaudhuri regards one aspect of the failure of India to develop an industrial revolution in the eighteenth century as due to the fact that there had been 'no marked progress in scientific knowledge for many centuries, and the intellectual apparatus for a diffusion and systematic recording of the inherited skills was seriously defective'.[15] If we rephrase Blotz's remarks in terms of the accumulation of scientific knowledge, as Chaudhuri does, then we are less inclined to dwell on 'uniqueness' (which becomes either meaningless or full of danger) or 'embeddedness', a concept that locates developments at the level of 'mentalities'. Of course mental processes are involved and they have obviously influenced the creation of knowledge. But to talk of mentalities, outlooks and even culture in this regard tends to overgeneralise the creative activity (not all members of society are involved) and to place it at a level others cannot attain since they do not have the right propensities. It is to place the cognitive processes, I have argued, at the level of abilities rather than capacities and therefore to underestimate the rapidity or even the possibilities of change.[16]

Once again, in Europe both the location and the timing of the knowledge 'revolution' are subject to dispute. Medievalists would stress the contribution of the thirteenth century, modern historians the contribution of the Renaissance or later, while philosophers emphasise the growth of learning in the 'Age of Reason' and Enlightenment in

[14] Blunden and Elvin 1983: 197.
[15] Chaudhuri 1978b.   [16] Goody 1986: 246.

Britain that followed the Restoration of the monarchy. As with changes in trade, in finance and in other features we have examined, that uncertainty among historians must induce hesitation about both the discontinuity and the continuity arguments, at least at the level of mentalities or of the deep structure of culture. These changes appear to take place over a longer term than most 'revolutionary', discontinuity or stage theories would allow. And at the same time the continuity thesis is threatened when the transformations are not confined to one country.

This discussion needs to take into account a further element. As we have seen, in a number of areas European knowledge in the Middle Ages was relatively backward compared to that of China, which had not been the case in the classical period. What Needham calls the Great Interruption occurred between the second and fifteenth centuries. Even after the brilliant insights and major achievements of the Greeks, China was 'much more advanced than Europe' in mathematics, astronomy, tidal theory, human geography, quantitative cartography and palae-ontology 'until modern science begins to appear'.[17] So that when expansion eventually came, it initially took the form of 'revolution' partly because of the earlier slump. In the subsequent revival against a history of 'backwardness' the actors were not always constrained in the same way as those in other intellectual milieux, at least once a breach had been made with the main local traditions. Puritanism and the study of Scripture may have been of little positive help, but Protestantism in the wider sense, together with the activities of other reformist movements, meant that in secular matters too the actors were freed from the restrictions which an established régime imposed, either explicitly through censorship or implicitly through the control of knowledge systems.[18] Or simply because of inertia, so that any stirring of the pot, in the fashion of the Hawthorne effect, led to higher productivity.[19] The 'freedom' from religious constraints affected a wide range of activity; for example liberating oneself from the bonds of the Catholic Church meant rethinking marriage arrangements, including the problem of 'incest'.[20] In a similar way, casting off papal chains meant in and of itself that England and Holland were free to attempt to break the trading monopolies in

---

[17] Needham 1959: 623. He is detailing subjects he has treated up to that point in time. The same was true of seismography (p. 626) and mineralogy (p. 646).

[18] On the application of this argument to the 'Scientific Revolution' in England, see Hill 1961; Kearney 1964; Raab 1962.

[19] The reference is to Elton Mayo's study of the Western Electric Company's Hawthorne Works at Chicago (1927–32). See G. C. Homans, *The Human Group* (London, 1951), chapter 3.

[20] Goody 1983.

west Africa and elsewhere which the Pope had awarded to Spain and Portugal. Their merchants no longer came under ecclesiastical jurisdiction and were now free to trade anywhere and in anything, including selling arms to 'pagans' which had been prohibited to Catholics; in northern Ghana muskets are known to this day as 'Dane guns', indicating their Protestant source. To gain such freedom it was not necessary to embrace Protestantism, only to be non-Catholic; it was not so much that Protestants were 'forced to be free' by their religion as that they were freed from numerous restraints by their very rejection of Catholicism.[21] The halo effect was powerful.

In both Europe and Asia literate cultures of a relatively open kind developed that were dominated by the merchants or the court rather than by the church. In particular the existence of merchant subcultures, which adapted and modified some features of the court as well as developing others, marked off those societies from Africa. That is not to say that African merchants do not have a separate identity. In Gonja, for example, long-distance traders were Muslims who existed as a distinct group but hardly constituted a separate subculture, except from the religious standpoint. Certainly they never developed an independent secular culture in the way they did in Hangzhou or Ahmadabad, in Osaka or in London, where they were very roughly on the same level of complexity and achievement.[22] In fact the broadly parallel developments of merchant cultures, for example, in the theatre in Europe, China and Japan, are an outstanding feature which most social or cultural history overlooks.

So, while it is certainly true that the West made important gains in knowledge following the Renaissance, gains that were partly due to the flourishing market and to the adaptation of movable print to an alphabetic script, many major achievements in the economy, in learning and the arts had already been recorded in the East.[23] Obviously these achievements had nothing to do with Protestantism, and little enough to do with any religious ideology. In terms of learning, attempts were constantly made by the Chinese court, by nobles and by scholars themselves to gather together the results of enquiry, as in the Song encyclopaedias, which Hawkes sees as a specifically Chinese invention. These works, which constituted compendia of information about the world, were varied in form, in content and in authorship.

---

[21] See Durkheim 1897.
[22] On Hangzhou see Rowe 1984; on Ahmadabad see Gillion 1968; on London see Thrupp 1962; on Osaka see Hauser 1974.
[23] On printing in China, which had already been available for some centuries, see Pelliot 1953; Tsien in Needham 1985.

So great were their achievements in a variety of practical fields that, looking at the fourteenth-century Chinese account of a spinning machine for hemp thread which could be powered by man, animal or by a water wheel, Elvin is irresistibly reminded of English inventions of the eighteenth century. That leads him to ask why later Europe rather than earlier China was the scene of an industrial revolution in textile production.[24] His answer is phrased in terms of 'the high-level equilibrium trap'. As a result his enquiry is directed not at the earlier backwardness of China but into 'the causes of the decline of invention in the traditional Chinese textile industries'. Explanations that refer to the absence of rationality, inventiveness or entrepreneurship become irrelevant, since all these features must have been present at the earlier period. Those discussions can be seen for what they are, as representing the understandable but distorting tendency of Europeans to inflate their overall contribution to world society and even to 'Western civilisation', a tendency reinforced by their undoubted achievements over the past few centuries. Such inflation of oneself inevitably involves the deflation of others; self-congratulation is a zero-sum game.

In view of this alternation, it is pointless to speculate about deep, continuing, cultural factors, such as individualism, that imply a semi-permanent pre-eminence for the West, or to try to isolate any 'necessary' sequence of events through which the West has passed – from 'ancient society' to 'feudalism' and so on. Instead we need to take into account the common heritage of the Bronze Age and ask on a much more specific level what factors enabled the East to advance at one period and in one sphere and the West at others. That is quite a different enterprise from the one that assumes the West to be marked by the presence or growth of rationality (or a special form of rationality) or by similar, unique features.

One such feature to be singled out was the Greek alphabet, undoubtedly an important development. Many Western humanists (including myself) concentrated on the Greek (consonants plus vowels) alphabet which they contrasted with the morphologically less developed logographic systems of east and west Asia. But while those traditions were more complicated to work with, being less easy to acquire in a definitive, exhaustive manner than was alphabetic literacy, they did provide many of the advantages which any form of writing gave to human societies, as a means of communication, as a way of storing and retrieving knowledge and as encouraging new techniques for processing that information. Both these forms of writing permitted the accumulation, synthesisation and

[24] Elvin 1972: 137.

formalisation of knowledge as well as having a profound effect on artistic genres.

The development of writing took place in societies that had a developed urban life during the Bronze Age, when more advanced forms of agriculture and craft had emerged. In this process the economic and the 'cultural' were closely linked, one feeding the other. The broad similarities between East and West (and to point to these is in no way to deny their many differences) contrast with black Africa, which until recently lacked both advanced agriculture and writing (except that developed under the influence of Islam). I have previously examined these broad similarities in Europe and Asia under three rubrics, that of family, food and flowers. In two earlier books I argued that, at the level of domestic groups, the family in Asia resembled its counterpart in Europe in a number of significant ways that are often overlooked.[25] It is an argument I have touched upon from a different angle in chapter 6, where I have suggested that household composition, interpersonal relationships, family strategies and the domestic economy are not as far apart in structure as many binary classifications and dualistic theories would require. For example, while there were important differences at the level of wider kinship groupings (such as the lineage or clan), these divergencies did not seem greatly to affect the development of mercantile and industrial processes, the accumulation of knowledge systems nor yet the level of 'cultural' performances. Indeed in China lineages themselves might well organise commercial enterprises, run schools and arrange festivals of various kinds.

In another study I have tried to compare 'cultural attainment' at the level of cooking. I suggested that within African societies forms of cooking were minimally differentiated: by and large even in kingdoms chiefs and commoners ate similar foods. It was in the complex states of Asia and Europe that we find a developed *haute cuisine* distinct (but not totally separated) from the food of ordinary folk and of ordinary occasions. One way of putting the point, not very satisfactorily, would be to say that the forms of cooking were structurally similar but culturally different. It could be better phrased without the resort to such all-embracing terms.[26] More recently I pursued a similar argument with regard to the culture of flowers. That I found only marginally relevant to black Africa but highly developed in the major states of Asia and Europe.[27]

Both food and 'aesthetic' horticulture were closely linked to the

[25] Goody 1976, 1990.
[26] Goody 1982.   [27] Goody 1993.

economy and to the existence of a surplus of ordinary foodstuffs. Though this was never the only relevant factor, it permitted extensive specialist production and hierarchical differentiation in usage. That hierarchy of custom was accompanied by an interesting reaction, an ambivalence, at the level of the individual, a contradiction at the level of the social system. The existence of 'class-based' subcultures within a single society laid open the possibility of explicit opposition resting on implicit contradictions between common societal membership (and language) and the varied customs and access to resources of different groups. It is the problem of the simultaneous unity and disunity of a culture, of equality and hierarchy, of membership and exclusion. In my view we can find similar problems in societies without writing, as in Africa, but there they rest largely implicit. Whereas in the major societies of Europe and Asia such concerns are openly expressed in writing and achieve not only a greater prominence but also a greater reflexivity. They become the stuff of philosophers and of priests, of reformers; the embarrassment of riches is embodied in an alternative tradition in cultures of luxury.[28]

Those situations are characteristic in their various ways of the problems and attainments associated with great differential access to substantial resources. That is not to assert an economic determinism but merely to claim that the Bronze Age, with its urban revolution, was an essential preliminary, at least in a temporal sense, to the kind of developments we are talking about. And those developments included changes in the mode of communication (initiated by the invention of writing) as well as in the sphere of production, both agricultural and artisanal.

A neglect of this common history over the long term lies behind a large body of research in sociology, in history, in economics and in anthropology that has dominated Europe over the last two hundred years and takes as its problematic the Rise and Uniqueness of the West. The development of industrial capitalism, of large-scale, mass production using water- and steam-powered machinery, first took place in western Europe. Some four hundred years previously the Renaissance was characterised not only by a great expansion of mercantile activity in the West but by the rapid growth of artistic production and of knowledge systems centring upon the courts and the urban bourgeoisie, who had increasingly liberated themselves from ecclesiastical control.

Some have seen this earlier expansion as representing the birth of capitalism. The notion of capitalism is not easy to define and some

---

[28] This theme is touched upon in *Cooking, Cuisine and Class* (p. 147ff.) and in *The Culture of Flowers* (final chapter), but is being developed in a forthcoming publication.

economic historians have tried to replace the concept with one of 'entrepreneurship' or of 'growth'.[29] From a longer historical and wider comparative perspective these two concepts seem equally inadequate. So too are many of the explanations. However it is widely held among historians that this development first took place in Venice.[30] Empirically the claim raises problems because the kind of trade and commerce that Europe experienced following the twelfth century was little different from that pursued over the centuries by many other communities stretching from Egypt to China. What it represented for Europe was not a birth but a rebirth of an earlier Mediterranean commerce which they had been unable to continue. The justification for the statement that Venice was the birthplace of capitalism must rest on the assumption that this mercantile activity was the necessary predecessor to the Industrial Revolution of the late eighteenth century. But were not other equivalent forms of economic activity in India, China or Japan equally open to the take-off provided by the investment of fixed capital in the factory system?

There is a problem in trying to reconcile general (often binary, but at least contrasting) views of the world offered by anthropologists, sociologists, economists, and development theorists, who stress the differences between the market and the marketless, with the facts of mercantile and later industrial activity of above all the Japanese, but also of the Chinese and Indians. In a perceptive discussion Timberg (1978) points to the deficiencies of the 'dominant school of thought among those who write on business entrepreneurship',[31] speaking of the 'psychological determinism' of writers like Weber and McClelland. Their perceptions are quite out of tune with subsequent developments in those areas, so that we get a series of *ad hoc* adjustments of theory to observation, giving rise to a number of articles, of which one title can stand as representative, 'Protestant Ethic and the Parsees'. In Max Weber's brilliant discussion of the development of capitalism, he called attention to the elective affinity between that institution and the Protestant Ethic, supporting his view by a survey of the economic ethics of the other major world religions and finding them wanting. Since then researchers have discovered the Protestant Ethic everywhere and nowhere.

The recourse to the notion of mentality which underlies this explanation has also been heavily criticised in the work of Lloyd (1990). What is problematic about the notion is that it tends to presume

[29] Lane 1969: 3.   [30] Lane 1963: 312.
[31] Timberg 1978: 16.

(though that is not absolutely intrinsic) total shifts of the kind from the non-rational to the rational, from magic to science. Whereas what we find is an interpenetration of opposites or, better, of alternatives. For example the astrologer, Girolano Cardono (1501–76), was not only a mathematician, a doctor and an astrologer but also a believer in chance.

In his book Lloyd undertakes a sensitive and intelligent study of Greek and Chinese science stressing the early differences that by implication relate to subsequent European achievements in knowledge systems. Lloyd draws attention to the number of features Greek science and philosophy had in common with the traditional forms of knowledge they were aiming to replace. But in one respect the differences he discerns are considerable, that is, in 'the degree of explicitness and self-consciousness of the inquiries'.[32] He sees this shift as due not to a change of mentality but to the self-definition of a style of inquiry which depends upon its polemical purpose. That he relates to the political system and its law courts where Greeks gained experience of argument and persuasion. However, as he recognises, many of those features go back to the archaic period.[33]

What is critical about Greek science, in Lloyd's view, is not that they invented medicine, mathematics or astronomy (which they did not) but that they were the first, in the West, 'to engage in self-conscious analysis of the status, methods and foundation of these inquiries, the first to raise, precisely, second-order questions'.[34] This is undoubtedly true, as far as explicit formalisation in the written word was concerned. However it is difficult to see, given their extraordinary achievements, that some of these questions were not raised in the course of Mesopotamian discoveries, even if they did not get preserved in cuneiform writing. Indeed the difficulties of that system would tend to discourage discursive reflections on methods. At a very general level we would see such discussion as encouraged by writing which promotes what Lloyd would rightly describe as self-consciousness (the reflexivity of the book in my terms) and the process I have called making the implicit explicit – because most of these processes are embryonically present in oral societies, even the comparisons between cures offered by herbalists and by sacrifice. The agonistic elements in Greek culture are certainly to be seen in politico-legal debate, but so too they are in some oral cultures where the techniques of rhetoric flourish.[35] That self-consciousness has no doubt multiple roots in Greek culture, but one is surely likely to be the explicit arguments which writing and especially the greater

[32] Lloyd 1990: 8.   [33] Lloyd 1990: 60.
[34] Lloyd 1990: 58.   [35] Bloch 1975.

facility offered by alphabetic writing and the papyrus offers, resulting
in those very extensive collections of authored books that fill the Loeb
collection.

Lloyd sees the notion of exact proof, at least of geometric proof, as
being a Greek invention, related to these methodological speculations.
He accepts that the Indians developed a geometrical method in the
context of building altars, in the course of which they showed themselves
confident in handling 'problems to do with the areas of squares,
rectangles, trapezia and right-angle triangles' based on considerable
geometrical knowledge. What he doubts is that there was a clear and
explicit *concept* of proof in the Sulbasūtra (composed between 500 and
100 BCE). For they failed to distinguish between approximations
and exact results (though they sometimes achieved the latter); they are
'interested in practical results and show no direct concern with proof
procedures as such at all'.[36] As Lloyd recognises, that is to take a narrow
view of proof procedures. It is possible to go a considerable distance in
science without necessarily employing the strict criteria formulated by
Aristotle and used by Euclid. Indeed, as he demonstrates, commitment
to such procedures may lead to a failure to pursue other possibilities.

While it seems plausible to maintain, as Lloyd does, that they made an
explicit distinction between metaphorical and literal statements,[37] I
would strongly argue that all cultures make this differentiation implicitly,
for they are bound to do so in the very use of language. I have used
the terms 'distinction' and 'differentiation' to correspond to what
Lloyd refers to as drawing a distinction and using one. In my sense, a
distinction is a terminological one; to use one for Lloyd means not
having the term. But a distinction may be drawn verbally without the use
of a precise word. The French have no special word, as we have, for the
meat of a dead sheep on the table (we have appropriated and transformed
terms from Anglo-Saxon and Romance roots under specific, socio-
economic circumstances). But there is no doubt that they make use of
a distinction between the living and the dead. Indeed it can be called
an explicit distinction, even though the explicitness does not take a
lexicographical form.

The general problem, as Lloyd sees it, is not how a new mentality came
to be acquired but the circumstances in which a certain rivalry between
claimants to knowledge could develop. In this the existence of categories
becomes critical to him: 'it is evident that where *there are no such explicit
categories as these*, statements of ideas and beliefs are less liable to a

---

[36] Lloyd 1990: 104.   [37] Lloyd 1990: 14.

certain type of challenge'.[38] As he admits, in relation to the Nuer of the southern Sudan, other cultures are not totally immune from challenge, especially from the enquiring anthropologist. But in any case that qualified immunity does not depend upon the absence of categorical distinction. That is to give too much emphasis to separate words as distinct from concepts, a criticism one can make of part at least of anthropological linguistics. The absence of a concept of blue does not mean the colour is not recognised. Clearly, however, the emergence of a specific category of blue is also significant in terms of cultural history.

Lloyd sees proto-science as developing in Egypt, Babylonia, India and China. How far therefore were Plato and Aristotle, in their rejection of metaphor (in for example the syllogistic in Aristotle's case), founders of 'a new style of inquiry'?[39] He attempts to link achievements in Greek science and philosophy with the polemic characterising the political system. He draws a comparison and contrast with China, in which he correctly rejects a discussion in terms of mentalities and concentrates on what I would describe as cognitive operations. He sees the similarities ('on a first superficial view') in the development of 'extensive interests in ethics, in natural philosophy, in mathematics, in aspects of logic and epistemology, and in literary criticism, as well as in medicine and in astronomy. We can exemplify from China at different periods, among many other features, the self-conscious study of arguments, the development of certain critical and sceptical traditions, and of explicitly innovative ones, the practice of proof and some related concepts – in mathematics, and a concept of metaphor – for example as characterizing a type of poetry.'[40] He also sees important differences in their use of dialectic as a mode of argument rather than formal logic, in practical enquiry rather than speculative, abstract theorising. These styles of intellectual activity he sees as related to the different political background and experience.

That may well be true as far as the differences are concerned. But what I am interested in in this context is not so much the differences, which have so often been seized upon to account for the apparent backwardness of the East, but the remarkable similarities to which Lloyd points. While the differences may be connected with the type of political system, the similarities seem to have much to do with the fact that we are dealing with two societies that benefited from the 'revolution' of the Bronze Age. In the context of these intellectual activities the advantages lay specifically in the development of writing, which as I have argued does

---

[38] Lloyd 1990: 25 (italics in the original).
[39] Lloyd 1990: 22.   [40] Lloyd 1990: 11.

precisely what Lloyd sees as characteristic of law courts, namely, makes the implicit explicit by throwing back to an individual his own words (as well as those of others) in a very particular way. It is a kind of internalised reflexivity which the verbal argument of the courts rarely achieves.

The difference in emphasis between Lloyd and myself comes partly from the different points at which we begin our enquiry. Coming from the study of an ancient literate society, Lloyd tends to look for the differences between say Indian and Greek geometry. I see them both as rather similar in comparison with spatial calculations in an African group such as the LoDagaa, where farms are paced out and the dimensions of a new house determined with the aid of a guinea-corn stalk.[41] So he tries to account for his differences in terms of socio-political structure (and the related context of discourse) whereas I look for broader differences in the mode of communication between oral and literate societies.

As we have seen, these various developments have been attributed by scholars to factors claimed to be unique to the West, such as rationality (or a special form of rationality), individualism, entrepreneurship, and even family forms whose absence supposedly inhibited a parallel process in the East. The family constitutes a paradigmatic case because when the economy of Japan advanced, the argument was adjusted to cope with the new entrant. The trouble is that no sooner are similarities found between the Japanese family and the western European one in contrast to that of China, than China itself begins to take off. We then have to deal with a Confucian version of capitalism dependent on familism (as indeed much of Japan's development was). Now India is about to do the same, so another *ad hoc* adjustment will have to be made with Hinduism and the Hindu joint family. As we have seen, much of India's earlier development was undertaken by family firms, leading Rudner, in his work on Chettiar bankers, to talk about a collectivist spirit of capitalism as distinct from the individualist one of the West.

This theoretical bricolage suggests we should look again not so much at the East but at the West in order to discover how these assumptions came to be made and if there is anything we can learn theoretically and empirically from what appears to be a misreading of the role, for example, of family and kinship in the East, where, far from being a hindrance to modernisation, the wider participation of kin has often been a positive advantage and not the drag that earlier social theorists and historians have thought. Skirting over the nineteenth-century writers

---

[41] In Gonja, there is evidence of more elaborate spatial calculations in the building of mosques and in the diagrams in the books of Islamic 'magic' coming from Northern Africa.

on the family, I turned to the more recent. In much German–American sociology there was a strong tendency to see the family not only as having been slimmed down under modern conditions but as becoming increasingly irrelevant as far as the macrostructure of society is concerned; or to put it more concretely, as increasingly irrelevant in the economic sphere, especially in business. The notion counts Weber among its ancestors, but it was developed in the writings of Talcott Parsons who saw achievement rather than ascription as one of the characteristic value orientations of modern society with the particularistic relations of kinship being superseded in significance by those of a universalistic kind. In modernisation theory this idea of progression, associated with the shift from traditional to modern societies, was linked with the growth of bureaucracy in which personal ties were replaced by those based on achievement. For them, the West had made this transition, the East (in the 1950s) had not. My argument has been that the West has tended to misunderstand even itself in drawing too sharp a contrast between *our* individualism, our rationality, our nuclear family, and *their* collectivism, their extended families. These differences are matters of degree rather than of kind and, if we are to absorb the lessons of the East, do not appear to have much to do with the onset of modernisation.

In looking at the Western sociology of the family (and anthropologists are not immune) we are often dealing with highly ethnocentric attitudes, to which national histories are especially prone. That is particularly clear in the case of England and of even the best of its historians in the nineteenth century when explanations directed to a temporary, economic advantage were often attributed to deep-structural factors. Vaunting oneself involves devaluing the other, whether that is French, eastern European, or Eastern more generally. At this period there was at least a temporary advantage that justified a measure of ethnocentricism but that advantage has now effectively disappeared.

Such attempts were mistaken in placing the weight of the explanation on features that were neither confined to the West nor always critical to the growth of industrial capitalism. It was ethnocentric bias that saw them as unique, bolstered by an overvaluation of the undoubted achievements which had occurred in Europe over the last five hundred years and which were especially important in the previous century. That overvaluation took the form firstly of underplaying the achievements of the East during the Middle Ages at a time when it was often Europe that could be considered 'backward'. And, secondly, the attribution of the advances in the West to permanent, deep-seated, structural factors that failed to account for the earlier imbalance and for the swings of the pendulum.

Many 'cultural' explanations tend to be of this very kind, resembling accounts of biological evolution in that the development of human groups, like that of species, is seen to involve the acquisition of quasi-permanent characteristics which marked their history and identity over the long run. But the lead in modernisation, and to a lesser extent in capitalism and industrialisation, are certainly temporary attributes of any particular group; even self-sustaining growth is self-sustaining at varying levels. The specific achievements indicated by these terms are the products of different groups or individuals at different periods; they are multiple and echeloned over time. One problem about the notion of stages of evolution or social development (such as ancient society, feudalism, capitalism) is that it tends to overlook this alternation and see the trajectories not only as unilineal but as marking one area (the West) rather than another (the East), allocating some universal priority over *la longue durée*. Some versions endow particular groups, often our own, with general qualities of a so-called cultural kind that are seen as persisting over the generations and as giving rise to that supremacy. The alternative view of historical development implies a decisive rejection of such approaches. Changes have to be looked at in much more specific terms than the notion of modes of production often allows, especially when it is further collapsed into considering primarily 'relations of production'. The major contributions to economic modernisation, resting on the basis of a developed, pre-industrial manufacture, advanced agriculture and extensive commodity production (hence the difficulties experienced by black Africa where these were and are very limited in extent), depended on advances in information and technology that were in their turn linked to the accumulation of knowledge made possible by changes in the mode of communication, in the graphic representation of the written word and of temporal and spatial co-ordinates.

Finally there is one argument that we have touched upon but need to face more squarely. It holds there is a great difference between initial emergence and subsequent development in this sphere, the first being beyond the capacity of the East, the latter not. It is clearly put by Ernest Gellner in the following terms: 'There is a difference between the social and cultural traits which favour advanced industrialism, and those which had made its emergence possible in the first place.'[42] He goes on to provide an example: 'The brilliant economic success of some Far Eastern societies suggests that whereas Calvinist individualism may have favoured the initial appearance of the new order, once it has come into being, and its advantages are clear to all, it can be better run in a

---

[42] Gellner 1992: 3.

Confucianist–collectivist spirit.' In my view this argument represents part of the unsatisfactory *ad hoc* adjustment of old theories to the changing world. Unsatisfactory because capitalism was never the subject of the precise kind of process that gave rise to the wheel, which was invented (apparently) only once. That is certainly true of mercantile capitalism, which had many beginnings, among Semites, among Indians, among Chinese and among Italian Catholics. It has been shown repeatedly, with the English borrowing of German iron technology in the sixteenth century and the Japanese use of the American video in recent years, that it is the capacity to utilise rather than invent a new technology that is often the significant factor. And if the factory production of industrial capitalism was developed in eighteenth-century Britain, the particular steps that led to its development hardly required Calvinist individualism to invent any more than did its later adaptation to Catholic Lille or to western India under Parsees, Jains, Hindus or Muslims. The reasons have to be much more contingent, the features to be explained much more precise.

Of course, it is not only the ability of Asian societies to industrialise that is at issue but whether they can do this without relinquishing all their earlier characteristics. Do they really have to become the equivalent of ascetic Protestants, Calvinists no less, to achieve higher production and continuous economic growth? Do they have to settle for the isolated nuclear family with its later development of high divorce rates, of domestic violence, child abuse, a high incidence of lone-parent house-holds and all the other features that can only be aggravated without the watchful eye of the extended family. Young reformers throughout the world wanted to escape its clutches (except where property is concerned). It is oppressive; all sanctions are. Nevertheless many wider ties persisted, despite modernisation.

A revaluation of the East is needed to set the record straight for Asia in the light both of the historical past and of contemporary developments. But it is also essential in order to reconsider the historical position of the West in the process of modernisation. This I have tried to do for a cluster of features that have been considered as unique to Europe's development of capitalism, namely certain types of rationality, of accounting and the family. Different candidates are offered by other scholars, 'law' (especially of contract), freedom (especially of the market) and similar virtues that are associated in Westerners' minds with the Greeks, the Renaissance or the Enlightenment, and that have been seized upon as differences relevant to the speed of later changes in Europe compared with Asia. But I have concentrated on the first set and tried to show that the differences are not so great, nor are the chosen features all that critical in the development of industrial capitalism. The same exercise could be undertaken for those other global variables. Such a reconsideration is as important for the history of the West as it is of the East. By looking back at the family, at accounting and at rationality in the West after reconsidering the situation in the East, we can attempt a better evaluation of 'our' past and present as well as that of the 'other'.

Appendix
Early links between East and West

The notion of the overall comparability of East and West, which much social theory denies or underplays, depends upon the idea that the major societies developed in parallel ways on the basis of their Bronze Age achievements. But it is also the case that they had common roots in Mesopotamia and continued to exchange goods and information, at different intensities over time varying with the particular historical circumstances.

The links between East and West clearly go back to the Mesopotamian world since it was there that many common features of Bronze Age civilisation such as the plough and the wheel had their source. Needham suggests that those features may also have included fundamental ideas such as the equatorial system of lunar mansions in astronomy or the general theory of pneumatic physiology in medicine, which were later developed by the Indians, the Chinese and the Greeks in different ways.[1] In more specific ways 'the essential unity of Europe and China' from well before the Shang dynasty (1500 BCE) has been brought out in a number of papers by Janse.[2]

Communication between 'Europe' and 'Asia' was of course a feature of the Greek world from the end of the Dark Ages because their world, as that of the Mycenaeans beforehand, extended across the Aegean down the coast of Asia Minor.[3] Indeed the great Ionian cities were located along the Anatolian coast, dating from the middle of the eighth century, and may have emerged out of Phoenician trading centres.[4] Bronze Age Mycenaean settlements had existed earlier, in the Cyclades, at Miletus and other places, and Mycenaean culture (e.g., chamber tombs) and

---

[1] Needham 1954: 213.
[2] Needham 1954: 159. See also Laufer 1919 on the distribution of the 'bird-chariot'.
[3] In early Greek literature, the name Asia seems to have been first applied to the central region of the Aegean coastland, possibly under the sway of the principality of Assuwa (Cook 1962: 20).
[4] Snodgrass 1972.

trading goods, as distinct from Mycenaean ethnicity, were widely spread over the Aegean, including Troy. The Hittites were in contact diplomatically with the Aegean coast, and their armies may have penetrated that region as well. In the classical period the Ionian settlements expanded inland and in the eighth century were in touch with the Phrygian kingdom with its capital, Gordion, on the Anatolian plateau. That state in turn had direct contact with Assyria and with the kingdom of Urartu (Ararat). So the Ionian Greeks had relations not only with 'Europeans' but with 'Asians'.

It was in the early eighth century that the Greeks established trading posts further south of the Asia Minor coast. Phoenicians had visited Greece during the Dark Ages but the Greeks of Euboea traded at Al Mina on the Syrian coast as early as the ninth or even the tenth century. Those exchanges brought Oriental influences to Greek art, religion and civilisation generally, as well as leading to the acquisition and development of the alphabet itself, which may have taken place as early as the eleventh century, if we accept the recent evidence of the brooch of Opheltas.[5] Subsequently Ionians and Carians served as mercenaries through the mediation of Lydia and raided the delta region of Egypt as well as serving in Babylon under Nebuchadnezzar. The significant direct contact was with the Milesian 'colony' (post) of Milesian Technos in the delta in the late seventh century but most important was the old Greek port of trade on the delta at Naucratis, exchanging Greek silver, oil and wine for Egyptian grain. This contact was a factor in leading the Greeks to realise the full potentialities of stone architecture and sculpture, although the influence of Bronze Age palaces and general Anatolian traditions must also be taken into account. The two activities of architecture and sculpture went hand in hand. It has been claimed that temples were 'only built at the stage when a deity required a house – that is to say, when there was a sizeable image, together perhaps with gear and dedications of great value, which must stay on the spot and be given protection'.[6] That seems doubtful since the first Heraion at Samos was built earlier in the eighth century. The temple of Athena at Gortyn may have been the result of Syrian influences while according to Aristotle the second temple of Hera at Samos dating from the later sixth century owes

---

[5] Cook 1962: 64. On the great importance of the discovery of the brooch of Opheltas, dating from the eleventh century, with a dedication to a god possibly in Arcadian script see Mossé and Schnapp-Gourbeillon 1990: 94.

[6] Cook 1962: 75, 103. Although the Greeks were familiar with the great stone effigies of Egyptian rulers, Cook thinks it doubtful they would have turned to monumental sculpture without the emergence of carving in marble on the island of Naxos in the seventh century.

its inspiration to the tyrant Polycratus who was a major channel for the influence of his close ally, Egypt.[7] That was the earliest known Ionic temple where stood one of the most venerable of Greek statues. It was the later years of the seventh century that saw the development of large-scale stone construction under Egyptian inspiration; at this time the earliest stone columns were made for use in a temple at Smyrna and adorned with capitals employing floral motifs. In the eastern Mediterranean the exchange of ideas and techniques between Europe, Asia and Africa had long been an established fact.

The major cities of eastern Greece that faced the Asian shore of the Aegean became important centres of commerce and learning. Trade with the Black Sea brought in grain, leaving the inhabitants freer to concentrate on their other activities. Miletus, famous for wool and furniture, was one of the great centres of Ionia for scientific speculation, being the home of Thales, sometimes spoken of as 'the inventor of rational thought', as well as of his pupil, Anaximander. Thales is said to have worked for Croesus, who came to the throne of Lydia in Asia Minor about 561 BCE and reduced all the Greek cities except Miletus itself. But when he challenged Cyrus, the Achaemenid king of Persia, he was defeated and Lydia in turn, together with the Greek centres of the Ionian coast, came under Persian domination. Some Ionians left for the west as they had done earlier. Pythagoras left Samos about 530 BCE and settled at Croton in southern Italy; the school of Eleatic philosophers, of which Zeno was one, consisted of descendants of those Phocaeans who founded Elea in Italy after they had been checked in Corsica. Other scholars moved in different directions. Hecataeus of Miletus travelled to Egypt about 500 BCE when drawing up his portable map. Greek seamen also made the voyage to Spain and down the west coast of Africa. Such movements of scholars emphasise that knowledge was not tied to places or cultures in any simple way. Since men were in touch with Egypt and Persia, knowledge travelled with them to and from the three continents.

The defeat of the Persian invasion of mainland Greece in 480 BCE led to the freeing of the Ionian cities, but they did not recover their prosperity under Athenian hegemony. So scholars from those cities moved either west to Athens like Anaxagoras and Herodotus or east to the Persian empire under Darius which from 522 BCE extended from Cyrenaica in north Africa to the valley of the Indus. The lingua franca of the empire was Aramaic, a Semitic language, but accounts of the royal

---

[7] Burkert 1985.

household were kept in Elamite and its mercantile procedures were Babylonian, while Greeks were preferred as court doctors.[8] An important result of the mixing of Babylonian and Greek culture in Babylon and Uruk was the further development of astronomy. The Babylonians contributed their methods of mathematical calculation and their observations accumulated over the centuries. 'The Greeks contributed their training in logical thinking.' Their co-operation laid the basis for later developments. For example around 280 BCE the Marduk priest, Berosus, founded a school for astrology and astronomy on the island of Cos, where he wrote a book about Babylonia in Greek.[9] The empire was multi-cultural. Greeks were later employed by Persia as shock troops as well as in other capacities; one man was sent by Darius down the Indus to explore the coast round to Suez. Some Ionians baked bricks or tiles, others were stone-carvers; indeed the new capital at Persepolis made much use of Ionic art. So Greeks travelled freely through the empire. Some received big estates; one court doctor, Ctesias, was employed as a diplomat and wrote a fantastic and romantic history of Persia as well as an account of India. Herodotus, who was the first serious historian of antiquity, also moved throughout much of the eastern Mediterranean and the Near East in the course of writing his *History* (originally, 'enquiry') of the Greeks and Persians, together with his famous book on the antiquities of Egypt.

Although the Ionian cities had been liberated, as a powerful neighbour the Persian empire continued to attract their inhabitants and used its wealth to employ Greek scholars, craftsmen and mercenaries as well as to exploit the divisions between Athens and Sparta. The ensuing uncertainty was followed by the establishment of the Athenian Empire but the many small city states survived until the decay of commerce in the Mediterranean in late antiquity or even until the Arab incursions. Civic life spread to the surrounding peoples, penetrating down the coast of Asia Minor as far as the Phoenician cities.

North-west India had already been in touch with the West since Cyrus, the Achaemenid emperor of Persia, crossed the Hindu Kush a little before 530 BCE and received tribute from the kingdom of Gandhara, with its capital at Taxila. It was from Persia that India borrowed and adapted the Aramaic script to form Karoshthi. In the opposite direction Buddhist influences flowed into Manichaeism, while later on Zoro-

---

8 The 'Hippocratic Corpus' continued to be developed in the eastern Aegean at this time, especially at Cnidus and Cos.

9 T. Jacobsen, 'Mesopotamian Religious Literature and Mythology', in *Encyclopaedia Britannica*, vol. XI, 1007–12.

astrianism made its mark on Mahayana Buddhism.[10] Persian ascendency vanished with the conquests of Alexander of Macedonia (356–323 BCE), beginning in the spring of 334 BCE. Hellenic influences spread throughout the Persian empire which he conquered and populated with new towns and new colonists, such as Alexandria in Egypt and the many other Alexandrias in Persia, Parthia, Bactria and Sogdiana. He established a base at Babylon (where he died) and the empire stretched beyond Samarkand to the Indus valley, linking eastern Europe with north India and with the outer limits of Chinese penetration. For as a result of the defeat of the last Persian ruler, Darius III, the new empire extended to central Asia. The Greek state of Bactriana arose in the valley of the Oxus in what is now northern Afghanistan, based on the cities of Balkh in the west and Ai Khanun in the east. At the latter place the settlers founded a city along Greek lines that included a gymnasium for learning and for physical training, and a theatre with 6,000 seats which performed a Greek repertory. Indeed Plutarch asserted that after Alexander's Asian expedition, people in the East read Homer and their children sang the tragedies of Sophocles and Euripedes. Such claims have some support from archaeology, since ink imprints show that the inhabitants read Greek literature and philosophy, while scenes from the Antigone decorate a vase of local manufacture.[11] Whether because of these foreign imports or because of the strength of the local culture, the Greeks of the Euthydemid dynasty who invaded India after Alexander regarded the inhabitants 'more as their equals'.[12] For the Greek expeditions had a profound effect, not only on central Asia, where many people were influenced by Greek law. Alexander himself became a mythical figure as far away as south-east Asia where he is embodied in genealogies in both Sumatra and Malaya, probably as the result of the spread of Islam.[13]

---

[10] Thapar 1966: 59.
[11] Bernard 1982.   [12] Tarn 1938: 411.
[13] I am greatly indebted to Dr Roxana Waterson of the Department of Sociology, National University of Singapore for the following comment: 'The Alexander link seems to be a distinctively Muslim phenomenon, deriving from Muslim folklore. Alexander is paired with Solomon as two great kings created by Allah. In South-East Asia he is known as Iskandar (often with the added Arabic epithet Zulkarnain, the "two-horned", which relates to his appearance on his coins). He is mentioned particularly in the *Sejarah Melayu* as the forerunner of Malay rulers. The rulers of Malay, Acehnese and Minangkabau kingdoms worked him into their genealogies, the latter with the aid of a myth recounted by Marsden (1811: 341), in which the Sultan of Rum (Constantinople) is pictured as the eldest brother, the Sultan of China as the second brother, and the Sultan of Minangkabau as the youngest brother. Legend has it that Iskandar married the daughter of the king of Rum and had three sons, each of whom was given a crown and told to go off and find his own kingdom to rule. In the

Equally the West learnt much from the East. A great trade route across Asia started from Patna on the Ganges and ran through Taxila, the Hindu Kush, to Bactria down to Seleucia, then westwards to Damascus (or Antioch) and to the seaports of Ionia.[14] Babylonian civilisation had continued under the Greeks, with both astronomical and astrological knowledge being transmitted to the conquerors, so Hellenistic astronomy is sometimes described as 'Graeco-Babylonian'.[15] Their astrology too was widely adopted in the West as well as spreading to the East and in both regions the current systems still hark back to Chaldean models. The Seleucid calendar also had an enormous success in the West. The continuing strength of the local tradition is indicated by the fact that the Babylonians retained many features of their own civilisation long after these conquests and continued to use cuneiform until 7 BCE in spite of the presence among them of both Greek and Aramaic writing.

With Alexander's death, the empire soon broke up into five separate kingdoms, including that of the Seleucids. The Indian conquests were relinquished to the new Mauryan emperor, Chandragupta, whose successor but one was Aśoka, while Parthian attacks from the north separated the east from the west. Afghanistan was lost but Bactria and Sogdiana, now largely independent, grew in strength and by about 180 BCE invaded north-west India. Helped by Buddhist sentiment, a Graeco-Indian empire was created that endured for 100 years after the Bactrian kingdom had collapsed. The rule of these Indo-Greeks brought Greece and India closer together culturally, influencing for example the form of Mauryan sculpture. Through a large part of the first century CE, the Greek language was used in a range of formal contexts.

The Greek advance into India led to the opening up of trade routes. India had an extensive coinage in the period of Greek rule, and under the Kushan kings, who were Indo-Scythian rulers holding sway over most of north India and central Asia (including Bactria) during the first three

Singapore Straits, they all tried in vain to put on the crown, which fell into the sea, after which they separated and established themselves in Rum, China and West Sumatra. The ruler of Aceh in the early seventeenth century styled himself (or else became known at a later date) as the "Young Alexander" (Iskandar Muda), as some Indian rulers had also since the fourteenth century claimed the title of "Second Alexander" (see Lombard 1967).' References: Marsden, W., *The History of Sumatra* (1811), reprinted, OUP, pp. 337–42; Winstedt, R., *The Malays: A Cultural History* (1965), pp. 2, 36, 70, 145; Josselin de Jong, 'Who's Who in the Malay Annals', *Journal of the Malay Branch of the Royal Asiatic Society* (1961), 34/2; Winstedt, R., two articles in JMBRAS, vol. 16/2 (1938), and vol. 18/2 (1940), Lombard, Denys, *Le Sultanat d'Atjeh au temps d'Iskandar Muda 1607–1636* (1967), Paris, Ecole Française d'Extreme-Orient, pp. 169–71, 226.

[14] Tarn 1938: 61.
[15] Tarn 1938: 57.

centuries of the Common Era, local monies continued to use that language on coins long after it had vanished as a spoken tongue. In west Asia, Seleucia experienced a great increase in prosperity resulting in the import of enormous quantities of ivory and spices from or through India. To the west, India exported ebony and other woods, peacocks, spices and ivory. To the south-west, Indian vessels sailed along the coast to Arabia although it was Arabs that dominated the trade until the Greeks and Romans began to sail directly to south India around CE 40–50. To the east, Greeks and Indians tried to get in touch with China through Khotan and during the first three centuries of the Common Era there were Indian settlements in what is now Chinese Turkestan.

What influence did the Greeks have on India and India on the Greeks? The Greek words for pen, ink and books passed into Sanskrit but there is no evidence of the parchment which Pergamum was mass-producing early in the second century; south Asia continued to use silk and split bamboo as writing materials long after the Chinese had invented paper some time before the beginning of the Common Era. Some well-educated Indians were acquainted with current Western literature, possibly the work of Plato, just as some Greeks knew the Mahābhārata.[16] As a result of these contacts, the setting of Indian drama may have been inspired by Greek productions, while medicine and astrology were both influenced by this interchange.[17]

However, the major impact on art forms came only in Roman times, with Parthia as an intermediary in the north, when the sculptural style of Gandhara began to employ Western forms. It was only in this later period that Buddhism, which the local Greeks had embraced, used human forms to depict the Buddha, for in the earlier period such figurative icons were avoided. The origins of the Buddha figure in India have been the subject of some dispute. What is clear is that early Buddhist art did not include any figurative representations of the founder; indeed there was 'a deep-seated repugnance to depicting Buddha in human form'.[18] His presence was indicated by the Bo-tree, the Wheel of the Law, by his footprints, his umbrella or by an empty throne. In the Greek or semi-Greek art of Gandhara he began to be represented in human form, and the same influence also entered into the Indian tradition of Mathurā, usually dated from the late Kushan period, the second century CE. The Gandhara figures are often thought to have been created in the first century BCE, but some local scholars have attempted to allocate priority to the Indian tradition. However the earlier date for the Greek figures

16 Tarn 1938: 378ff.
17 Cook 1962: 166.   18 Tarn 1938: 396.

seems confirmed by representations of a Buddha statue on a coin of Maues (*c.* 80 to *c.* 58 BCE).

The adoption of these figurative forms may have been the result of the spread of Bakhti, not only in Hinduism (as in the Bhāgavadgītā) but in Buddhism too. Bakhti is the 'passionate self-oblivion to a deity who in return bestows grace'[19] and it was incorporated in the personal cult of Viṣṇu-Krishna as an all-embracing god as well as in the devotion to the person of Buddha that was one of the factors leading to the divine Buddha of the Mahāyāna, the 'Great Vehicle'. It may have been under these pressures that Buddhists adopted the type of Greek Apollo for their sculptures in the early first century, leading to a Hindu reaction in the form of the Mathurā figures.

The Greek (Yavana) king, Menander, who reigned in the middle of the second century BCE, ruled an empire extending from Mathurā in the east to Broach or Baruch in Gujarat in the west. His fame was widespread and he became the subject of the Milindapañha, or Questions of Milinda, found in a Pali text, in which the monarch engages in a dialogue with the Buddhist sage, Nāgasena. The form has classical prototypes and the work was translated into Chinese already in the fourth century.

Buddhism influenced other rulers. The great conqueror, Aśoka, left an inscription in Kandahar (Afghanistan) consisting of parallel Greek and Aramaic texts that recorded his abstention from eating living creatures as a way of improving the quality of life. By the third century BCE Buddhism had an influence on some speakers of Greek, just as they in turn influenced Buddhist artistic styles.[20] Whether Buddhism played any part in the development of the Neoplatonic vegetarianism of Porphyry or of the monastic régimes of Christianity is a matter for speculation.[21] In post-Bronze Age societies abstentionism does not, I have argued, require a specific point of origin; it is there as an intellectual possibility because of the potential cognitive contradiction involved in spilling some blood of animals and not of humans.[22] Nevertheless it requires some stimulus for this potentiality to take one form rather than another, and in this sphere as in others the lines of communication between the Greek and the Indic worlds may have provided just that.

The East was known to the Greeks not only through conquest but through trade, and that was reciprocal between relatively equal

---

[19] C. Eliot, *Hinduism and Buddhism* II (London, 1921), p. 180.
[20] See Thapar 1992b: 26 for examples of the way 'Yavanas did take to Indian religions'.
[21] But see Grant 1971.
[22] Goody 1981.

partners.[23] In addition to the northern land route there was the seaborne traffic in the Indian Ocean that went back to Mesopotamian and Harappan times and continued in the form of local circuits.[24] According to a probably mythical story, around 120 BCE Egyptian guards on the Red Sea found an exhausted Indian on a drifting ship. He was taught Greek and then offered to head an expedition to the Indian coast.[25] Egyptian ships made the voyage to India by coasting but about 15 BCE they had probably discovered the use of monsoon winds to take them directly from the Red Sea as far as the very south of India.[26] That more direct route flourished under the impact of the Roman conquest of India and the search for eastern luxuries. From the first to the middle of the third century CE 'Roman' ships (actually Graeco-Egyptian) sailed to ports all around India, perhaps as far as Indo-China and China. A Greek, Eudoxus, had already made the journey twice in the second century BCE on behalf of the Ptolemaic king of Egypt and returned with spices and jewels. Earlier the trade had been through intermediaries, but Eudoxus opened up direct contacts which only developed on any large scale under Augustus. Believing it possible to circumnavigate Africa, he then sailed down the Atlantic coast with doctors, craftsmen and cabaret girls for the Indian princes. While this route failed, the other soon became well travelled by Mediterranean sailors voyaging to the mouth of the Indus as well as to more southerly ports for pepper.[27] Indo-Greek merchants carried out business in the north-west. Down the Malabar coast silk and cotton cloth, ivory and cosmetics were acquired in exchange for women, metals, clothing, wine, gold and silver. Mediterranean merchants settled in Indian ports. Local princes may have employed 'Greek' bodyguards, and 'Greek' engineers were also in demand.[28] Some seamen travelled up the east coast to the Ganges, a few visited the Far East. Early in the second century CE one traveller sailed up the coast of Indo-China, possibly further. The Romans left many reminders of their commerce throughout the Indian sub-continent. The excavations at Arikamedu, Pondichery, in the south-east turned up evidence of wine jars (*amphorae*)

---

[23] Our best early example is Megasthenes, Seleucid ambassador to Chandragupta Maurya between 302 and 288 BCE.

[24] On 'local circuits' of later times, see Thapar 1992a: 3.

[25] Thapar (1992a) cites cases of Indians in Egypt.

[26] So it is often assumed, but did the East find this out before the West?

[27] 'Mediterranean' because it is difficult to tell the nationalities involved after Augustus. Italian and even Carthaginian merchants were involved in the India trade (Casson 1989: 31–4; Tchernia 1992).

[28] The guards at Kaveripattinam may have been for the foreign quarters of the port-of-trade rather than for princes. In such ports a number of languages may have been spoken.

and the red polished Arretine ware, and finds of similar objects have been made widely throughout India. In Gujarat in the north-west evidence is provided by the remains of wine jars (from Akota, Devnimori), a bronze figure of Atlas (locally made) and shards of the red polished ware which have turned up in houses and even in Buddhist monasteries (from Devnimori Stupa).[29] Architectural innovations and the use of acanthus leaves as a decorative theme constitute other ways in which this influence was felt. Much information on the East filtered back to Rome as we see from the extensive writings of Pliny the Elder.

Even in the south of India, familiarity with Hellenistic ideas on medicine and horoscopy is evident from various early texts. While in the contrary direction there is a tradition of Buddhist missions having been sent to proselytise in Yavana (western) lands just as Christian missions came to India almost as early as they did to western Europe. Votive inscriptions in the Deccan even mention some Westerners as Buddhists.[30] Did the cult of Isis have any impact on India?[31]

The most extensive information on the maritime routes comes from the well-known Greek work, *The Periplus of the Erythraean Sea*, written between CE 40–70. Indian and Singhalese vessels were using some of the same sea routes as the Westerners and by the second century CE the Indian expansion to Java, Sumatra and Cambodia was at its height, an expansion that may well have led to the decline of westward voyages. The east had become a more important destination. At the beginning of the Christian era Indian influence began to make itself felt in the east of the Indo-Chinese peninsula, which is the period when Romano-Indian trade goods were found in Burma, Java, Thailand and the Mekong delta.[32] From the third century BCE relations were established with China; although the *Periplus* gives evidence of Chinese goods in Indian ports, some came through intermediaries overland. At the same time Chinese goods were also being brought to the Ganges valley by sea.[33] By this period, Indians had established themselves in the Indonesian peninsula, bringing first Hinduism. Buddhism arrived at the beginning of the sixth century CE, possibly a century or so earlier, being brought by travellers on the way to China, with which close relations were maintained through the port of Canton (Guangzhou) from the seventh century.

---

[29] See also Thapar 1992a.

[30] Thapar 1992a: 21.

[31] See R. Fynes, 'Cultural transmission between Roman Egypt and Western India' (DPhil dissertation, Oxford, 1991), cited Thapar 1992a: 20.

[32] On the role of Sri Lanka in Indo-Roman trade see de Romanis 1988.

[33] Bagchi [1951] 1971: 17.

It was only after the third century that the Chinese engaged in long-distance voyages, which achieved their zenith in the thirteenth century. They reached Penang in Malaya about 350 CE, Sri Lanka towards the end of that century and probably the mouth of the Euphrates and Aden by the following one. Those contacts continued until about 900, after the rise of Islamic Arab shipping. The first Muslim embassy reached China in 651 and a century later in 758 their presence was powerful enough to lead to the burning and looting of Canton. In the following century they established 'factories' in areas of Guangdong where they had been preceded by Syrians and by Graeco-Egyptians as long ago as the third century.

There was no direct contact with China along the land route after the Greek period, since the first caravans from China to Iran only began in 106 BCE as the result of the missions of the ambassador, Chang-K'ien. But goods nevertheless passed between East and West through a series of intermediaries.[34] Chinese silk was imported into Rome from India.[35] The opening up of the direct route took place in the context of the trade in silk between East and West. In the time of Julius Caesar and Augustus, the Chinese were referred to as Seres, the silk-producers. Previously silk in the West came mostly from the wild silkworm of western Asia. Other goods travelled eastwards. When Chang-K'ien returned to China, he brought back collections of strange plants, including the pomegranate, the alfalfa and the vine.[36] Imports of that period were the great war horse, the cataphract and Greek influences on Han art, with silk, furs and high-class iron, cinnamon and rhubarb being exported in return.[37] From the Mediterranean again came glassware, some wool and linen textiles, but above all payments had to be made in bullion or specie which may have amounted to the equivalent of what has been estimated at £1 million sterling a year (at 1954 values). This direct silk trade continued for only a century or two, providing a link between the Mediterranean and the Far East. However even when the caravan trade was interrupted, causing a silk shortage in the Roman empire, beginning in CE 166 contacts were made with the Han Court by sea from the south. During the reign of Marcus Aurelius an embassy (but probably no more than a private trading enterprise) was sent, mentioning a route via Vietnam (Jih-nan) and hence by sea. East–West trade was now an established fact.

Following the Greek expansion in the East and the settlement of the Bactrian Greeks in India after the downfall of the Aśokian empire,

[34] Tarn 1938: 87.   [35] Casson 1989: 26.
[36] Laufer 1919.   [37] Tarn 1938: 364.

Indo-Greek culture penetrated to central Asia. With the beginning of a unitary government in China in the third century BCE, attempts were made to secure the western marches then under the control of the Hun. In 138 BCE, when Chang K'ien was sent to the Buddhist kingdom of Bactriana (Balkh), he found bamboo and cloth from south-west China being sold in the local market, suggesting that the silk route to India may have already been in existence. When he reported back to the Emperor, attempts were made to open up and secure the routes to the West. Traders as well as missionaries came from all directions and this period saw the advent of Buddhism to the Chinese court, probably around 65 CE. The routes to northern India crossed to the south and north of the Tarim desert and met up on the Chinese frontier at 'the Jade Gate', near to which were the later caves of Dun-huang, one of the major centres of Buddhist learning. These caves, constructed between the fifth and eighth centuries, became the meeting place of Buddhist scholars, the home of Buddhist art, the depository of innumerable texts, and a centre for translating them into Chinese.

These connections between India and China did not depend on missionaries alone. Under the Tang dynasty (618 CE) 'thousands of Indians were found in the metropolitan cities'.[38] There they aroused the opposition of the literati but a desire to keep up relations with central Asia meant giving some patronage to Buddhism. Buddhist teachers knew about more than the religious canon in the narrow sense. Bodhisuci from southern India had first trained in a Brahman school, studying philosophy as well as sciences such as the Sāṅkya, phonetics, astrology, mathematics and medicine. He was converted to Buddhism, invited to China in 692 CE and reached there by sea the following year. He eventually joined the court at Ch'ang-an where the Emperor helped him set up a unit where he translated fifty-three volumes of the canon.

The advent of Buddhist teachers from central Asia and India encouraged a counterflow of Chinese pilgrims to India, seeking further knowledge and returning with texts of various kinds. Already in the third century a party of Chinese monks reached that country along the Yunnan–Burma route which had been of early significance. The end of the fourth century saw the fifteen-year voyage of Fa-hein starting by the desert route, returning by sea through Sri Lanka and Java and finally landing in Shan-tung. These connections took the peach and the pear, vermilion and Chinese silk to India, while some of the visitors were interested in the mathematics, astronomy and medicine of that country as well as in its religion.[39]

[38] Bagchi [1951] 1971: 49.   [39] Bagchi [1951] 1971: 68

Contacts between the Far East and Far West developed. By the sea route the Arabs firmly established themselves in Canton from the middle of the eighth century and they made many voyages to China during the next 200 years. From the ninth century Jewish merchants known as the Radhanites travelled regularly between China and Spain both by land and by sea, bringing back perfume, spices, medicinal plants and possibly porcelain and other Chinese inventions, in exchange for slaves, swords and brocades. Another centre of Judaism was the Khazar kingdom north of the Black Sea, many of whose Turkic inhabitants were converted about 740 when it became an important area in the exchange of goods and information with the Far East. By the beginning of the twelfth century a Jewish community was established in Khaifêng. Nestorian Christians had also settled in China as did Zoroastrians fleeing from the Muslims. Representatives of all the creeds and many nations were found in that country, attracted by its wealth, its manufactures and its hospitality. With these migrants, merchants and refugees came ideas, techniques and materials from other lands, so that the empire was never totally isolated from the outside world. Equally ideas and goods were continually being exported to the West, leading up to the great burst of trade that followed the entry of Europeans into the sea route at the beginning of the sixteenth century. These were the major connections that made possible the exchange of goods and ideas between East and West, for these never existed in the kind of total isolation from one another that is implied by the categorical distinctions between those areas that has been the hallmark of so many modern social and historical theories and speculations.

Bibliography

Abrahams, M. 1988 *Two Medieval Merchant Guilds of South India*. New Delhi

Abu-Lughod, J. L. 1989 *Before European Hegemony: the world system AD 1250–1350*. New York

Adams, R. M. 1965 *The Evolution of Urban Society*. Chicago

Adas, M. (ed.) 1993 *Islamic and European Expansion: the forging of a global order*. Philadelphia

Aghassian, M. and Kévonian, K. 1985 Le commerce arménien dans l'océan indien aux XVIIe et XVIIIe siècles. In D. Lombard (ed.) *Actes du colloque, Les Milieux marchands asiatiques dans l'océan indien*. Paris: Editions EHESS

Alaev, L. B. 1964 *Yuzhnaya India: sotsialno-ekonomicheskaya istoriya XIV–XVIII vekor* (South India: social and economic history, 14th–18th centuries). Moscow (English summary)

Al-Azmeh, Aziz 1986 *Arabic Thought and Islamic Societies*. London

Albright, W. F. 1968 *Yahweh and Gods of Canaan*. London

Anderson, P. 1975a *Passages from Antiquity to Feudalism*. London

1975b *Lineages of the Absolutist State*. London

Andreski, S. (ed.) 1983 *Max Weber on Capitalism, Bureaucracy and Religion: a selection of texts*. London

Arasaratram, S. 1980 Weavers, merchants and Company: the handloom industry in south-eastern India 1750–1790. *Indian Economic and Social History Review* 17: 257–81

Ariès, P. 1962 *Centuries of Childhood: a social history of family life*. New York (French edn 1960)

Aristotle 1938 *Prior Analytics* (ed. and trans. H. Tredennick). London: Loeb

1960 *Posterior Analytics* (ed. and trans. H. Tredennick). Cambridge, MA: Loeb

Arkell, A. J. 1936 Cambay and the bead trade. *Antiquity* 10: 292–305

1951 Meroe and India. In W. F. Grimes (ed.) *Aspects of Archaeology in Britain and Beyond*. London

Ashburner, W. 1909 *Rhodian Sea-Law: nomos Rodion nautikos*. Oxford

Ashton, T. S. 1939 *An Eighteenth-Century Industrialist: Peter Stubbs of Warrington, 1756–1806*. Manchester

Astuti, G. 1932 *Origini e svolgimento storico della commenda fino al secolo XIII*. Turin

1934 *Il libro dell'entrata e dell'uscita di una compagnia mercantile senese del secolo XIII (1277–1282)*. Turin

Ayoub, M. R. 1966 The family reunion. *Ethnology* 5: 415–33

Backer, S. 1972 Yarn. *Scientific American* 227 (6): 47–56

Bagchi, P. C. [1951] 1971 *India and China: a thousand years of cultural relations.* New York (2nd edn)

Balacz, E. 1964 The birth of capitalism in China. In E. Balacz (ed.) *Chinese Civilization and Bureaucracy: variations on a theme.* New Haven, CT

Barbosa, D. [1918–21] *The Book of Duarte Barbosa*, ed. M. L. Dames, 2 vols. London

Bardhan, P. 1982 Agrarian class formation in India. *Journal of Peasant Studies* 10: 33–94

Barker, E. 1948 *The Politics of Aristotle.* Oxford

Barnes, J. 1982 *Aristotle.* Oxford

Begley, V. 1983 Arikamedu reconsidered. *American Journal of Archaeology* 87: 461–81

Bellah, R. N. 1957 *Tokugawa Religion: the values of pre-industrial Japan.* Boston

Bendix, R. 1960 *Max Weber: an intellectual portrait.* New York

Benedict, B. 1968 Family firms and economic development. *Southwestern Journal of Anthropology* 1: 1–19

Berengo, M. 1965 *Nobili e mercanti nella Lucca del Cinquecento.* Turin

Berger, P. 1987 *The Capitalist Revolution: fifty propositions about prosperity, equality and liberty.* Aldershot

Bergeron, L. 1978 *Les Capitalistes en France, 1780–1914.* Paris

Berle, A. A. and Means, G. C. 1932 *The Modern Corporation and Private Property.* New York

Bernard, P. 1982 An ancient Greek city in central Asia. *Scientific American* 246: 126–35

Bernstein, H. 1979 African peasantries: a theoretical framework. *Journal of Peasant Studies* 6: 421–43

Berrill, K. 1964 Historical experience: the problem of the economic 'take-off'. In K. Berrill (ed.) *Economic Development with Special Reference to East Asia.* New York

Binsbergen, W. van and Geschiere, P. (eds.) 1985 *Old Modes of Production and Capitalist Encroachment: anthropological explorations in Africa.* Monographs from the African Studies Centre, Leiden. London

Blitz, R. C. 1967 Mercantilist policies and the pattern of world trade, 1500–1750. *Journal of Economic History* 27: 39–55

1978 Some reflections on the world trade of the XVIIth and XVIIIth century: a comment on the findings of Professor Chaudhuri. *Journal of European Economic History* 7: 214–22

Bloch, M. (ed.) 1975 *Political Language and Oratory in Traditional Societies.* London

Blois, G. 1984 *The Crisis of Feudalism.* Cambridge (French edn 1970)

Blunden, C. and Elvin, M. 1983 *Cultural Atlas of China.* Oxford

Bocheński, I. M. 1961 *A History of Formal Logic.* Notre Dame, IN (German edn 1956)

Bottéro, J. 1977 Les noms du Marduk, l'écriture et la 'logique' en Mésopotamie ancienne. In M. de Jong Ellis (ed.) *Essays on the Ancient Near East: in memory of Jacob Joel Finkelstein.* Hamden, CT

1987 *Mésopotamie: l'écriture, la raison et les dieux.* Paris

Bouvier, J. 1967 *Les Rothschild*. Paris

Braimah, J. A. and Goody, J. 1967 *Salaga: the struggle for power*. London

Bratchel, M. E. 1978 Italian merchant organisation and business relationships in early Tudor London. *Journal of European Economic History* 7: 5–32

Braudel, F. 1985 *Le Dynamique du capitalisme*. Paris (French edition of *Afterthoughts on Material Civilization and Capitalism*, 1977)

Bray, F. 1984 Patterns of evolution in rice-growing societies. *Journal of Peasant Studies* 11: 3–33

Brenner, R. [1976] 1985 Agrarian class structure and economic development in pre-industrial Europe. *Past and Present* 70: 30–75. Reprinted 1985 in T. H. Aston and C. H. E. Philpin (eds.) *The Brenner Debate: agrarian class structure and economic development in pre-industrial Europe*. Cambridge

Brook, T. 1981 The merchant network in 16th century China: a discussion and translation of Zhang Han's 'On Merchants'. *Journal of Economic and Social History of the Orient* 24: 165–214

Buchanan, D. 1934 *The Development of Capitalistic Enterprise in India*. New York

Buchanan, F. 1807 *A Journey from Madras through the Countries of Mysore, Canara and Malabar*. London

Burkert, W. 1985 *Greek Religion: archaic and classical* (trans. J. Raffan). Oxford

Buss, A. E. (ed.) 1955 *Max Weber in Asian Studies*. London

Caldwell, J. C. 1976 Toward a restatement of demographic transition theory: an investigation of conditions before and at the onset of fertility decline employing primarily African experience and data. *Population and Development Review* 2: 321–66

Casson, L. 1989 *The Periplus Maris Erythraei: text with introduction, translation and commentary*. Princeton, NJ

Chandler, A. D. 1977 *The Visible Hand: the managerial revolution in American business*. Cambridge, MA

Chandra, S. 1982 *Medieval India: society, the jagirdari crisis and the village*. Delhi

Chao, K. 1984 La production textile en Chine. *Annales: ESC* 39: 957–76

Chapman, S. D. and Chassagne, S. 1981 *European Textile Printers in the Eighteenth Century: a study of Peel and Oberkampf*. London

Chaudhuri, K. N. 1965 *The English East India Company: the study of an early joint-stock company, 1600–1640*. London

1968 Treasure and trade balances: the East India Company's export trade, 1660–1720. *Economic History Review* 21: 480–501

1974 The structure of the Indian textile industry in the seventeenth and eighteenth centuries. *Indian Economic and Social History Review* 11: 127–82

1975 The economic and monetary problem of European trade with Asia during the seventeenth and eighteenth centuries. *Journal of European Economic History* 4: 323–58

1978a Some reflections on world trade of the XVIIth and XVIIIth century: a reply. *Journal of European Economic History* 7: 223–31

1978b *The Trading World of Asia and the English East India Company, 1660–1760*. Cambridge

1979 Markets and traders in India during the seventeenth and eighteenth centuries. In K. N. Chaudhuri and C. J. Dewey (eds.) *Economy and Society: essays in Indian economic and social history*. Oxford

1982 Foreign Trade. 1. European trade with India. In T. Raychaudhuri and I. Habib (eds.) *The Cambridge Economic History of India*, vol. I. 1200–1750. Cambridge

Chaudhuri, K. N. and Dewey, C. J. (eds.) 1979 *Economy and Society: essays in Indian economic and social history*. Oxford

Chaudhuri, M. R. 1964 *The Iron and Steel Industry of India: an economic–geographic appraisal*. Calcutta

Chen, Chi-yun 1983 Kung-sun Lung: white horse and other issues. *Philosophy East and West* 33: 341–54

1990 Chinese language and truth – a critique of Chad Hansen's analysis. *Chinese Culture* 31: 49–80

Cheng, Chung-Ying 1965 Inquiries into classical Chinese logic. *Philosophy East and West* 15: 195–216

Chicherov, A. I. 1971 *India, Economic Development in the 16th–18th Centuries: outline history of crafts and trade*. Moscow (revised edn)

Childe, G. 1939 *What Happened in History?* Harmondsworth

Chingming, Hou 1963 Some reflections on the economic history of modern China (1840–1949). *Journal of Economic History* 23: 594–605

Chinoy, S. 1968 *Pioneering in Indian Business*. London

Chittick, H. N. 1971 The coast of East Africa. In P. L. Shinnie (ed.) *The African Iron Age*. Oxford

Chmielewski, J. 1962 Notes on early Chinese logic (1). *Rocznik Orientalistyczny* 26(1): 7–21

Clanchy, M. T. 1979 *From Memory to Written Record: England 1066–1307*. London

Claverie, E. and Lamaison, P. 1982 *L'impossible mariage: violence et parenté en Gévaudan, XVIIe, XVIIIe et XIXe siècles*. Paris

Cohen, M. 1976 *House United, House Divided: the Chinese family in Taiwan*. New York

Cole, M. *et al.* 1971 *The Cultural Context of Learning and Thinking: an exploration in experimental anthropology*. London

Coleman, D. C. 1977 *The Economy of England, 1450–1750*. Oxford

Colless, B. E. 1969 Persian merchants and missionaries in medieval Malaya. *Journal of the Malayan Branch of the Royal Asiatic Society* 42 (2): 10–47

1969–71 The traders of the pearl: the mercantile and missionary activities of Persian and Armenian Christians in south-east Asia. *Abr-Nahrain* 9 (1969–70): 17–38; 10 (1970–1): 102–21; 11 (1971): 1–21

Collins, R. 1986 *Weber's Sociological Theory*. Cambridge

Commissariat, N. S. 1938 *History of Gujerat*. 2 vols. Bombay

Cook, J. M. 1962 *The Greeks in Ionia and the East*. London

Coquery-Vidrovitch, C. 1978 Research on an African mode of production. In D. Seddon (ed.) *Relations of Production*. London (trans. from the French, 1969)

Coser, L. 1968 Sociology of knowledge. *International Encyclopedia of the Social Sciences* 8: 428–35. New York

Crawcour, E. S. 1963 Problems of Japanese economic history. *Journal of Economic History* 23: 619–28

Creighton, C. 1980 Family, property and relations of production in western Europe. *Journal of Peasant Studies* 9: 129–67

Cumont, F. 1906 *Les Religions orientales dans le paganisme romain*. Paris

Curtin, P. D. 1984 *Cross-cultural Trade in World History*. Cambridge

Damerow, P. and Englund, R. K. 1989 *American School of Prehistoric Research Bulletin* 39. *The Proto-elamite Texts from Tiepe Yahya*. Cambridge MA: Peabody Museum of Archaeology and Ethnology, Harvard University

Das Gupta, A. 1979 *Indian Merchants and the Decline of Surat, c. 1700–1750*. Wiesbaden

Dasgupta, P. 1993 *An Inquiry into Well-being and Destitution*. Oxford

Dasgupta, S. N. 1922–55 *A History of Indian Philosophy*. 5 vols. Cambridge

Davis, J. C. 1973 *A Venetian Family and its Fortune, 1500–1900*. Philadelphia

Dawson, R. (ed.) 1964 *The Legacy of China*. Oxford
1967 *The Chinese Chameleon: an analysis of European conceptions of Chinese civilization*. London

Defoe, D. [1745] 1841 *The Complete English Tradesman*. Oxford

Delille, G. and Rizzi, F. (eds.) 1986 *Le Modèle familiale Européen: normes, déviance, contrôle du pouvoir*. Rome

Dermigny, L. 1960 *Cargaisons indiennes: Solier et Cie, 1781–1793*. 2 vols. Paris
1964 *La Chine et l'Occident: le commerce à Canton au XVIIIe siècle, 1719–1833*. 4 vols. Paris

Desai, K. 1964 *Indian Law of Marriage and Divorce*. Bombay

Dietler, M. 1990 Driven by drink: the role of drinking in the political economy and the case of early Iron Age France. *Journal of Anthropological Archaeology* 9: 352–406

Dihle, A. 1978 Die entdeckungsgeschichtlichen Voraussetzungen des Indienhandels der römischen Kaiserzeit. *Aufsteig und Niedergang der Römischen Welt*, II, 9.2. Berlin

Dobb, M. 1947 *Studies in the Development of Capitalism*. New York (revised edn)

Duggan, C. 1981 Equity and compassion in papal marriage decretals in England. In W. van Hoecke and A. Welkenhuysen (eds.) *Love and Marriage in the Twelfth Century* (Mediavalia Lovanensia), ser. 1, no. 8. Leuven

Dumont, L. 1970 *Homo Hierarchicus: the caste system and its implications*. Chicago (French edn 1966)
1977 *From Mandeville to Marx: the genesis and triumph of economic ideology*. Chicago
1985 *Essays on Individualism*. Chicago

Dumont, W. A. 1976 Family migration and family reunion. *International Migration* 14: 53–83

Dunbabin, T. J. 1957 *The Greeks and their Eastern Neighbours*. London: The Society for the Promotion of Hellenic Studies

Duncan, P. 1963 Conflict and co-operation among trawlermen. *British Journal of Industrial Relations*. 1: 331–47

Durkheim, E. 1897 *La Division du travail*. Paris (English translation 1933)

Dutt, S. 1962 *Buddhist Monks and Monasteries of India*. London

Dyson, T. and Moore, M. 1983 On kinship structure, female autonomy and demographic behavior in India. *Population and Development Review* 9: 35–60

Edler, F. 1934 *Glossary of Mediaeval Terms of Business, Italian Series, 1200–1600.* Cambridge, MA

Einarson, B. 1938 On certain mathematical terms in Aristotle's logic. *American Journal of Philology* 57: 34–54, 151–72

Eisenstein, E. L. 1979 *The Printing Press as an Agent of Change.* Cambridge

Elias, N. 1978 *The Civilizing Process.* Oxford

Elvin, M. 1972 The high-level equilibrium trap: the causes of the decline of inventions in the traditional Chinese textile industries. In W. E. Wilmott (ed.) *Economic Organization in Chinese Society.* Stanford, CA

Evans-Pritchard, E. E. 1934 Lévy Bruhl's theory of primitive mentality. *Bulletin of the Faculty of Arts, Cairo University* 1: 1–36

  1937 *Witchcraft, Oracles and Magic among the Azande.* Oxford

  1940 *The Nuer.* Oxford

Factor, R. L. 1983 What is the 'logic' in Buddhist logic? *Philosophy East and West* 33: 2, 183–8

Farrell, B. G. 1993 *Elite Families: class and power in nineteenth-century Boston.* Albany, NY

Faure, D. 1989 The lineage as business company: patronage versus law in the development of Chinese business. *The Second Conference of Modern Chinese Economic History,* January 5–7, The Institute of Economics, Academia Sinica, Taipei.

Fei, Hsiao Tung 1939 *Peasant Life in China.* London

Feldhaus, A. 1984 *The Deeds of God in Rddhipur.* New York

Feuerwerker, A. 1958 *China's Early Industrialization: Sheng Hsuan-Huai (1844–1916) and Mandarin enterprise.* Cambridge, MA

Finley, M. 1973 *The Ancient Economy.* London

Flandrin, J. 1979 (1976) *Families in Former Times: kinship, household and sexuality.* Cambridge

Fortes, M. 1954 Mind. In E. E. Evans-Pritchard (ed.) *The Institutions of Primitive Society.* Oxford

Fortune, R. 1857 *A Residence Among the Chinese: inland, on the coast, and at sea.* London

Frantz-Murphy, G. 1981 A new interpretation of the economic history of medieval Egypt. *Journal of Economic and Social History of the Orient* 24: 174–297

Fung Yu-lan 1953 *A History of Chinese Philosophy* (trans. D. Bodde). Princeton, NJ

Furber, H. 1976 *Rural Empires of Trade in the Orient, 1600–1800.* Minneapolis, MN

Gadd, C. J. 1932 Seals of ancient Indian style found at Ur. *Proceedings of the British Academy* 18: 191–210

Gadgil, D. R. 1959 *The Origins of the Modern Business Class.* New York

Garcin de Tassy, J. H. 1847 *Histoire de la littérature Hindoui et Hindoustani.* 2 vols. Paris

Gardella, R. P. 1982 Commercial bookkeeping in Ch'ing China and the West: a preliminary assessment. *Ch'ing-shih Wen-t'i* 4: 56–72

  1983 The development of accounting in the West, China and Japan. Working Paper Series. Harrisonburg, VA: The Academy of Accounting Historians

1992 Squaring accounts: commercial bookkeeping methods and capitalist rationalism in late Qing and republican China, *Journal of Asian Studies* 51: 317–39

Garelli, P. 1969 *Le Proche-Orient asiatique: des origines aux invasions des peuples de la mer*. 2 vols. Paris

Gellner, E. 1992 *Reason and Culture*. Oxford

Gerschenkron, A. 1962 *Economic Backwardness in Historical Perspective*. Cambridge, MA

Geschiere, P. and Raatgever, R. 1985 Introduction. Emerging insights and issues in French Marxist anthropology. In W. van Binsbergen and P. Geschiere (eds.) *Old Modes of Production and Capitalist Encroachment: anthropological explorations in Africa*. Monographs from the African Studies Centre, Leiden. London

Ghosh, A. 1992 *In an Antique Land*. London

Gillion, K. I. 1968 *Ahmedabad: a study in Indian urban history*. Berkeley, CA

Glick, T. F. 1979 *Islamic and Christian Spain in the Early Middle Ages: comparative perspectives on social and cultural formation*. Princeton, NJ

Glover, I. C. 1990 *Early Trade between India and South-east Asia: a link in the development of a world trading system*. Hull: University of Hull, Centre for South-East Asian Studies (2nd edn)

Gluckman, M. 1949–50 Social beliefs and individual thinking in primitive society. *Memoirs and Proceedings of Manchester Literary and Philosophic Society* 91: 73–98

Goitein, S. D. 1954 From the Mediterranean to India: documents on the trade to India, south Arabia, and east Africa from the eleventh and twelfth centuries. *Speculum* 9: 181–97

1963 Letters and documents on the India trade in medieval times. *Islamic Culture* 37: 188–205

1964 Commercial and family partnerships in the countries of medieval Islam. *Islamic Studies* 3: 315–37

1966 Bankers' accounts from the eleventh century AD. *Journal of Economic and Social History of the Orient* 9: 28–67

1967 *A Mediterranean Society, the Jewish Communities of the Arab World as Portrayed in the Documents of the Cairo Geniza*, vol. I. Berkeley, CA

1973 *Letters of Medieval Jewish Traders*. Princeton, NJ

1980 From Aden to India: specimens of the correspondence of India traders of the twelfth century. *Journal of Economic and Social History of the Orient* 23: 43–66

1987 Portrait of a medieval India trader: three letters from the Cairo Geniza. *Bulletin of the School of Oriental and African Studies* 50: 449–64

Gokhale, B. G. 1969 Ahmedabad in the XVIIth century. *Journal of Economic and Social History of the Orient* 12: 187–97

1979 *Surat in the Seventeenth Century: a study in urban history of pre-modern India*. London

Goldthwaite, R. 1980 *The Building of Renaissance Florence: an economic and social history*. Baltimore, MD

Goody, E. 1973 *Contexts of Kinship: an essay in the family sociology of the Gonja of northern Ghana*. Cambridge

270   Bibliography

1982a *Parenthood and Social Reproduction: fostering and occupational roles in west Africa*. Cambridge
1982b Introduction. In E. Goody (ed.) *From Craft to Industry: ethnography of proto-industrial cloth production*. Cambridge
1989 Apprenticeship, learning and the division of labor. In M. Coy (ed.) *Apprenticeship: from theory to method and back again*. New York
1995 (ed.) *Anticipatory Interactive Planning*. Cambridge
Goody, J. 1956 *The Social Organisation of the LoWiili*. London
1962 *Death, Property and the Ancestors*. Stanford, CA
1971 *Technology, Tradition and the State in Africa*. London
1972a The evolution of the family. In P. Laslett and R. Wall (eds.) *Household and Family in Past Time*. Cambridge
1972b *The Myth of the Bagre*. Oxford
1972c *Domestic Groups*. Addison-Wesley Module in Anthropology. Reading, MA
1973 Polygyny, economy and the role of women. In J. Goody (ed.) *The Character of Kinship*. Cambridge
1975 Population, economy and inheritance in Africa. In R. P. Moss and R. J. A. R. Rathbone (eds.) *The Population Factor in African Studies*. London
1976 *Production and Reproduction: a comparative study of the domestic domain*. Cambridge
1977 *The Domestication of the Savage Mind*. Cambridge
1979 Slavery in time and space. In J. L. Watson (ed.) *Asian and African Systems of Slavery*. Oxford
1980 Rice-burning and the green revolution in northern Ghana. *Journal of Developmental Studies* 16: 136–55
1981 Sacrifice among the LoDagaa and elsewhere: a comparative comment on implicit questions and explicit rejections. *Systèmes de pensée en Afrique noire: le sacrifice IV*. Cahier 5. Ivry: Centre national de recherche scientifique
1982 *Cooking, Cuisine and Class*. Cambridge
1983 *The Development of the Family and Marriage in Europe*. Cambridge
1986 *The Logic of Writing and the Organisation of Society*. Cambridge
1990 *The Oriental, the Ancient and the Primitive: systems of marriage and the family in the pre-industrial societies of Eurasia*. Cambridge
1993 *The Culture of Flowers*. Cambridge
Goody, J. and Gandah, J. D. K. 1981 *Une Récitation du Bagré*. Paris
Goody, J. and Goody, E. N. 1990 Marriage and the family in Gujarat. In J. Goody, *The Oriental, the Ancient and the Primitive: systems of marriage and the family in the pre-industrial societies of Eurasia*. Cambridge
Goody, J. *et al.* 1981a On the absence of implicit sex preference in Ghana. *Journal of Biosocial Science* 13: 87–96
1981b Implicit sex preferences: a comparative study. *Journal of Biosocial Science* 13: 455–66
Gopal, S. 1975 *Commerce and Crafts in Gujarat, 16th and 17th century*. Delhi
Gough, K. 1979 *Dravidian Kinship and Modes of Production*. The Irawati Karve Memorial Lecture for 1978, Indian Council of Social Science Research. New Delhi

Graham, A. C. 1964 The place of reason in the Chinese philosophical tradition.
In R. Dawson (ed.) *The Legacy of China*. Oxford
1978 *Later Mohist Logic, Ethics and Science*. Hong Kong
1989 *Disputers of the Tao: philosophical argument in ancient China*. La Salle,
IL

Grant, R. M. 1971 Early Alexandrian Christianity. *Church History* 40:
133–44

Gray, A. (ed.) 1887–9 *The Voyage of Frances Pyrard of Laval*. London

Greenhalgh, S. 1987 Families and networks in Taiwan's economic development.
In S. M. Greenhalgh and E. A. Winckler (eds.) *Contending Approaches to the
Political Economy of Taiwan*. Armonk, NY
1990 Land reform and family entrepreneurialism in east Asia. In G. McNicoll
and M. Cain (eds.) *Population and Rural Development: institutions and policy*.
A supplement to *Population and Development Review*

Grove, L. and Esherick, J. W. 1980 From feudalism to capitalism: Japanese
scholarship on the transformation of Chinese rural society. *Modern China* 6:
397–438

Gunawardana, R. A. L. H. 1979 *Robe and Plough: monasticism and economic
interest in early medieval Sri Lanka* (Association for Asian Studies, No. 35).
Tucson, AZ

Habermas, J. 1971 *Towards a Rational Society*. London
1984 *The Theory of Communicative Action*. Boston

Habib, I. 1960 Banking in Mughal India. In T. Raychaudhuri (ed.) *Contributions
to Indian Economic History*, vol. I. Calcutta
1964 Usury in medieval India. *Society and History* 6: 393–423
1969 Potentialities of capitalistic development in the economy of Mughal
India. *Journal of Economic History* 29: 32–78
1972 Potentialities of change in the economy of Mughal India. *Socialist Digest*
6: 74–137
1976 Notes on the Indian textile industry in the seventeenth century. *S. C.
Sarkar Felicitation Volume*. New Delhi

Hajnal, J. 1965 European marriage patterns in perspective. In D. V. Glass and
D. E. C. Eversley (eds.) *Population in History: essays in historical demography*.
London
1982 Two kinds of pre-industrial household formation systems. *Population and
Development Review* 8: 449–94

Hall, J. A. 1985a *Powers and Liberties: the causes and consequences of the rise of the
West*. Oxford
1985b Religion and the rise of capitalism. *Archives Européenes de Sociologie* 26:
193–223

Hall, K. R. 1980 *Trade and Statecraft in the Rise of the Cholas*. New Delhi

Hanley, S. B. and Wolf, A. P. (eds.) 1985 *Family and Population in East Asian
History*. Stanford, CA

Hansen, C. 1983 *Language and Logic in Ancient China*. Ann Arbor, MI

Harper, E. B. 1959 Two systems of economic exchange in village India.
American Anthropologist 61: 760–78

Harrell, S. 1985 Why do the Chinese work so hard? Reflections on an
entrepreneurial ethic. *Modern China* 11: 203–6

Hartwell, R. W. 1969 Economic growth in England before the Industrial Revolution: some methodological issues. *Journal of Economic History* 29: 13–31

Hauser, W. B. 1974 *Economic Institutional Change in Tokugawa Japan: Osaka and the Kinai cotton trade.* Cambridge

Hayashi, R. 1975 *The Silkroad and the Shoso-in.* New York

Heers, J. 1974 *Le Clan familial au moyen âge.* Paris

Heimann, J. 1980 Small change and ballast: cowry trade and usage as an example of Indian Ocean economic history. *South Asia* ns 3: 48–9

Herlihy, D. 1969 Family solidarity in medieval Italian history. In D. Herlihy, R. S. Lopez, and V. Stessarev (eds.) *Economy, Society, and Government in Medieval Italy. Essays in memory of Robert L. Reynolds.* Kent, OH: Kent State UP

   1971 The economy of traditional Europe. *Journal of Economic History* 31: 153–64

   1977 Deaths, marriages, births and the Tuscan economy (c. 1300–1550). In R. D. Lee (ed.) *Population Patterns in the Past.* New York

   1985 *Medieval Households.* Cambridge, MA

Hervouet, Y. (ed.) 1978 *A Sung Bibliography.* Hong Kong

Higham, C. 1989 *The Archaeology of Mainland Southeast Asia: from 10,000 BC to the fall of Angkor.* Cambridge

Hill, C. 1961 *The Century of Revolution.* London

   1964 Puritanism, capitalism and the scientific revolution. *Past and Present* 29: 88–97

Hill, P. 1970 *The Migrant Cocoa-farmers of Southern Ghana: a study in rural capitalism.* Cambridge

Hilton, R. 1985 Introduction. In T. H. Ashton and C. H. E. Philpin (eds.) *The Brenner debate: agrarian class structure and economic development in pre-industrial Europe.* Cambridge: Past and Present Publications

Hindess, B. and Hirst, P. Q. 1975 *Pre-capitalist Modes of Production.* London

Hirschmeier, J. 1964 *The Origins of Entrepreneurship in Japan.* Cambridge, MA

Hirschmeier, J. and Yui, T. 1975 *The Development of Japanese Business 1600–1973.* London

Hirst, P. 1975 The Uniqueness of the West. *Economy and Society* 4: 446–75

Hobson, J. A. 1902 *Imperialism: a study.* London

Hodges, R. 1982 *Dark Age Economics: the origins of towns and trade AD 600–1000.* London

Hollis, M. and Lukes, S. (eds.) 1982 *Rationality and Relativism.* Oxford

Homans, G. C. 1941 *English Villagers of the Thirteenth Century.* Cambridge, MA

Honneth, A. *et al.* 1992 *Cultural and Political Interventions in the Unfinished Project of Enlightenment.* Cambridge, MA

Hopkins, K. 1980 Brother–sister marriage in Roman Egypt. *Comparative Studies in Society and History* 22: 303–54, reprinted in K. Hopkins *Sociological Studies in Roman History* vol. III. Cambridge

Horton, R. and Finnegan, R. (eds.) 1973 *Modes of Thought.* London

Hossain, H. 1979 The alienation of weavers: impact of the conflict between the revenue and commercial interests of the East India Company, 1750–1800. *Indian Economic and Social History Review* 16: 323–45

Hou, Chi-Ming 1963 Some reflections on the economic history of modern China (1840–1949). *Journal of Economic History* 23: 595–605

Hourani, G. E. 1951 *Arab Seafaring in the Indian Ocean*. Princeton, NJ

Howard, R. 1978 *Colonialism and Underdevelopment in Ghana*. London
    1980 Formation and stratification of the peasantry in colonial Ghana. *Journal of Peasant Studies* 8: 61–80

Hoyt, S. H. 1993 *Old Malacca*. Kuala Lumpur

Hsu Tzu-fen 1991 Traditional Chinese bookkeeping methodology. *Chinese Business History* 2: 1–2

Hudson, P. 1992 *The Industrial Revolution*. London

Hufton, O. 1974 *The Poor of Eighteenth-Century France, 1750–1789*. Oxford

Hughes, D. O. 1975 Urban growth and family structure in medieval Genoa. *Past and Present* 66: 3–28

Hu Shih 1922 *The Development of the Logical Method in Ancient China*. Shanghai

Huyghues des Etages, M.-F. *et al*. 1994 *A la Rencontre de Sinbad: la route maritime de la soie*. Paris

Inalcik, H. 1969 Capital formation in the Ottoman Empire. *Journal of Economic History* 29: 97–140

Irwin, J. and Brett, K. B. 1970 *Origin of Chintz*. London

Irwin, J. and Hall, M. 1971 *Indian Painted and Printed Fabrics*. Ahmadabad

Irwin, J. and Schwartz, P. R. 1966 *Studies in Indo-European Textile History*. Ahmadabad

Jackson, H. 1920 Aristotle's lecture room. *Journal of Philology* 35: 191–200

Jacobs, N. 1958 *The Origins of Modern Capitalism and Eastern Asia*. Hong Kong

Jain, L. C. 1929 *Indigenous Banking in India*. London

Jashemski, W. F. 1979 *The Gardens of Pompei: Herculaneum and the villas destroyed by Vesuvius*. New Rochelle, NY

Jha, S. C. 1963 *Studies in the Development of Capitalism in India*. Calcutta

Johnson, M. 1970 The cowrie currencies of west Africa. *Journal of African History* 11: 331–53

Johnson-Laird, P. N. 1983 *Mental Models*. Cambridge

Johnstone, R. F. 1910 *The Lion and the Dragon in Northern China*. New York

Jones, E. L. 1981 *The European Miracle*. Cambridge

Kantowsky, D. 1984 *Recent Research on Max Weber's Studies of Hinduism: papers submitted to a conference held in New Delhi*. Munich

Kapadia, K. M. 1966 *Marriage and Family in India*. Oxford (3rd edn; 1st edn 1955)

Kearney, H. F. 1964 Puritanism, capitalism and the scientific revolution. *Past and Present* 28: 81–101

Kennedy, Jnr, R. E. 1962 The Protestant ethic and the Parsis. *American Journal of Sociology* 68: 11–20

Khachikian, L. 1962 Le Registre d'un marchand arménien en Perse, en Inde et au Tibet (1682–1693). *Annales: ESC* 22: 231–78

Kneale, W. and M. 1962 *The Development of Logic*. Oxford

Korson, J. H. 1975 Some aspects of social change in the Muslim family in West Pakistan. In D. Narain (ed.) *Explorations in the Family and Other Essays*. Bombay

Kou Pao-koh 1953 *Deux Sophistes chinois – Houei Che et Kong-souen Long*. Paris

Kramer, S. N. 1954 Ur-Nammu Law Code. *Orientalia* s. 2 23: 40–51

Labib, S. Y. 1969 Capitalism in medieval Islam. *Journal of Economic History* 29: 79–96

Lach, D. F. 1965 *Asia in the Making of Europe* vol. I. Chicago

Ladinois, R. 1986 L'Ordre du monde et l'institution familiale en Inde. In A. Burgière *et al.*, *Histoire de la famille*. Paris

Lamoureaux, N. R. 1986 Banks, kinship and economic development: the New England case. *Journal of Economic History* 46: 647–67

Landis, D. 1969 *The Unbound Prometheus*. Cambridge

Lane, F. C. 1944 Family partnerships and joint ventures in the Venetian Republic. *Journal of Economic History* 4: 178–96

    1963 Recent studies on the economic history of Venice. *Journal of Economic History* 23: 312–34

    1969 Meanings of capitalism. *Journal of Economic History* 29: 13–31

    1973 *Venice: a maritime republic*. Baltimore, MD

Larsen, M. T. 1976 *The Old Assyrian City State and its Colonies*. Copenhagen

Laslett, P. 1972 Mean household size in England since the sixteenth century. In P. Laslett and R. Wall (eds.) *Household and Family in Past Time*. Cambridge

Laslett, P. and Wall, R. (eds.) 1972 *Household and Family in Past Time*. Cambridge

Laufer, B. 1919 *Sino-Iranica: Chinese Contributions to the History of Civilization in Ancient Iran with Special Reference to the History of Cultivated Plants and Products*. Field Museum of Natural History, publication 201, Anthropological Series XV: 185–597. Chicago

Leakey, M. 1983 *Africa's Vanishing Art: the rock paintings of Tanzania*. New York

Ledderose, L. 1992 Module and mass production. *Proceedings of the International Colloquium on Chinese Art History, 1991, Painting and Calligraphy*, Part 2. National Palace Museum, Taiwan

Le Goff, J. 1967 Culture cléricale et traditions folkoriques dans la civilisation mérovingienne. *Annales: ESC* 22: 780–91

    1984 *The Birth of Purgatory*. Chicago (1st French edn 1981)

Leur, J. C. van 1955 *Indonesian Trade and Society: essays in Asian social and economic history*. The Hague

Levine, D. 1977 *Family Formation in an Age of Nascent Capitalism*. New York

Levine, N. E. 1987 Differential childcare in three Tibetan communities: beyond son preferences. *Population and Development Review* 13: 281–304

Levkovsky, A. 1966 *Capitalism in India*. Bombay

Levy, M. J. [1949] 1963 *The Family Revolution in Modern China*. New York

Lévy Bruhl, L. 1922 *La Mentalité primitive*. Oxford

Lhote, H. 1960 *The Search for the Tassili Frescoes*. London

Li, L. M. 1981 *Chinese Silk Trade: traditional industry in the modern world, 1842–1937*. Cambridge, MA

Lieber, A. E. 1968 Eastern business practice and medieval European commerce. *Economic History Review* 21: 230–43

Lindahl, M. W. and Back, K. W. 1987 Lineage continuity and generational continuity: family history and family reunions. *Comparative Gerontology* B 1: 30–4

Linschoten, J. H. van [1598] 1974 *Discours of Voyages into ye East and West Indies*. London (reprinted Amsterdam, 1974)

Litchfield, R. B. 1969 Demographic characteristics of Florentine patrician families, sixteenth to nineteenth centuries. *Journal of Economic History* 29: 191–205

Lloyd, G. E. R. 1979 *Magic, Reason and Experience: studies in the origin and development of Greek science*. Cambridge
1990 *Demystifying Mentalities*. Cambridge

Lopez, R. S. 1943 European merchants in the medieval Indies: the evidence of commercial documents. *Journal of Economic History* 3: 164–84
1945 Silk industry in the Byzantine empire *Speculum* 20: 1–42
1952 Chinese silk in Europe during the Yuan period. *Journal of the American Oriental Society* 72(2): 73–4

Lopez, R. S. and Raymond, I. W. 1955 *Medieval Trade in the Mediterranean World*. New York

Lüthy, H. 1961 *La Banque protestante en France de la révocation de l'Edit de Nantes à la révolution* vol. II *De la banque aux finances (1730–1794)*. Paris: Ecole pratique des hautes études, VIe section

MacCormack, G. 1944 The traditional Chinese law of homicide, Po-Chüni and the *euisdem generis* principle. *Chinese Culture* 35 (3): 7–14

McDermott, J. P. 1990 The Chinese domestic bursar. *Asian Cultural Studies*, special issue, no. 2: 15–32
1991 Family financial plans of the southern Sung. *Asia Major* 3rd ser., 4, ii: 15–56

McElderny, A. L. 1976 *Shanghai Old-Style Banks (Ch'ien-Chang) 1800–1935*. Ann Arbor, MI

Macfarlane, A. 1978 *The Origins of English Individualism: the family, property and social transition*. Oxford

Mackay, E. 1931 Further links between ancient Sind, Sumer and elsewhere. *Antiquity* 5: 459–73

McNicoll, G. and Cain, M. 1990 Population and development issues and policies. In G. McNicoll and M. Cain (eds.) *Population and Rural Development: institutions and policy*. A supplement to *Population and Development Review*.

Macve, R. H. 1994 Some glosses on 'Greek and Roman accounting'. In R. H. Parker and B. S. Yamey (eds.) *Accounting History: some British contributions*. Oxford

Maine, H. S. 1861 *Ancient Law*. London

Malinowski, B. 1913 *The Family among the Australian Aborigines: a sociological study*. London
1948 *Magic, Science and Religion, and other essays* (ed. R. Redfield). Boston

Mallowan, M. E. L. 1970 An early Mesopotamian link with India. *Journal of the Royal Asiatic Society*: 192–4

Manandian, H. A. 1965 *The Trade and Cities of Armenia in Relation to Ancient World Trade*. Lisbon

Mannsåker, F. 1990 Elegancy and wildness: reflections of the East in the eighteenth-century imagination. In G. S. Rousseau and R. Porter (eds.) *Exoticism in the Enlightenment*. Manchester

Marcus, G. E. 1986 Generation-skipping trusts and problems of authority: parent–child relations in the dissolution of American families of dynastic wealth. In M. J. Aronoff (ed.) *The Frailty of Authority* (Political Anthropology, vol. V). New Brunswick

Markowits, C. 1985 *Indian Business and Nationalist Politics, 1931–39: the indigenous capitalist class and the rise of the Congress Party.* Cambridge

Marris, P. H. 1968 The social barriers to African entrepreneurship. *Journal of Development Studies* 5: 29–38.

Marris, P. H. and Somerset, A. 1971 *African Businessmen: a study of entrepreneurship and development in Kenya.* Institute of Community Studies Report. London

Marx, K. [1867] 1970 *Capital.* New York

Matthews, G. 1975 The dating and the significance of *The Periplus of the Erythraean Sea.* In N. H. Chittick and R. I. Rotberg (eds.) *East Africa and the Orient: cultural syntheses in pre-colonial times.* New York

Mazzarino, S. [1947] 1989 *Fra Oriente e Occidente: ricerche di storia Greca arcaica.* Milan

Medick, H. 1976 The proto-industrial family economy: the structural function of household and family during the transition from peasant society to industrial capitalism. *Social History* 3: 291–315

Mehta, M. 1982 *The Ahmedabad Cotton Textile Industry: genesis and growth.* Ahmadabad

Meilink-Roelofsz, M. A. P. 1962 *Asian Trade and European Influence in the Indonesian Archipelago between 1500 and about 1630.* The Hague

1970 Asian trade and Islam in the Malay–Indonesian archipelago. In D. S. Richards (ed.) *Islam and the Trade of Asia.* Oxford

Meillassoux, C. 1964 *Anthropologie économique des Gourou de la Côte d'Ivoire: de l'économie d'autosubsistence à l'agriculture commerciale.* Paris

1986 *Anthropologie de l'esclavage.* Paris (English edn 1991)

Melis, F. 1950 *Storia della ragioneria.* Bologna

Mendels, F. 1972 Proto-industrialization: the first phase of the industrialization process. *Journal of Economic History* 32: 241–61

Mennell, S. 1985 *All Manners of Food: eating and taste in England and France from the Middle Ages to the present.* Oxford

Merton, R. 1957 Science, technology and society. In R. Merton, *Social Structure and Social Change.* Glencoe, IL

Miller, J. I. 1969 *Spice Trade of the Roman Empire.* Oxford

Mills, J. V. G. (ed. and trans.) [1433]1970 Ma Huan, *The Overall Survey of the Ocean's Shores.* Cambridge: Hakluyt Society

Mintz, S. W. 1985 *Sweetness and Power: the place of sugar in modern history.* New York

Misra, S. C. 1963 *The Rise of Muslim Power in Gujarat.* Bombay

Montesquieu, C. de S. [1989] *The Spirit of the Laws.* Cambridge (trans. from French)

Moore, O. K. 1957 Divination: a new approach. *American Anthropologist* 59: 69–74

Morikawa, H. 1992 *Zaibatsu: the rise and fall of family enterprise groups in Japan.* Tokyo

Morishima, M. 1982 *Why Has Japan Succeeded?* Cambridge

Morris, M. D. 1963 Towards a reinterpretation of nineteenth-century Indian economic history. *Journal of Economic History* 23: 606–18

1967 Values as an obstacle to growth in south Asia: an historical survey. *Journal of Economic History* 27: 588–607

Mossé, C. and Schnapp-Gourbeillon, A. 1990 *Précis d'histoire Grecque: du début du deuxième millénaire à la bataille d'Actium.* Paris

Mote, F. W. 1977 Yuan and Ming. In K. C. Chang (ed.) *Food in Chinese Culture.* New York

Moulder, F. V. 1977 *Japan, China, and the Modern World Economy: toward a reinterpretation of east Asian development (c. 1600 to c. 1918).* Cambridge

Mueller, E. 1976 The economic value of children in peasant agriculture. In R. G. Ridker (ed.) *Population and Development.* Baltimore, MD

Mukhia, H. 1981 Was there feudalism in Indian history? *Journal of Peasant Studies* 8: 273–310

Mungello, D. E. 1989 *Curious Land: Jesuit accommodation and the origins of sinology.* Honolulu, HI (1st edn Wiesbaden, 1985)

Muramatsu, Y. 1966 A documentary study of Chinese landlordism in late Ch'ing and early republican Kiangnan. *Bulletin of the School of Oriental and African Studies* 29: 566–99

Murra, J. V. 1980 *The Economic Organisation of the Inka State.* Greenwich, CT

Murray, A. 1978 *Reason and Society in the Middle Ages.* Oxford

Nakamura, H. 1964 *Ways of Thinking of Eastern Peoples: India, China, Tibet, Japan.* Honolulu, HI (revised edn, 1st English edn 1960)

1967 *A History of the Development of Japanese Thought AD 592–1868.* 2 vols. Tokyo (2nd edn 1969)

1975 *Parallel Developments: a comparative history of ideas.* Tokyo

Nakane, C. 1972 An interpretation of the size and structure of the household in Japan over three centuries. In Laslett, P. and Wall, B. (eds.) *Household and Family in Past Times.* Cambridge

Needham, J. 1954 *Science and Civilisation in China.* vol. I. *Introductory Orientations.* Cambridge

1956 *Science and Civilisation in China.* vol. II. *History of Scientific Thought.* Cambridge

1959 *Science and Civilisation in China.* vol. III. *Mathematics and the Sciences of the Heavens and the Earth.* Cambridge

1985 *Science and Civilisation in China.* vol. V. *Chemistry and Chemical Technology.* Cambridge

Nehru, J. 1951 *Discovery of India.* London (3rd edn)

Neville, G. K. 1984 Learning culture through ritual: the family reunion. *Anthropology and Education Quarterly* 15: 151–66

Nicholas, D. 1985 *Domestic Life of a Medieval City: women, children and the family in fourteenth-century Ghent.* London

Nissen, H. J., Damerow, P. and Englund, R. J. 1990 *Frühe Schrift und Techniken der Wirtschaftsverwaltung im alten Vorderen Orient.* Berlin

Nussbaum, F. L. 1933 *A History of the Economic Institutions of Modern Europe.* New York

Oakley, F. 1979 *The Crucial Centuries: the medieval experience.* London

Oppenheim, A. L. 1964 *Ancient Mesopotamia: portrait of a dead civilization.* Chicago

Oppong, C. and Bleek, W. 1982 Economic models and having children: some evidence from Kwahu, Ghana. *Africa* 52: 15–33

Orenstein, H. 1962 Exploitation or function in the interpretation of jajmani. *Southwestern Journal of Anthropology.* 18: 302–15

Orme, R. [1792] 1805 *Historical Fragments of the Mogul Empire, of the Morrattoes, and of the English Concerns in Indostan, from the year MDCLIX.* London

Palmade, G. 1961 *Capitalisme et capitalistes français au XIXe siècle.* Paris

Parker, R. H. and Yamey, B. S. (eds.) 1994 *Accounting History: some British contributions.* Oxford

Passow, R. 1918 *Kapitalismus, eine begrifflich-terminologische Studie.* Jena

Patlagean, E. 1977 *Pauvreté économique et pauvreté sociale à Byzance 4e–7e siècles.* Paris

Paul, G. 1993 Equivalent axioms of Aristotelean, or Traditional European, and Later Mohist logic: an argument in favor of the universality of logic and rationality. In H. Lenk and G. Paul (eds.) *Epistemological Issues in Classical Chinese Philosophy.* Albany, NY

Pavlov, V. I. 1964 *The Indian Capitalist Class: a historical study.* New Delhi (English edn)

1979 *Historical Premises for India's Transition to Capitalism.* Moscow

Pearson, M. N. 1976 *Merchants and Rulers in Gujarat: the response to the Portuguese in the sixteenth century.* Berkeley, CA

Pelliot, P. 1953 *Les Débats de l'imprimerie en Chine.* Paris

Peragallo, E. 1938 *The Origin and Evolution of Double Entry Bookkeeping.* New York

Perera, B. J. 1951 The foreign trade and commerce of ancient Ceylon I: the ports of ancient Ceylon. *Ceylon Historical Journal* 1: 109–19

1952a The foreign trade and commerce of ancient Ceylon II: ancient Ceylon and its trade with India. *Ceylon Historical Journal* 1: 192–204

1952b The foreign trade and commerce of ancient Ceylon III: ancient Ceylon's trade with the empires of the eastern and western Worlds. *Ceylon Historical Journal* 1: 301–20

Perlin, F. 1983 Proto-industrialization and pre-colonial south Asia. *Past and Present* 98: 30–95

1984 Growth of money economy and some questions of transition in late pre-colonial India. *Journal of Peasant Studies* 11: 97–106

1987 Money-use in late pre-colonial India and the international trade in currency media. In J. F. Richards (ed.) *The Imperial Monetary Systems of Mughal India.* Delhi

Pirenne, H. 1914 *Les Périodes de l'histoire social du capitalisme.* Brussels

1928 Le commerce du papyrus dans la Gaule mérovingienne. *Comptes rendus des séances de l'Académie des Inscriptions et Belles-Lettres* 178–91

1929 L'Instruction des marchands au moyen âge. *Annales d'histoire économique et sociale* 1: 13–28

1969 *Medieval Cities: their origins and the revival of trade.* Princeton, NJ (French edn 1927)

Pires, Tome [1944] *The Suma Oriental*. London: Hakluyt Society (trans. A. Cortesao)

Polanyi, K. 1945 *Origins of our Time: the great transformation*. London (revised edn)

1957 *Trade and Market in the Early Empires*. Glencoe, IL

Postan, M. M. 1928 Credit in medieval trade. *Economic History Review* 1: 234–61

1932–4 Medieval capitalism. *Economic History Review* 4: 212–27

1957 Partnerships in English medieval commerce. *Studi in Onore di Armando Sapori* vol. I. Milan

Priouret, R. 1963 *Les Origines du patronat français*. Paris

Pullan, J. M. 1968 *The History of the Abacus*. London

Purchas, S. 1905–7 *Hakluytus Posthumus, or Purchas his Pilgrimes* (20 vols.) Glasgow

Qaisar, A. J. 1974 The role of brokers in medieval India. *Indian Historical Review* 1: 220–46

Quine, W. V. 1970 *Philosophy of Logic*. Englewood Cliffs, NJ

Raab, T. K. 1962 Puritanism and the rise of experimental sciences in England. *Journal of World History* 7: 46–67

Ramaswamy, V. 1980 Notes on textile technology in medieval India with special reference to the south. *Indian Economic and Social History Review* 17: 227–41

1985a The genesis and historical role of the masterweavers in south Indian textile production. *Journal of the Economic and Social History of the Orient* 28: 294–325

1985b *Textiles and Weavers in Medieval South India*. Delhi

Randeria, S. 1992 The Politics of Representation and Exchange among Untouchable Castes in Western India (Gujerat). PhD thesis, Free University, Berlin

Raschke, M. G. 1978 New studies in Roman commerce with the East. In H. Temporini and W. Haase (eds.) *Aufstieg und Niedergang der Römischen Welt*. Berlin

Rawson, J. 1984 *Chinese Ornament: the lotus and the dragon*. London

Raychaudhuri, T. 1962 *Jan Company in Coromandel 1605–1690: a study in the interrelations of European commerce and traditional economics*. The Hague

Raychaudhuri, T. and Habib, I. (eds.) 1982 *The Cambridge Economic History of India*. vol. I. 1200–1750. Cambridge

Razi, Z. 1993 The myth of the immutable English family. *Past and Present* 140: 1–44

Redding, S. G. 1990 *The Spirit of Chinese Capitalism*. Berlin

Reid, A. 1988 *Southeast Asia in the Age of Commerce, 1450–1680*. vol. I. *The Lands below the Winds*. New Haven, CT

Reynolds, R. L. 1951 Bankers' account in double-entry in Genoa, 1313 and 1316. *Bollettino Ligustico per la Storia e la Cultura Regionale* 3: 33–7

Richards, J. F. 1981 Mughal state finance and the pre-modern world economy. *Comparative Studies in Society and History* 23: 285–308

Robb, P. 1993 Intermediaries and change in eighteenth-century Gujarat: a note on G. D. Sharma's view of credit, revenue and commerce. In G. Austin and K. Sugihara (eds.) *Local Suppliers of Credit in the Third World, 1750–1960*. London

Rodinson, M. 1973 *Islam and Capitalism*. London (French original 1966)

Roe, M. 1994 *Strong Managers, Weak Owners: the political roots of American corporate finance*. Princeton, NJ

Roetz, H. 1993 Validity in Chou thought: on Chad Hansen and the pragmatic turn in sinology. In H. Lenk and G. Paul (eds.) *Epistemological Issues in Classical Chinese Philosophy*. Albany, NY

Rogers, S. C. 1991 *Shaping Modern Times in Rural France: the transformation and reproduction of an Aveyronnais community*. Princeton, NJ

Romanis, F. de 1988 Romanukharaṭṭha e Taprobane: sui rapporti Roma–Ceylon nel 1 sec. DC *Helikon* 28: 5–58

Roover, R. de 1937 Aux origines d'une technique intellectuelle: la formation et l'expansion de la comptabilité à partie double. *Annales: ESC* 9: 171–93, 270–98

1942 The commercial revolution of the thirteenth century. *Bulletin of the Business Historical Society* 16: 34–9

1948 *Money, Banking, and Credit in Medieval Bruges: Italian merchant-bankers, Lombards, and money-changers: a study in the origins of banking*. Cambridge, MA

1953 *L'Evolution de la lettre de change (XIVe–XVIIIe siècles)*. Paris

1954 New interpretations of the history of banking. *Journal of World History* 2: 38–76

1956 The development of accounting prior to Luca Pacioli according to the account books of medieval merchants. In A. C. Littleton and B. S. Yamey (eds.) *Studies in the History of Accounting*. London (reprinted 1974)

1963 The organization of trade. In *The Cambridge Economic History of Europe* vol. III (eds. M. M. Postan, E. E. Rich and E. Miller). Cambridge

1974 *Business, Banking, and Economic Thought in Late Medieval and Early Modern Europe: selected studies of Raymond de Roover* (ed. J. Kirschner) Chicago

Rosenberg, N. 1974 Science, invention and economic growth. *Economic Journal* 84: 90–108

Rostovtzeff, M. I. 1926 *The Social and Economic History of the Roman Empire*. Oxford

Rougé, J. 1980 Prêt et sociétés maritimes dans le monde romain. In J. H. D'Arms and E. C. Kopff (eds.) *The Seaborne Commerce of Ancient Rome*. Memoirs of the American Academy in Rome, 36. Rome

Rowe, W. T. 1984 *Hankow: commerce and society in a Chinese city, 1796–1889*. Stanford. CA

Roy, J.-A. and Dansette, J.-L. 1958 Origines et évolution d'une bourgeoisie: le patronat textile du bassin lillois (1789–1814). *Revue du Nord*: 49–69

Rudner, D. 1989 Banker's trust and the culture of banking among the Nattukottai Chettiars of colonial south India. *Modern Asian Studies* 23: 417–58

1992 *Caste and Capitalism in Colonial India*. Berkeley, CA

Rungta, R. S. 1970 *Rise of Business Corporations in India*. Cambridge

Sabean, D. 1990 *Property, Production, and Family in Neckarhausen, 1700–1870*. Cambridge

Sabloff, J. A. and Lamberg-Karlovsky, C. C. (eds.) 1975 *Ancient Civilization and Trade*. Albuquerque, NM

Sahlins, M. 1972 *Stone Age Economics*. Chicago

Said, E. 1978 *Orientalism*. London

Sanborn, F. R. 1930 *Origins of Early English Maritime and Commercial Law*. London

Sankalia, H. D. 1987 *Prehistoric and Historic Archaeology of Gujarat*. New Delhi

Saul, M. 1983 Work parties, wages and accumulation in a Voltaic village. American Ethnologist 10(1): 77–96

Scanlon, G. T. 1971 Egypt and China: trade and imitation. In D. S. Richards (ed.) *Islam and the Trade of Asia*. Oxford

Schluchter, W. 1981 *The Rise of Western Rationalism: Max Weber's developmental history*. Berkeley, CA

Schlumberger, J. 1934 *Eveils*. Paris

Schoff, W. H. (ed.) 1912 *The Periplus of the Erythraean Sea: travel and trade in the Indian Ocean by a merchant of the first century*. New York

Schwab, R. [1950] 1984 *The Oriental Renaissance – Europe's discovery of India and the East 1680–1880*. New York (original edn Paris 1950)

Scott, J. 1979 *Corporations, Classes and Capitalism*. London

Segalen, M. 1991 *Fifteen Generations of Bretons: kinship and society in lower Brittany, 1720–1980*. Cambridge (French edn 1985)

Shahar, S. 1990 *Childhood in the Middle Ages*. London

Sharma, G. D. 1993 Urban credit and the market economy in western India, c. 1750–1850. In G. Austin and K. Sugihara (eds.) *Local Suppliers of Credit in the Third World, 1750–1960*. London

Shiba, Y. 1970 *Commerce and Society in Sung China*. Ann Arbor, MI

Shorter, E. 1975 *The Making of the Modern Family*. New York

Simkin, C. G. F. 1968 *The Traditional Trade of Asia*. London

Singer, M. 1968 The Indian joint family in modern industry. In M. Singer and B. S. Cohen (eds.) *Structure and Change in Indian Society*. Chicago

Sivin, N. 1982 Why the scientific revolution did not take place in China – or didn't it? In Li Guohao *et al.* (eds.) *Explorations in the History of Science and Technology in China*. Shanghai: Chinese Classics Publishing House

Sleen, W. G. N. van de 1967 *A Handbook on Beads*. Liège

Smith, J., Wallerstein, I. and Evans, H. (eds.) 1984 *Households and the World-Economy*. London

Smith, R. (ed.) 1989 *Aristotle, Prior Analytics*. Indianapolis, IN

Smith, R. M. 1979 Some reflections on the evidence for the origins of 'European marriage pattern' in England. In C. Harris (ed.) *The Sociology of the Family*. Keele

Smith, T. C. 1959 *The Agrarian Origins of Modern Japan*. Stanford, CA
  1973 Pre-modern economic growth: Japan and the West. *Past and Present* 60: 127–60

Snodgrass, A. 1972 *The Dark Age of Greece: an archaeological survey of the eleventh to the eighth centuries BC*. Edinburgh

Sombart, W. 1930 Capitalism. In *Encyclopaedia of the Social Sciences*. vol. III. New York.

Somda Nurukyor, M. K. n.d. Les cauris du Lobi. MS

Speiser, J.-M. 1985 Le christianisation de la ville dans l'Antiquité tardive. *Ktema: civilisations de l'orient, de la Grèce et de Rome antiques* 10: 49–55

Spodek, H. 1965 The 'Manchesterisation' of Ahmedabad. *Economic Weekly* 17: 483–90

Ste Croix, G. de 1956 Greek and Roman accounting. In A. C. Littleton and B. S. Yamey (eds.) *Studies in the History of Accounting.* London

Steensgaard, N. 1972 *Carracks, Caravans, and Companies: the structural crisis in the European–Asian trade in the early seventeenth century.* Copenhagen

1974 *The Asian Trade Revolution of the Seventeenth Century: the East India companies and the decline of the caravan trade.* Chicago (1st edn Copenhagen 1972)

Stein, B. 1980 *Peasant, State and Society in Medieval South India.* New Delhi

Stock, B. 1983 *The Implications of Literacy: written languages and models of interpretation in the eleventh and twelfth centuries.* Princeton, NJ

Stockman, N. 1994 Gender inequality and social structure in urban China. *Sociology* 28: 759–77

Stokes, E. 1973 The first century of British colonial rule in India: social revolution or social stagnation? *Past and Present* 58: 136–60

Stone, L. [1977] 1979 *The Family, Sex and Marriage in England, 1500–1800.* London (abridged edn 1979)

1986 Inheritance strategies among the English landed elite, 1540–1840. In G. Delille and F. Rizzi (eds.) *Le Modèle familial Européen: normes, déviances, contrôle du pouvoir.* Collection de l'École Française de Rome, vol. 90. Rome.

Streefkerk, H. 1985 *Industrial Transition in Rural India: artisans, traders, and tribals in South Gujarat.* Bombay

Stützner, H. and Szöllösi, D. 1985 The development of technical education during the second stage of the industrial revolution in Saxony. *History and Technology* 2: 269–82

Tai, Huang-chao 1989 *Confucianism and Economic Development: an oriental alternative?* Washington, DC

Takenaka, Y. 1969 Endogenous formation and development of capitalism in Japan. *Journal of Economic History* 29: 141–62

Tambiah, S. J. 1990 *Magic, Science, Religion and the Scope of Rationality.* Cambridge

Tarn, W. W. 1938 *The Greeks in Bactria and India.* Cambridge

Taylor, R. M. 1982 Summoning the wandering tribes: genealogy and family history in American history. *Journal of Social History* 16: 21–37

Tchernia, A. 1992 Le dromadaire des *Peticii* et le commerce oriental. *Mélanges de l'Ecole Française de Rome. Antiquité* 104: 293–301

Tenbruck, F. H. 1984 *Die unbewältigten Sozialwissenschaften, oder, Die Abschaffung des Menschen.* Graz

Terray, E. 1974 Long-distance exchange and the formation of the state: the case of the Abron Kingdom of Gyaman. *Economy and Society* 3: 315–45

Thapar, R. 1966 *A History of India.* Harmondsworth, Middlesex

1992a Black gold: south Asia and the Roman maritime trade. *South Asia* 15 (2): 1–27

1992b Patronage and community. In B. S. Miller (ed.) *The Powers of Art: patronage in Indian culture.* Delhi

Thrupp, S. L. 1962 *The Merchant Class of Medieval London (1300–1500).* Ann Arbor, MI

Tien, Tsuen-Hsuin 1985 *Paper and Printing*. Part I. *Chemistry and Chemical Technology*. vol. V. J. Needham, *Science and Civilisation in China*. Cambridge

Timberg, T. A. 1978 *The Marawaris: from traders to industrialists*. New Delhi

Trevor-Roper, J. H. 1966 *The Rise of Christian Europe*. London

Tripatni, D. 1981 *The Dynamics of Tradition: Kasturbhai Lalbhai and his entrepreneurship*. New Delhi

Tyan, E. n.d. *Le Notariat et le régime de la preuve par écrit dans la practique du droit musulman*. Beirut (2nd edn)

Tylor, E. B. 1871 *Primitive Culture*. London

Udovitch, A. L. 1962 At the origins of the western *commenda*: Islam, Israel, Byzantium? *Speculum* 37: 198–207

  1967a Credit as a means of investment in medieval Islamic trade. *Journal of the American Oriental Society* 87: 260–4

  1967b Labor partnerships in early Islamic law. *Journal of the Economic and Social History of the Orient* 10: 64–80

  1970 *Partnership and Profit in Medieval Islam*. Princeton, NJ

Usher, A. P. 1934 The origins of banking: the primitive bank of deposit, 1200–1600. *Economic History Review* 4: 399–428

Vaughan, J. D. 1971 *The Manners and Customs of the Chinese*. Singapore (1st edn 1879)

Veenhof, K. 1972 *Aspects of Old Assyrian Trade and its Terminology*. Studia et Documenta ad Iura Orientis Antiqui Pertinentia. vol. X. Leiden

Veyne, P. 1978 La famille et l'amour dans le haut empire romain. *Annales: ESC* 33: 35–63

Vogel, E. 1979 *Japan as Number One*. Cambridge, MA

Ware, H. 1978 The economic value of children in Asia and Africa; comparative perspectives. *Papers of the East–West Population Institute*, Honolulu, HI

Weber, M. 1947 *Theory of Social and Economic Organisation*. Edinburgh

  [1916] 1951 *The Religion of China* (trans. H. H. Gerth). New York

  1952 *Ancient Judaism*. Glencoe, IL

  1958 *The Protestant Ethic and the Spirit of Capitalism*. New York

Westermark, E. 1926 *A Short History of Marriage*. New York (reprinted 1968)

Wheatley, P. 1961 *The Golden Khersonese*. Kuala Lumpur

  1975a Satyānṛta in Suvarṇadvjpa: from reciprocity to redistribution in ancient southeast Asia. In J. A. Sabloff and C. C. Lamberg-Karlovsky (eds.) *Ancient Civilizations and Trade*. Albuquerque, NM

  1975b Analecta Sino-Africana recensa. In N. H. Chittick and R. I. Rotberg (eds.) *East Africa and the Orient: cultural syntheses in pre-colonial times*. New York

Wheeler, R. E. M. *et al.* 1946 Arikamedu: an Indo-Roman trading-station on the east coast of India. *Ancient India* 2: 17–124

Whitehouse, D. and Williamson, A. 1973 Sasanian maritime trade. *Iran* 11: 29–49

Wickham, C. J. 1984 The other transition: from the ancient world to feudalism. *Past and Present* 103: 3–36

  1985 The uniqueness of the West. *Journal of Peasant Studies* 12: 166–96

Wilmot, W. E. (ed.) 1972 *Economic Organization in Chinese Society*. Stanford, CA

Wilson, B. (ed.) 1977 *Rationality*. Oxford

284   Bibliography

Wittfogel, K. A. 1957 *Oriental Society*. New Haven, CT
Wolf, A. P. and Hanley, S. B. 1985 Introduction. In S. B. Hanley and A. P. Wolf (eds.) *Family and Population in East Asian History*. Stanford, CA
Wolf, A. P. and Huang, C.-S. 1980 *Marriage and Adoption in China 1845–1945*. Stanford, CA
Wolf, E. R. 1982 *Europe and the People without History*. Berkeley, CA
Wolters, O. W. 1917 *Early Indonesian Trade: a study of the origins of Srivijaya*. Ithaca, NY
World Bank 1986 *Population Growth and Policies in Sub-Saharan Africa*. Washington, DC
Wright, T. 1861 *Essays on Archaeological Subjects and on Various Questions Connected with the History of Art, Science, and Literature in the Middle Ages*. 2 vols. London
Wrigley, E. A. 1969 *Population and History*. London
    1988 *Continuity, Chance and Change: the character of the Industrial Revolution in England*. Cambridge
Wrigley, E. A. and Schofield, R. S. 1981 *The Population History of England 1541–1871*. Cambridge
Yamey, B. S. 1949 Scientific bookkeeping and the rise of capitalism. *Economic History Review* 1: 99–113
    1964 Accounting and the rise of capitalism: further notes on a theme by Sombart. *Journal of Accounting Research* 2: 117–36
    1975 Notes on double-entry bookkeeping and economic progress. *Journal of European Economic History* 4: 717–23
    1994 Balancing and closing the ledger: Italian practice 1300–1600. In R. H. Parker and B. S. Yamey (eds.) *Accounting History: some British contributions*. Oxford
Yamey, B. S. *et al.* 1963 *Accounting in England and Scotland, 1543–1800: double-entry in exposition and practice*. London

Index

Both general areas (eg Indian Ocean) and specific locations (eg Socotra) are indexed.